"Drawing from Sebastian Moore's use of an extraordinarily wide variety of disciplines, Deominic Arcamone offers us a detailed presentation of Moore's thought—a thought that is both contemplative and entirely relevant for a Christian construal of spirituality. By doing so, Arcamone helps his readers to correct many traditional distortions in Catholic theology and to suggest helpful understandings."

—LOUIS ROY, professor of systematic theology, Dominican University College

"Dominic Arcamone presents a comprehensive exposition and appreciation of the thought of English Benedictine Sebastian Moore by one whose life was transformed by his encounter with Moore."

—WILLIAM LOEWE, professor emeritus of historical and systematic theology, The Catholic University of America

"Dominic Arcamone has done the theological community a great service in bringing the work of Sebastian Moore to a new audience. Moore's work is a constant challenge to 'know thyself,' to enter into the depths of human interiority. Arcamone's nuanced and detailed exposition renews that same challenge for those willing to take the risk."

—NEIL ORMEROD, honorary professor of theology, Alphacrucis University College

"If we imagine Sebastian Moore as a spirited, piebald wild horse filled with life, curiosity, and enthusiasm, in this book Arcamone has tamed the wild stallion. Arcamone has done a great service by transforming Moore's sustained mercurial flashes of insight into ideas and inspirations that even the novice rider can confidently handle. *A New Awareness* is exhilarating, at times challenging, but ultimately very satisfying. Take up and read!"

—JOHN FRANCIS COLLINS, lecturer, Sydney College of Divinity

"Sebastian Moore's writings are familiar in their core goal of healing from brokenness through encounter with Jesus, but strange in the many ways Moore starts us off and gets us there. Dominic Arcamone's book clearly and comprehensively presents Moore's thought, his greatest influences, and their topics, from hidden desires to Trinitarian doctrines. It is a pleasure to read and is richly informative to anyone wanting to know more about Moore and apply his thought to contemporary issues."

—MARK MILLER, associate professor of systematic theology, University of San Francisco

A New Awareness

A New Awareness

The Theological Insights of Sebastian Moore

DOMINIC ARCAMONE
Foreword by Neil Ormerod

WIPF & STOCK · Eugene, Oregon

A NEW AWARENESS
The Theological Insights of Sebastian Moore

Copyright © 2024 Dominic Arcamone. All rights reserved. Except for brief quotations in critical publications or reviews, no part of this book may be reproduced in any manner without prior written permission from the publisher. Write: Permissions, Wipf and Stock Publishers, 199 W. 8th Ave., Suite 3, Eugene, OR 97401.

Wipf & Stock
An Imprint of Wipf and Stock Publishers
199 W. 8th Ave., Suite 3
Eugene, OR 97401

www.wipfandstock.com

PAPERBACK ISBN: 979-8-3852-0601-8
HARDCOVER ISBN: 979-8-3852-0602-5
EBOOK ISBN: 979-8-3852-0603-2

02/28/24

All Scripture quotations taken from New Revised Standard Version Bible, copyright © 1989, the Division of Christian Education of the National Council of the Churches of Christ in the United States of America. Used by permission. All rights reserved.

For all who have felt insignificant in their lives

Contents

Foreword by Neil Ormerod — ix

Acknowledgments — xi

Introduction — 1

1. Moore, Lonergan, and the Turn to the Subject — 20
2. Moore: Theologian and Poet — 47
3. Conversion, Contemplation, and Eckhart Tolle — 79
4. Moore and Becker: Personal Significance and Death — 102
5. Moore and the Psychology of Ego and Self — 128
6. Moore, the Grammar of Desire, and Girard — 167
7. Moore and the Person of Jesus I — 203
8. Moore and the Person of Jesus II — 233
9. Moore and the Community of the Church I — 268
10. Moore and the Community of the Church II — 299
11. Moore and the Trinity — 324
12. Moore and Sexuality — 360

Bibliography — 399

Index — 409

Foreword

I FIRST CAME ACROSS the writings of Sebastian Moore in the early 1980s as I was transitioning from a career as a mathematician and branching out into theology. I had already delved into the writings of Bernard Lonergan, and I was aware of some connection between the two thinkers. I had an opportunity to meet Moore during one of his visits to Australia, at the Lonergan Centre in the Jesuit house in Pymble, Sydney. I gave him a copy of something I had written on the work of Edward Schillebeeckx, using Lonergan's cognitional theory, and he was very appreciative, always a generous interlocutor.

During that decade I devoured his writings, *The Crucified Is No Stranger*, *The Fire and the Rose Are One*, *The Inner Loneliness*, *Let This Mind Be in You*, and *Jesus the Liberator of Desire*, as well as various articles in Lonergan Workshops and *Downside Review*. As Lonergan said of his encounter with Aquinas, Moore's writing changed me utterly, attuning me to my own interiority, the whole world of affectivity, of symbol, that I had never developed as a mathematician. By this stage I was a working theologian, if a bit green and underdeveloped, but his work became central to my own thought on grace, sin, salvation, and original sin. In 1992 I published a book, *Grace and Disgrace*, largely informed by what I had learnt from Moore. With great generosity, he wrote a blurb for this work, though at the time I was a relatively unknown young theologian outside Australia.

Moore's work took on a very personal dimension as my wife and I struggled with our encounter with the problem of clergy sexual abuse. Moore's exploration of human brokenness, in both the victims and the perpetrators of abuse, helped us navigate the emotional currents that threatened to overwhelm us at the time. Out of this experience we wrote

When Ministers Sin, which included the voices of a number of survivors of clergy abuse.

While I remained in contact with Moore in the 1990s, including another meeting with him in one of his trips to Australia, my theological interests began to focus more and more on the writings of Lonergan and Robert Doran. Doran's work on psychic conversion, culminating in his magnum opus, *Theology and the Dialectics of History*, provided an ongoing source of theological enrichment for my theological researches. I doubt that I would have made as much headway with Doran were it not for my schooling in interiority through Moore's writings.

Reading Dominic Arcamone's manuscript on Moore was a powerful reminder to me of how much Moore's writings meant to me, and their continuing power to illuminate the inner life. Arcamone has drawn on an extensive range of Moore's writings, from the early publications prior to his encounter with Lonergan, to his final blogs on sexuality. He analyzes Moore's influences and sources, his key themes and concerns, to open up his thought for those willing to learn. Arcamone is a generous reader of Moore and has clearly had a similar experience of Moore's writing to my own, one of deep gratitude.

Still, I wonder what the current generation of theologians will make of Moore. Theology has been overtaken by a multitude of concerns—feminism, racism, anti-colonialism, eco-theology, queer theology, and the like. All these are pressing and important issues that theology needs to engage with urgency. Yet there is a fragmentation in these range of concerns that the writings of Moore can help heal. For we are all have an interior realm that bears the wounds of being both victim and perpetrator, of wounded and wounding. Unless and until theologians become familiar with their own interiority, and take responsibility for it, the ongoing danger is simply to repeat the old patterns of victimhood into the future. Arcamone's book can assist a new generation of theologians to do this inner work by making the breadth of his writings available to a new readership.

Neil Ormerod

Acknowledgments

I WANT TO ACKNOWLEDGE my beloved wife Anita, who died on the fifth of December 2022. She gave me twenty-three years of immense joy and delivered to me my significance as a person. I would also like to thank Neil Ormerod for his untiring help. Also, I would like to thank Father Michael Kelly OSB, William Loewe, Mark Miller, Father Louis Roy OP, and John Collins for their encouragement, comments, and suggestions.

Introduction

WHY WRITE THIS BOOK?

Every book has the author's story above, underneath, and around its pages. I first came across the writings of Sebastian Moore in the early 1990s when a then-younger Australian theologian, Neil Ormerod, published his book *Grace and Disgrace: A Theology of Self-Esteem, Society, and History*. Neil's book surprised me for no other reason than the fact that he gave an intelligent and responsible account of the Catholic doctrine of original sin. One of his main dialogue partners in that endeavor was Sebastian Moore. Although the doctrine of original sin indirectly touches the life of any person when parents present their children for baptism into the Catholic Church, very few preachers speak to it or try to unpack its significance in our day-to-day lives or attempt to help the faithful understand its relationship to the life, death, and resurrection of Jesus. Moore did this very task over his lifetime. Reading Ormerod's book was my first intersection with the philosophy and theology of Sebastian Moore.

Later, I was to discover that Moore's writings were central to at least three doctoral theses: "Soteriology Based on a Reformulation of Human Desire: Sebastian Moore and Raymund Schwager" by Rev. James F. Hurlbert (1991); "The Encounter with Jesus Crucified and Risen in the Soteriology of Sebastian Moore" by Tuan Le Quang (2011); and "Dying to Live: The Paradox of Christian Salvation, the Terror of Death and the Developmental Stages Theory" by Alexander T. Blondeau (2016). Moore was featured in several single chapters in such books as *What Are They Saying about Salvation?* by Denis Edwards, *Introducing Contemporary Theologies: The What and the Who of Theology Today* by Neil Ormerod; *Trinity: Nexus of the Mysteries of Christian Faith* authored by Anne Hunt; *Jesus Crucified and Risen: Essays in Spirituality and Theology in Honour of Dom Sebastian Moore*, edited by William P. Loewe and Vernon

A New Awareness

J. Gregson; chapter 6 of *Coherent Christianity: Towards an Articulate Faith* and *Embracing Desire*, both books by Louis Roy; and *Suspended God: Music and a Theology of Doubt* by Maeve Louise Heaney. I was also to discover that Moore was a significant contributor to the British-based Catholic newspaper *The Tablet*, where, from the 1950s to 2014, there were some 160 plus entries, including articles by him, letters to the editor penned by him, reviews of his books by others, and comments made by subscribers about his letters to the editor or his writings. He was well known to English Catholics who subscribed to *The Tablet*.

In the beginning, having read Ormerod's book, I did not become an avid reader of Moore. My interest in him took some fifteen years to peak when I set about writing my second book, *Conversion as Transformation: Lonergan, Mentors, and Cinema*. When I spoke about Christian conversion, a key word for understanding it was "desire." Again, Moore wrote extensively about human desire: our desire for God and our interpersonal desire for one another. I was captivated by his persistence in speaking about desire right up to his death at the ripe age of ninety-six. By late 2020, and amid the COVID-19 restrictions, I began researching by reading everything I could get my hands on written by Moore. The mandatory laws around movement within our country amid the COVID-19 crisis gave me the time to do this research.

I continued the research till late 2021, and then I stopped. In early 2019, my beautiful, beloved wife, Anita, was diagnosed with lung cancer. I had just retired from work. She began a course of treatments that went over three years. I was at her side whenever she visited doctors or treatment centers, except when the COVID-19 restrictions prevented family members from accompanying their spouses into the hospital precinct. The medical appointments included doctor consultations, monthly blood tests, and scans between treatment sessions. During my research, Moore's insights provided a voice to our committed love over twenty-three years and how important Anita had been in my life. Then, around May 2022, the doctors told Anita that all treatments would stop since no treatment could eliminate or contain the spread of cancer throughout her body. The doctors gave her radiation to stem the suffering, where appropriate, and pharmacological palliation to stop the pain. This change in direction began a new stage of our journey together, and I knew that I had to entirely hand over all my time to her as she progressively became incapacitated. For me, it was the most privileged period of our lives and, for us both, the most challenging. Slowly, the cancer spread and progressively incapacitated her, but never without love surrounding her. She died on Monday, December 5, 2022, at 9:55 a.m.

I had been a Catholic priest in Sydney, ordained in 1980 before my departure to marry Anita in October 1998. She was and remains simply the most important person in my life. We had known each other for over thirty years. We were married for twenty-three years. In Moore's words, she gave me immeasurable significance, which opened me to be myself for her and others and helped me awaken to God. Over those last few years, I shared many of Moore's insights with her. As I write this introduction, it is approaching eight months since my wife's death, and I miss her terribly. About a week after her death, consumed by sadness, I began to write our autobiography as an act of devotion to her. Nothing can assuage the sadness I feel. As I approach each new day, I am still gripped by sheer disbelief at her death.

I wanted to complete the task of writing this book on Moore for these reasons. First, I deeply respect Sebastian Moore since his theology has touched many people of my generation. Moore is not currently well-known, and I agree with Maeve Louise Heaney's assessment when she states that Moore's lack of readership may be due to "the complexity of his thought, the specific knowledge of psychological categories presumed in his books and his eccentric combination of prose, colloquialisms, and poetry."[1] However, even as an eclectic thinker, he possessed the capacity to integrate insights from a wide variety of disciplines and throw fresh light on important questions of the Christian journey.[2]

Most serious Catholics believe this task is crucial for several reasons. First, in our post-COVID-19 context, many Catholics have not returned to their place of worship. The Sunday Eucharist lacks young people, representing 5 percent or less of the congregation. Many young people who still seek to follow Jesus have migrated to more Pentecostal communities, if at all. In the wake of the sexual abuse scandals in the Catholic Church, many people have lost faith in church leaders and have been discouraged from hearing that the official church protected itself and the clergy when they knew abuse was happening. For many younger Catholics, there exist several issues that divide Catholics at the level of the local church and thus discourage their appreciation for the Catholic wisdom of life. There is a division within the local church over many social issues: climate change

---

1. Heaney, *Suspended*, 218.
2. Melling, "Sebastian Moore," 1.

and global warming, global economic inequalities, the separation of the prosperous global North from the poor global South, and the failed experiment of globalism in the hands of transnational corporations and its negative impact on poorer countries, to name a few.

In general, Catholics are either captive to a post-modern atheistic culture or a scientifically based understanding of life, often relying on a technologically driven culture. They have stopped believing in God and, subsequently, lost a feeling for God in their lives and, therefore, the felt need to surrender to God. Conversely, for many, the official church's stance on women and gay people in the life of the church remains a bone of contention and has caused them to decide to opt out of the faith community.

Specifically, Moore wrote for an audience who saw their life direction through a psychological awareness and were willing to take up the challenge of knowing their conscious and psychic lives. Whenever people gather to reflect, the categories of the psychological disciplines have become second nature in their desire to make sense of their lives; whether the categories are taken from the depth psychology of Sigmund Freud and Carl Jung or the height psychology of Victor Frankl, the terms used are second nature to us. These forms of communication have become part and parcel of the language of our commonsense meaning-making, at least from the 1960s. This cultural orientation presents us with a specific and significant insight: navigating the issues that confuse, divide, and discourage Catholics today requires a return to human consciousness, to ourselves as feeling, thinking, and valuing beings and, therefore, involves self-knowledge and self-appropriation, without which we will be more reactive than responsive to social and cultural issues.

Firmly planted in the awareness that we must own our conscious and "unconscious" selves, Moore seeks to meld together psychological and religious insights. The title of my book comes from this insight. In one of his later books, *The Body of Christ: The Shudder of Blissful Truth*, Moore writes rather awkwardly what could arguably be the leitmotif of his life. He states: "Our desperate need today is for a new consciousness, a new awareness, not a sharper or a cleaner or a better awareness, or an awareness of more, but a new awareness. In all our experience, the you you never notice, open to God in the silence that the new atheists are filling with the mental noise of their angry words. Feel your silence, and you might even find yourself praying for them, poor men."[3]

---

3. Moore, *Body of Christ*, 103–4.

Second, Moore will not readily appeal to systematic thinkers since many of his writings are more exploratory than explanatory. He would say, "This is where I am up to so far." His books and articles mostly lack footnotes and references, which may be a turn-off to a systematic mind or someone who wants to pursue one of Moore's insights from within its primary source. There are some explanatory flourishes amid the descriptive writings, which are worth the effort of reflection. I am not setting out to be particularly critical of his writings; however, throughout this book, I will engage in a dialogue between Moore and other writers who, similar to Moore, are trying to appreciate similar texts and theological concerns. For example, Moore could have wrestled, in a far more comprehensive manner, with the thought of Freud and Jung and their use of the terms *ego* and *self* and the relationship between their understanding of these terms and Christian revelation. Despite this, I maintain that the overall corpus of his work affirms a thoroughly Christian anthropology, even if Moore does not systematically engage such terms in the way Robert M. Doran did so brilliantly.

Third, I remain saddened that a person who wrote so profoundly about religious faith and the human condition can easily be forgotten by the next generation. I know that we can easily forget people of enormous insight. This fact could also be said of other great theologians of the Catholic Church: Karl Rahner, Hans Urs von Balthasar, Hans Küng, and Johann Sebastian Metz, to name just a few. The fact that they passed over us and are replaced by other emerging theologians has much to do with the theologian's preoccupation with current issues in the world and new perspectives such as those that champion the cause of inclusivity within LGBTI communities.

This book is my attempt to demonstrate that Moore still has something to offer our current generation of faithful Christian and Catholic disciples of Jesus. Therefore, my approach is generous towards Moore's insights. Moore's writings have thrilled me and helped me understand myself and my life with my wife, Anita, and the reason why I daily surrender to Jesus. His insights have deposited before me many pieces of wisdom: the centrality of desire and the weakening of desire, and restoration of desire through love, our self-understanding as the church, our appropriation of the doctrines of faith, for example the doctrine of original sin, the Trinity, and the significance of salvation in Jesus. I am a better person for having set myself the task of understanding him, and I hope to impart this same joy to others.

Fourth, my original intention was to start reading Moore, and then I realized that this book's publication might coincide with the tenth anniversary of Moore's death in 2024. I was amused to find that the wiki page from the internet about Downside Abbey had a section on notable people to have come out of that Benedictine community, and the author of the wiki pages did not include Moore in that list.

Fifth, following my wife's death, I spent the first few months writing an autobiography of our life together. I think this book's writing has been a way of managing my ongoing sadness. The writing of the autobiography and the writing of this book have helped me express some of the deepest truths of my life. If I did not have the book to research and write, I would always be sad. Writing has been my way to recovery.

THE STRUCTURE OF THE BOOK

I have structured the chapters intending to present the significant theological and philosophical influences on Moore's writings and his critical theological concerns for Christian living.

Chapter 1 examines the relationship between Bernard Lonergan's writings and Moore's insights. Even until his final days of writing, Lonergan features strongly in Moore's approach to theology.

Chapter 2 presents Moore as a theologian with his unique theological method and Moore as a poet, trying to examine what kind of method informs his theologian writings and what he is trying to do through his poetry.

Chapter 3 outlines Moore's understanding of prayer, contemplation, conversion, and the significance of Eckhart Tolle in his journey of faith. His thoughts on contemplation open us to a fundamental distinction between a direct and an indirect awakening to God. His reflections on the experiences of Eckhart Tolle demonstrate that conversion can occur to people from theistic and non-theistic backgrounds. They are a mark of the Holy Spirit working in their lives even when interpreting the events does not have a Christian framework. It also alerts us to Moore's insistence that mysticism and being a mystic is an essential orientation for the Christian in the modern and post-modern world.

Chapter 4 expounds on Moore's engagement with the writings of Ernest Becker and his understanding of the importance of self-esteem, personal significance, our dependency on meaning, our denial of death,

INTRODUCTION

and what that denial does to our whole orientation toward God, others, and life.

Chapter 5 examines the two psychological categories of ego and self, as presented originally by Sigmund Freud and Carl Jung and the post-Freudian school of psychology. For Moore, these categories contain a key to understanding the meaning of redemption and sin for the believer. I will primarily engage these terms and their precise relationship to psychology, reoriented by Christian revelation.

Chapter 6 unpacks Moore's central category of desire in human living and draws on the influence of René Girard and the triangulation of desire. The nature of desire in Girard and Lonergan is very different, so there is a need to explore where they converge and diverge. In this chapter, I will outline Moore's understanding of the doctrine of original sin, which one could understand as the origin of the weakening of our desire, and what such weakening means for those who profess to be self-made people.

Chapters 7 and 8 explore the meaning and significance of Jesus for our lives drawing on Moore's engagement with the terms *ego*, *self*, *original sin*, *moral sin*, *generic guilt* and *moral guilt*, *sorrow*, and *forgiveness*. I have decided in chapter 8 to give an extended preamble on the theology of redemption to understand Moore's insights better.

Chapters 9 and 10 will examine Moore's theology of the church and other related questions to do with the life of the church, which Moore championed over a lifetime, including women, homosexuality, and mandatory celibacy for clergy and religious. Within the context of the church, I have included Moore's appreciation for the meaning of the Eucharist for Christian living, given that the Eucharist has been called the source and summit of the life of the church.

Chapter 11 unpacks Moore's theological explorations around the Trinity as a doctrine that must have a central place in the day-to-day life of the church but which often is met with glazed eyes, especially when preached about on Trinity Sunday. I have decided that speaking about Moore and the Trinity would only confuse the reader unless the reader already had some understanding of a traditional Trinitarian theology. Therefore, I have attempted to give some appreciation of a traditional Trinitarian theology before working out what Moore is saying and whether his insights help us understand the Trinity better or whether he confuses the theological concerns.

Chapter 12 unpacks Moore's insights into sexuality and outlines some of the gaps in the official church's pronouncements on sexual desire in a culture and social setting where sexual desire is expressed and accepted so openly by many Catholics.

Finally, there is Moore's cherished poetry. Most especially, he made it his whole life's concern to understand the poetry of T. S. Eliot. In *Little Gidding*, Eliot writes that we shall never cease our explorations and arrive at the end of such explorations only to realize that we know the place originally and uniquely for the first time. This poem sums up exactly how I feel about Moore's writings and the light he shines on my life journey. He also was interested in the poetry of Samuel Taylor Coleridge and the modern American poet Wallace Stevens.

I can honestly say that I know my life and soul better, illuminated by the insights of Sebastian Moore. I wish the same for the reader.

A BRIEF BIOGRAPHY OF MOORE

These few biographical details about Moore come from an article written by Joseph Melling, emeritus professor at Exeter University, on the occasion of a symposium for Sebastian Moore in 2017 and subsequently published in the *Downside Review* in 2018. I have since discovered that Melling was successful in publishing a work containing a complete biography in 2020 through Paulist Press. The title was *Sebastian Moore: An Uncommon Monk*. I have not been able to obtain a copy despite my best efforts.

Moore was born in Madras (now Chennai), Tamil Nadu, British India, on December 17, 1917. His father was Pierce Langrishe Moore (1873–1944), a chief of police, and his mother was Muriel Moore, whose maiden name was Strange (1882–1953). He was baptized by his uncle, the Bishop of Madras, with the name Charles Patrick Moore. His family always called him Patrick, even after he took his religious vows with the monastic name Sebastian. He spent his schooling years at Downside School in Somerset until he left in 1934 to join the Royal Navy. The school community at Downside was considered, at the time, to be one of the three best private Catholic boarding schools for young men in the whole of Britain. The other two schools included the Benedictine monastery and school of Ampleforth and the Jesuit Catholic boarding college of Stonyhurst. Students received a humanist education in the classics, studying history, mathematics, sciences, languages, and the arts. Sebastian emerged well-versed in French. He joined the Royal Navy in 1934 until he resigned in 1938 for the Benedictine monastic community of Downside

Abbey with a recommendation from the captain of the battleship HMS Rodney that he would have made a fine executive officer and could make a fine monk.

Any decision to enter monastic life comes with certain vows after the entrant completes his postulancy and novitiate. These include the vows of Obedience (including chastity), Conversation Morum (fidelity to monastic living), and Stability. In those days, there was a short period of postulancy, and then the aspirant was allowed to join the novitiate. Upon entering the monastery at Downside and adjusting to monastic daily life, Moore would have been struck by the imposing architecture of the buildings, constructed from Bath stone under a red tile roof. The monastery's collection of books and medieval manuscripts was probably one of the most important in the southwest of England.

The Divine Office would have been prayed communally each day, including the Readings of the Day, Lauds, Midday Prayer, Vespers, and Night Prayer before the great silence till the morning. Meals would have been eaten in silence, except when a person read some pious text during the meal. Women would not have been allowed to visit the interior of the monastery. In the case of Downside, the chapel possessed a relic of Blessed Oliver Plunket, an Irish martyr. The monks engaged in pastoral work in parishes, but the principal occupation would have been teaching in the abbey school. During Moore's time, the *Downside Review*, devoted to philosophical and theological studies, had already been established, and in time Moore became an editor of the journal.

The following years presented a most turbulent time for the monastery, the school, and Great Britain. In 1939, Hitler declared war on Great Britain, and the years that followed, till the end of the war in 1945, meant that the monastery and school community were expected to respond by doing their part toward the war effort. This duty to the war effort included housing medical staff, nursing staff, and other military personnel.

In 1947, Sebastian was ordained to the priesthood. He then studied English Literature at Christ College, Cambridge, and his supervisor was F. R. Leavis, for whom he wrote an obituary many years later. Moore emerged from his studies with a double first but later admitted that he wasn't sure whether his examiners considered him a genius or mad. He went on to obtain a doctorate in sacred theology at St. Anselmo in Rome and, there, came in contact with the theological thought of Bernard Lonergan. Upon his return to Downside, Moore became the master of studies for the novices and was awarded an academic chair in dogmatic theology. He kept that role till at least 1964 when he was asked to become parish priest of a Benedictine-run parish, St. Mary's Church, Highfield Street in Liverpool, England.

The Benedictines took the vow of Stability, which meant that the house they entered as novices was the house they stayed with for their whole lives. Sebastian served seven abbots during his time as Downside. Sebastian's mother died in 1953, and this caused him to fall into a deep crisis of confidence about his sexuality, especially fearing that "his homosexual desires would destroy his personal life and professional career."[4] This early emotional collapse led him to seek counseling and therapy with Freudian and Jungian psychoanalysts. At the same time, this series of therapeutic interventions interested Moore in the language of psychology and psychoanalysis as a way to self-understanding and self-knowledge. Through various poems, we can capture the intensity of Moore's relationship with his mother. Moore expresses the loss felt by his mother at not having her husband around and the loss felt by Moore at not having his father around to raise him, following the death of his father when Moore was only twenty-seven years old.[5] In the poem "To My Mother," Moore recalls the tearful consolation given him by God for what he missed emotionally through not having his father and through the fact that his mother had to live alone and without her partner.[6] In another poem, "The Old Monk Remembers His Mother,"[7] Moore hints at the lack of emotional affection between his mother and him. He speaks, however, of a dream in which his mother either appears to him or speaks to him. Following that dream experience, Moore felt healing from a sadness that had endured for many years whenever he thought of his mother. Others close to Moore assess that he appeared "as an outsider, even in those few years when he was a young monk resident in the Downside cloisters."[8]

Moore's thinking and speaking were gaining a reputation as innovative as the monastery witnessed various reform movements within the church in the postwar years. Rees states that while, in 1898, there had been seventy-eight English Benedictine parishes, by 1993, the number had gone down to thirty-one.[9] The postwar years saw several parishes

---

4. Melling, "Sebastian," 2.
5. Moore, "2012–2014 Blog," Dec 11, 2013.
6. Moore, *Contagion of Jesus*, 181.
7. Moore, *Contagion of Jesus*, 180–81.
8. Melling, "Sebastian," 3.
9. Rees, "Monastic Mission," 241.

handed back to the Diocese. The handing back of parishes, especially those that were a significant geographical distance from the monastery, was balanced by an increasing commitment to villages and mass centers in the monastery's direct neighborhood. A renewed commitment to the apostolate of Catholic schools also matched these services. The vocations to priesthood were abundant till the decline in the early 1970s. During the Second Vatican Council (1962–65), Melling assesses that divisions between traditionalists and innovators hardened into firm battle lines. The changes brought about by the Council were felt by the believer, especially in the Sunday liturgy. These changes to the liturgy included the introduction of the Mass of Pope Paul VI, concelebration by clergy, and the permission to use the vernacular. Each monastery was permitted to devise its scheme of community prayer instead of the Latin Office or Prayer of the Church and to submit its new programs to Rome for approval. The Bible was enjoying a higher status among the people of God. Sermons became an integral part of the mass, and the laity became participants rather than spectators in the liturgy. The Council decrees also promoted ecumenism, and in Great Britain, ecumenism between the various Anglican and Catholic monasteries was the place to start.

It was through the experience of being a parish priest that Moore would feel a significant amount of change. The change was not only coming from the deliberations of the Council but also from the broader challenges of the church's relevance in the modern world, the pace of change within society, the thought of atheistic thinkers that had moved out of academia and penetrated the wider society, and the question as to the continuing relevance and meaningfulness of religious faith for Catholics who were still linked to the community of faith by their Sunday mass.

Upon his appointment to parish ministry as parish priest of St. Mary's parish Liverpool, in the early 1960s, with his fellow monk Peter Harvey, on whom he had had a profound influence, Moore had little contact with the monastery. Years before, Moore was visiting Cambridge to discuss theology with young Catholic intellectuals, and Harvey' encounter with Moore influenced his decision to enter the novitiate at Downside. Now they would share a common parish ministry. Moore and Harvey represented a new spirit within the parish church community. Moore settled into parish life with Harvey and, by 1967, was joined by Kevin Maguire and Anselm Hurt as part of an experimental parish. Melling states that Moore's parish ministry comprised "a multiplicity of preaching, teaching, writing during a ceaseless round of activities."[10] I would add to this list the daily requirements of usual monastic life. These requirements include the Prayer of the Church of Divine Office recited in common. Moore published two works with Maguire: *The Experience of Prayer*, which showed their mutual love for poetry and their desire to speak on the topic of personal prayer, and *The Dreamer Not the Dream*, which was a reflection on the church community in the parish following the Second Vatican Council. He also published *Before the Deluge*, which he co-authored with Anselm Hurt, a book containing several short reflections for lay Catholics on various religious topics relevant to their lives. Only Moore remained in the priesthood and monastic life from that group of priests.

Then, something quite life-changing happened to Moore. As Melling states: "The liberation of Sebastian during the 1960s empowered him to venture beyond the realm of the intellectual and the introspective into the domain of physical intimacy."[11] Moore was fifty years old and had lived in a celibate monastic community with little to no experience or dialogue around sexuality. The formation in the monastery, in his earlier years, would not have included, in any way, the topic of human sexuality or the monk as a sexual person, apart from the importance of acknowledging sexual sins that needed to be confessed, for example masturbation. Melling asserts that his "clumsy attempts at romantic connections and predictable disappointments led to the recurrence of crisis and a return to psychotherapy. He subsequently fell deeply in love with the younger priest, and when the affair became known to his Abbot the humiliating confrontation resulted in his exclaustration from his community."[12]

Following this event, Moore was appointed to the United States in 1971 as part of the Jesuit chaplain ministry at Marquette University in Milwaukee, which became a more permanent role, including teaching theology to undergraduate students. Perhaps Moore's appointment was an attempt by his superiors to distance him from the events of Liverpool. Gordon Stewart recalls meeting Moore at a campus ministry meeting. He writes: "There was this strange monk who said nothing. He just observed. He was weird, but his eyes were penetrating."[13] At Marquette University, he came in contact with fellow theologians to discuss their dreams under

10. Melling, "Sebastian," 7.
11. Melling, "Sebastian," 3.
12. Melling, "Sebastian," 3.
13. Stewart, "God as Policeman."

the tutelage of Charlie Goldsmith, a United Church of Christ chaplain at Deaconess Hospital. This group also included Robert M. Doran, Tad Guzie, Vernon Gregson, and William Loewe. Doran had just completed eleven years of Jungian studies at a Jungian Institute in Switzerland. Moore was subsequently appointed to Boston College, Boston. At Boston College, he joined the Lonergan Workshops organized by Frederick Lawrence and attended by many others attracted to the approach of Bernard Lonergan. He became a regular contributor to the conferences held yearly. One workshop (Lonergan Workshop 14) was dedicated to Moore.

In those years at Boston College, he started to recognize the writings of René Girard, who helped further shape his thought around the nature of desire. Later in the nineties, he became friends with James Alison, another Girardian scholar, who lectured in theology while ministering to gay and lesbian people in Britain. They remained firm friends till Moore's death. Moore remained at the college till 1992, after which he returned to Downside Abbey, England. The years between 1970 and 1992 were among the most effective regarding Moore's writings and publications. By 1992, he had been absent from Downside for thirty years and was now seventy-five years old. On his return to the abbey, he struggled with a monastery needing an extensive overhaul. Moore felt that at his age the most productive contribution he could make was to teach monks how to best communicate the Christian faith to their students. The abbot also appointed him to teach theology to the novices. Those who attended the abbey's Easter retreat would receive copies of his prose pieces or sonnets, even if composed overnight. He liked to distribute these leaflets both to his fellow monks and to those who attended Sunday by placing copies in the pews.

Throughout his teaching and writing career, Moore provided several personal markers that influenced the direction of his theology. The markers were never clearly or deeply probed. Still, they indicate a man who was always reflecting on where he was up to in the journey of discovering God and self by means of a truthful ownership of his conscious and psychic self. Moore was never far from a personal assessment. He wrote of his life: "a Jewel-in-the-Crown; birth; sulk; bully; monk obsessed with Jesus crucified!"[14] Ever self-effacing, Moore relates how, in the latter part of his life, "I wake sometimes these days to my past as a parade of absurd

---

14. Moore, "Our Love," 29.

posturing."¹⁵ On one occasion, a person approached him about his school days, which they had shared with Moore, and pointed out how he was a bully during the period when he was eight or nine years old. Later, Moore wrote a poem about this event titled "Why I Was the Worst Bully." In the poem, he states that his bullying came from a place in his soul of self-punishment, the dread of being happy, loneliness, self-hatred, and cruelty.¹⁶ These feelings of disesteem and self-rejection were part of his sense of self in his early years of monastic formation. He states: "In the early days of Downside, I used to speak of a sense of being insubstantial."¹⁷ He was saddened by the memory of the early formative years of Downside when there was an emphasis on suffering renunciation and self-punishment. In the Tumblr blog, he writes: "I have always been prone to self-punishment, indeed to self-hatred and 'feeling bad about feeling good' was an accurate description of my self-punishing attitude."¹⁸

At other times, Moore was very self-effacing, not only about how he badly treated people but also about his reactions to those who badly treated him. Powering these occasions of reactions and hurts was "the need to be right," which became the title of yet another poem.¹⁹ While in the States, what irritated him the most was being asked what he was doing teaching in a US university and not in his monastery. Moore states: "I notice that I hate being asked, especially by women about my life's motives why I came to the States. It's the wobble. I'm protecting from them and, in the end, from Jesus wounded."²⁰ Yet on another occasion, after an invitation to share intimacy with a woman, Moore writes: "Here, I'm doing me in the universal first person is when I recall the verdict of a woman who fell in love with me that I had never loved anyone in my life [and] in falling in love with me, she had come slap up against my inertness."²¹ His diagnosis of inertness was Moore's obtuse reaction to an invitation to love, and he knew he had to change. He writes: "I have expressed dangerous feelings and numb to myself at dangerous spots. A woman I was very closely involved with told me this."²² Moore received

15. Moore, *Contagion of Jesus*, 129.
16. Moore, *Contagion of Jesus*, 129.
17. Moore, *Let This Mind*, 154.
18. Moore, "2012–2014 Blog," Jun 11, 2012.
19. Moore, "2012–2014 Blog," Aug 2, 2012.
20. Moore, *Let This Mind*, 165.
21. Moore, *Contagion of Jesus*, 129.
22. Moore, *Contagion of Jesus*, 124.

religious insight from various sources, which helped him come to terms with his wobble. Over and over, through cryptic autobiographical details, Moore affirmed that divine grace gets in at a point of acknowledged weakness within us. He admits: "I could never crumble till I felt refelt, recovered, my wonkiness . . . Rosemary Haughton's 'weak spot,' the point of [God's] breakthrough."[23] Indeed, there are three distinct religious conversion moments in his life. I will speak about these in chapter 3.

Moore felt the sting of being a Christian writer and publisher, often misunderstood and misquoted. When writing on Mary, the mother of the Lord, but put in a way that sounds somewhat autobiographical, he states: "Mary [the Lord's mother] has no difficulty in matching the expectations and disappointments [by others around her son] . . . being misunderstood [was met with] . . . perseverance through thick and thin . . . [And now, applying more to himself] above all, the exposure to the powers of 'superiors' with their limitations, with the conditions laid down in the rule of St Benedict."[24] Obedience was not always an easy vow to follow. Moore had his fair share of being misunderstood by those who listened to his preaching. The axiom *desire is love trying to happen* landed him in the most trouble. He writes: "Seen by an intelligent fanatic in a paper of mine never published that impelled him to take the paper to the CDF in Rome," a letter was received by his abbot from Rome asking for an explanation. Moore admits that "[the intelligent fanatic] had the intelligence to see that this formula creates insuperable problems for the official line on homosexuality."[25] In humor, he speaks of the letter and his name gathering dust on a hit list somewhere in Rome.

Moore's achievement was to communicate his feelings, meanings, and religious values through the art and mediation of the written word. For some seventy years, Moore pursued an intellectual life and a love of learning through writing theology, philosophy, and poetry. His academic style is not predominately systematic in scope but a series of explorations into issues, problems, and topics to do with religious faith and life that focus our attention on the task of becoming happy individuals. From his first article in *The Downside Review* on the poetic style of Gerard Manley Hopkins[26] to the final entry of his online blog on January 13, 2014,

---

23. Moore, *Contagion of Jesus*, 167.
24. Wolff-Salin, *Journey into Depth*, x.
25. Moore, *Contagion of Jesus*, 131.
26. Moore, "Gerard Manley," 184–95.

A New Awareness

Moore sets about to explore the meaning of our lives and how to become better the person God desires us to be.

In a *Lonergan Workshop* dedicated to Moore, Fred Lawrence recounts speaking to Moore about his intellectual life and asking about its origins. Moore attributes his academic pursuits to reading a book from the Downside Library by Père A. Gratry when he (Moore) was a schoolboy. At the time of Lawrence's question, Moore could not recall the book's title but later remembered. It was titled *The Well-Springs*, and Lawrence goes on to quote Gratry: "What you will ask me is the meaning of listening to God? What am I to do in reality? . . . Here is my answer: you are to write."[27] Gratry then goes on to quote Augustine's *Soliloquies*, which impresses Moore. In the *Soliloquies*, Augustine writes: "'Listen! Ask for strength; ask for help to find what you seek. Then write it, that this offering of your mind may animate and strengthen you. Think not of the generality of those who may need your pages. Some few will know how to appreciate them.'"[28] In Moore's mind, what Augustine said applied just as much to Moore's endeavors as to Augustine. Again, Lawrence quotes Gratry:

> Therefore to write one needs, not presence of mind only but the presence of one's soul. The heart too must be in it, nay the whole man. It is the real soul that we must get down to . . . you need the presence of your soul and the presence of God, that is your whole soul that must be awakened and the light of God shone upon you . . . you must write. You must strive to picture forth the grand whole and the delicate details of that inward scene of which you are catching so fleeting a glimpse. You must listen to and translate the hidden "veins of the divine whisper," you must follow up and capture the most delicate emotions of this newly awakened life.[29]

Finally, there are four biographical details worth mentioning that give us a picture of the man's identity. First, as a scholar and theologian, Moore felt deeply saddened at the plight of those theologians whom the Congregation for Doctrine and Faith, under the leadership of Cardinal Ratzinger and supported by Pope John Paul II, silenced in the name of church unity. He writes about his utter disappointment, sadness, and anger at how "the teaching of some of the more splendid [were silenced],

---

27. Quoted in Lawrence, "Dedication," ix.
28. Lawrence, "Dedication," vii–ix.
29. Lawrence, "Dedication," x.

including Jon Sobrino, who changed my theology forever."[30] He grieved the creativity lost to the church because of these actions.

Second, another personal issue near and dear to Moore was the place of gay people in the church. Late in life, Moore accepted that he was gay. He writes: "Now there is the whole matter of my homosexuality. What about my self-acceptance as a gay? Self-acceptance, whether gay or straight, is essential, the ground of well-being. And to be wholly self-accepting is to be free of the need to be right. But self-acceptance is historically complex, for until the condition is socially accepted, a man or woman's attitude to himself [or herself] is a potential binge for the pain-body."[31] Moore acknowledges the tremendous suffering he experienced over the non-acceptance of homosexuality in the church. This condition produced in him homophobic attitudes before he accepted himself. Moore admits that "looking back on my 22 years working in the States, I would have to say that I was homophobic."[32] Moore's resolution around issues of sexual identity was a pain felt bodily, an emotional suffering (anxiety and fear), and a personal challenge over many years.

In a radio interview given to ABC Radio National's "Religion Report" in Sydney, Australia, Moore was asked about the relationship between sexual desire and the monastic life that he chose. I will unpack his response more extensively in chapter 12. On the question of his calling to monastic life in the same interview, Moore tells the interviewer Noel Debien: "I think I chose the monastic life because I couldn't cope with people, with getting married, what everyone did . . . I suppose in being alone and obscurely knowing that that's where something was going to happen."[33]

Third, Moore's writings and occasional biographical details show him to be a man always in search of the truth about the emotional side of himself in his early years. This fact may partly explain why his writings deal with childhood and the early formative years and the influence of primary caregivers on emerging self-esteem and sense of self. As a man in his seventies, Moore confesses: "Having most of my self-analytic life seen myself as over-mothered, I now realize that I am hugely under-mothered, a condition that I share with most men of my nation, class, and time . . . The under-mothered child finds him or herself subsequently harking back to a never had closeness in an orbital relationship to the

30. Moore, "2012–2014 Blog," May 8, 2012.
31. Moore, "2012–2014 Blog," Aug 7, 2012.
32. Moore, "2012–2014 Blog," Aug 7, 2012.
33. ABC Radio National, "Dom Sebastian Moore."

mother."³⁴ Moore calls this condition of under-mothering an "original woundedness."³⁵ Again, in the same vein, Moore acknowledges: "For years I have known that the leitmotif of my life is panic. I now understand this panic as flowing out of the original lack in the ecstasy of trust."³⁶ On several occasions, Moore acknowledges that his community noticed that he never talked about his family of origin. Although, he may have relented on this point when it came to his celebrated nephews and English actors Ralph and Joseph Fiennes.

As a man in his mid-nineties, reflecting on his childhood upbringing, his decision for monastic life, and his early homosexual feelings, he writes: "[My mother] had to wriggle through the turmoil of an unusually heavy pain-body [unhappiness and perhaps depression] the memory of a mother who was sadness personified and always dressed in brown. This turmoil was accentuated by an adoption of the monastic life [on my part] as an alternative to a failed homoerotic adolescence, the life called 'family.'"³⁷

Fourth, three people mention meeting Moore and their recollections are worth repeating. Dan Carpenter met Moore when Moore came to the States. Dan was the editor of the Marquette University paper, *Tribune*. He speaks of spending a great deal of time conversing with Moore together with Joseph and Darlene McCook. Joe and his wife took Moore to Las Vegas on at least one occasion. In conversation with Carpenter, Moore never considered himself to be unfaithful to or rejecting the undivided tradition of the Catholic Church, even though his writings would have been innovative in the eyes of many people and beyond what the institutional church would have affirmed. This innovativeness was especially the case when it came to his interpretation of the doctrine of original sin. Though many considered his ideas to be stimulating, Carpenter also states that people generally thought that Moore

> had too many thoughts churning around his mind—possibly as a result of reading a diverse series of "gurus" without judiciously considering them in a wider context. Since he was not always the most lucid of writers, the absence of footnotes in his books added to the unease . . . . Scholars were attracted to his seminars on the Canadian theologian Bernard Lonergan, the Downside abbot John Chapman, and T. S. Eliot. But he could

---

34. Moore, "In Water," 94.
35. Moore, "In Water," 95.
36. Moore, "In Water," 95.
37. Moore, "2012–2014 Blog," Apr 11, 2013.

be surprised by innovations, as when he woke up shocked at having apparently wet his bed then discovered that he had been sleeping in a waterbed which had burst.... In extreme old age, he continued to attract a variety of visitors including American theologians and his cousin the actor Ralph Fiennes. He became even more outspoken, enthusing about the Clint Eastwood film *Dirty Harry* and praising his favorite American feminist, Gloria Steinem.[38]

David McCarthy blogs almost two years after his death:

> Sebastian was my mentor during my vocation as a potential postulant in the Order of St. Benedict. This occurred back in 1964, when the church in its wisdom had decided to conduct an experiment involving the installation of a three-man team of Benedictine monks to run a parish church in one of the more intensely working-class dockland areas of Liverpool.... The result was mixed reception from the hard-core doctrinal Catholic hardliners and a relatively short-lived tenure. Old Moore himself actually upset the applecart by stating from the pulpit that if the Sacrament of Penance could actually forgive sins, Jesus' death would have been entirely unnecessary.... Anyway, he didn't last too long after that, having effectively removed the absolution guilt trip from many of the previously guilt-bound congregation.[39]

Dwight Longenecker recalls being introduced to the French thinker René Girard when he lived in England and made a retreat at Downside Abbey. He states: "The Benedictine theologian Dom Sebastian Moore was a monk there and he would knock on my door after compline (when we were supposed to be observing the Great Silence) to discuss Girard. Dom Sebastian was usually armed with a bottle of scotch to lubricate the God-talk. I didn't know much about Girard's thought at the time but have come to share Sebastian's enthusiasm for the great man."[40]

Moore died on February 28, 2014, aged ninety-six. He was buried at Stratton-on-the-Fosse, Mendip District, Somerset, England.

---

38. Carpenter, "Recovering Dom Sebastian."
39. David McCarthy, comment on Prodigal Kiwi(s), "Dom Sebastian Moore."
40. Longenecker, "Picking a Bone."

1

Moore, Lonergan, and the Turn to the Subject

INTRODUCTION

In this first chapter, I will explore several points of intersection between the Canadian philosopher and theologian Bernard Lonergan and Moore. These intersections include the meaning of consciousness, self-awareness, and reflective self-awareness, the importance of self-discovery, the priority of the dramatic pattern of experience, how meaning works in our life, the various carriers of meaning, the multiple dimensions of conversion, and Lonergan's Mysterious Law of the Cross. Each of these topics becomes significant to Moore.

MOORE ABOUT LONERGAN

In a memorial article at the death of F. R. Leavis, Moore speaks about another profound influence in his life, the Canadian Jesuit philosopher and theologian Bernard Lonergan. He writes: "Leavis was one of those very rare men who opened my eyes. There has been one other such teacher in my life, the Canadian Jesuit Bernard Lonergan. I have long felt that there must be a profound connection between these two crucial influences.... One of Lonergan's most transformative ideas was that there are other conversions besides religious [conversions]."[1] Describing Lonergan,

---

1. Moore, "F. R. Leavis," 221.

Moore writes that he is a master "in the intellect as well as the heart."[2] He notes Lonergan's openness to psychological conversion: "There is moral conversion. The feeling drawn to a good that is not simply (the) advantageous as some others whom Lonergan has taught and changed have been convinced and Lonergan has strongly agreed that there is still another conversion of feeling perhaps, of imagination, of (the) psyche of our mythic, or symbolizing consciousness."[3] He asserts: "God knows we need this conversion today when a murderous defense policy is insinuating itself through a systematic murder of the language in euphemistic phrases like 'acceptable losses,' 'surgical strikes,' (and) fratricide."[4] It is evident to Moore that Lonergan's thought offers profound and practical insights from which any person might address today's religious, cultural, social, and political problems.

In a special edition of *Compass*, a Jesuit journal dedicated to the memory of Bernard Lonergan, Moore writes:

> What I have from Lonergan is a haunting, persistent and systematic conviction that the movement of my heart to the unknown God, of which I am more certain than I am of anything else in my life can be understood as felt-after by all my other desires as their fundamental direction and that, therefore, to help students to understand themselves as desiring beings is to move them toward the point where this fundamental direction of consciousness can show itself.[5]

He goes on to justify this claim by pointing to Lonergan's focus on the person, often called Lonergan's "turn to the subject," which is also a "zeroing in on consciousness as the central reality whose bewildering polymorphism is the reason for the dizzying variety of conflicting philosophies and policies whose being laid-hold-by the ultimate mystery makes it luminous and revelatory."[6] Moore describes Lonergan's ideas around mysticism and the mystic, the immediacy of knowing in the mystic's experience of God, and the conviction that "in this knowing all experience finds its meaning."[7] He notes that Lonergan always said that "concepts have dates. That was said in the late fifties. The

---

2. Moore, *Fire and the Rose*, xiv.
3. Moore, "F. R. Leavis," 222.
4. Moore, "F. R. Leavis," 222.
5. Moore, "For Bernard," 9.
6. Moore, "For Bernard," 9.
7. Moore, "For Bernard," 9.

Church—especially church authority—has still to learn it."[8] He concludes his short piece by saying, "I love that man .... In the seeming night of the world, thank God for this quiet, steady, and humorous light."[9]

LONERGAN'S INSIGHTS

I will now expand on Lonergan's insights into consciousness.[10] Moore started using the notion of consciousness in the 1950s, signifying his shift away from what previously was called the language of faculty psychology: possible intellect, passive intellect, agent intellect, and the will. Lonergan always suggests that a person would do well to be attentive to themselves and to their conscious performance, whether that person is a believer in the sacred, a lover, a moral agent, a researcher, a scholar, or simply a person who is trying to understand something in the drama of their life. Lonergan applied the phrase "the turn to the subject" to illuminate one's conscious performance. He speaks to the importance of self-presence, that is, "a person present to [oneself] for others to be present to [self]."[11] Consciousness is a dimension of presence, and Lonergan understands "presence" in three ways: first, inert objects are present in a space but are not present to each other; second, people can be present to each other; and third, a person cannot be present to another person unless the other person to whom they are present were not in some way present to themselves.[12] Being present to ourselves is being conscious. Moore calls this self-awareness.

Beyond Lonergan's self-presence and Moore's self-awareness, Lonergan's notion of self-appropriation invites the person to self-knowledge, and Moore is committed to self-discovery. Lonergan states that self-appropriation is the effort to discover the kind of person that one is. He employs an ocular metaphor, asserting that "what is important, in other words, is the looker, not the looked at, even when the self is what is looked at."[13] By self-appropriation, one comes to an ultimate point of

---

8. Moore, "For Bernard," 9.

9. Moore, "For Bernard," 9.

10. I know that Moore published an article on consciousness in *Downside Review* 75, 1957. I was unable to get a copy.

11. Lonergan, "Self-Appropriation," 352.

12. Lonergan, *Understanding and Being*, 15–17.

13. Lonergan, "Self-Appropriation," 353.

reference to deal with various questions.[14] Self-appropriation concerns both the subject as subject or our self-presence and the subject as object, the process by which we can arrive at a thoroughgoing knowledge of ourselves. In attaining self-knowledge, the subject intends to be the object of inquiry. While gaining knowledge of themselves, the subject can be present to or attend to oneself as a subject.[15] Therefore, the metaphor of "looker" should not mean that self-appropriation is accomplished through introspection as if one could take a long and hard look at oneself and become thoroughly knowing of oneself. Self-appropriation means that we are engaged in reflective practice by which we can analyze what we are experiencing when we are feeling, symbolizing, learning, choosing, and loving. This reflective practice reveals a presence to and of oneself as empirical when simply experiencing, a presence to and of oneself as intelligent when understanding, a presence to and of oneself as rational when making judgments, and a presence to and of oneself as existential when deliberating, making decisions, and choosing a loving course of action.[16]

Intellectual self-appropriation is grasping what is going on when we know. This form of self-appropriation involves sustained or heightened self-awareness of our concrete performance.[17] Moore calls this reflective self-awareness. This process makes demands and begins in a "sufficiently cultural consciousness," one aware of the complexity and range of human knowing.[18] Lonergan's theory about knowing is grounded in attaining insight. He is saying that within all our efforts to learn and to know about the world, ourselves or other people, there lies implicitly within human consciousness an ideal about understanding and knowledge. Since seeking knowledge is seeking an unknown through questioning, Lonergan states that the implicit ideal of knowledge is each person's ideal of asking questions, being intelligent, having insights, formulating hypotheses and concepts, weighing evidence, making judgments, and deliberating about choices.[19]

---

14. Lonergan, "Self-Appropriation," 359.
15. Lonergan, "Cognitional Structure," 209–10.
16. Arcamone, *Religion*, 46.
17. Lonergan, *Method*, 11–14. Lonergan's approach is more an analysis of the performing subject than a conceptual analysis.
18. Lonergan, *Method*, 22.
19. Lonergan, "Self-Appropriation," 351–52.

Moral self-appropriation involves attending to self as one deliberates on values, choosing what is better and more loving, and making the self a lot more aware of one's possible growth in freedom in a way that "to be aware of possibility is to be anxious."[20] Our conscious intending notices when we are oriented towards values by way of feelings, through such questions as: Is this worthwhile to pursue or not? Can I do better? Existentially, we can name the conscious and unconscious biases that prevent moral insights from emerging.

Religious or spiritual self-appropriation helps us articulate our awareness that God loves us and allows us to affirm God's solution to the problem of evil in faith. The problem of sin and evil brings about personal and cultural breakdown and solidifies the social issues of violence and alienation.[21] Religious development brings us to the awareness that there is a divine-originated solution to evil, offered to our freedom as a gift and whose acceptance makes possible a new direction for growth, a capacity for discerning the will of God and attaining transformation.[22] In religious self-appropriation, presence to self is a matter of articulating what is going on when we are in love with God and how this love affects the whole of human consciousness.[23] It is our self-understanding grasped by the love of God and oriented towards what is valuable.

Through the self-appropriation of one's intellectual, moral, and religious consciousness, a person can assemble, review, evaluate, compare, and identify the underlying roots of diverse accounts about any reality since the one thing we share is the human mind. Intellectual self-appropriation, moral self-appropriation, and religious self-appropriation can form a community in dialogue, seeking to shape an authentic critique of culture.[24] To deal with questions of profound significance through concrete performance, theologians and believers must commit to self-presence (Moore's self-awareness) and self-knowledge (Moore's reflective self-awareness). We can still live morally and religiously good lives without self-appropriation. Still, with self-appropriation, we can express more accurately what we are feeling, thinking, and doing and why others feel and think differently. Without commitment, we are all vulnerable to accepting destructive feelings uncritically, to being deluded by blind

---

20. Morelli, "Reflections on the Appropriation," 186.
21. Doran, "Jungian Psychology I," 396–97.
22. Doran, "Jungian Psychology I," 398–401.
23. Doran, "Jungian Psychology I," 407.
24. Lonergan, *Second Collection*, 213–15.

spots, entrapped by an unwillingness to seek what is truly good, and compromised by appealing ideologies and distorted inherited traditions. Trying to negotiate an open inquiry into what is better for us when fear, panic, anxiety, envy, and jealousy fill our minds and hearts is challenging. Beyond this challenge, there is also the difficulty of appropriating the experience of God in human consciousness, given the cultural and social conditions that promote a bias away from encountering God and toward a solely practical and one-dimensional approach to life.

Lonergan is well aware of these challenges and understands the problem of appropriation as threefold: learning, identification, and orientation.[25] The task of learning is about the slow acquiring of habitual insights or sufficient understanding so that a person can move from one viewpoint to another—a process of education facilitated by committed mentors in contexts of social stability and development.[26] The danger in religious communities where education is minimal is that religious authorities might use words as weapons of power. There may also be an implicit or explicit attitude that believers must not think for themselves but placidly receive beliefs when imparted to them. The task of identification is locating in oneself the data that confirms the account of what one is doing when one is feeling, knowing, and choosing through a heightening of consciousness, involving a shift in focus from the intended object to the subject intending.[27] The task of orientation highlights that, though we may be capable of intelligent inquiry and critical reflection, we may still "fail to orient ourselves towards truth, [thus] we both distort what we know and restrict what we might know," pointing to a bias away from a disinterested desire to know, to value and love.[28]

In *Insight* and *Method in Theology*, Lonergan explains the structure and operations of intentional consciousness that become foundational to appropriating the intrinsic norms for uncovering the intelligible, the real, the genuinely worthwhile, and the path towards self-transcendence.[29] Human experiencing, knowing, valuing, and deciding are all parts of a dynamic and invariant structure, a self-constituting whole of several

---

25. Lonergan, *Insight*, 582.
26. Lonergan, *Insight*, 582.
27. Lonergan, *Insight*, 582.
28. Lonergan, *Insight*, 582–83.
29. Lonergan, *Method*, 11.

parts.[30] Each part is related to the other parts of the structure so that if one part breaks down, the other parts are affected.

Flawed perceptions, incorrect understandings, false judgments mistaken for reality, and distorted values give rise to a situation where relevant questions are ruled out, insight is denied, falsehood is held to be true, and choices become destructive towards oneself or others. Distorted judgments and values lead to delusional attitudes that keep inaccuracies in place, potentially worsening a situation. On the other hand, by attuning ourselves to the operations of human consciousness, we achieve self-transcendence, moving beyond illusions and half-truths about reality toward what is truly good and worth doing.

Human knowing and acting are a compound of consciousness's four distinct yet interrelated levels issuing into practical action: experience, understanding, judgment, deliberation of values, and ultimately issue into the decision to love.[31] As we progress from lower to higher levels, we become more fully ourselves. Moore often spoke about the fully conscious person being a person of love. Empirical consciousness, or the level of experience where the word *experience* is technically understood, has conscious experience presented as data, the data of sense, and the data of consciousness.[32] To the extent that one is guided by wonder, where wonder acts like a hinge to a door of possibility, and to the extent that we are attentive to the relevant data of a given inquiry, one is better able to understand. Conversely, failing to attend to or notice the relevant data leads to a lack of understanding. The precept for this level is to be attentive.

Questions arising from empirical consciousness (What is it? How is it so? Why is it the case? What is its purpose? How does it work?) lead to the second level of intellectual consciousness (concerned with acts of understanding, direct insights, inverse insights), which gives rise to hypotheses, formulations, and concepts. Understanding requires we experience a field of data, wondering, inquiring, being curious about the data, ruminating over that data, waiting for insight (sometimes the wait can be very long since we cannot force insights), apprehending insight, and conceptualizing insight. We are getting to the nature of things and the intelligible content of specific data before us. The precept for this level is to be intelligent.

---

30. Lonergan, *Method*, 14.
31. Lonergan, *Method*, 9–10.
32. Lonergan, *Method*, 9.

These insights and their formulations give rise to questions for reflection or verification (Is it so? Is the insight correct?) that are concerned with existence or reality, constituting the level of rational consciousness or judgment. We return to our original understanding, anticipating that if our insight is correct, we will find sufficient evidence to verify it. Many fields of endeavor use evidence-based learning for ongoing knowledge in that field. Evidence needs to be brought to bear on insight before we can pronounce a judgment. A correct judgment follows the posing of questions for reflection and the weighing up of evidence, culminating in a reflective insight in which all conditions have been fulfilled to render a judgment. For Lonergan, a grasp of the objective veracity of judgment rests upon an understanding of the virtually unconditioned; namely, all conditions for that insight have been fulfilled. The precept for this level is to be reasonable.

Further questions arise beyond a judgment of truth and reality concerning deliberating, valuing, and choosing (Is it worthwhile or valuable? What am I going to do?), constituting the fourth level of rational self-consciousness or moral consciousness.[33] At the level of moral consciousness, one is concerned with intending the truly good and truly valuable so that knowing leads to doing, and the subject moves away from satisfaction as the criterion for what is good and towards what is genuinely valuable. Accordingly, the precept for the fourth level is to be responsible.

From this account of the operations within consciousness, Lonergan focuses on appropriating the polymorphic nature of our consciousness.[34] Polymorphism is constituted by several patterns of experience that orient our understanding in various directions: biological, aesthetic, artistic, intellectual, practical, dramatic, mystical, and religious.[35] I will demonstrate how Moore privileges the mystical, the intellectual, and the dramatic for the task of writing theology. Empirical consciousness is prepatterned by our interests and concerns, affecting our data choice.[36] For example, a person constituted predominantly by the biological pattern has physical survival as their primary concern, so when faced with threat or fear, the person is concerned above all to protect their life. It is also possible for patterns to coexist; for example, when dramatic and religious patterns dominate the experiential flow, the person can think and act

33 Lonergan, *Method*, 34–36.
34. Lonergan, *Insight*, 410.
35. Lonergan, *Insight*, 202–12.
36. Lonergan, *Insight*, 205.

religiously and practically. One implication is clear: cultural meanings and values influence the concerns that each of us has, and the different combinations of patterns shape differing personal horizons. These affect the selection of our values and, thus, culture. The exclusion of specific patterns due to the influence of less developed or distorted cultures may result in a lack of needed insights into reality and the lack of authentic moral values.

These insights into human consciousness and its operations underpin the reality that people are both discoverers of meaning (the meaning of the natural world) and makers of meaning (meanings and values that shape their lives and the lives of others). The world is mediated by meaning and motivated by value. Moore delights in speaking about the meaning or significance we impart to one another as a foundation for loving others. Lonergan explains the "meaning of meaning" through a forensic examination of what we do when we are meaning discoverers and meaning makers. To speak to all of Lonergan's insights regarding the meaning of meaning would be too broad, so I will focus on four particular points: the acts of meaning, the functions of meaning, the realms of meaning, and the carriers of meaning.

Lonergan asserts five acts of meaning: potential, formal, full, constitutive, and effective.[37] A potential act of meaning is one in which the meaning of a word or phrase and what is "meant" by the word are not distinct in the seeker's mind. For example, a person may smile at someone, but its complete meaning may need further investigation. We know the sense of the smile but do not know what the person meant by the smile. A person may use symbols in a poem to communicate the reality of God. The poetic symbols immediately affect the person reading the poem with a deep sense of God's love. Formal acts of meaning do distinguish between meaning and "meant" through conceiving and formulating insights. Full acts of meaning judge what is or is not the case and declare, "This is what was meant." Constitutive and effective acts of meaning are our decisions and actions according to the proposed meanings.

Lonergan asserts four functions of meaning: cognitive, constitutive, effective, and communicative.[38] These functions of meaning are a helpful tool to understand Moore's difficulties with Benedict XVI's assessment of the legacy of the Second Vatican Council, which I will discuss in chapter

---

37. Lonergan, *Method*, 73–76.
38. Lonergan, *Method*, 76–79.

9. Cognitive meanings are our efforts to get to reality and the objective world through understanding and judgments. From a young age, we are taught to distinguish between the real and the imaginary, myth and history, truth and fantasy, and well-founded adult and childish beliefs. It is a world in which we name objects, their distinctiveness, and connections with one another. In Christianity, we have Church doctrines that teach us that this is the truth about God and that is not the truth about God. Theological systems try to bring these doctrines into a meaningful whole and relate the world of the objects of faith to the world of the things of physical sciences, philosophy, and social sciences.

Constitutive meaning is the kind of person we become through the meanings worked out in our lives. As a believer, I am more than someone who accepts specific, clear affirmations of faith, primarily as expressed in the Creed. I am constituted in a certain way by these affirmations. I am formed into the person I am. The critical dimension to this meaning function answers the question: What kind of subjectivity or lived identity does this affirmation of faith bring me? It is centrally concerned with the transformation of human consciousness. It affirms that we live in a universe constituted by an all-enfolding and all-attracting love. Moore's theological enterprise is primarily situated in this function of meaning.

Effective meaning relates to what we do with the meanings when they are translated into our lives through building institutions and whole cities. The plans we make, the laws we keep, and the cultural and political concerns we bring to a situation conspire toward a world-making and world-transforming energy. If the Christian faith calls for authenticity and promises to bring genuine love to bear on the earth, following the example of Christ, then its meaning must be effective. There is also communicative meaning. Anthony Kelly states: "Christian faith communicates a range of meanings that sets us in the community of creation that identifies us as members of the body of Christ, that assures us of the shared 'Holy Breath' of the Spirit that discloses their identity as sons and daughters of the 'Father.'"[39] Communicative meaning secures that meanings can become a rich source of connectedness, making us into a specific "we" whether we achieve this bonding through all or any of the carriers of meaning such as artistic, intersubjectivity, symbolic, linguistic, or incarnate carriers of meaning.[40]

---

39. Kelly, *Expanding*, 85.
40. Lonergan, *Method*, 57–73.

It is also possible to recognize within consciousness various realms of meaning. These differentiations account for our control over the products of meaning that constitute our identity and mediate the difference between reality and illusion, value and disvalue. These realms are called common sense, theoretic, interiority, and transcendent.[41] The realm of common sense is concerned with our day-to-day practical lives.[42] Common-sense knowing and valuing are practically oriented through descriptive thinking, expressed in everyday language, and concerned with how an issue affects us now. In the normal and good sense of the word, common-sense thinking is egocentric, intellectual, widespread, practical, and intersubjective. The person of common sense asks: How do I do this in the most practical way to address the issue for us here and now? Religious expression in common-sense thinking is the identification of spiritual experience with its outward manifestations: the external (for example, the text), the spatial (for example, a piece of land), the practices of a group (for example, the way of life), and the human (this community).[43]

In terms of spiritual transformation, there may have been a time when being practical was enough to sustain people. However, there are indications today that simply a practical approach is insufficient to overcome the distortions in communities divided by hatred. Lonergan puts the matter urgently: "But if man's practical bent is to be liberated and turned toward the development of science, if his critical bent is to be liberated from myth and turned towards the development of philosophy, if his religious concern is to renounce aberrations and accept purification, then, all three will be served by a differentiation of consciousness, a recognition of the world of theory."[44] Yet, our understanding of and solutions for complex and challenging problems require "fully differentiated consciousness," which Lonergan was convinced "is the fruit of an extremely prolonged development."[45] Common sense is not concerned with complexity, long-term solutions to problems, an ultimate resolution of ongoing issues, or the most optimum way of thinking, evaluating, and acting. Indeed, people may even resentfully brush aside or ignore any attempts to raise questions about long-term solutions.

---

41. Lonergan, *Method*, 81–85. Lonergan also proposes a fourth differentiation, the realm of art. See Lonergan, *Insight*, 187; *Method*, 303–4.
42. Lonergan, *Method*, 81.
43. Doran, "Psychic Conversion," 52.
44. Lonergan, *Method*, 258.
45. Lonergan, *Method*, 257.

The realm of theory gives rise to more explanatory ways of thinking, knowing, and valuing in all fields of study and is illustrated in religious traditions by the introduction of dogmas, theology, and juridical terms.[46] Rather than understanding how this issue relates to me or this group practically, theory is concerned with reaching a systematic exigency by introducing terms and the relations between the terms to expand our understanding of issues. The explanations advanced are meant to deliver objective knowledge and objective morality that go beyond the immediate practical interest of this subject or community. Theory and common sense are often mistakenly pitted against one another rather than seen as complementary ways of knowing.

The realm of interiority makes it possible for us to distinguish between common sense and theory.[47] I have concluded that Moore's theology prioritizes this realm of meaning. Interiority moves from consciousness of self and objects of the world to self-knowledge by means of grasping the structure and operations of knowing, valuing, and loving. By inhabiting the realm of interiority, we will also learn when we make progress and why we engage in human breakdown. The move to human interiority means that knowledge of truth and values is attained through faithfulness and attunement to intrinsic norms. Interiority helps us identify and value which operations within consciousness are active at any given moment, especially as we move from practical common sense to the realm of theory, with its technical and precise knowledge. An interiorly differentiated consciousness allows us to develop the categories of all our knowledge, whether for philosophical or religious understanding. For Moore, these categories include psychological categories including self and ego, guilt and shame, self-love and love-gift, and self-for and self-against, to name just a few.

Finally, Lonergan identifies the realm of transcendence as our experience of surrendering to the Divine with devotion, prayer, and acts of love.[48] Moore grounds theological writing in the theologian as contemplative. The gift of God's love is, therefore, itself a realm of meaning, transforming us through the experience of the forgiveness of sin, cultivated by a life of prayer and self-sacrifice and then "intensifying, purifying, clarifying, the objectification(s) referring to the transcendent whether in the realm of common sense, or of theory, or of other

---

46. Lonergan, *Method*, 82–83.
47. Lonergan, *Method*, 83.
48. Lonergan, *Method*, 83–84.

interiority."⁴⁹ As consciousness differentiates, theoretical questions about the transcendent will emerge. With the person's differentiation into common sense, theory, and religious interiority, self-appropriation leads to operations of experiencing, understanding, judging, and deciding and an appreciation for religious experience and religious conversion.⁵⁰

The realms of meaning help us appreciate the insufficiency of practical, common-sense knowing (whose focus is getting a job done) and the insufficiency of theory alone, with its technical precision and specializations. The realms also highlight the importance of not only being religiously and morally upright but also of being able to articulate intelligently and with precise self-knowledge what is going on in human consciousness. Yet, the realms of meaning articulate a ground beyond theory and common sense that would help us avoid relativism. The realms also reveal that human development is about human creativity and self-transcendence and the power of God acting in our lives. The power of God becomes the ground for doing what God wants, choosing responsibly, and gaining an accurate knowledge of God.

Finally, Lonergan offers insights to help us understand how meanings and values develop. I want to mention four notions central to Moore's theology and spirituality: self-transcendence, horizon, dialectic, and conversion. Lonergan states that self-transcendence "is the achievement of conscious intentionality."⁵¹ Since achieving conscious intentionality has many parts to be sustained over a long period of development, so does the process of self-transcendence. I have already stated that moving from lower to higher levels of consciousness is to achieve a richer measure of self-transcendence. Lonergan also warns of the challenge to self-transcendence. He says: "But it is one thing to do this occasionally, by fits and starts. It is another to do it regularly, easily, spontaneously; it is finally only by reaching the sustained self-transcendence of the virtuous man, that one becomes a good judge, not on this or that human act, but on the whole range of human goodness."⁵²

Following Lonergan, Conn states: "The fundamental desire of the self is to transcend itself in [the form of] relationship—to the world, others, and God."⁵³ Conn recognizes two focal points in this fundamental

---

49. Lonergan, *Method*, 266.
50. Lonergan, *Method*, 266.
51. Lonergan, *Method*, 35.
52. Lonergan, *Method*, 35.
53. Conn, "Understanding," 3.

desire: the drive to be a self, a center of strength, and the dynamism to move beyond the self into the various relationships of our lives. Conn asserts that these two elements are inextricably connected and must always be understood; therefore, we experience separation *and* attachment, independence *and* belonging, and autonomy *and* relationship.[54] As Tad Dunne affirms, our developing lives are not so much "an interest *in* self [self-interest] but an interest *of* self in what transcends the self: intellectual objectivity, collaboration with others, the true well-being of others, personal openness to all things good and allowing love to take the lead in our heart."[55]

Horizon is the full scope of everything we feel, think about, value, love, and care about. The image of a horizon gives rise to another image: standing on the beach, looking out to the visible horizon before us as far as the eye can see. For Lonergan, the horizon metaphor is "the scope of one's knowledge and the range of one's interests."[56] Moore uses the term several times, especially when he speaks to the horizon of death. Within each person's horizon there are things we care about that are remote and so in the distance and things that are proximate and near to us. More often than not, we attend to the near horizon while the things in our remote horizon need more time and attention. We do not care about everything with the same intensity. Our patterns of experience are shaped by the things we care about within our horizon. As our horizon expands, so does the possibility of further insights and building on other insights in our lives. The existential truth that we affirm shapes our identity. Our feelings are a crucial part of our horizon, and one of the most essential is the feeling we have of ourselves, which we call self-esteem. Moore makes ownership of our feelings and achieving self-esteem a central concern for human living.

Our horizons change, and the best way to understand this change is to employ Lonergan's notion of dialectic and conversion. A dialectic is the recognition of two opposed drivers of change mutually conditioning one another when they operate and take into account the existence and relevance of each other. In terms of transforming a person's horizon, dialectic can inform a general notion of development, which involves a tension between limitation and transcendence where the pole of limitation is the integrator in the dynamic, and the pole of transcendence is the

54. Conn, "Understanding," 3.
55. Dunne, "Rights," 13–14.
56. Lonergan, *Method*, 237.

operator in the dynamic. The integrator brings harmony and stability to a thing and a base from which change can happen; the operator functions to transform the current situation in the direction of transcendence. The operator is always ceaselessly transforming the integrator.[57] There are dialectics of contraries and dialectics of contradictories. When the opposing drivers work together in a creative tension towards the direction of transcendence, we have a dialectic of contraries. There are also dialectics of contradictories when the two drivers work against one another in opposite directions. Moore articulated several dialectics in human living. His dialectics of contraries are self-love and self-gift, finite and infinite, grace and nature, and oneness and separation. His dialectics of contradictories are good and evil, "This is my body for you," and "This is your body for me," and self-for and self-against.

Finally, conversion helps us understand precisely how we develop within our horizons. Conversion indicates a whole reevaluation of our feelings, thinking, valuing, and acting that make up our horizon, from one ruled by distortions to one more authentic. Often, conversion can have a traumatic effect on our lives. Moore often mentions Eckhart Tolle's experience and his descent into the vortex. Religious conversion is the core of religion, the light of faith, capable of healing people so that their wounded creativity and derailed capacity for responsibility can be rediscovered and restored. It is grounded in the gift of the love of God poured into our hearts.

Moral conversion is a change in the criteria by which we make commitments and choices from "satisfactions to values."[58] Lonergan's satisfaction is closer to the sense of paralysis that gives rise to indolence and is the condition of the person who drifts through life. Values are a reasonable assessment as to what truly is worthwhile. Related to moral conversion is affective conversion. Affective conversion is a wholehearted commitment to the unrestricted range of love. It is a state of being where feelings respond to the highest values, orienting and motivating us towards moral self-transcendence. Lonergan states that affective conversion is present in our lives when "our questions for intelligence, for reflection, and for deliberation constitute our capacity for self-transcendence. That capacity becomes an actuality when one falls in love. Then, one's being becomes being-in-love . . . once it has blossomed forth and as long as it lasts, it

---

57. Arcamone, *Conversion*, 38–39.
58. Lonergan, *Method*, 240.

takes over. It is the first principle. From it flow one's desires and fears, one's joys and sorrows, one's discernment of values, one's decisions and deeds."[59]

Intellectual conversion is the elimination within human consciousness of the myth that reality is grasped by simply taking a look and recognizing the radical difference between taking a look and facts affirmed through reasonable judgments. Much of what I have said about human consciousness and its activities is the fruit of intellectual conversion. Finally, there is psychological conversion. Here, we must distinguish between psychic and psychological. Psychic conversion is very nuanced and specific. It is a radical change in the human psyche that becomes a means to the constructive generation of feelings, images, memories, and symbols and away from a repressed stance towards these psychic products. More generally, psychological conversion is a shift away from any neurotic functioning of the human person, that is, a change from a state influenced by anxiety, fears, the possibility of paralyzing guilt, unrecognized or acknowledged anger, depression, debilitating tension, a sense of partial loss of control of the self and life and other symptoms so that by removing these neurotic aspects, the person can move towards a healthier functioning.[60] Moore's concern is for feelings and psychic wholeness, and with this in mind, he speaks to the relationship between psychological breakdown and the doctrine of original sin, conversion, and desolation. I will talk extensively about religious conversion in chapter 3.

MOORE APPROPRIATING LONERGAN

Moore states that Lonergan's focus on the "turn to the subject" is "massive in nature."[61] He often uses the term *existential subject*. By existential, Moore is denoting the person striving for authenticity. Following Lonergan, authenticity is acquired by affirming true value judgments and putting them into action. Authenticity is an ideal and becomes an achievement through ongoing conversion moments and activity. Religious conversion is very central to Moore. The disposition of being in love made possible by religious conversion brings us a new awareness for understanding values and a new awareness of other people. As Moore

---

59. Lonergan, *Method*, 105.
60. Arcamone, *Conversion*, 222.
61. Moore, "For a Soteriology," 229.

would explore throughout his life, it makes a significant difference to any God-talk if a person has already decided that there is no God, that we are the product of our self-making, including independence from others. Alternatively, if someone has already decided that the world's order is underpinned by violence and confrontation, they will make other decisions. Similarly, it makes an enormous difference if we are convinced that the natural world is passive and ripe for our self-making in whatever way we choose. By contrast, if we prioritize becoming the best version of ourselves through our love for others and God, our lives develop on a different path.

Self-Awareness, Reflective Self-Awareness, and Consciousness

First, Moore always speaks about the importance of self-awareness. Self-awareness is grounded in Lonergan's account of consciousness. With a proper understanding of consciousness, we can understand the meaning of self-awareness. Self-awareness has two different stages. In the first stage, the self-aware person is being conscious. I am aware of my feelings and my intended operations. Moore can, therefore, say, "I am self-aware or having myself not as an object of my awareness, but rather myself as a subject of awareness, self-awareness is something I bring and have to bring to every act of thought or feeling or decision, it is my end, the me-end of everything I do. Whenever there is awareness, there is self-awareness."[62]

Here, Moore distinguishes between self-awareness as our "first knowing" or self-presence and reflective self-awareness as our "second knowing" or self-knowledge. I don't know whether Lonergan would agree with Moore's first and second knowing language. However, Moore and Lonergan are in sync regarding the difference between self-presence and self-knowledge. The latter is objective knowledge of ourselves and knowledge of our inner activities.[63] Lonergan presents far more detail about human consciousness and the knowing subject, and Moore gives more detail on consciousness and the feeling subject. For Lonergan, knowledge of consciousness is more than simply introspection or "taking a look" at consciousness and its emotions, states, and acts. Knowledge is far more precise. Knowledge is equivalent to Moore's "second knowing," or the difference between mere interests, introspection, and an accurate

---

62. Moore, *Let This Mind*, 10.
63. Moore, *Let This Mind*, 10.

introspective process that he calls "second knowing." Nor is knowledge simply a matter of formulating concepts about what we observe through mere introspection. Knowledge comes about through reflective self-awareness or reflective acts of questioning, understanding, and judging. Reflective self-awareness as second knowing requires that we exercise a heightened consciousness: we wonder about our inner world and come to insights and judgments about our inner world. This process is directed by the desire to know, value, and grow into a more responsible and loving human through greater inner awareness.

Louis Roy, a theologian and advocate for Moore's insights, distinguishes two stages within consciousness. He speaks about consciousness-in and consciousness-of, as well as a third form of consciousness, mystical consciousness.[64] Moore's self-awareness as "first knowing" is what Roy calls consciousness-in. Consciousness-in is the condition for the possibility of self-awareness as "second knowing" or reflective consciousness. In the consciousness-in form, we discover that consciousness is never inert. Consciousness is ever in process, accompanying our inner acts and operations and making them events for us and to us. In the second form or consciousness-of, or what Moore calls reflective self-awareness or "second knowing," consciousness has the subject, you and I, taking ourselves as an object of inquiry to have more significant and more precise self-knowledge and self-understanding. Moore, following Lonergan, is engaging in the turn to the subject simply by moving from thinking about intellect and will to thinking about consciousness. Consciousness permeates all intra-personal and interpersonal knowing, valuing, and loving awareness. Yet, consciousness is not what I know, but who I am and what I am, and how I am existentially in my daily life as well as my direction and final destiny and will consist in actualizing my identity and the person I become. The more conscious and intentional my life is, the more I desire God.

Critical Realism and Moore

Second, Moore accepts Lonergan's critical realism. Moore is well aware of Lonergan's analysis of intentional consciousness and the process of human knowing and is fully convinced of it.[65] In a talk given to the

64. Roy, *Engaging the Thought*, 142–44.
65. Moore, "New Life," 148–51.

BBC Third Program on Radio on the twenty-eighth of September, 1961, and as "a subjective tribute to Lonergan," Moore explains to his audience the difference between saying "I saw something" and calling that knowledge and the process of human intentionality from experience to understanding and judgment, in which the act of judgment gives us a possible, probably or certain knowledge of reality.[66] Reality is not what we see. The mind has an invariant structure through which it advances to lay hold of reality unless the mind is hopelessly biased. We see, understand, and judge. Reality is the whole to which the mind advances. This insight helps us to understand the relationship between the mind and reality as not one of "looker" to "looked at" but instead as an affinity between the structure of the mind as knowing and the structure of reality as known. Moore concludes that in understanding the mind's real object, reality is understanding something of the nature of metaphysics.[67] In an early article on the difference between empiricism and realism, Moore points out that Lonergan set out to prove in *Insight* a "realist bias is the structure of the human mind" as distinct from a naïve realist or even an idealist bias of the human mind. A realist bias is based on the insight that knowledge is not the "already-out-there-real," but knowledge is attained through experiencing, understanding, and judgment.[68] The only way to grasp truth is by being attentive to our conscious performance.

Moore: Noticing and Focusing

Third, Moore appreciates that noticing or being attentive is a challenging act. We can be distracted by all sorts of things around us. We live in an age of distraction, and we need some technique to help us be attentive. Due to the many distractions, it is easy to become subtly civilized into a lack of truth and values. Our minds and hearts can be colonized with untruth. We can exercise specific psychological mechanisms for good or away from the good. They are hidden from sight: projection, denial avoidance, suppression, resentment, and even repression that prevent the truth from emerging. Being attentive and noticing who we are, day-to-day, and in our relationship with God and others is a vital step to self-discovery and growth. Being focused and noticing are the first steps in

---

66. Moore, "Discovery of Metaphysics," 122.
67. Moore, "Discovery of Metaphysics," 123.
68. Moore, "Realism," 99–100.

the journey of self-discovery. Then, we can better follow the imperatives to be intelligent by asking questions and searching for insights. We are better able to be reasonable so that those insights relate to everything else we know, value, and love.

What appeals to Moore is that we are always trying to make sense of our experiences. To arrive at some point, noticing our personal experience is a vital starting point. It presumes that what is real is mediated by meaning. The goal is to arrive at intelligent insights that mediate what our experience means. From the grasp of what is real and true, we can ask: What do I need to do? What is my responsibility, given this affirmation of reality? Where is reality taking me in terms of presenting what is worthwhile for my life? My feelings, symbols, and memories link what I understand as real and what I judge as valuable.

Moore is committed to finding ways to determine what he is feeling, symbolizing, and remembering. He introduces the technique of focusing. Self-appropriation requires taking time to be with ourselves, and focusing becomes a technique for accomplishing this task. Focusing, in the first instance, is a process of self-presence. We can then ask about ourselves by first attuning to our embodiment. The focusing technique is a pathway into feelings and a means to truly understand what it means to be embodied as a person. To focus, one must first reach a plateau in one's life from which one can sink a plumb line. Moore states that focusing "introduces the practiser to the place a Shakespeare is working from, the mint of metaphor and symbol, the very 'how' of the process whereby images of ordinary things become endowed with overwhelming power."[69]

Focusing is allowing the body to tell us how we are feeling. The only way to move on from feelings of fear, panic, and anxiety is first to name them. To name them, one must be quiet through focusing and wait for insight to emerge that might help to change troubled feelings.[70] If the right words come, a "body shift" occurs, a release of tension.[71] The presupposition is that the body has a memory, and the memory it carries is what we are feeling or what we have felt, and there is wisdom to be gained from staying in the feeling and waiting for insight. Moore alludes to the expressions we often use: that person is "a pain in the neck." Instead of dealing with negative and stressful feelings through a flight or fight reaction, Moore encourages his readers to stay with the feeling and wait. There may

---

69. Moore, "Poetry of the Word."
70. Moore, "Body Speaks," 155.
71. Moore, *Let This Mind*, 18.

not be any solution that emerges immediately to the hurtful or anxious feeling. Still, I will better understand their origins and possible direction by staying with the feelings.[72] Alternatively, it may be possible to call up "the happy body" in stressful situations so that our body is at its best to deal with the stress.

Moore provides an example in an autobiographical note where he mentions his obsessive struggles with panic.[73] Moore's emphasis on focusing comes from his personal experience of wanting to fix things immediately whenever a problem causes panic. Focusing is Moore's alternative to panicking and the overwhelming impetus to "fix things." He affirms that the same could be said about religion: "We come to God as a super-fixer."[74] By staying with his feelings of panic and applying the method of focusing, he discerns what he most wants: dignity. The body speaks a language, and when it is denied its opportunity to speak, it becomes a victim, either victimized by others or ourselves. The body's language can give us clues into what we seek in life, what we are trying to discard, and what is unhelpful to living. Moore states that when the body speaks and we listen, we notice the "language [of the body] in which I am finding myself, free from some captivity that has been synonymous with civilized consciousness."[75] When our body speaks, its concrete "human cover" is blown, and rather than allowing ourselves to lapse into self-rejection, love paves the way for the self-acceptance of this blown cover and the sign that the body is coming alive fully.[76]

Moore again writes in an autobiographical note about the importance of noticing, especially when it uncovers the "feeling like I was a mistake," a feeling state that he returns to many times during his journey of self-discovery. The pain of disesteem and self-rejection can have no relief while it stays in the head and continues to cause so much unstated anger that stifles creative writing and artistic expression. Until the body is heard, there will be no resolution to painful inner moods or states. For Moore, "spiritual pain is pain inflicted on the body,"[77] and personally manifested in him by "never having felt allowed, or invited, or loved, to be me."[78]

---

72. Moore, "Body Speaks," 156.
73. Moore, "Body Speaks," 159.
74. Moore, "Body Speaks," 156.
75. Moore, "Body Speaks," 160.
76. Moore, "Body Speaks," 161.
77. Moore, "Body Speaks," 163.
78. Moore, "Body Speaks," 164.

Moore asserts: "This existential angst cannot be dealt with in the head. It is in the body! So, until the body is 'heard,' there is no resolution to the anguish. When the body is heard, resolution, or at least movement and change, begins. In fact, an elementary map of the body's feeling life begins to emerge . . . *Spiritual pain denied is pain inflicted on the body.*"[79] He defines spiritual pain as pain that hurts so much one has to deny it to oneself and everyone else.[80] Moore asserts, "I must go into myself where I find what that little boy in the story may have found a gnawing disbelief in me as someone in my own right. Something in me fits with, or lets in, the non-respect that I seem to hear from others. It is perfectly clear to me that my story is only one [story] form of the human story under the reign of death."[81] The method of focusing is ripe for discovering himself or beginning the process of self-appropriation and can be the first step toward a fuller sense of his goodness. In religious faith born of religious love, we become convinced that life's worth is mysteriously upheld and continued by the mystery of God at the heart of the universe. Moore's "turn to the subject" has become "a turn to the body."[82] Moore is not saying that intelligence and responsibility are not necessary, but rather, since intelligence and responsible commitment rely on noticing and asking questions, only by turning to the body can a person notice what is happening to themselves, name it, and then try to understand what to do about it.

THE AFFIRMATION OF ORDER AND THE ACT OF JUDGMENT

As well as focusing on the world of feelings, Moore also shows respect for the process of understanding, especially the act of judgment. With his colleague and friend Glenn Hughes, Moore maps out the relationship between the process of knowing and an affirmation of order that God has placed into creation. Any exploration into the process of bringing about an ordering of our lives has enormous ramifications if we do not start from the right place. For example, in gender politics, the official Church has argued for centuries that our gender orientation is grounded in our physical nature alone. In contrast, many people today speak about having

---

79. Moore, "Body Speaks," 163.
80. Moore, "Body Speaks," 165.
81. Moore, "Body Speaks," 165.
82. Moore, "Body Speaks," 170.

the right to choose their gender orientation or, indeed, to be known by both genders or no gender, as each person sees fit.

Usually, people argue that order is apprehended in one of two ways. First, we affirm that there is a pre-existent order already in nature and given by God, and all we have to do is surrender to it. The order within nature is revealed in the Scriptures by God. Lonergan assesses this kind of thinking as underpinned by a classicist view of culture. The classicist notion of culture is normative and permanent. There is an attitude of facticity toward nature that requires no interpretation.

Second, we make meaning and impose our order on chaos as we choose and see fit. This trajectory does not give any criterion for judging how we interpret or whether our actions will lead to more authentic living. In our present culture, authenticity is often grounded in emotivism, where the criterion for decision-making is placed on how we feel, choosing to do what we think is good when the criteria for decision-making are feelings alone and pleasurable consequences for ourselves.

Both Moore and Hughes opt for a third way, namely, that being human means being a creative participant in the order of being.[83] They speak about the cognitional process by which we know and value anything, distinguishing between direct insights, reflective insights, and oversights. Direct insights grasp an intelligent pattern in the data of experience according to questions that are asked. Reflective insights affirm insights to be true or false, real or unreal, since correct insights are grounded in evidence. These are two different acts within the one process of cognition. The first is an act of intelligence. The second is an act of judgment. They conclude that if we collapse judgment into intelligence, the reduction represents a significant shift in how we experience our relationship to order in reality. When we collapse judgment, order derives from the creative process of understanding alone, and this amounts to order based on some brilliant conception of the mind.[84]

Losing the distinction between understanding and judgment leads to the experience of thinking that we alone are the creators of order. We become trapped in an idealist understanding of human knowing and move away from critical realism. Thus, what we declare real and valuable is mistakenly grounded solely in our feelings, understanding, and will. As we impose our order on the chaos, there forms the idea that there is a

---

83. Hughes and Moore, "Affirmation," 109.
84. Hughes and Moore, "Affirmation," 110.

split between the order of things and reality itself since order is imposed on what we term pre-existing reality. The consequence of this position for our modern values and meanings, what we call the culture of modernity, is that any order we design or devise is doomed to end when we die.

This view about order distorts our understanding of death. The fact of our death, pointing to our finiteness, has no part to play in how God might have structured reality. We can only then accept death with courageous comportment.[85] The worst outcome of this option is to see the countless victims of human evil within history brought on by actors who are heedless to their pretensions. Nietzsche's madman running down the streets of his town crying out that God is dead and that we have killed him echoes the hypothesis that without God, all things become possible, even the evilest of crimes. This condition is grounded in the conviction that we are the sole source of order in the universe. To believe that we are the sole source of order either by power over others or some other act of the will is to be in love with chaos, the extinction of all God-given order, with nothingness, and eternal death.

This worldview is one of the hallmarks of an emerging modern culture that has downplayed the importance of the moment of judgment and the imperative to be reasonable. We, therefore, must ask ourselves: "Does the order I have, through insights discovered, conceptualized, hypothesized, reflect the order that this world is?" At this point in the argument, Moore's voice comes to the fore when he asks: Do we recognize Hitler in ourselves? Why does intellectual sin attract us? Intellectual sin is "the lack of surrender to contemplation to the Divine order in which we exist."[86] When we are open to contemplating the Divine order in which we exist, there remains the possibility of a profound ennoblement. When we refuse the contemplative moment, we are in danger of bringing upon ourselves an impossible burden, confused anxiety, and doom.[87]

While Samuel Beckett views life as the contradiction between two opposing principles of change, the principle of the imperishable human spirit and the principle of the de-limiting reality of death, other authors including Søren Kierkegaard view life as two contrary, opposite poles, the pole of the finite and the pole of the infinite in mutual creative tension with one another. For Beckett, the grace of God is imaginary and delusory. For Kierkegaard, the grace of God heals our unfreedom and

85. Hughes and Moore, "Affirmation," 111.
86. Hughes and Moore, "Affirmation," 115.
87. Hughes and Moore, "Affirmation," 116.

draws us to higher realities.[88] Freedom happens when we break out of our imagined freedom (freedom from impediments) into the order of the universe. Healthy living comes about through our creative participation and correct understanding of human participation in the order of reality. Knowing the truth leads to doing the truth.

Both Hughes and Moore are following Lonergan's discovery of human understanding. We search for insight into our sensory, feeling, and symbolizing experiences in response to questions we wonder about. Questions lead to direct understanding. Direct understanding asks the question, But is it so? This question hopefully leads to correct understanding. The order in the world sends us to specific points in our experience that we would never have otherwise alluded to so that evidence is discovered for prospective judgments. In the light of evidence, our judgment of the true and real becomes possible. Until there is evidence, there remains a perhaps-ness in the mind in dialogue with a world order to which the hypothesis brings us. Judgment means we move through evidence into the order of things as they are.[89] We become a participant in an order that transcends us and includes us, creative participants, since on us, the exigence to apprehend truth and value depends, forming the basis for continuing action. The good of order unfolds then into the good of value, where our original desire successively reaches into love.[90] Rather than one's feelings dictating the order, the whole mind process "is a liberation in which feeling becomes the passion at the heart of good judgment and right action."[91] Real happiness is a participation in the order of all that is, and so, we are enabled to anchor ourselves in a Divine ordering of the world. Thus, Moore is committed to helping people understand the nature of mysticism, one of the realms of meaning spoken about by Lonergan. I will discuss mysticism in the next section and also in chapter 3.

LONERGAN INTERPRETING MOORE

I want to talk about how Lonergan's insights interpret Moore. Earlier, I spoke about Lonergan's understanding of consciousness and the

---

88. Hughes and Moore, "Affirmation," 117–18.
89. Hughes and Moore, "Affirmation," 122.
90. Hughes and Moore, "Affirmation," 129.
91. Hughes and Moore, "Affirmation," 130.

pre-patterning of experience. Experiencing is noticing the raw material of the senses, memories, feelings, symbols, and other spontaneous bodily movements and thoughts (distinct from thinking). Everyone's experience enters consciousness in a pre-patterned form. Intelligence and imagination select specific patterns of experience according to what we care about or demonstrate a concern for or are interested in out of a whole range of neurological configurations for representation as images. This selection process indicates that our concerns shape the kind of world we believe in. Expanding the breadth of what concerns us expands our world. The content of experience comes into our essential awareness according to what we love, value, and our interests shaped by what we like and dislike. These patterns become habitual patterns.

First, Moore privileged the dramatic pattern of experience. Mark Morelli defines the dramatic pattern: "My and other's sensible beauty, my and other's intellectual respectability, my and other's critical and moral authority, my and other's worthiness to play the leading roles in the unfolding dramas of our lives."[92] Morelli describes the characteristics of the dramatic pattern:

> Our sensing becomes heightened sensitivity to raised eyebrows and rolling eyes, disapproving frowns and grimaces, encouraging nods and nudges, discouraging shakes of the head, congratulatory smiles and pats on the back, condemning glares, condescending gazes, puzzled and uncomprehending stares, tentative glances, bold and suggestive advances, aloof withdrawals, welcoming waves, extended hands, and open arms, bored yawns, wide-eyed surprise, insulting tones, thoughtless remarks, aggressive postures, dismissive or offensive gestures.[93]

> The emphasis of the dramatic pattern can be captured in several "I" affirmations: "I seek not the practical or the aesthetic or the intellectual meaning, but the dramatic meaning of the present situation in which I play the leading role; I pursue the dramatic, interpersonal understanding, I submit my dramatic ideas to critical assessment and make judgments on my understanding of the dramatic significance . . . (I desire my actions to be) . . . deliberatively authored."[94]

---

92. Morelli, *Self-Possession*, 228.
93. Morelli, *Self-Possession*, 229.
94. Morelli, *Self-Possession*, 229–30.

Moore is aware of the task of deciding what kind of person each of us chooses to become in the context of the drama of our lives. The drama of our lives is an inter-individual drama. It necessarily includes the influences of others on our lives, their reaction or responses to us, and how such effects impact the various moments of our development. It consists of the institutions we are a part of and, especially, leaders of institutions who are charged with our formation, whether the institution of the family or the monastery. Moore speaks of our positive responses to our life circumstances in terms of "I am" affirmations. He recognizes the suffering that might be present in the life of a person when there is inattention to illusory directions, pretensions, self-deception, arrogance, self-pride, and what he comes to call through his encounter with Eckhart Tolle, the "pain-body."

Second, Moore prioritizes a second pattern of experience: the mystical pattern, which Roy calls mystical consciousness. Moore also uses another term, "cosmic consciousness," which seems to indicate a mystical consciousness applied to the conviction of "God being all in all." The mystical pattern of experience reveals our interest in God alone. Moore judges that when our interest is in God alone, we are sent back to people in love. I will explore this more thoughtfully in chapters 4 and 7. Morelli states, "The mystical interest is an interest in the Ultimate, the All, the mysterious Beginning, the mysterious end and the mysterious ground and the point of our existence. It emerges to pattern the flow of experience from the combination of our presence to ourselves as inescapable limited beings with an inescapable unlimited aspiration for all truth, objectivity, knowledge, reality, and value. Our presence to ourselves in our basic commitment is at once (present) to ourselves as unfinished striving and incomplete and (present) to ourselves as radically dissatisfied with anything less than meaning, objectivity, knowledge, truth, reality, and value in all their absoluteness."[95] In the next chapter, I will explore Moore's attempt to bring the mystical and dramatic patterns of experience into conversation with of the intellectual pattern of experience through the task of doing theology.

---

95. Morelli, *Self-Possession*, 238.

2

Moore: Theologian and Poet

INTRODUCTION

I want to explore Moore as a theologian and poet in this chapter. By describing his theological method, we will better appreciate Moore, "the theologian," and how he chooses to reflect theologically. In the previous chapter, I noted that Moore privileged a dramatic and mystical pattern of experience. As a theologian, he inhabits an intellectual pattern of experience so as to be attentive to distinctions and precise terms, reaching up to a certain control of meaning. However, I want to first place Moore in the context of how he received his theology during his formation years and demonstrate the Copernican revolution toward writing theology in his middle and senior years. I also want to introduce Moore, the poet, thus highlighting the critical directions of his writing that helped him communicate his ideas about God and living the Christian way, as well as helping him to pray differently.

MOORE'S THEOLOGICAL FORMATION

To open a whole discussion on theological methods would be beyond the scope of this book. However, I can state some brief comments on this vast field of study. Lonergan judges theology to be a function best accomplished by the converted theologian. In chapter 1, I explored the multidimensional nature of conversion and proposed an interaction between these dimensions. Religious and affective/moral conversion and transformation are most important for the theologian. Since theology is an intellectual enterprise, intellectual conversion, and transformation are also important. Since the theologian seeks to express the Divine Mystery, feelings, images, and symbols become an essential means of communication and, therefore, psychological conversion is also vital. Lonergan presents two stages or vectors to theological writing with four distinct steps in each phase: the mediated phase of theology (research, interpretation, history, and dialectic) and the mediating phase of theology (foundations, doctrines, systematics, and communication). Both stages delineate the steps in a "creative, faith-filled process, which moves from data to final results, that constitutes theology."[1]

However, it is essential to state that Moore (and Lonergan) was schooled in an approach to theology that privileged certain elements but, to his credit, moved beyond these learnings. Neil Ormerod suggests that theological method was already in transition during the 1940s and 1950s. Moore received his theological training in the monastery and Rome during that period. The way of doing theology that dominated the Church for centuries could be characterized as having four elements.

First, the language of theology was metaphysical, using concepts from the philosophy of Plato and Aristotle. Philosophy was considered the handmaid of theology and faith was informed by reason. Terms such as "essence, existence, substance, potency, act, and habit" were common when dealing with questions concerning grace, the being of Christ, and the nature of the Eucharist.[2] Second, theology was scholastic in methodology; that is, theology began with a question seeking an answer, striving for conceptual clarity.[3] Moore's earlier theological articles demonstrate a concern with clarity and precision through question upon question. His later writings are far more exploratory.

Third, theology had nothing to do with history, that is, "there was little sensitivity to the changing contexts and meanings that history gives rise to," and so "revelation was set of revealed truths of divine realities rather than related to a series of concrete historical events, centering on the life death and resurrection of Jesus and resulting in the offer of salvation to all peoples."[4] This lack of historical consciousness was characteristic of a classicist mentality of culture. The classicist mentality

1. Ormerod, *Introducing*, 50.
2. Ormerod, *Introducing*, 28.
3. Ormerod, *Introducing*, 28–29.
4. Ormerod, *Introducing*, 29–30.

understands that theology written in one period is a permanent achievement for all periods. By the end of his life, Moore is wholly convinced of the importance of historical consciousness and has moved away from a classicist mentality.[5] Fourth, theology was dogmatic. Its concern was to defend the dogmas of the Church and use Scripture to proof-text what had been affirmed in the doctrines.[6] While Moore respects the dogmas of the Church, progressively, he aims to aid self-discovery through religious conversion. Therefore, he uses insights from cultural anthropology, psychological and sociological sciences, and literature to break open the human condition and better appreciate the uniqueness of Jesus risen. While having an appreciation for the significance of the Word of God found in Holy Scripture, a mature Moore would ultimately come to a position about writing theology referencing sources beyond scripture where "outside the Bible there is to be found the rudiments of a spiritual culture, of a met-anthropology unknown or at least not consulted by Ratzinger and Balthasar as the prime human datum. . . . It can make manifest the beauty and humanity of our transformation in Christ, more deeply human, and vividly than does Holy Writ."[7]

Moore came out of a tradition that was already changing when he was studying theology. Here are three examples. First, in an article published in the *Downside Review* of winter 1947–48, Moore pleads for theologians to return to the biblical tradition for a healthy and more vibrant understanding of the Blessed Trinity. No doubt he had in mind preachers who, on Trinity Sunday, spoke to their congregations in theological categories unknown to the laity to explain the intelligibility of the doctrine. Moore asks for greater attention to a prayerful appropriation of doctrine grounded in meditating on the biblical text rather than using Scripture in the tradition of proof-texting.[8] His appeal for a change of approach in the use of Scriptures is to bring the theology student and Christian believer into an experience of participating in the life of the Trinity before seeking an understanding through such terms as *processions*, *nature*, *persons*, and *relations*. To receive an intelligible meaning about the Trinity before hearing and praying the words of Christ that one finds in Saint John's Gospel is to fail to understand that the "gift whereby Christ in the Last Supper room implanted in his apostles' doctrine and

5. Moore, "2012–2014 Blog," Sep 28, 2008.
6. Ormerod, *Introducing*, 30–31.
7. Moore, "2012–2014 Blog," Sep 28, 2008.
8. Moore, "Blessed Trinity," 17.

life has to be repeated. It is only Christ who gave the doctrine and it is only Christ who gives it."[9]

Second, as an example of the scholastic influence in theology, there is an article by the theologian P. D. Chenu OP that Moore was asked to translate from French to English for the 1942 publication of the *Downside Review*. In the article, Chenu argues for the priority of divine revelation before we can be moral and intelligent about what to believe and how to put it into practice. He bases his argument on the two planes of the intellect: the lower plane, which he calls *ratio inferior*, and the higher plane, which he calls *ratio superior*. Without divine revelation, neither the higher nor the lower planes (a light called *synderesis*) is appropriately ordered. Correct understanding cannot be gained without first contemplating God. These arguments are scholastic in nature and rely on a terminology derived from a faculty psychology typical of scholastic thinking.

Third, Moore was schooled in an approach to theology where philosophy was considered the handmaid of theology. Philosophy and theology always interacted. In the article "Analogy and the Free Mind," Moore explains the importance of analogy in theological reflection, outlining the distinction between the analogy of proper proportionality and the analogy of improper proportionality. This article is an excellent example of philosophy being the handmaid of theology. He talks about "being" when applied to God and "being" when applied to human beings. God is the principle of all whose identity is known by sheer light, and human beings are created beings whose identity is known by their creaturehood or finitude.[10]

Moore argues that the mind can manage analogy at a created level but breaks down at the level of contemplating the infinite since the infinite is the source of all analogy when it comes to human thinking. Therefore, whatever analogical term we apply to God, for example, God's goodness, we are applying it appropriately to God. When we use the same word for human beings, the meaning of goodness in the created reality must first be appropriated by understanding God's goodness and then derived to human goodness.[11] Knowing God means we know ourselves better. While analogy is essential in writing theology, Moore also acknowledges the importance of metaphor and symbol. Metaphor has been a powerful

9. Moore, "Blessed Trinity," 18.
10. Moore, "Analogy," 10.
11. Moore, "Analogy," 11.

tool in the writing of spirituality over centuries. An example of metaphor is to speak of the presence/absence of God as a "cloud of unknowing." The use of metaphor often communicates a surplus of meaning and intimates a presence beyond the clear concepts of analogy. Given Moore's disposition to write religious poetry to make God real for his audience and himself, in his mind, theology needs both analogy and metaphor.

Moore's critical shift in theology is through reflection on one's personal experience, the importance of recognizing the contexts and cultures in which ideas historically emerge, the skilled task of finding the meaning of a text, and then passing on that meaning from one epoch to another. This critical exigence includes interpreting past texts for the present world while remaining faithful to their significance in the world in which they were written.[12] Moore recognizes that culture changes and the world of his youth, especially the Western world pre-World Wars I and II, no longer exists. In this new context, theologians must find a new language of communication about God. In writing theology, he takes on board the concerns of his time: the brotherhood and sisterhood of all people, the sexual revolution, the rise in affluence through Western societies, the increase in leisure, the rise in consciousness to be and become, and the voice of a new form of atheism, strident and angry.

THEOLOGY: GOD AS REAL

In light of so many theological shifts in the twentieth century, Moore takes a simple approach to theology, which is genuinely a Copernican revolution for him. The purpose of theology is to make God real to people and, therefore, to present a new language about God that can speak to contemporary audiences. He sees himself securing theology from an "old language, a dead language," which he views as "encased or encapsulated."[13] Convinced by the sterility of an older theology, he states: "The question of Christian belief . . . may be showing itself to be a crisis of poetry."[14] He asks fellow priests to speak honestly about faith and life, especially when preaching, without defaulting to Catechism answers and doctrines.[15]

---

12. Ormerod, *Introducing*, 34–37.
13. Moore, *God Is a New Language*, 9–10.
14. Moore, *God Is a New Language*, 11.
15. Moore, *God Is a New Language*, 20.

A New Awareness

What motivates Moore is the conviction that God desires everyone to turn away from false images. Making God real is equivalent to helping people let go of false images. Faith is made possible when we have escaped from false gods to the true and real God. These false images are projections of our inadequacies and remain images in which we find no real reason to believe or employ. As Michael Paul Gallagher points out, false images of God abound, including God as the faraway and stern judge who ultimately spies on us from afar; God as a non-communicator who lacks warmth; God who pronounces that only the ideal is acceptable; God who induces in us the futile quest for approval; God who is always displeased with frown and pointed finger; God who is somewhere out there as some gigantic super-power; and God who did not give me what I asked for.[16]

Instead, Moore insists that we must turn toward a concept of God grounded in human experience and revelation.[17] The critical human experience shaping our image of God is our union with others through love. Gallagher states: "The only God worth believing in is the God who believed enough in people to die for us. The only God worth living for is the One who calls us to live with him, through dark faith in this life, and beyond death in face-to-face fullness. The only God worth searching for is the One who searched for us and who struggles within us in order that we may become more free to believe."[18] Chapters 7 and 8 on the significance of Jesus highlight these trajectories spoken about by Gallagher and pursued by Moore.

Moore wants us to begin with our concrete personality, the "appropriation of self-awareness," which reveals us to be in the process of becoming the best persons we can be and engaged in a "flow" of life around and through our being.[19] He wants to present God in a language that overcomes two lies: that each of us is primarily aware of ourselves, in a mode of being over and against others, and in the way of being over and against God and, therefore, ultimately self-made individuals.[20]

Moore is trying to find a common ground on which our diverse religious and human experiences grow. He judges the common ground to be found through an exploration of religious and mystical intersections.

16. Gallagher, *Free to Believe*, 52–55.
17. Moore, *God Is a New Language*, 39.
18. Gallagher, *Free to Believe*, 59.
19. Moore, *God Is a New Language*, 41–42.
20. Moore, *God Is a New Language*, 43.

He realizes the importance of the psyche and the "unconscious," which becomes the storehouse of our feelings and memories and provides a place for our myths and symbols to take shape. Myths should not be discounted as primitive by a new rationalist perspective, nor should they be interpreted as literal. He takes the power of myth seriously as communicating a narrative story that tells us what life feels like from the inside. Further, the language of poetry speaks to the heart. The ideas, symbols, and words of myth and poetry are what Lonergan calls elemental meaning. Elemental meaning is bound to our experiential level of consciousness when the meaning of something and its concrete embodiment is indissolubly united. One encounters the meaning of something through experience, and the meaning cannot be separated from the experience. Another example of elemental meaning is the experience of intersubjectivity or our communion with others.

MOORE: A NEW THEOLOGICAL AWARENESS

I want to examine the revolution in Moore's mind and heart. In 1967, Moore published *God in a New Language*. Moore begins with the contemporary experience of faith. His opening question is: What is a concept of God adequate for our time?[21] He starts with this assertion: an understanding of God based on past certainties has nothing to do with people's lives as they currently experience it and cannot be the center of our striving. To speak about God adequately and intelligently requires that we go back to human experience so that our understanding of God is relevant, fruitful, and able to be preached to the world, a sense of God coming from the Scriptures and lived in the life of the Church.[22] In this period, Moore believes that the theologian's task is to dismantle all the images of "a dead God."[23] He wants to rescue the understanding of faith from the "mental citadel"[24] of liberal theology, approach the problem of understanding faith as "a crisis of poetry," and understand religious faith as an adventure toward human authenticity.[25] He wanted to move away

---

21. Moore, *God Is a New Language*, 38.
22. Moore, *God Is a New Language*, 38–39.
23. Moore, *God Is a New Language*, 9.
24. Moore, *God Is a New Language*, 11.
25. Moore, *God Is a New Language*, 11, 143.

from a mindset that determined revelation to be simply a series of propositions that, to his mind, made God remote and unreachable.[26]

For example, concerning the doctrine of the Trinity, Moore advocates that we must switch from the "Penny Catechism" version of God as three Persons in one God to understanding God as the "essence" of and within our relationships. This shift is incarnational. We discover God through the incarnate meaning of people who live lovingly. Any theology must find its true center in the self-aware person becoming a better person towards others and not becoming over against others.[27] He believes the best place to start is with the healing of the self and its hunger for authenticity. Recovery would only be possible through conversion and when Christ's story becomes our story, liberating us from the objectivist notions of God to experience the transformation of the Spirit.

In as much as the theologian writes theology within a cultural setting, the society Moore finds himself in imbues a cultural outlook that sees God as a question since the God whom people once found gave meaning to their lives no longer provides that meaning. For Moore, the new human identity crisis cannot be addressed with a God language that knows nothing of this cultural problem.[28] At the same time, modern culture cannot be accepted without critique but must be dialectically engaged since it shows all the signs of a refusal to face human finitude and instead posits a denial of death.[29]

Moore understands the modern world as searching for and demanding meaning about human existence and believes that it is the Church's role to present meaning honestly, intelligently, and responsibly. The Church has a vocation, therefore, to speak theologically. However, the Church cannot expect to deliver tried and old answers about God, especially when many people have discounted God.[30] The meaning of God for human existence must also incorporate an evolutionary worldview, an understanding of our complex ecology, and the emergence of a uniquely human consciousness. Theological reflection must consider that humanity is no longer a spectator in the created order. Human beings exercise "consciousness in which and to which the universe reveals

---

26. Moore, *God Is a New Language*, 50.
27. Moore, *God Is a New Language*, 40–41.
28. Moore, *God Is a New Language*, 47.
29. Moore, *Crucified Is No Stranger*, 71.
30. Moore, *God Is a New Language*, 87.

its meaning."[31] Any theology that speaks to the people of his generation must start with the world and the questions that involvement in the world generates and not with our past answers about God.[32] From these exploratory reflections, Moore advocates a theology that shifts to the human person's experience and the problem of meaning and recognizes the change in culture in which theology speaks.

THEOLOGY, CONTEMPLATION, AND CHRISTIAN CONVERSION

In *The Fire and the Rose Are One*, published in the early 1980s, Moore states that "mutual invigoration of speculative intelligence and the heart is fundamental to the Catholic theological tradition. Would that we could recover it! . . . If we have built for centuries on the denial of that weddedness of mind and heart, what is there to do, but in some way to begin again?"[33] Moore advocates the importance of prayer and contemplation as a prerequisite for theological reflection. He writes: "Theology is the sustained attempt to understand religious experience."[34] Religious experience is a unique state of the heart that forms us into a person in love with the Divine in an unrestricted manner. The essence of religious experience is the experience of love. Religious experience is not primarily rational but affective and penetrates our whole being. It does not begin with knowledge but in an immediate, affective, and undifferentiated awareness preceding knowledge. It leads to self-surrender and commitment. This awareness is an experience felt before it is formulated into words and, as such, relies on the judgments, evaluations, and language of a religious tradition to identify its authenticity. It originates in the Divine initiative, the gift of grace. It brings us from a natural way of being to a higher and more authentic way without destroying what is created. Religious experience, in its most authentic form, brings to fulfillment everything else in our lives and turns us from a life of triviality to a life of full realization.[35]

---

31. Moore, *God Is a New Language*, 89–90.
32. Moore, *God Is a New Language*, 93.
33. Moore, *Fire and the Rose*, xiv.
34. Moore, *Fire and the Rose*, 3.
35. Arcamone, *Conversion*, 62–63.

Through an understanding of religious experience, we can better understand religious conversion. To do theology, Moore affirms the importance of religious experience and Christian conversion in the theologian's life. This theme would occupy his understanding of theological reflection for the whole of his life. Religious conversion is a complete change of mind and heart born from religious experience, and specifically in the Christian context from the event of the love of God poured into our hearts by the gift of the Holy Spirit (Rom 5:5). When there is a transformation of our mind and soul through the religious experience of falling in love with God, religious faith, hope, and love is born. In the early eighties, from the perspective of the importance of conversion to Jesus as Lord and Savior, Moore stated: "At last, I am able to state my method [for theology]. Its principle is that the gospel story has to be interiorized: that until I have discovered in my own experience and as a dynamic of my spiritual-psychic existence, the important moments in the story—I do not understand them for what they are—moments in God's communication to me."[36] From the perspective of salvation in Jesus, Moore affirms: "According to my method, each of these interactions [with those disciples whom Jesus met] represents a condition of affection or disaffection in my relations with 'the free person' [the unique freedom of Jesus] with the one who challenges my own free life with his freedom."[37] Again, Moore affirms: "Method demands I see in Jesus's claim to an intimacy with God (ontological), the supreme affront to me and my consciousness controlled by envy . . . with an insatiable need to be meaningful . . . [and] a lack of experienced support from God, whose approval must be earned."[38] Moore affirms the importance of religious conversion for a new feeling for God, a new surrender to God, and a unique knowledge about God through theological reflection.

Moore couches spiritual experience in the language of contemplative prayer and mysticism. The theologian who does not pray contemplatively and abide within a mystical consciousness cannot write theology well. Moore's understanding of theology rests on the distinction between the knowledge of God and the knowledge about God. Without some felt knowledge of God, we cannot speak about God. As indicated earlier, his turning point in 1944 came about when he left behind a sterile form of mental prayer and sought a more contemplative approach. For God to be

36. Moore, "Language of Love," 100.
37. Moore, "Language of Love," 100.
38. Moore, "Language of Love," 100.

more clearly expressed in thought, there must first be a non-conceptual awareness of God. Concepts can become barriers to the exploring of new frontiers. The birth of contemplative prayer means that "this peace treaty between God and myself is broken and I come to a sense that any point in my world may certainly be touched and brought newly to my attention as a new territory for his gracious occupation."[39] Therefore, the touch of God (direct knowledge of God through prayer) makes way for better concepts (knowledge about God), which leads to a more profound indication of God. Contemplative prayer validates our ideas of God. It does not modify, amplify, or change them, but it does help to critique them.[40]

THEOLOGY AND THE PRE-RELIGIOUS

As much as Moore acknowledged the need for conversion to Christ, he also recognized the importance of being attentive to our felt humanity. Moore states: "The greatest need in theology today is to discover and to name this pre-religious emotional involvement with God."[41] First, Moore highlights the importance of an emotional involvement with God so that the theologian might communicate effectively their love of God to an audience. Secondly, and just as importantly, Moore recognizes the different cultural settings in which believers find themselves and the need to consider each cultural context when communicating. First, I will speak to the significance of an emotional involvement with God and later to the second point regarding cultural context. One possible way of unpacking Moore's insistence on an emotional involvement with God is through a distinction made by Louis Roy. Roy asks: "How can faith experience be balanced and avoid falling into extremes? On the one hand, how can it escape subjectivism, namely the addiction to specific feelings. The pursuit of fanciful meanings or the acting out of aberrant behavior? On the other hand, how can it shun objectivism, that is, the mindless acceptance of non-interiorized devotions, dogmatic formulas and rules of conduct?"[42]

The theologian must engage with three kinds of dynamism within human consciousness. First, the consciousness of God invites the life of surrender to the Mystery of God in obedience to God's

---

39. Moore, *God Is a New Language*, 202.
40. Moore, *God Is a New Language*, 206.
41. Moore, *Fire and the Rose*, 26.
42. Roy, "Three Faith," 542.

self-communication, which is "to believe God" with the faithfulness of an interpersonal relationship. This dynamism is centrally about one's surrender and assent and could be called the authority of faith. Second, the consciousness of God must also include the vitality of affectivity or feeling, which is "to believe in God," which suggests an impulsion into or unto God and a definite thrust of affectivity. This dynamism is central to trust and the heart of faith. Third, the consciousness of God must include the vitality of human intellectuality or "to believe that . . ." the human mind adheres to a set of truths. This dynamism is about reasonable knowledge and could be called the reason for faith and flows from affectivity and surrender.[43]

To better seek an emotional engagement with God, Moore explores a pre-religious starting point for theology. I want to present two pre-religious starting points offered by Moore. First, in his book *The Inner Loneliness*, Moore presents a pre-religious starting point in the experience of inner loneliness. Moore begins with the question: What propels us to form relationships? Answer: Our sense of personal significance, worth, uniqueness, and a sense of myself as priceless urges us to develop relationships. However, since we form relationships with other people, we find that "no one can know me as I know myself, no one can touch me as I thus feel myself. No one can be present to me as I am thus present to myself. So, there is a loneliness in each person that no other person can relieve."[44] From a pre-religious starting point, Moore moves to an understanding of God, "who is 'the idea of me existing' an unimaginable thought which is of me and of all that is" and therefore, we can affirm that "God unconditionally desires me into being—[God] the mystery that 'thinks' us."[45]

Thus, our inner loneliness can only be relieved by: first, Someone who knows us thoroughly and inwardly; second, Someone who is limitless since the limits of others prevent them from receiving us as we ought to be received; third, Someone who is other than us; and fourth, Someone who would have to be different in a unique way, that is, an otherness of ultimate Mystery.[46] As the desire for relief demonstrates our wish that there be Someone who can take away our inner loneliness, Moore concludes that our questioning and searching is fundamentally a wish

---

43. Roy, "Three Faith," 543–44.
44. Moore, *Inner Loneliness*, 1.
45. Moore, *Inner Loneliness*, 1.
46. Moore, *Inner Loneliness*, 12.

for God. However, Feuerbach's assertion that God is *only* a product of our wishful thinking and, therefore, not "real" does not hold. The desire coming out of a longing to assuage our inner loneliness is not in vain, and an act of trust will affirm that Someone exists and is real beyond the desire since "faith means trusting our radical desire even when it reached beyond our familiar world."[47] God is the Other within who ends our inner loneliness and partners us through life. This partnership serves to orient us more responsibly toward people since "the effect of experiencing the more radical fulfillment of our desire to be-for [in God] is that one will experience that desire more intensely in relation to other persons." In experiencing ourselves as unique or ultimately significant in the eyes of God, who relieves our inner loneliness, a much fuller conviction emerges, namely that in our specialness, we can be a gift to others.

Moore offers two examples of our pre-religious experience: the experience of restlessness illustrated in the life of Saint Augustine and the understanding of direction and purpose reflected in the life of Dag Hammarskjöld. He often mentions both experiences. Saint Augustine's path to God begins, in part, through acknowledging the restlessness of the heart. In his *Confessions*, he states: "Our hearts are restless, Lord, till they rest in you." Hammarskjold articulates a pre-religious experience when he says:

> I don't know who—or what—put the question, I don't know when it was put. I don't even remember answering. But at some moment I did answer Yes to Someone—or something—and from that hour I was certain that existence is meaningful and that, therefore, my life, in self-surrender had a goal. From that moment I had known what it means "not to look back" and "to take no thought for the morrow." Led by the Ariadne's thread of my answer through the labyrinth of life, I came to a time and place where I realized that the Way leads to a triumph, which is a catastrophe, and to a catastrophe, which is a triumph that the price for committing one's life would be reproach and that the only elevation possible to man lies in the death of humiliation. After that, the word courage lost its meaning since nothing could be taken from me.[48]

Second, in *The Fire and the Rose Are One*, Moore states that we are born with a radical uncertainty about our being, and the critical question

---

47. Moore, *Inner Loneliness*, 15.
48. Hammarskjöld, *Markings*, 169.

for us is: "Am I significant to anyone?"[49] Moore begins with our self-awareness, which leads to the desire to find significance in ourselves. Our desire to feel significant gives us intense satisfaction in our attraction to another person and their attraction towards us. Moore concludes that our need to feel alive and meaningful reaches its proper intentionality in enhancing the life of another. He proposes that a good definition of being human and our most fundamental need is the need "to be myself for another." To be consciously alive is to be a gift. Even if our desire to find our significance seems like an act of self-absorption, "at root," our self-absorption is a dialogue with an unknown origin who answers the question: "Am I ultimately significant?"[50] The answer is realized in the affirmation that each of us is genuinely significant for the unknown reality that originates us. Therefore, the human definition of "being myself for another" is grounded in a pre-religious relationship with God. In God, our hunger for meaning and our sense of dependence coalesce in "our dependence for meaning."[51]

THEOLOGY AND THE AUTOBIOGRAPHICAL THEOLOGIAN

Moore's understanding of theology reaches a new awareness when he states that "theology has become autobiographical."[52] What does he mean? Moore is saying that our genuine or authentic story mediates the incredible story of God, and it is the story of Jesus who can awaken in us our real story. Moore's use of the metaphor "story" emphasizes his conviction that our lives are a drama and that to live the gospel is to live the drama of salvation.[53] Our true story of grace and sin will more likely persuade others of God's presence. God's story is the story of revelation and how he reveals himself in the death and resurrection of Jesus and the sending of the Spirit.

Moore states that Christian theology "is the work of understanding and communicating the interaction of our story with the Jesus story."[54]

---

49. Moore, *Fire and the Rose*, 12.
50. Moore, *Fire and the Rose*, 13.
51. Moore, *Fire and the Rose*, 19.
52. Moore, "Four Steps," 81.
53. Moore, "Four Steps," 100.
54. Moore, "Four Steps," 88.

The real story is God's ultimate story for all humankind. Moore proposes that the only way to do theology autobiographically is to seek our true self through prayer, contemplation, and a following of Jesus. Our true self accepts the tension between the finite and the infinite. Nothing of our creaturehood is rejected, but our hearts are restless till they rest in God. To do theology well, one must have a contemplative faith in Jesus.[55]

Moore concludes with five steps in the doing of theology autobiographically. Step one is God giving us freedom from all that holds us back from loving God and our neighbor. Step two is the self-revelation of God in Jesus, with whom we enter into dialogue and who stretches us beyond our own story. Step three is a dialogue between ourselves set free and the story of Jesus. Step four is our story becoming a mission in the world empowered by the Holy Spirit that becomes our story spoken to others, mediating the great story. Step five is the Divine life of the Trinity, recapitulating all that has gone before.[56]

THEOLOGY AND THE DRAMA OF SALVATION

Within the context of understanding theology as autobiographical, Moore adds another insight: the importance of appreciating the drama of salvation within the human heart.

Mark Morelli explains that a person sensing that their life is a drama generally acquires a sensitivity to their movements, recall, remembering, and feelings.

> Our *movements* are graceful or awkward, agile or bumbling, confident or hesitant in halting. We *recall* with pride our past successful performances. We *remember* with embarrassment our foolish *faux pas*. Our *feelings* are of pride or humility, embarrassment or self-assurance contentment, pleasure or elation at our achievements, unhappiness with our mediocre performances, depression in the wake of our failures and hopeful anticipation of approval or fearful expectation of disapproval. We feel loved or we feel hated. We feel liked or disliked. We feel cared for or ignored and dismissed. We feel suspected or we feel trusted. We feel offended or appreciated. We feel respected or disrespected, equal or unequal better or not as good. We imagine how we might deliberately impress others or we worry about

---

55. Moore, "Four Steps," 82.
56. Moore, "Four Steps," 89.

how we might inadvertently expose ourselves to derision and ridicule.[57]

Moore's account as to the importance of God's love poured into our hearts, the centrality of desire for God and interpersonal desire, and the interior experiences of envy and jealousy, guilt, sorrow, forgiveness, anxiety, self-esteem, self-rejection, and self-hatred, self-love, and self-gift give us a deeper awareness of our lives as a drama where we are involved in becoming the best edition of ourselves.

Furthermore, regarding Moore's theology of salvation in Christ, the rightful point of entry is through the eyes of the disciples, whose lives were a drama. He affirms that Jesus' divinity became an affirmation of faith for them only after they were drawn into his life through the climatic drama of his crucifixion and in the healing and forgiveness of his resurrection. The truths of faith subsequently affirmed in the Church derived from the experience of being saved. For Moore, the direction is clear: if we desire to do the task of theology, we need more to work with than the dogmas of the faith or the doctrine of salvation in Jesus. We need to first get into the skin of the disciples and ponder the kind of impression that Jesus made in their lives, starting from the premise that we are dealing with One for whom the being of God meant everything to him and touched every moment of his humanity.[58] We need to deeply appreciate how much we are convicted to the assertion that we are "death-bound, and that's all there is!" Peering through the dogma to the originating drama that eventually gave rise to the doctrine, we discover, as did the disciples, an interwovenness of the fall of Jesus in the crucifixion with our fall. We need to appreciate how Christ gets under our lostness to a distorted horizon of death, that has psychically created a division between God on one side and death on the other.[59]

Moore states that "what was 'there' as their first pre-sacramental involvement of men and women with Christ . . . was their humiliation in his, their shame in his, their fall in his, their underpinning with him as giving full expression to it, of that fall out of glory, that is the story of being human."[60] We must recover the disciple's original mutual involvement in the shame of the cross and the deep drama of that moment if

---

57. Morelli, *Self-Possession*, 228–29.
58. Moore, "Spirituality and the Primacy," 279.
59. Moore, "Spirituality and the Primacy," 294.
60. Moore, "Spirituality and the Primacy," 283.

we are to do theology well. Even today, Jesus' self-identification in our shame leaves us in no doubt of our association with him in his return to glory. Thus, the Christian way is not so much that we identify with him in his passion but rather that Christ self-identified with us in our degradation, which means we can be lifted by him.[61] The emphasis on capturing the drama of our lives nudges us towards an adequate metapsychology: "Otherwise resurrection comes to be nothing but the name they gave to *some* experience of Jesus after his death."[62]

THEOLOGY AND CULTURE

During Moore's lifetime, the culture of theology was undergoing a shift: a shift to critical-historical thinking in all areas of knowledge, including theology; concerned with questions of meaning (hermeneutics); pluralistic in orientation; suspicious of authority alone as the justification for truth; philosophically personalist in direction; scripturally oriented in wanting to know Jesus, the disciples, and the Church in their concrete historical manifestations; and, finally, a set of foundations on which to build the truths of the faith grounded in conversion that is religious, moral, intellectual, affective, and psychic.[63] I am not saying that Moore set about the task of thoroughly exploring all the issues behind these critical changes to the doing of theology. However, he did subscribe to them.

The final iteration by Moore on the process of doing theology comes from his penultimate book, *The Contagion of Jesus: Doing Theology as If It Matters*. Moore turns to the "dense definition" Lonergan gave as a guide to theological reflection.[64] Lonergan states: "Theology mediates between a cultural matrix and the significance and role of religion in that matrix."[65] Lonergan's definition needs some unpacking.

First, identifying the cultural matrix in which we do theology is essential. Our culture gives us a set of meanings and values about human living. Not only does culture seek to express meanings and values, but the way culture expresses them is the outcome of a particular mindset: the

---

61. Moore, "Spirituality and the Primacy," 284.
62. Moore, "Spirituality and the Primacy," 287.
63. Ormerod, *Introducing*, 38–40.
64. Moore, *Contagion of Jesus*, 69.
65. Lonergan, *Method*, 1.

classicist and the empirical mindset. Lonergan distinguishes between a classicist notion of culture and an empirical notion of culture. He states:

> The classicist notion of culture was normative: at least *de jure* there was but one culture that was both universal and permanent; to its norms and ideals might aspire the uncultured, whether they were the young or the people or the natives or the barbarians. Besides the classicist, there also is the empirical notion of culture. It is the set of meanings and values that informs a way of life. It may remain unchanged for ages. It may be in process of slow development or rapid dissolution. When the classicist notion of culture prevails, theology is conceived as a permanent achievement. When culture is conceived empirically, theology is known to be an ongoing process, and then one writes on its method.[66]

There is no doubt that Moore stands with an empirical notion of culture. He states that the cultural clothes we once wore were those of a culture that was saturated with Christian thinking. But today, those clothes have been removed, and "the soul shivers."[67] Whereas the church saw itself as the happy possessor of a uniform culture held together by an unreflective adherence by many, this situation has completely changed in our contemporary world. Therefore, the doing of theology, which must speak to a cultural matrix, is an ongoing process and must not think of itself as a permanent achievement since, within cultures, various groups espouse differing meanings and values. It is essential for the theologian to dialectically engage with each of these groups, hopefully in a spirit of conversation and dialogue. The dialectic process presents opposing points of view, which can be mutually complementary or radically different. When a theologian dialectically engages with a set of meanings and values fundamentally different from the values of the gospel, then a dialectic of contradiction emerges. When a theologian dialectically engages with a set of meanings and values complementary to the values of the gospel, there occurs a dialectic of contraries. To discern which cultural meanings and values are true, good, and loving requires a theologian to be converted.

Moore identifies both contraries and contradictories within the culture of modernity and the subculture of the Church. For example, Moore asserts that the pre-religious starting point of "inner loneliness" for the

---

66. Lonergan, *Method*, xi.
67. Moore, "2008 Blog," Sep 28, 2008.

doing of theology is a starting point that our modern culture cannot accept. To accept it as a valid universal experience would be to canonize it.[68] To canonize it would be to render false the claims of our consumerist culture and its promises of relief from inner loneliness. Similarly, our modern culture has a distorted understanding of God. A malformed atheistic culture contains within it the premise that our independence and personal autonomy are our greatest strengths and judges independence as the only means to discover our significance. The more independence one has, the more personal worth can be found. Further, our independence must include the process of outgrowing God since independence means we do not need God and can go it alone.[69] Moore concludes that the statement "I am absolute" that our distorted culture implicitly affirms through independence is not the absolute of outgrowing God but rather an appreciation for the dream of myself being the dream for others. Only by "being myself for another" do we possess a quality that compels us to say that the self is absolute, unique, and non-derivative.[70]

Second, Lonergan's definition of the function of theology also speaks to the role and significance of religion. Moore knows one can distinguish between authentic faith and distorted belief. Any genuine account of religion must have the value of love at its core. Love is the experience of going out toward others for their good. Love grounds theological reflection, prayer, and religious expression. Meanwhile, any spiritual tradition that encourages its adherents to seek violence as a change method is a distorted religion. The distortion may come from the malformed inherited tradition passed on or the unintelligent and irresponsible interpretation and behavior of the adherents promoted to others.

Third, in the doing of theology, the categories we use can be classified as both special and general categories.[71] Special categories have become a part of the Church's theological tradition, often taken from the Bible or various philosophical traditions and used to explain dogma and answer questions surrounding Christological, ecclesiological, and Trinitarian controversies. Special categories include nature, person, grace, sanctifying grace, sacraments, processions, *homoousion*, cross, resurrection, etc. General categories are those drawn from contexts outside of theology, usually human and social sciences, but which could contribute

---

68. Moore, *Inner Loneliness*, 38–39.
69. Moore, *Inner Loneliness*, 50–51.
70. Moore, *Inner Loneliness*, 52.
71. Lonergan, *Method*, 285–93.

to the writing of theology. General categories include words such as oppressors and oppressed, exploited workers and the proletariat, the latter being drawn from the context of liberation theology, as well as general words such as society, culture, and values, desire and scapegoat, self-esteem, self, shadow, and ego.

Moore's theology was open to categories from various sources outside the usual theological and traditional circles. He drew categories from René Girard, Ernest Becker, Sigmund Freud, and Carl Jung. He sought to better understand the human condition under the reign of sin by reading Friedrich Nietzsche and Fyodor Dostoevsky. He found the work of Eckhart Tolle and Eugene Gendlin helpful for spiritual understanding. He encouraged the tools of Enneagram and the Myers-Briggs for self-discovery. Subsequent chapters will examine the contribution of all these people to his theology.

OTHER THEOLOGIANS SPEAKING ABOUT MOORE

Finally, I want to present the insights of other theologians who have engaged with Moore's theological thoughts. Before doing so, it is worth noting that the British title of Moore's book on soteriology was *The Crucified Is No Stranger*. The US publishers insisted on putting "Jesus" in the title, because people would not know what the title meant. Some have sought to address the method that grounds his theological writings. First, in response to his reading, *The Crucified Jesus Is no Stranger*, David B. Burrell CSC characterizes Moore's theological method as an inner work responding to an "anxious query in himself."[72] The query stems from the human experience of suppressing goodness, an action grounded in a profound self-disesteem and felt self-rejection coupled with the orientation, "in for a penny in for a pound." Our suppression of goodness reaches its most evil manifestation in the crucifixion of Jesus, the innocent and sinless one, where self-rejection reaches a point of intensity that we crucify and kill our True Self, Jesus. Yet, God raises him to impart healing and forgiveness.

Further, Moore's theological quest is a fine example of theology struggling for the right words to illuminate and illustrate the drama of salvation. It is worth noting that Moore argued for a theology of "the revelation of God in Jesus not to be adjudicated according to pro-Christian

---

72. Burrell, "Torment," 14.

verification list scheme but pointing to a fresh and refreshing use of language, we have come to know . . . . That language has to try to express rather than to suppress our longings. Once we begin to sensitize ourselves to the new rhetoric of the Gospels, we ourselves can also imagine new uses of language."[73] His method gives rise to a theology "at once an interior and a communal affair. Yet grammar, in the sense of a struggle for appropriate formulation, grammar remains crucial to both concerns: interior and communal, for we need clarity to breathe, especially to unscramble our conflicted emotions and desires."[74] Burrell asserts that it is out of this tangle that Moore keeps trying to find his way and thus names his orientation "torment as method."

Burrell concludes that

> his inestimable worth as a guide turns on the fact that we all live enmeshed in that tangle, yet few of us are able or willing to acknowledge it. Perhaps it was Ignatius's grasp of the power of images to illuminate the twists and turns of desire that moved Sebastian along the paths he has taken but there is no doubt that his experience with the *Exercises* has shaped his theological explorations. For that is precisely what his writings amount to: decidedly *not* a revisionist theological program, but rather a continual struggle to find the formulations that will release the dynamism hidden in revelation to unleash the Spirit to "truly live."[75]

Moore explicitly realizes a theology that goes beyond mere logic and toward a theology that powerfully communicates with both mind and heart. Since all human beings desire to be desired by the one they desire, the purpose of all Christian theology is to recognize that the one who desires us without restriction is Jesus, crucified and risen. It is Jesus who brings us to the peace and truth of God.[76]

Second, in her book *Trinity: Nexus of the Mysteries of Christian Faith*, Anne Hunt gives her assessment of Moore's theological method:

> One might, without much ado or delay easily relegate Sebastian Moore's work to the realm of spirituality and concomitantly dismiss it from the more rigorous area of properly systematic theology. Indeed, many do! He is writing is sketchily developed; the

---

73. Burrell, "Torment," 15.
74. Burrell, "Torment," 14.
75. Burrell, "Torment," 14.
76. Burrell, "Torment," 15.

terminology is loose and not well-defined. The usual raft of scholarly references is notably absent; he daringly breaks into poetry at various points in the focus of his attention is not so much of God per se, as the process of conversion and the associated psychological changes in the consciousness of the human subject. At first glance, Moore's work is simple and uncritical and seemingly even naïve; but, in fact, it demands a kind of psychological workout . . . That requires a sophisticated level of self-awareness and a very serious effort to examine one's own interiority. Moore's contribution is in fact neither naïve nor uncritical, but rather the fruit of a refined post-critical religious consciousness and a keenly honed methodological awareness of the dynamics of consciousness that aims at a distinctly post-critical retrieval.[77]

It is worth noting that Hunt's assessment of Moore focuses on a term coming from the thought of Lonergan when he explains the various realms of meaning that consciousness might inhabit. In Moore's writings, it is the realm of interiority. From our exploration of Lonergan and Moore in chapter 1, we were able to appreciate that we are meaning discoverers and meaning makers. The world is mediated by meaning and motivated by value through conscious acts of noticing, understanding, judgment, and deliberation on values, choices, and decisions. These acts have intentionality: to fulfill the desire to know, value, and ultimately be in love. Each of these acts is interior. The heightened intentional consciousness that attends not to objects external to the conscious subject but to their acts might be called "inhabiting" the realm of interiority. Interiority is not just a theory about how our consciousness operates. It is an act of self-appropriation, and when we use the word *self*, we mean the whole self of any person, including feelings, symbols, images, memories, questions, insights, formulation of concepts, judgments of truth, deliberations of what is worthwhile and valuable, choices and decisions. Interiority means achieving self-appropriation to identify the movement from theory to common sense and back again. It also means identifying the difference between the procedures and canons of each realm.

To be attuned to the realm of interiority helps us grasp the depth and breadth of religious conversion. Moore states:

> It seems to me that the primary theological need in our time is for the psychological to mediate the transcendent. Until this comes about, the psychological dimension remains subjective,

---

77. Hunt, *Trinity*, 79.

the transcendent dimension extrinsic. The perennial vigor of Christianity stems from a dangerous memory of the experience of a group of people being brought to a crisis whose issue was such a freedom in the face of our mortality can only come from the transcendent ground of being. The psychological mediation of the transcendent is remembered . . . . To awaken at this level is to have one's answer to the common view that the Christian myth has lost its power.[78]

There are multiple examples of religious interiority explored by Moore throughout his writings. Perhaps one of the best examples in his writings is the process he describes by which the disciples were first awakened to the desire for God, brought to a desolation of desire and a feeling that was for them the death of God in Jesus' suffering and death, and lastly, healed into a transformation of desire in the resurrection and sending of the Spirit.

MOORE THE POET

Moore loved writing theology that made use of precie terms, analogies, metaphors, and a wide range of symbolic expressions and stories, as well as composing theological poetry. In the previous chapter, I indicated that meaning is carried in several ways. There is an artistic carrier of meaning, where even before the desire to objectify the work of art in language and concept emerges, the symbol within the artwork already has a profound influence on our minds and hearts. These symbols are dense with affectivity and rich in felt meaning. Symbols awaken feelings, and feelings orient us to values, including the value of Ultimate Mystery. They can also frighten, disturb, and turn our thinking upside down. Since symbols are images evoking feelings or evoked by feeling, they carry in their stead a vast array of memories that impact our religious and psychological development.

In his early writings, Moore speaks of the need for theology to be more poetic. By "poetic," he does not mean that a theologian must now take a course on writing poetry. Instead, Moore is articulating a way of doing theology that has in the foreground a feeling for God as a "consuming fire in our hearts." When reflecting on the religious poet Gerard

---

78. Moore, *Jesus the Liberator*, x.

Manley Hopkins, Moore affirms a unique bodily quality to Hopkins's language. This language springs from

> a certain way of feeling the things around him, which forms the core of his personality.... An intense realization of the uniqueness of each experience. To perceive to be fully conscious is to come to an edge to a point which is absolutely unlike any other point.... To enter into an organic relation with the whole of being. We must contract to a point that seems the antithesis of that whole. The universal is only perceived in the particular.... To realize one's organic harmony with trees, flowers, and springs is to come into relation with the source of being.[79]

To this end, the emerging field of theopoetics seeks to bring together diverse perspectives through symbolic and artistic carriers of meaning to engage people in fresh ways to experience the Divine in our world. Theopoetics comprises two words, *theos* and *poiein*, meaning to make or shape the experience of God and to ponder on ways that people can come to know the Divine Spirit. Speaking to the purpose of theopoetics, Heaney states:

> The intent is much more than a theology in poetic form, but an embodied attempt to say something, experienced and accessible about the God we can host but not control a conversation opener towards further truth so that whether theology is inscribed in the genre of poetry, in the form of narrative, it remains a *poiesis*: an inventive, imaginative, active composition performed by authors. Theology implies radical engagement with the lived human experience of embodiment in all its dimensions ... implying that kinaesthetic, embodied knowing has a trustworthy role to play in making sense of the faith we believe. For theopoetics, the knowledge of God, born of embodied knowing, is nothing more than the consequence of taking the Incarnation seriously.[80]

Moore also wrote poetry. Moore judges that the poet's use of symbol and metaphor to communicate the transcendent is a more powerful means for drawing people to God and conversion than concise rational thought. Poetry can draw people to ask about God and communicate God in a manner that will illuminate the reader's feelings just as the poet feels them. The illumination of feeling is what Moore particularly loved in Hopkins's and Eliot's poetic writings. In the whole corpus of Moore's

79. Moore, "Gerard Manley," 184–86.
80. Heaney, *Suspended*, 35.

writings, which includes his final published work, *Remembered Bliss: A Book of Spiritual Sonnets*, specifically containing only poems, I count at least 160 long or short sonnets.

Moore loved writing religious sonnets on religious conversion, self-discovery, Jesus, the crucifixion and resurrection, the state of the Church, monastic life, and his inner thoughts about himself. On the occasion of a Lonergan Workshop in 1983, Moore paid tribute to his supervisor at Cambridge University, F. R. Leavis. It was Leavis who convinced him that good literature was "to be troubled and excited in those deepest reaches of the spirit where damnation, purgation, and salvation are appropriate concepts."[81] At Cambridge, Leavis introduced Moore to the poetry of Gerard Manley Hopkins and T. S. Eliot. Eliot's poetry would remain a constant companion to him throughout his life. What poetry helped us to do was to become more self-aware and conscious human beings. Ultimately, religious poetry aids our surrender to God.[82]

What is Moore trying to do through his poems? First, Moore is not concerned with giving a philosophical understanding of religious poetry. However, he believes in the importance of symbols and agrees with the assertion that a symbol is the tip of an ontological iceberg.[83] Therefore, Moore suggests that symbols can change our minds and hearts. The bread and butter of the poet are the symbols that they employ to communicate existential and religious truth.

Second, when a symbol of transcendence illuminates our hearts and minds with the Mystery of God, the call we hear from within is the call to change our lives. The truth within the symbol "invades and permeates the whole process and catches up the data of sense [indicated by the image chosen within the symbol] into a new intensity of luminosity."[84] Therefore, it is possible that symbols within religious poetry not only "stand for" the truth but partake of it, and we become overwhelmed in seeing, hearing, and speaking them.[85] Our participation in the truth of God's love is undoubtedly the case through the symbols of the sacraments, especially the symbol of the Eucharist (the bread and wine) and

---

81. Moore, "F. R. Leavis," 214.
82. Moore, "F. R. Leavis," 219.
83. Moore, "Critical and Symbolic Realism," 147.
84. Moore, "Critical and Symbolic Realism," 159.
85. Moore, "Critical and Symbolic Realism," 160.

marriage (the couple in mutual self-sacrificing love). Symbols "mediate transcendent mystery so as to transform us."[86]

This mediation also can occur through poetry. The words used by the poet contain the Mystery of God. Moore, paraphrasing M. Jadwiga Swiatecka, OP, states: "The symbol is not a pale reflection of a noetic heaven: it is [heaven] among us. God with us, incarnate transcendent meaning."[87] As Hughes indicates, the symbols and images of poetry communicate what Lonergan called elemental meaning:

> meaning that is more primordial, more basic, more concrete, more densely contacted than that of conceptualized explanation. This is a way of explaining how art is able to bypass, as it were, through its use of the symbolic languages of music, tactile, visual, and verbal media, the realm of explanatory ideas, which gives art a unique power to allude to the reality of divine transcendence, a power both more primal than that of intellectual concepts and one that surpasses the suggestive reach of all conceptual definitions.[88]

Third, in so far as religious poetry presents us with images that seek to overwhelm the soul with the Mystery of God, it also communicates the importance of staying between the balance of finite and infinite, thus affirming the finite and created universe and the Beyond of the infinite. Religious poetry will affirm that the Mystery of God is active as a divine formative presence in the world's order and that the Mystery of God reveals Godself to human consciousness. The images and symbols will seek to elicit fidelity to the Mystery of God, which surpasses all understanding and who is the source and final goal of reality. Images illuminate the value of the world as sacramental and promote inwardly a love for people and the world God has created. Images indicate how we are all involved in a drama, at the center of which is God's story for each of us, toward unfolding an intelligent, responsible, and loving universe.[89] The most significant barriers to embracing God's story in our culture are the positions of skepticism, scientism, pessimism, and a false utopianism through consumerism that stands against the Mystery of God, vitally active in our lives, immediately present in our lives, and in whom we participate.

---

86. Moore, "Critical and Symbolic Realism," 173.
87. Moore, "Critical and Symbolic Realism," 173.
88. Hughes, *More Beautiful*, 34–35.
89. Hughes, *Transcendence*, 172.

Moore's particular style of poetry is that of the sonnet, where the poem becomes a form of devotional or prayer poetry. In the foreword to *Remembered Bliss*, published in the year of his death, 2014, Abbot Krombach, Hayo Benedict E. Desire OSB, writes: "[Moore] stirs and invigorates humanity at large about the cultural malaise of faithlessness, the fragility of life, and the lack of moral compass and direction."[90] Moore's poetry addresses a culture of unbelief. However, the themes of his poetry also speak of human beings trying to find the balance within themselves between the finite and the infinite so that others may be prompted to "listen to their own inner longing for a blissful awakening to true selfhood . . . [where] finite and infinite are brought together and expressed in poetry."[91] In as much as Moore invites us to appreciate our inner longings, he also invites us into the simplest yet most difficult of all encounters: the encounter with ourselves. When the task is done well, religious poetry "reflects the essence of what happens to man. It reconnects us with that part of our being that is not touched by compromise. It mediates us to our carefree childhood to the freshness of our reactions to boundaries and bandages. And in that poetry returns us to ourselves, it also links us to the company of others, gives us back the possibility of communication."[92] In Krombach's estimation, "Moore is concerned about the intersubjectivity of human existence and the subjectivity of each person."[93]

In Moore's mind and heart, the poem invites the reader to have "courage" in the face of life's sufferings, disappointments, and uncertainties. Krombach states: "The courage which the poet needs is threefold: the courage to speak, which is the courage of the poet to be himself instead of the image of someone else; the courage to name, which is the courage of the poet not to name wrongly; and the courage to call which is the courage of the poet to believe that others can be called upon to be themselves instead of becoming subjects of suppression."[94] The call to courage comes from a conviction that only by being truthful to ourselves and others can one be joyful and alive, and the poet bears responsibility for helping people become truthful. The call to be honest indicates that Moore, the poet, is a human being first and then a monk who "is blessed to fathom human nature at its finest and fiercest. He values and trusts

---

90. Moore, *Remembered*, vii.
91. Moore, *Remembered*, vii.
92. Moore, *Remembered*, viii.
93. Moore, *Remembered*, viii–ix.
94. Moore, *Remembered*, ix.

the word and is careful not to waste." A random selection of his poetry indicates a man who, for a long time, "was filled with tormenting crises, but for that reason also, with a lasting yearning to be helped into the *refugium* of heaven." His crises gave him an intuitive feel for the hearts and souls of others and the need to listen to the call to change one's life. Thus, his poetry helps the converted reader find himself "transformed in a flash from a remote and frightened spectator of the self into an immediate non-resisting participant in his existential expression."[95] But above all, his poetry echoes a cosmic confidence in the power of love.[96]

Moore and His Poetic Themes

Before leaving this chapter, I want to present some of the main themes central to Moore's poetry. His book *Remembered Bliss* was ready for distribution on the day he died. It contains only poems with a brief introduction by Moore and Father Hayo Benedict E. Desire Krombach (friend, philosopher, and author). But sadly, it is not available for purchase, and I could not get a copy. I am relying on the partial copy on the internet for knowledge of the poems within their pages. A full critique of Moore's poems is beyond the scope of this book. And therefore, I can offer only a tiny selection. Further, Moore titled some of his poems and did not title others. Where a poem is rendered untitled, I have indicated the first line of the poem in inverted commas to identify it for the reader.

First, in the poem "Light and Half-Light,"[97] Moore reflects on the importance of living one's human existence to the full, having a desire to exist, live, grow, be, know, and do all that one can do. Human existence can only be lived when we have interacted with our brother and sister from the heart and a place of love. Truth, reality, and knowledge are born of love; until we love, the stars cannot reveal their glory to us. Moore urges his reader to move beyond simply espousing opinions, which he calls a decent rule for not getting to the truth, a shadowy knowledge, which is characteristic of the "anti-man" and something that we get used to, instead of undergoing the pain of finding the truth and living it through love. To arrive at the truth and to communicate truth to the people of our current generation requires that we be historically conscious rather than relying on the language and forms

---

95. Moore, *Remembered*, xi.
96. Moore, *Remembered*, xi.
97. Moore and Maguire, *Experience of Prayer*, 46–47.

of past culture (the move from the classicist notion of culture to the empirical notion of culture) that does not speak to our contemporaries. Moore captures this insight in his poem "Time has a history, is not absolute."[98] Living human existence requires attending to our historicity, especially when it comes to understanding our faith. We must be imbued with the trajectory of being historically conscious, for only then can we say that the truth has uncovered its light in us. In the poem "Pain-Body Disclosed," Moore calls on theologians to write theology that seeks to awaken people and transform them inwardly as if they were rewiring a house.[99]

Second, in several poems Moore reflects on the importance of conversion in our lives. In the poem "Liturgy not about our transformation,"[100] Moore alerts us to the danger of religious life and liturgical worship becoming a routine rather than a liturgical celebration being an occasion for listening deeply to God and undergoing transformation. The words of Jesus at the Last Supper, "Do this in memory of Me" are meant to wake us from an ignorance similar to being awakened from deeper sleep, rather than finding us remaining in our complacency like sheep. This theme of transformation continues in the poems "With the Lenten Exercise"[101] and "Awoken"[102] in which transformation is referred to as overcoming the heart of stone and replacing it with a heart of flesh. In several poems, Moore speaks to the process of conversion undergone by Eckhart Tolle and its impact on his feelings and thinking about God, himself, and others. Moore expresses the revolution in Tolle's life, and by implication our lives, in the poems "The Tolle Moment and Gethsemani,"[103] "I seek the Bliss of being One not Two,"[104] and "Tolle."[105] Tolle's transformative experiences so illuminate Moore that he writes of coming to know for the first time that there is only one self and, in that knowledge, Moore feels his heart accessible and attuned to whatever each new day might bring.

Third, Moore's poetry focuses on Jesus, his death and resurrection, and its transforming power in his life and every Christian life.

---

98. Moore, *Contagion of Jesus*, 4–5.
99. Moore, "2012–2014 Blog," Aug 13, 2012.
100. Moore, *Contagion of Jesus*, 42.
101. Moore, *Contagion of Jesus*, 113.
102. "2012–2014 Blog," Jan 21, 2013.
103. "2012–2014 Blog," Jul 9, 2013.
104. Moore, "2008 Blog," Oct 3, 2008.
105. Moore, *Contagion of Jesus*, 9.

A New Awareness

In "Stripped Bare,"[106] Moore contemplates the Mystery of the Cross of Jesus, from his entering the "void" of Gethsemani until the "letting go" of the crucifixion and the new dawn of the resurrection and sending of the Spirit, which signals that God has made all things new and that God is all in all. In "Jesus Stripper of God,"[107] Moore expresses the Mystery of the Cross, which is our killing of Jesus, who is a threat to us, and Jesus' free choice to accept death and return good for evil so that we might be divested of all guilt and stand before God full of love and at last feel at home. In the poem "Ours is the death that Jesus has destroyed,"[108] Moore addresses the new found freedom that comes from experiencing the power of the death and resurrection of Jesus. He expresses the hope that our graced freedom has the propensity to liberate humanity from all forms of domination and enable the inner movement from rivalry into ecstasy. These same themes of liberation through Jesus are continued in the poems "The man we love we call the Lamb,"[109] "Those hands we crucified to keep our fear,"[110] "Vilanelle" (Jesus is the "one who's always coped with me and changes me to leave me always free"),[111] "Vindication with love,"[112] "Was it a terrifying act of love,"[113] "What is my fear?"[114] "Learn of Me,"[115] and "See, I make all things new."[116] In other poems related to the theme of the saving actions of Jesus, Moore focuses on the Eucharist and its significance for our lives. These poems include: "A meal that takes a long time over grace,"[117] "At Mass,"[118] "Gethsemani,"[119] "Make It New,"[120] and "The Taste of Eucharist."[121]

---

106. Moore, *Contagion of Jesus*, 32–36.
107. Moore, *Contagion of Jesus*, 39.
108. Moore, "2012–2014 Blog," May 9, 2012.
109. Moore, "What God Has Joined," 163.
110. Moore, *Contagion of Jesus*, 41.
111. Moore, *Contagion of Jesus*, 186.
112. Moore, *Body of Christ*, 78–79.
113. Moore, *Body of Christ*, 67.
114. Moore, *Body of Christ*, 59.
115. Moore, *Contagion of Jesus*, 104.
116. Moore, *Body of Christ*, 46.
117. Moore, *Contagion of Jesus*, 31.
118. Moore, *Contagion of Jesus*, 55.
119. Moore, *Contagion of Jesus*, 188.
120. Moore, *Contagion of Jesus*, 189.
121. Moore, *Contagion of Jesus*, 189.

Fourth, Moore also explores in his poetry the themes of disesteem, personal sin, victimization of others and victimization of self, original sin, the reality of the pain-body, which signals that things are not right with us, the need for healing so that sadness may be replaced by happiness, and the need to be released from our addiction to unhappiness and self-punishment. These poems include: "Confession" ("I think I must have been born to be sad"),[122] "The need to be right holds us in our form,"[123] "Pain-Body Disclosed,"[124] and "No More to Sadness."[125] Moore was formed in a monastic spirituality emphasizing self-punishment as a form of humility. He affirms in "Let me Cry" that low esteem is not the same as humility.[126] The poem "Happy Synergy" captures part and parcel of our propensity for self-victimization, where Moore states, "I don't want to believe that God loves me."[127] A central reason for his victimization of others is articulated in "Why I Was the Worst Bully," where he states that his violence toward others came out of his dread of happiness and his self-punishing attitude, which then gave rise to cruelty.[128] In light of what Moore says about the crucified Jesus being no stranger but the true selves that we are crucifying, the poem "Break-out" points to sin being a form of self-crucifixion with self-hatred as its root.[129]

Fifth, Moore also delves into the themes of Church life, the example of Mary, the mother of the Lord, sexuality, women in the Church, the centrality of love and affectivity in our lives, the importance of contemplation and prayer (especially in the poem "God," where Moore speaks of being surprised by a form of prayerfulness not needing many words),[130] and the template for the Christian life found in the experience of the Lord's death and resurrection felt by the disciples (especially in the poem "Psalm Ninety New Style," where Moore speaks of the community of disciples touched in their darkness and made one by the Spirit of the risen

---

122. Moore, *Remembered*, 16.
123. Moore, "2012–2014 Blog," Aug 2, 2012.
124. Moore, *Remembered*, 19.
125. Moore, "2012–2014 Blog," Sep 8, 2012.
126. Moore, *Remembered*, 16.
127. Moore, *Remembered*, 14.
128. Moore, *Remembered*, 18.
129. Moore, *Contagion of Jesus*, 186.
130. Moore and Maguire, *Experience of Prayer*, 41.

Lord).[131] In the poem "Sickness unto Death,"[132] we find Moore within a community facing the prospect of the sickness of despair overwhelming them, the Church more broadly, and humanity generally. Moore writes a poem that addresses multiple themes: our common fear and anxiety, the possibility of having to face death, concerns at diminishing vocations to the priesthood and religious life, anxiety over a spirituality that does not speak to people, the way to peace through the desolation of the cross and the coming of the Spirit, the call to conversion, and an invitation to come into the heart of God. In the poems "In a Troubled Time for the Church"[133] and "For the Conclave,"[134] Moore urges his listeners to be reassured that God has the future in his hands even as the Church goes through difficult times and, above all else, to remember the call to love.

In several poems about Mary, Moore highlights her deep faith, perfect surrender to God, and our need to imitate her in her discipleship.[135] As he poetically reflects on Mary as a model of faith, he is well aware of all women in the Church and their desire to live with the "dangerous memory" of Jesus despite the distortion of patriarchy.[136] Never far from his thoughts and considerations are the themes of healing, the importance of wholesome affectivity in our lives, and an acceptance of the gift of our sexuality ("Tears"[137]). In the poem "Having Known,"[138] Moore speaks to the goodness of sex and our embodiment, the realization that to be gay is not to be "wrong," and the importance of accepting gay people fully into the life of the Church. Most significantly, Moore lays his soul bare as a gay man and priest in the two poems "The Last Place Where It Dare Not Speak Its Name"[139] and "A Gay Man Speaks."[140]

---

131. Moore and Maguire, *Experience of Prayer*, 44.
132. Moore and Maguire, *Experience of Prayer*, 81–83.
133. Moore, *Contagion of Jesus*, 184.
134. Moore, *Contagion of Jesus*, 184–85.
135. Moore, *Contagion of Jesus*, 80, 83, 86–87, 91, 96.
136. Moore, *Contagion of Jesus*, 183.
137. Moore and Maguire, *Experience of Prayer*, 36–37.
138. Moore and Maguire, *Experience of Prayer*, 39.
139. Moore, *Contagion of Jesus*, 159.
140. Moore, *Contagion of Jesus*, 192.

3

Conversion, Contemplation, and Eckhart Tolle

INTRODUCTION

In the last chapter, I explored how Moore appreciated that the vocation of the theologian is about making God "real" to oneself and others. In this chapter, I will unpack Moore's insights into prayer and contemplation as essential tools for embracing God as real and living in Christ. Religious conversion is at the heart of making God real. As a religious seeker, discoverer, and Christian believer, Moore probes the relationship between the person and the mystery of God, primarily through the experience of conversion, which leads to and flows from prayer and contemplation. All discovery of God, self-discovery, and discovery of others is also potentially an awakening to God through prayerfulness.

CONVERSION

Lonergan proposes that conversion is

> a change in direction, and indeed a change for the better [whereby] one frees oneself from the inauthentic. One grows in authenticity. We drop our harmful dangerous misleading satisfactions. Fears of discomfort, pain, [and] privation have less power to deflect one from one's course. Values are apprehended, whereas before, we overlook them. Scales of preference shift.

> Errors, rationalizations, [and] ideologies, fall and shatter to leave one open to things as they are and to man as he should be.[1]

As indicated in chapter 1, religious conversion is falling in love with God, who loves us unconditionally. The sense of being loved unconditionally gives rise to a reevaluation of our feelings, thinking, valuing, and actions. However, conversion can be traumatic. Even when we have access to illuminating insights and enriching values, experience shows that we may not accept the invitation to change. Change may prove too challenging for us. The suffering of change might mount up in waves of fear within us. Yet, to reject genuine insights and responsible values is to settle for old routines. Conversion invites us to take a risk. Accepting conversion enlarges our thinking and feeling, creating greater openness to meaning, truth, goodness, beauty, and love. Moore highlights the importance of conversion through the notion of "self-transcendence," that is, the change from the subject one is to the subject one is called to be in order to become authentic.[2] Further, Moore is well aware that delusion can paralyze us. We can delude ourselves into thinking that transformation is too arduous, even believing that one's current way of life is the best one can do. Moore does not hold back on the difficulties of realizing one's true identity and personhood in God. The obstacles to self-discovery are "formidable, torturous, and perverse."[3]

Self-identity, growth, and conversion go hand-in-hand. Moore states: "The discovery of the self carries the discovery of self-transcendence within it."[4] Self-transcendence presupposes conversion, and conversion brings a change to our distorted horizon. Who we are now in our particular identity has self-transcendence as its structure so that we may fully flourish. The imperative to which self-transcendence leads can be stated as "I love."

Further, conversion is multifaceted. Moore acknowledges not only religious conversion but also moral and psychological conversion, that is, "of feeling perhaps of imagination, of psyche, of our mythic or symbolizing consciousness."[5] One aspect of psychological conversion involves healing our neurotic and distorted feelings so that authentic feelings might motivate us toward values and happiness. Moore's studies into

---

1. Lonergan, *Method*, 52.
2. Moore, "Christian Self-Discovery," 187.
3. Moore, "Christian Self-Discovery," 188.
4. Moore, "Christian Self-Discovery," 187.
5. Moore, "F. R. Leavis," 222.

Freud and Neo-Freudian schools of thought demonstrate to him that our feelings about ourselves and others can become grossly distorted. Our values are grounded in our emotions and rely on healthy self-worth and self-love to guide us. Moore affirms: "I am not only convinced of our desire for worth but of the radical self-experience of worth, a self among selves, a being in relationship and communication, a dreamer of shared dreams, a co-celebrant of the being of things through language."[6] The healing of our disordered affective life amounts to a form of conversion. Alternatively, the disvalues pursued by people often originate in a radical disvaluing of themselves and give rise to a disvaluing of others.

Moore's own experience of moments of intense religious conversion happened at least three times throughout his life. His first religious conversion experience happened very early in his monastic life. He relates how, until 1944, the practice of "head-breaking mental prayer" left him sterile. Thus, Moore's first religious conversion comes when he discovers the power of contemplative prayer and, from that moment, can break from the "torture" of mental or discursive prayer taught to novices according to the Ignatian tradition.[7] From this experience he notes that the anxiety brought on by a failure in mental prayer is not necessarily self-centered. It has more of an invitation to a new direction, though it often needs clarification. Saint John of the Cross calls it "anxious love."[8] Moore knows a new desire is coming to birth as he feels this anxious love. It is "new in that I do not know what I desire except times of solitude."[9] Moore describes the process and aftermath of identifying the new desire: "I told God he bored me and I felt like packing in the whole silly business. Nothing happened at the time, but half an hour later, walking outside, I knew that I had been completely changed and would give him anything he wanted. I was in love."[10] The contemplative moment leads to surrender. Shortly after this moment, Moore exposes himself to God layer by layer, and "at each exposure, I said that too, take that too! I was being stripped down to a first awareness of un-differentiated trust."[11]

His second religious conversion came around 1959, when Moore, at the time studying theology in Rome, was wandering with friends in the

6. Moore, "For a Soteriology," 231.
7. Moore, *Remembered*, v.
8. Moore, "In Water," 92.
9. Moore, "In Water," 92.
10. Moore, "In Water," 92.
11. Moore, "In Water," 92.

Roman countryside. He relates: "It was the feast of the Sacred Heart, and they were seeing the first anthem of Vespers, 'One of the soldiers opened his side with a spear, and immediately there came out blood and water.' Quietly and with part of the mind that does not wrestle with concepts, I knew that the whole thing was there: the act of aggression, the sin, releasing the waters of grace."[12] This experience seemed like a vision in which he felt a symbolic concentration of truth. Moore relates that upon hearing those words, at that time in Latin, "I had what I can only describe as a sense of fullness of truth. Somehow, everything that was to be said about life and its renewing was in those words. Somehow *my* life, *my* destiny, was in those words."[13]

His third religious conversion was in the 1970s when he participated in a thirty-day Ignatian retreat. Moore calls the occasion "the turning point," which became the title of another poem: "Just where I, for fear must fly, you for love, have to die."[14] Moore adds: "What is this love that overcomes the insecurity of being itself? It comes of God overcome by my insecure violence. Embraced by this bleeding love, 'I feel I was never right, it was never well with me till now. Though I did not know it. I never felt right.'"[15] Again, Moore links his conversion to the ongoing healing of feeling himself never right.

Moore interprets the experience of self-surrender and love as akin to "the intrusion into our adult world of the simple, undifferentiated awareness, in which our life starts of being held helpless and trusting, of being in love."[16] He uses the metaphor of the mother-child relationship to deepen the meaning of this experience, a relationship he often calls "oceanic consciousness." There is an objectless character around the desire that emerges from the experience. He states: "I simply am desire, as originally, I simply was ecstasy."[17] However, while the mother-child experience is akin to returning to the womb, all experiences that follow conversion are a grace-initiated rebirth. There is no going back to the womb. Moore affirms that rebirth is "a fact of consciousness that contains the very meaning of consciousness."[18]

12. Moore, *Crucified Is No Stranger*, ix.
13. Moore, *Inner Loneliness*, 119.
14. Moore, *Let This Mind*, 170.
15. Moore, *Let This Mind*, 172.
16. Moore, "In Water," 92.
17. Moore, "In Water," 93.
18. Moore, "In Water," 93.

DRAWN TO CONTEMPLATIVE PRAYER

Most significantly, Moore feels his own rebirth occurring through being drawn to contemplative prayer, or as he calls it, "immediate prayer." He states that "a person comes to this pivotal moment where the simple being in trust of the beginning reaffirms itself in the midst of present complexity, 'in the middle of the way' (T. S. Eliot) and looks with serenity towards the unknown end."[19] For Moore, his conversion, paving the way for the gift of praying contemplatively, brings about a second ecstasy of which the mother-child relationship is a paradigm. He also accepts that mystics can come to contemplative prayer either through recovering an original trust felt at birth with one's mother or healing the absence of initial trust that wounds. The former generates a mysticism that builds on and transforms a sense of actual and original abundance, giving rise to a new ecstasy, as if, once again, one is being held by the mother. The latter focuses on a new ecstasy through healing an original woundedness, where the mother was absent, and the child felt little to no first ecstasy at being alive.[20] In either path, the second ecstasy lifts the goodness of the first ecstasy between mother and child to a higher level. This higher level is a rebirth of "real freedom, the being in love with God."[21] As we mature and think of death as our dissolution and destruction, the contemplative moment is the graced moment of the Spirit and amounts to "freedom in dissolution, intention in unmeaning, life in death."[22]

In later chapters, I will examine how Moore understands the centrality of Jesus for self-discovery, conversion, and self-transcendence. In this context, however, Moore states that Jesus' ecstasy comes about because of his Abba experiences and affirms that the experience of his ecstasy was nothing more than "a living by and in and to the ground of being as simple as the infants loving in the mother-love" and his experience of the Father was "a revolution in consciousness into which all will be summoned."[23] Jesus, though victim, is completely free to love, and his love is grounded in the contemplative moment of his Abba experience. Further, Jesus' resurrection and sending of the Spirit becomes the other

---

19. Moore, "In Water," 93.
20. Moore, "In Water," 95.
21. Moore, "In Water," 95.
22. Moore, "In Water," 97.
23. Moore, "In Water," 96.

side of the Abba experience, therefore, the point of conversion for the disciples, and becomes a social fact in the birth of the church.

Moore does not understand the contemplative moment as a solitary experience. It can be encountered in the liturgy, where we are drawn out of ourselves to God and one another. What prevents the liturgy from communicating its powerful public message is that we sacrifice others on the altars of our felt dis-esteem, self-hatred, apathy, and malice as individuals or as social bodies. As we become conscious of any distorted orientation in our lives, the forgiveness of Christ is the ground of contemplation, and the liturgy can become a socializing and sharing of the contemplative moment.[24]

PRAYER AND MONASTIC LIFE

While the constitutions of various Benedictine congregations may be slightly different, all share common characteristics: allegiance to the Rule of Saint Benedict; community life, supporting each other with patience despite weaknesses and poor behavior; ownership of all goods in common; the communal prayer of the Liturgy of the Hours; prayerful reflection on the Scriptures and related literature called *Lectio Divina*; and the performing of monastery-oriented and apostolic tasks: agriculture, hospitality, education, retreats, craft work, scholarship, counseling, and parish ministry. As members of a religious community, each monk dedicates themselves to the search for God within their community under the monastic vows of obedience, stability of place, and conversion of manners.

Prayer, prayerfulness, and contemplation are at the heart of the monk's life. Such prayer can be done corporately or individually. However, while prayer and the search for God may be at the top of the hierarchy of invitations in the monk's life, work and recreation often take prime positions. From the year that Moore first entered the monastery up to the 1960s, there was little to indicate how prayer and contemplation increased the monk's wisdom, deepened his relationship in love with others, and contributed to the other aspects of his life. Therefore, little direction was given regarding the emotions one ought to experience when in prayer. For this reason, Moore speaks of the torture of discursive prayer. The obligation to practice mental prayer bearing no relationship to life made prayer burdensome for some individual monks, which

---

24. Moore, "In Water," 101.

meant they would only come across the insight that prayer was the center of one's life by some other means.[25]

This boredom also affected some monks when praying the Liturgy of the Hours. The monks felt it to be a vain repetition and, for some monks, an exercise devoid of meaning. They would see that a set of monastic imperatives through blind obedience and an obligation to pray had replaced a whole-hearted search for God. In this context, Moore spoke about praying the psalms. He argues that the music and rhythm of plainsong chanting in Latin manifests the human person as embodied and human spirit inspired by grace.[26] The body in chant manifests the spirit searching for God and witnesses the monk's participation in the life of God. The rhythm of the chant is not just the metric time in which the chant is sung but is symbolic of a "still point of the turning world."[27] The fact that the psalms are prayed in Latin enables the monk to be even more rhythmic than if it were prayed in the vernacular. Psalms are meant to be prayed and sung in a chant that breathes the soul into the voice. Speaking the psalm in a monotone voice is no substitute. This aspect of communal prayer enthuses Moore when he states: "The opinion that singing is beautiful but not necessary separates function [of words] from beauty."[28]

PRAYER AND LIFE

There is a relationship between our concrete lives and the act of prayer. Prayer arises from our concrete lives. It is not a compartmentalized experience separate from life. Yet, Moore's experience living in a monastic community may have been quite different, and according to Harvey, his good friend, prayer and how monks lived seemed disconnected. Spiritual reading was simply a preparation for prayer, not a means to spiritual growth. Work was how the monk supported the community and was, therefore, functional. Personal relationships were interpreted as being kind and helpful to others rather than growing together in love.[29] When Moore entered the monastery, human relationships were low on the essential list of being a monk. Growth with others meant being careful of

25. Moore and Maguire, *Experience of Prayer*, 4.
26. Moore, "Rhythm and Psalmody," 74.
27. Moore, "Rhythm and Psalmody," 74.
28. Moore, "Rhythm and Psalmody," 76.
29. Moore and Maguire, *Experience of Prayer*, 5.

intimate relationships and "particular friendships" with other monks. The experience of having feelings of love for someone had to remain private and quickly became dangerously inward and sterile. Harvey points out that "love had to remain a privileged and ambiguous accidental happening."[30] Prayer was not viewed as the "creative factor drawing together and giving a unified direction to all the facets of their experience."[31] Instead, prayer was seen as a safety-first factor or device for keeping in touch with God and away from the dangers of living in common. It was often thought that if one stopped praying, the risk was that worst things could happen, for example, the threat of particular friendships spiraling out of control accompanied by neurosis and depression.

For Moore, these factors needed reorientation. He was convinced that life provides a womb from which prayer is born.[32] To illustrate the concreteness of prayer, Moore gives the example of two people who have fallen in love. When we fall in love, the task of self-disclosure is primary. While love continues and is felt powerfully, the self-disclosure is easy. Someone is accepting us as we are, and we are receiving them. So, with prayer, when we are powered by the experience of God's valuing us, our desire to self-disclose to God is easy. When we fall out of love with someone or when someone we have loved over many years dies, we feel an emptiness and nothingness. The question becomes: Can you still live after an experience of emptiness and nothingness when there was once fullness in our lives? If prayer, at this time, is born in us even in the face of all the paradoxical scenarios that life throws up for us, it can break the psychic limits that such suffering experiences leave us with and "quicken our life at lower (psychic) levels."[33]

PRAYER AND THE UNKNOWN GOD

Moore begins to understand prayer as a desire to open to the Unknown God. He states prayer "is a response to that dark initiative that fills the world of people with ordinary life and beauty."[34] Therefore, prayer is born of our desire for God "felt in our bones and not in our senses, singing a

---

30. Moore and Maguire, *Experience of Prayer*, 7.
31. Moore and Maguire, *Experience of Prayer*, 8.
32. Moore and Maguire, *Experience of Prayer*, 13.
33. Moore and Maguire, *Experience of Prayer*, 14.
34. Moore and Maguire, *Experience of Prayer*, 16.

wild song in our heads, bringing into play our whole terrible, vulnerable desire for happiness, our whole existence, making us feel that the outcome here will be either the beginning or the end of the world."[35] In a relationship that is sometimes new to us, one aims to get to know the other person and to open oneself honestly and with full disclosure to them. So, in prayer one strives to get to know God and open ourselves honestly in disclosure to God just as we are and not as we may think God wants us to be. This act of openness may be shut down by feelings of fear and threat or, alternatively, opened by trust and acceptance. When our intentions are powered by fear and danger, God is usually understood to threaten our being. The threatening attitude derives from the experience of being insubstantial and self-disesteeming. When openness is powered by trust and acceptance, God is understood to be intimate, in love, very fond of us, and our constant companion.[36] Even at this stage of his writings on prayer, Moore believes that our experience with the unknown leads us to feel lovable and to love since the unknown is present in all our concrete experiences of love. In his mind, prayer and our felt sense of lovableness are ultimately connected. For this reason, he writes: "The greatest courage there is, is the courage to be wholly and unfailingly a person in the face of the unknown. The source of this courage is itself unknown, but most certain. No one can give you the courage, but you can catch it off others when they aren't looking but are themselves attuned to this source."[37]

PRAYER AND LOVE

Prayer is also the completion of something we are already doing when doing the work of love. Prayer is oriented to love and love is an orientation in myself that I have to cultivate. God is in our relationships of love. God makes someone highly attractive to me. The task of self-discovery through prayer is "to find somehow in the depths of myself, how to love, what it is to love—which of course is the way he wants it, for it is only in self-knowledge that a man can know God."[38] By loving another person, "you are learning to be for another person rather than to possess him. Through this painful process, two people are coming out of their shells

---

35. Moore and Maguire, *Experience of Prayer*, 18.
36. Moore and Maguire, *Experience of Prayer*, 12.
37. Moore and Maguire, *Experience of Prayer*, 16.
38. Moore and Maguire, *Experience of Prayer*, 18.

into a real meeting. But it is terribly hard at first to love another person with your whole self and not with your appetite for gain. Yes, I think that's the point, learning to love with yourself, learning that infinite respect which is the tribute I pay to another person, his freedom his immense variety, his horror of being engulfed, his selfhood."[39] As oriented to love, prayer is the completion of something we are already doing and something that is already going on within us, something that we are.[40] Through prayer, God calls us out of our tiny world into "the joy of his fullness."[41]

CHAPMAN AND CONTEMPLATIVE PRAYER

With these opening remarks on prayer and its importance to the task of love in our concrete lives, Moore explores the place of contemplative prayer drawing from the writings of Abbot John Chapman, a former abbot of Downside Abbey. Abbot John Chapman's *Spiritual Letters*, published posthumously in 1938, became a fertile field of exploration for Moore's discovery of contemplative prayer.

In appendix 1 of his *Spiritual Letters*, Chapman speaks to several "simple rules,"[42] when it comes to contemplative prayer, which has a bearing on Moore's approach to prayer. First, for those who find mental prayer unhelpful, Chapman suggests that when entering a period set aside for prayerfulness, "cease *all thinking*" and only be in that space because you want to be there and give that time as your gift to God.[43] In other words, use meditation on the words and scenes of Scripture or the practice of mental prayer with pious imagination whenever it is possible for you, and not when it has become fruitless and barren. This approach echoes one of Chapman's important axioms about prayer: "pray as you can and do not try to pray as you cannot."[44] Chapman also proposes discursive and imaginative meditation as a method of prayer that will not suit, especially when it is grounded in some anxious need to praise God for his Almighty power and putting ourselves down as his lowly subjects, because mistakenly that

---

39. Moore and Maguire, *Experience of Prayer*, 19.
40. Moore and Maguire, *Experience of Prayer*, 21.
41. Moore and Maguire, *Experience of Prayer*, 19.
42. Chapman, *Spiritual Letters*, 289–91.
43. Chapman, *Spiritual Letters*, 289.
44. Chapman, *Spiritual Letters*, 109.

is what we think God expects of us.[45] Any self-loathing in prayer only brings about an inappropriate self-berating for the lack of enthusiasm and inattentiveness to meditation. When in prayer, do not force imaginative images, feelings, or emotional thoughts to come. Instead, start with who you are before God and tell God you will allow him to do what he will do with you. It is all about wanting or desiring God.

Second, Chapman notes that

> the strangest phenomenon is when we begin to wonder whether we mean anything at all, and if we are addressing anyone, or merely repeating a formula we do not mean mechanically. The word God seems to mean nothing. If we feel this curious and paradoxical condition, we are starting on the right road, and we must beware of trying to think about what God is and what he has done for us, etc., or what we are before Him, etc. because this takes us out of prayer and spoils God's work.[46]

Chapman's description of contemplative prayer is apt: It feels like an "idiotic state" and a "complete waste of time."[47] We will even get distracted in prayer, but that does not mean all is useless. In the end, prayer is about wanting nothing but God. Prayer's efficacy will reflect how we live the rest of our day.

Third, Chapman has much to say about the night of the soul, which becomes a powerful key for Moore to unlock the disciples' experience after the crucifixion. Through reading Chapman, Moore became interested in the mystical writings of st John of the Cross and especially the dark night of the soul. Chapman speaks to the darkness, dryness, and strangeness of contemplative prayer, likely producing worry, anxiety, and bewilderment in people.[48] Still, if one persists, there will emerge, for some, a consciousness "of being in the presence of something undefinable yet above all things desirable without any the more arriving at being able to think about it or speak about it..."[49] Most of Chapman's responses to questions regarding blankness and darkness are words of reassurance that such things are not abnormal though unusual.[50] He urges people not to give up but to be prepared to accept the violent trials that may come

---

45. Chapman, *Spiritual Letters*, 104.
46. Chapman, *Spiritual Letters*, 290.
47. Chapman, *Spiritual Letters*, 290.
48. Chapman, *Spiritual Letters*, 42.
49. Chapman, *Spiritual Letters*, 291.
50. Chapman, *Spiritual Letters*, 85.

A New Awareness

with attempting contemplative prayer.[51] These experiences may be God's way of shaping us into the likeness of Christ.[52]

MOORE INTERPRETING CHAPMAN

Moore speaks of two kinds of awakening to God: an indirect and a direct awakening to God. An indirect awakening to God occurs when we fall in love with another, and, in that love, feel the presence of God in our lives. I will also speak about this indirect awakening to God in chapter 6. Let us examine contemplative or centering prayer as a pathway toward a direct awakening to God.[53]

Moore's appreciation for Chapman's insights into contemplative prayer is no less controversial than when Chapman first articulated it. Contemplative prayer was considered the reserve of the most committed to God, who were vowed religious and priests, especially those enclosed in religious orders, and certainly not the preserve of the laity. Moore follows Chapman in appreciating that contemplative prayer belongs to everyone. It is not idiosyncratic but normative for the life of the believer. The division between beginners in worship, and therefore, more suited to mental prayer, and advanced people in the life of prayer and, therefore, more suited to contemplative prayer, did not hold for Moore and many other people, for whom the more discursive prayer only leaves them feeling empty. All people are being invited into a new awakening to God. For this reason, Moore, drawing from Basil Pennington, gives a short six-point instruction into contemplative prayer and invites the reader to try it.[54]

There are several insights underpinning contemplation that Moore returns to over and over again. First, following Chapman, Moore affirms that all human desire, whether the desire for truth, goodness, and beauty, is, first and foremost, a desire for God since to desire these realities is to seek the source and terminus of these desires. When one surrenders to God, or what Moore calls being in love with God, one has come to the Source and ground of all contemplative prayer. Seeking God through contemplative prayer comes with a surrender and desire for God and leads to a deepening surrender to God.

---

51. Chapman, *Spiritual Letters*, 84.
52. Chapman, *Spiritual Letters*, 143.
53. Moore, *Let This Mind*, 35–36.
54. Moore, *Let This Mind*, 64.

CONVERSION, CONTEMPLATION, AND ECKHART TOLLE

Moore also describes the path of contemplative prayer as entering a void, where one is oriented not to any object but more essentially to "nothing in particular."[55] We are awakened directly to God when our desire breaks the rules and reaches out to nothing or nobody. Direct awakening primarily concerns our desire for God, giving ourselves to God interiorly, wanting God intensely, turning to God, and seeking to remain united. Without any object in mind, we learn the practice of just being and resting in our existence or what we might call the "I am" experience. In the mystery of God, to be significant is to be. This attentive presence to "nothing in particular" in centering prayer, concurrent with the feeling of a new and intense sense of self, is God.[56] Moore states that the

> condition of being suddenly alive and wanting I know not what cannot be induced. It simply happens. But from time immemorial, in different cultures and religious climates, people have used a method for quieting or simplifying consciousness so that a person may be better *disposed* for the moment of awakening. Thus, while the awakening moment consists of *wanting* nothing in particular, the method consists of *thinking* of nothing in particular.[57]

Second, through a direct awakening, we come to our core selfhood or desirability not through some object before us desiring us but through feeling the unknown God simply and directly. While this desirability has no object, Moore asserts that all desirability reaches for intimacy. The mysterious reality, which seeks affection with us and with whom we seek intimacy, is God's mystery. This intimacy leads to a desire to surrender entirely to God. In the words of Saint Ignatius, we can pray: "Take, Lord, and receive all my liberty, my memory, my understanding, and my entire will, All I have and call my own. You have given all to me. To you, Lord, I return it. Everything is yours; do with it what you will. Give me only your love and your grace that is enough for me."[58] In this case, we do not desire some object but God, who first desires us. God's loving of us causes us to notice our desirability and to respond.

Third, God's desire for us creates a "luminous identity," generating a desire for God and the new horizon that the experience opens up to us.

---

55. Chapman, *Spiritual Letters*, 248.
56. Moore, *Let This Mind*, 55.
57. Moore, *Let This Mind*, 65.
58. Ignatius, "Prayer of Surrender."

Luminosity gives rise to a sense of personal significance. I am made significant by God's choice of me, and in God's desire for me, I experience all our other desires for lovers, family, and friends.[59]

Fourth, the felt knowledge of my desirability through a direct awakening to God turns our perspectives on their head. Instead of saying that the bride's love for her groom and the groom's love for his bride is an image of God's love for us, we can now say that *God's love for us* (my italics) helps us grasp the bride's love for her groom and the groom's love for his bride. From this, Moore distinguishes two modes of being religious: romantic and mystical. Romantic religiousness proceeds from created analogies to help grasp the love of God. Mystical religiousness has the human mind and heart illuminated by a more profound source wherein desirability is awakened directly by God. The shift from the romantic to the mystical is the nerve to becoming religiously adult.[60]

Fifth, Moore suggests that God causes in us a form of desire, which he calls "we know not what"[61] while simultaneously making our lives sure of our meaningfulness and ultimate significance. Our oneness with God as the cause of desire is likened to a river overflowing its banks, pressured by the waters flowing down from some source high in the mountains. According to Moore, the heart of religion is reaching toward the origin or the cause of our desirability, being, and goodness.[62] This breakthrough grounds any other image or thought we might wish to use to communicate the quality of the relationship between ourselves and God.[63] Moore sums up his thoughts in this Coda: "God desires us before we desire God because God's desire makes us desirable, which we must be in order to desire anything at all. In the new creation, we feel the creative touch of God's desire stirring us in our desirableness to desire nothing that can be named until this nothing is named as the cause of our desire, which (is) the cause of desire, is desirable."[64]

---

59. Moore, *Let This Mind*, 38.
60. Moore, *Let This Mind*, 42.
61. Moore, *Let This Mind*, 65.
62. Moore, *Let This Mind*, 43.
63. Moore, *Let This Mind*, 39.
64. Moore, *Let This Mind*, 47.

MOORE AND CONTEMPLATION

For Moore, the terminus of God in contemplation points to the mystery of the indwelling of God within the human soul. First, Moore refers to Thomas Merton's "hidden ground of Love" or the *point vierge*. Merton also writes of the importance of inwardness and contemplation and where it takes us, namely to that place where we discover the presence of God. Merton writes that

> *le point vierge* (at) the center of our being is a point of nothingness which is untouched by sin and by illusion, a point of pure truth, a point or spark which belongs entirely to God, which is never at our disposal, from which God disposes of our lives, which is inaccessible to the fantasies of our own mind or the brutalities of our own will. This little point of nothingness and absolute poverty is the pure glory of God within us. It is so to speak his name written in us, as our poverty, as our indigence, as our dependence, as our sonship. It is like a pure diamond, blazing with the invisible light of heaven. It is in everybody, and if we could see it, we would see those billions of points of light coming together in the face and blaze of the sun that would make all the darkness and cruelty of life vanish completely . . . I have no program for seeing this. It is only given. But the gate of heaven is everywhere.[65]

Christian tradition names this reality the dwelling place of God within our innermost being. The innermost region is no longer just ourselves naturally as we are, but the place of grace, where the gift of God is poured into our hearts by the Holy Spirit (Rom 5:5). Paul of Tarsus can then say, "It is no longer I who live, but it is Christ who lives in me" (Gal 2:20). For Moore, the dwelling place that Merton speaks of is the seat of our true self. I will explore the term *true self* more fully in chapter 5.

Second, contemplation requires an "act of attention to God (and) an act of inattention to everything else."[66] When we inhabit an attitude of attentiveness, we let go of any number of thoughts one by one.[67] When we stumble into seeking nothing in particular but only to desire God, a dramatic demotion of our ego as the power in charge of awareness happens in us, and it feels right.[68] Moore encourages us to choose

---

65. Merton, *Conjectures*, 158.
66. Moore, *Body of Christ*, 65.
67. Moore, *Let This Mind*, 65.
68. Moore, *Body of Christ*, 24.

a path of transformation, "a journey beyond our world full of mental noises into the silence that is . . . the silence of contemplative prayer."[69] In the hidden ground, one discovers the True Self, "the Nazarene crucified, of course, by our violent world and raised from the dead to spread the happiness of God."[70]

Third, contemplation means that one ceases in thought, waits, and gropes towards nothing in particular, which "is, of course, God."[71] Moore states that the groping experience "is letting myself into an enclosed presence that is nothing but love."[72] It is "a wasting time in God. The waste of time (feeling) vies with a feeling of direction. The groping for nothing, in particular, is a groping *into all*, the all that is enclosed love."[73]

Fourth, Moore surmises that our fear and misunderstanding of contemplation, even as believers, comes from a disordered interior orientation that could be nothing more than an "addiction to unhappiness" and a view of religion that privileges renunciation and suffering, a climate that typified his early years of formation and monastic life.[74] Those who disparage the contemplative way usually have a fundamentalist mindset, relying on religious certainty and privileging a rigorous and clear articulation of the truths of the faith. They fear a feeling for God and surrender to God.

Fifth, Moore advocates for the silence of contemplative prayer in contrast to the mental noise and angry words of the new atheists. Moore encourages us to "feel your silence and you might even find yourself praying for them, poor men . . . take to the words 'be still and know that I am God!' and say them to yourself slowly. The purpose of having a stretch of prayer time or *Lectio* is to give the new consciousness a chance to become stronger . . . you give this new awareness a chance to become tenderness and this is likely there when something annoying happens."[75]

Lastly, Moore claims that removing contemplative prayer from priestly formation in the centuries following Quietism "has surely been a background factor to the present moral crisis in the priesthood."[76]

---

69. Moore, *Body of Christ*, 25.
70. Moore, *Body of Christ*, 25.
71. Moore, "Contemplation in a World," 18.
72. Moore, "Contemplation in a World," 18.
73. Moore, "Contemplation in a World," 18.
74. Moore, "Thoughts in a Defence," 19.
75. Moore, "In Water," 104.
76. Chapman, *Spiritual Letters*, vii (Moore's introduction).

MOORE AND THE MYSTICAL

In chapter 1, I noted that mystical consciousness preoccupies Moore's life and writings throughout his monastic career. For Moore, the mystical brings to mind such great people as John of the Cross, Teresa of Avila, and Saint Augustine. His interest in the mystical helps configure his consciousness with a radical and humble anticipation of its absolute fulfillment by God and, through that completion, a guide to living daily. It is a fulfillment grounded in the experience of falling in love with God, who first loved us.

Reflecting on mystical experience, Morelli states,

> The love we feel is a love that has no bounds. The acceptance we feel is an acceptance that has no conditions. It is unconditional and unrestricted love that sustains us and enables us to persist in our basic commitment to the pursuit of meaning, objectivity, knowledge, truth, reality, and value despite our dramatic failures and psychological suffering, our intellectual confusion, our aesthetic numbness, our practical obstacles and debacles, our physical pain. Our distracting derailing and debilitating desires and fears and our undermining victimization by others.[77]

Moore's appreciation for Augustine helps him to express what can be the outworking of the mystical in our lives. Speaking of Augustine, Moore relates religious and moral conversion to the mystical. He states: "The terror of being without what seemed to be absolutely needed is removed by the New Plan within [the event of conversion in Augustine] surrender to whom is pure delight and swallows up all the fear of life without lusting."[78] He goes on to assert: "The mystical is not some kind of pure essence boiled off the melting pot of the human. It throws its roots into the depths of the human, into the darkest reaches of our dreams . . . this is only true within the ambit of a faith that is being known and loved by God and thus are valuable in one's own eyes."[79]

In the church of late antiquity, mystical experiences were expressed through the categories of Neoplatonist thought. Neoplatonism was the dominant philosophical tradition that began with Plotinus, an interpreter of Plato. It was a way for Christian believers to marry Platonic philosophy and spirituality. Plotinus describes a system of thought that

---

77. Morelli, *Self-Possession*, 240.
78. Moore, "Doxology of Joy," 143.
79. Moore, "Doxology of Joy," 144.

focuses on three [spiritual] substances: "The One, fount of all being, but itself beyond being and prediction; Mind emanating eternally from the One as its image containing the eternal ideas on which the sensible universe is modeled; and World Soul, which penetrates and enlivens the sensible world based on the rational principles it receives in its generation from Mind."[80]

Moore's critique of Neoplatonic spirituality is simple. Spirituality based on Neoplatonic categories degenerates genuine mystical knowledge to an apolitical and spiritually impotent piety. The knowledge of God is divorced from any sense of relationship with another. In Moore's view, Neoplatonism is alive and well and killing monastic life. While Neoplatonism can account for being overcome by the sense of God's transcendence, for Moore, it falls short of describing how each of us knows that we are loved "in the way a man knows when he is in love and loved that the transcending one loves me?"[81] At the basis of all mysticism is the assurance and conviction that one is loved. Moore states: "As I look back on all my experience and experiments with sexuality and love, the one thing I find I have most wanted, most avoided, most forgotten, is primitively and immediately to know that another loves me."[82] Being convinced that the mystical is grounded in love, Moore is also confident that while the mystical and the sexual are poles apart in the mind of the Church, they should not be. Indeed, there should be no division and separation between God in the abbey chapel and God in my sexual fantasies.[83]

THE TOLLE FACTOR

Drawing together the importance of conversion and the contemplative moment in our lives, Moore speaks continually about the experience of Eckhart Tolle. Here is the experience Tolle underwent that Moore relates to:[84]

> Until my thirtieth year I lived in a state of almost continuous anxiety interspersed with periods of suicidal depression. It feels now as if I am talking about some past lifetime or somebody else's life. One night, not long after my twenty-ninth birthday, I

---

80. Cavadini, "Neoplatonism," 910.
81. Moore, "Doxology of Joy," 153.
82. Moore, "Doxology of Joy," 154.
83. Moore, "Doxology of Joy," 156.
84. Tolle, *Power of Now*, 3–4.

woke in the early hours with a feeling of absolute dread. I had woken up with such a feeling many times before, but this time it was more intense than it had ever been. The silence of the night, the vague outlines of the furniture in the dark room, the distant noise of a passing train—everything felt so alien, so hostile and so utterly meaningless that it created in me a deep loathing of the world. The most loathsome thing of all, however, was my own existence. What was the point in continuing to leave with this burden of misery? Why carry on with this continuous struggle? I could feel that a deep longing for annihilation, the nonexistence, was now becoming much stronger than the instinctive desire to continue to live. "I cannot live with myself any longer." This was the thought that kept repeating itself in my mind. Then suddenly I became aware of what a peculiar thought it was. "Am I one or two? If I cannot live with myself, there must be two of me the 'I' and the 'self' that I cannot live with." Maybe I thought only one of them is real. I was so stunned by this strange realization that my mind stopped. I was fully conscious, but there were no more thoughts. Then I felt drawn into what seemed a vortex of energy. It was a slow movement at first and then accelerated. I was gripped by an intense fear and my body started to shake. I heard the words "resist nothing" as if spoken inside my chest. I could feel myself being sucked into a void. It felt as if the void was inside (me) rather than outside. Suddenly, there was no more fear, and I let myself fall into that void. I have no recollection of what happened after that.

Moore makes several observations about Tolle's experiences. First, Tolle experiences a complete breakdown in the meaning and significance of his life. It is a profound point of trauma and crisis. He feels himself pulled into a vortex or void or nothingness. The vortex is a symbol of dissolution or death. Moore is convinced that the presence of God pulled Tolle into the vortex.[85] Tolle's experience is a moment of conversion. The state of being pulled into the void complements other authors who speak of a conversion experience as a kind of death. For example, Paul states, "For me living is Christ and dying is gain" (Phil 1:21). Jerome Miller states:

> Where must human beings place themselves for the Sacred to become real to them? The only answer I can give to that question is this text as a whole. My purpose from the beginning has been to follow the footsteps of a pilgrimage toward the heart of crisis. If we have been led to think that at the heart of crisis is

85. Moore, "2012–2014 Blog," May 1, 2012.

A New Awareness

an encounter with the Sacred, that means, conversely, that the only way to find what is Ultimately Sacred is to take the road that leads past all the way stations of crisis, to its dreadful center. If a human being is to find the Sacred, his will to control must give way to generosity, his generosity to heroism, his heroism to shame, his experience of shame to worship of that reality which he was avoiding all along because it requires identifying with nothingness. If the encounter with the Sacred is the consummate anguish of all crises, it is also true that the anguish of radical crisis is the unknown but inevitable destination of a person intent on encountering the Sacred. Just as all horrors only approximate, the experience of one's nothingness before the Sacred, all religious worship is authentic only to the degree that it participates in what we have called suffering.[86]

In the above passage, Miller identifies the traumatic passage by which we give up the will to control and surrender into the hands of God. At such a point, and in the depths of one's abyss, we can only look up and speak words that suggest a stance of humility and poverty. Miller continues his analysis:

If our reflection has not been mistaken, when the boundaries of ordinary existence collapse, they leave us exposed in sudden dereliction to the powers over which we have no control; awful realities which seem to bear down on us from above and surge up from below, ready to overwhelm us like gods of old, by letting go of the ordinary, and allowing these realities, to have their devastating effect, we open life for the first time to the things that really matter, ultimately. In breaking with ordinary existence, we discover that the awful realities which rupture our life possessed by virtue of that very fact a sublime terrible, stature .... Giving up that desire for control is a terrible ordeal, but one which, for that very reason initiates us into the religion of the heroic where the Sacred is identified with whatever causes us to be overwhelmed.[87]

Second, Moore, following Tolle, affirms that there are not two selves in us: an authentic self and a false self, where the true self is victorious at certain times and the false self at other times. There is only one self, the self of goodness that God has created. We suppress the authentic self and in that suppressed state begin to feel the palpability of evil within,

---

86. Miller, *Way of Suffering*, 166.
87. Miller, *Way of Suffering*, 167.

with an intensity that gives the impression of an evil false self. Still, such feelings do not indicate a separate and false self. We may speak about our inner self (how we feel inwardly) and our outer self (how we feel responding to the world). But we are always and everywhere, only a single self. For Moore, Tolle recognizes "the pseudo-relationship of me with me as though I am two is faced with the possibility that I am one."[88]

Third, in God's eyes, I am not two but one, and that oneness in God is what we have come to know as God's dwelling in the depths of the human heart. In any experience of feeling anxious about some matter to the point of fear, we can interpret what is going on by stating two alternatives: either the anxious soul is me, or the anxious soul is not me. I am not two people. I cannot be an anxious self and a self at peace with oneself and the world simultaneously. One cannot be the anxious self and the self who comes to a knowledge about anxiety and beyond. There is no dualism of true self and false self, straining against each other for supremacy. Anxiety and fear get attached to the one self, and we feel alone. If the person is alone, the experience of meditation through which one meets God gives way to an understanding of not being alone, an enlightenment that comes about by God's grace and away from a feeling of attachment to "me-alone." In being passive to the Spirit of God, the fear linked to "me-alone" melts away. The alone and terrified self that has been attached to the one self, melts away by the power of God.[89]

In addressing the indwelling, Moore alludes to Saint Augustine when Augustine writes: "Late have I loved you, O Beauty, ever ancient, yet ever new, late have I loved you. For you were within me." There is only one true self, and it is the self that lives when "Christ lives in me,"[90] a spiritual reality that has taken Moore many years to realize.[91] His response to Tolle is immediate: "And when I read it, I saw the tragic side of my earlier life no longer as an isolated misery but only as a strong example of a common human phenomenon."[92]

Fourth, Tolle is asked to "resist nothing." On the one hand, Tolle is asked to surrender everything, allowing the layers of his life that have formed a hard crust around who he truly is to disappear. For Moore, the hard crust that Tolle is resisting is the reality of utter bliss. He is invited to

88. Moore, "2012–2014 Blog," Apr 23, 2012.
89. Moore, "2008 Blog," Oct 3, 2008.
90. Moore, "2012–2014 Blog," May 5, 2012.
91. Moore, "2012–2014 Blog," Apr 23, 2012.
92. Moore, "2012–2014 Blog," Jun 6, 2012.

move from the fear of happiness to the embrace of love. To not resist, for Moore, means letting happiness dwell in us and letting ourselves live in joyfully, and accepting the invitation to discover that life is not ultimately sad.[93]

Fifth, when we surround ourselves with a rigid encrusted envelope, we develop what Tolle calls the pain-body, especially when convinced that life is ultimately sad and we are cursed to unhappiness. The pain-body is our body feeling the pain of some distorted attitude. It is every effort we make to remain unhappy for a long time. The pain-body reveals how we hang on to sadness and despair and decide that happiness will never be for us. It is really "the fear of 'being.'"[94] Here, Moore articulates what he understands as the basis of psychological conversion. Liberation from the pain body is possible, and as discussed in chapter 1, focusing is an essential method in addressing our pain-body.

Sixth, Moore sees Tolle as undergoing a conversion experience to come to a place of bliss. He realizes that religion is often presented poorly as a pathway of toughness, sadness, and renunciation. If a conversion is genuine, then it addresses those aspects of our affectivity that give rise to the pain-body: fear, anxiety, unhappiness, controller, disesteem, self-hatred, and apathy felt in our bodies.[95] Conversion becomes "a radical change in one's horizon, from one horizon to a dialectically opposed horizon, from a horizon determined by inadequate, false and disordered dis-esteem to one determined by proper, undistorted, true self-esteem."[96] But genuine religion is an awareness that we are loved unconditionally.

Seventh, the process of conversion is traumatic. In his own words, it is a "presence" that gives rise to a desire for the infinite that comes down on Tolle similar to an enormous pressure, causing a colossal reaction away from something addictive and a lonely sadness toward bliss and love. Yet, conversion awakes in Tolle a contemplative moment where he discovers his true self, which is our life in God and God dwelling in us. Moore surmises that "the void receives him and births him into blissful light."[97] Conversion and rebirth are another way to discuss the contemplative moment.

---

93. Moore, "2012–2014 Blog," Jun 11, 2012.
94. Moore, "2012–2014 Blog," Jun 16, 2012.
95. Moore, *Body of Christ*, 77.
96. Ormerod, *Grace and Disgrace*, 26.
97. Moore, "2012–2014 Blog," Apr 23, 2012.

Yet, the moment of rebirth can at first feel death-like. Jerome Miller states:

> The death of one mode of life makes possible the birth of radically different alternatives. Life as a whole collapse; but thus a new whole with a new center becomes possible... Thus, a crisis to be radically disruptive, must rupture not just the structure I want my life to have but the underlying attitude of the will, its demand that life conforms to it. We have discovered that this calling into question can always be avoided. No matter what happens to us, we can treat it as a problem to be solved by some technique or therapy. This means that the heart can suffer a crisis only to the degree that it allows its will to control to be questioned-and this very active consenting to its loss of control is itself the crucial event of all [crises]: to give up one's stature as the director of one's own existence: this is for us, the ultimate death, the crisis that undermines our being in the most radical way.[98]

The moment of conversion helps the seeker ask: How am I in the world? Am I at home, or am I suspicious and alienated (and) feeling as if the universe is unfriendly?[99] The moment helps him discover the real or true "I," which is "the presence of God, the true self to which we are asleep. That the 'I' within is God is not new to our mystical tradition... that God is closer to me than I am to myself is commonplace since Augustine who said it frequently."[100]

Eighth, conversion gives rise to contemplative prayer, and prayer gives rise to the power to love. Moore states that, in his conversion moment of 1944, "desire became the want to give, desire broke into love and bliss. And I was happiness itself in those days. I was taught at last to mistrust what I had always lived with, a sense of unhappiness as my response to reality. I was (instead) taught that happiness is ok."[101]

---

98. Miller, *Way of Suffering*, 171–72.
99. Moore, "In Water," 95.
100. Moore, "2012–2014 Blog," May 1, 2012.
101. Moore, "2012–2014 Blog," Jun 6, 2012.

4

Moore and Becker: Personal Significance and Death

INTRODUCTION: THE INSIGHTS OF BECKER

In this chapter, my attention turns to the influence of the cultural anthropologist Ernest Becker (1924–74) on Moore's theological thought. Becker's writings are vast; however, I intend to focus, as Moore does, primarily on his ninth book, *The Denial of Death* (1973), the Pulitzer Prize–winning publication, in which he outlines his insights regarding each person's significance and the denial of death in modern society.

BECKER, SOCIETY, AND THE DENIAL OF DEATH

Becker begins with the question: Why are people violent, hurtful, hateful, and intolerant toward one another? He argues that human beings, similar to all animal creatures, have a physical body that is born and dies. However, the primary and largely unattended motivation for human behavior is repressed anxiety and fear around death. This anxiety forming and demotivating experience shapes everything we do, even if it escapes our attention. The fear of death concerns not only the physical end of the body but in the death of meaning, for it is meaning that defines the human self. The primary function of culture and society is to articulate humanity's intentions and values through myth, symbol, and story. However, it is impossible for society to function, especially if we are constantly in a state of paralysis due to our fear of death. To function, we must keep a lid on our fear and anxiety. To control fear, we need self-esteem. Self-esteem reaches a point of assurance in us that despite all that may happen around us, even death, our lives have "cosmic significance."[1] The paradox for Becker is that each of us is an "individual within finitude," with "a symbolic identity that brings (man) out of nature," and yet he is both out of nature and hopelessly in it.[2] Both our physical extinction and the death of meaning give rise to a fearful sense of our vulnerability, even to the point of being anxious and terrified of that vulnerability.

Becker assesses that humanity's response to anxiety is repression and suppression. How do culture and society engage in the task of suppressing our mortality? First, the psychological denial of death becomes one of the most basic drivers in forming our cultural meanings and values. Everything that man does in his symbolic world "is an attempt to deny and overcome his grotesque fate."[3] Faced with the immensity of the universe, the universe's disregard for an individual's fate, and the terror of death that such immensity elicits in us, we lie to ourselves about ourselves. Second, we create death-denying hero systems that help us believe our lives surpass our mortality. These assure us that our lives are of enormous value. How does society do this? Society facilitates the feeling that everything in our lives is permanent, invulnerable, and eternal. Society gives us heroic enterprises to carry out so that we feel an existential self-esteem deep within.[4]

Our denial of death happens in several ways. First, we build a very high sense of ourselves and our importance. Culture works towards establishing and reinforcing our significance. Our significance can grow out of a natural self-absorption experienced in childhood towards greater altruism in adulthood. However, when altruism is not achieved, the person becomes trapped in a narcissistic self-absorption. Becker states that "we are hopelessly absorbed in ourselves."[5] From our early years, the natural narcissism of the child gears towards banishing from awareness its impotence, and "not only impotence to avoid death, but his impotence to stand alone, firmly rooted in his own powers."[6] We are self-absorbed for self-esteem. But self-esteem comes only from making sure we feel

1. Becker, *Denial of Death*, 3.
2. Becker, *Denial of Death*, 26.
3. Becker, *Denial of Death*, 27.
4. Becker, *Denial of Death*, 3, 7.
5. Becker, *Denial of Death*, 2.
6. Becker, *Denial of Death*, 54.

meaningful and powerful by bolstering the conviction that we can control life and death, act as a willful and free individual, and have a "unique and self-fashioned identity, that [we are] somebody."[7] This kind of self-absorption is natural, but we are meant to grow beyond it. Combining a natural narcissism with the need for self-esteem, "you create a creature who has to feel [himself] as an object of primary value."[8] In all our projects and practical affairs, the human person seeks to show that "[he] counts more than anything or anyone."[9] When the experience does not occur, we suffer the ache of "cosmic specialness."[10]

Second, it is the function of society to provide what Becker calls "immortality systems." Systems promise to connect our lives with something that will not perish but that endures. Society is "a mythical hero-system in which people serve in order to earn a feeling of primary value, of cosmic specialness, of ultimate usefulness, to creation, of unshakable meaning."[11] What is most alienating is when we are unconnected to others and a stranger to ourselves. We may double our efforts to stay connected to people even when the truth invites us to separate from them to live a more authentic life. For example, we might identify with some religious group or be part of some cultural activity in which we invest ourselves and which imparts to us significance, even though that group may not have the right intentions toward others. This may also require us to attack and degrade the immortality systems of others so we can claim that we hold absolute value.

Third, our lifestyle produces what Becker calls a "vital lie ... a necessary and basic dishonesty about oneself and one's whole situation."[12] We move towards those things that will support the lie of our character. Our stance distorted by Becker's vital lie is only to be expected since "if [one's] character is a neurotic defense against despair and you shed that defense, you admit the full flood of despair, the full realization of the true condition, what men are really afraid of, what they struggle against, and are driven towards and away from."[13] However, Becker praises those people who can break away from these cultural meanings and social networks

7. Becker, *Denial of Death*, 55.
8. Becker, *Denial of Death*, 3.
9. Becker, *Denial of Death*, 4.
10. Becker, *Denial of Death*, 4.
11. Becker, *Denial of Death*, 6.
12. Becker, *Denial of Death*, 55.
13. Becker, *Denial of Death*, 57.

that perpetuate the vital lie and move towards an ability to grasp and hold the precariousness of human living, even with its inevitable anxiety.

Fourth, Becker critiques the symbol of "immortality." While immortality is one of those symbols that has a justifiable meaning and function, helping us to make sense of the difference between the finite and the infinite, our experiences of non-finite being, and our hopes that arise from our participation in the life of God, Becker assesses that we have distorted the notion. Our distorted idea of immortality emerges from our self-delusions to escape our death and morality. We treat immortality as if it were something that we should rightfully possess and own.

Overcoming the Denial of Death

To overcome our denial of death, Becker speaks about the importance of religious faith and genuine religion, the attitude of humility and living in the tension of the finite and infinite. First, religious faith is the belief that despite the felt sense of insignificance that death may inchoate, we live guided by an infinite creative force.[14] The two alternatives that stand before each of us are: either we cling to the so-called absolutes of our immortality systems, turning away from death and claiming and creating our absolutes all around us, or we grow an authentic faith in a mystery of enduring meaning, tasting our mortality, and placing our trust in the Divine Mystery.[15]

Second, genuine religion encourages an attitude of humility before our creaturehood and the mysterious and threatening universe. To live authentically, we must be aware of our finitude and creatureliness.[16] The implication is that only through humility can human consciousness deal creatively with the dread of death, whether the end of our physical existence or the spiritual death of meaning. Transformed by humility, death will no longer be able to sap our energy or drive us toward illusory projects, even when the shadow of death emerges from some hidden and deep cave in the recesses of our psyche.[17] Owning our mortality could bring wisdom into our lives and lead us to realize that each person, or even humanity, is not the center of the universe. If one is not the center

---

14. Becker, *Denial of Death*, 90–91.
15. Hughes, "Denial of Death," 2.
16. Becker, *Denial of Death*, 58.
17. Kelly, *Touching on the Infinite*, 57.

of the universe, then we may ask: Who is the center and real force of the universe?

Third, according to Eugene Webb, Becker owes much to the writings of Søren Kierkegaard and Otto Rank.[18] Kierkegaard points out the ways we deny our responsibility to self-conscious freedom, through immersing ourselves in bodily experience or the givens of society and through denying our finitude or animal limitation by "soaring into fantasies of unlimited possibility, including the fantasy of preservation from death and destruction."[19] Kierkegaard shows how "the fatalist, the determinist, the social conformist, the happy consumer, the hedonist, the dreamer or fantasist, the worshipper of technology" can all be assessed to be living the vital lie, that is, the lie being that we are immortal.[20] Rank urges us to face our terror and fear and "the shedding of one's character armor," a difficult task since it is one we have built up since childhood.[21] We must accept the paradox of our being and the knowledge that death is part of our lives. However, to do so requires some religious faith in a power greater than ourselves. Faith is accepting our finitude while reaching out to the infinite. Our inner self sits within the tension between the infinite and the finite. When we do, we find ourselves linked to the source of creation.

In these ways, Becker subscribes to the anthropology offered by Kierkegaard regarding being a human being, namely, that each of us is

> a synthesis of the infinite and the finite, of the temporal and the eternal, of freedom and necessity . . . . The self is the conscious synthesis of infinitude and finitude that [in our minds and hearts] relates itself to itself, whose task is to become itself which can be done only through the relationship with God. To become oneself is to become concrete. But to be concrete is neither to become finite nor to become infinite, for that which is to become concrete is indeed synthesis . . . [faith becomes a process that] in relating itself to itself and in willing to be itself, the self [stays restfully and] transparently in the power [of God] that established it.[22]

We live in the in-between of finiteness and infiniteness.

18. Webb, *Worldviews and Mind*, 65.
19. Hughes, *Transcendence*, 205.
20. Hughes, *Transcendence*, 206.
21. Webb, *Worldviews and Mind*, 66.
22. Kierkegaard, *Sickness unto Death*, 29–30.

Rank focuses on breaking the armoring of our character against the terror of physical death and meaninglessness. The problem for humanity deepens when "the vital lie of character" becomes a prison of our own making and when the projects and hero system of our culture no longer function in a way to roll back the fear of death.[23]

Becker died at the age of forty-nine years old. Though he did not pursue the theme of religious faith, its relevance to meaningfulness, and the kind of life that the virtue of humility brings, he does state that it is the role of genuine religion to stand for a larger version of the truth about ourselves and the universe. When religious faith does this, it enables persons to "wait in a condition of openness toward miracle and Mystery, the lived truth of creation, which would make it easier to survive and be redeemed because men would be less driven to undo themselves and would be more like the image which pleases their creator: awe-filled creatures trying to live in harmony with the rest of creation. Today we would add . . . they would be less likely to poison the rest of creation."[24]

Equally, Becker points to the damaging effects of distorted religion. In his book *Escape from Evil*, published posthumously, he articulates how distorted religious faith can promote the dark side of heroism.[25] Again, even when it is religiously motivated, one of the root causes for evil actions is our inevitable urge to "deny mortality and achieve a heroic self-image."[26] We deny others their belief systems by dehumanizing them since their system threatens to expose the relative character of our systems. Hughes states that "through humiliating, damaging, and self-defeating the enemy; through mass deportations, through ethnic cleansing and genocide, we can at once eliminate threats to our heroic self-esteem and prove that it is we who are living and fighting the service of everlasting truth."[27]

Becker encourages a non-destructive system to guide living. Webb concludes that Becker

> suggested, rightly I think, that any worldview that is to be effective in eliciting human trust and loyalty must offer satisfaction to "the basic general motive of man—the need for self-esteem, for the feeling of primary value," by promising victory over

23. Webb, *Worldviews and Mind*, 66.
24. Becker, *Denial of Death*, 282.
25. Webb, *Worldviews and Mind*, 67.
26. Webb, *Worldviews and Mind*, 67.
27. Hughes, *Transcendence*, 204.

"extinction and insignificance" . . . offer something worth believing in and living for. But it must do so without tempting us to believe in utopian absolutism and without yielding to the allure of polarizing visions of the world divided into heroes and eternal enemies.[28]

Again, Becker stops short of interpreting what living between finiteness and infiniteness could mean for us. He has amassed the clues for unlocking a better understanding of authentic living but needs to take us where these clues lead. According to Hughes, Becker might have unpacked the meaning of authentic living if he had a more precise grasp of authenticity and acknowledged the primary experience of the cosmos for ancient peoples. In the primary experience, reality, including what we now call the natural world and its transcendent ground, was experienced as an undifferentiated oneness. What followed in Western culture was the subsequent differentiating of the conceptual difference between the natural order and what is an intrinsic and a transcendent realm within the one reality.[29]

MOORE INTERPRETING BECKER

How does Moore engage with these insights? It is essential to remember that Moore felt insubstantial through his earlier years in the monastery and speaks of his monastic formation as emphasizing self-punishment and renunciation. The question of significance was vital to him personally. Therefore, the theme of self-esteem and the journey away from disesteem becomes significant in Moore's appreciation of the human condition. In chapter 1, I spoke of Moore's relationship to Lonergan and his appreciation of Lonergan's insight into the importance of "feeling," an insight that emerges between the writing of *Insight* and *Method in Theology*. Feelings are a pre-apprehension of what we value, and what we value is an integral part of our self-identity. We evaluate any number of things in our lives all the time, and the manner of our evaluation, to a certain extent, depends on how we feel about them and ourselves. Self-esteem is how we feel about ourselves and is essential to living well.

Moore takes up the insights presented by Becker out of his conviction around the need for personal significance. Moore asks: "Is there

---

28. Webb, *Worldviews and Mind*, 69.
29. Hughes, *Transcendence*, 213.

one feeling we all desire to have, the need for which may therefore be said to constitute the fundamental and universal human need?"[30] The feeling that Moore is searching for would not depend on the absence of life's snags nor the absence of challenges tripping us up nor a kind of life free of suffering. The feeling would endure throughout all these realities. Moore states that the feeling is "that whatever happens to me, I am significant. I have worth, value, I *am* someone."[31]

Moore states that Becker's achievement highlights the "essential need of the human being to feel significant, worth-full, worthy, someone."[32] In the development from animal to human consciousness, humans experience the birth of self-awareness. With self-awareness growing, we search for personal significance. Self-aware human beings desire importance for themselves. Even our desire to survive comes from the feeling that we are worth surviving. We attach far more importance to ourselves than we dare to admit. The feeling of personal significance is often known best by its non-fulfillment when we are not afforded personal relevance. There is an ache within us that wants self-esteem. How does the feeling come about? It begins in childhood when each of us seeks attention from our parents. It reaches a second level in adolescence, where we strive to be desired by the person we desire. It gets to a third level in adult life when we live by the axiom "to be myself for another."[33]

In adult life, the self-aware being finds their whole meaning and satisfaction as an act of love that creates happiness in another. Therefore, there is no opposition between self-fulfillment and our desire to make someone else happy, and our growing into mature people is a progressive clarification of this goal. Thus, what begins in a zest for being in infancy ends in the need to feel significant for another. The feeling of personal significance has an intentionality that reaches its consummation in making someone else happy. What we discover is that to be alive is to be a gift.

To analyze the axiom, "to be myself for another," we can divide it up into three parts: "to be myself," "for," and "another." First, there is the phrase "to be myself." To be myself is to feel all of one's being with joy and to feel happy and fulfilled in the presence of another. To be myself is to be self-aware. Second, there is the word "for." The word "for" refers to both my experience of attraction to another and the life-enhancing

30. Moore, *Fire and the Rose*, 6.
31. Moore, *Fire and the Rose*, 7.
32. Moore, *Fire and the Rose*, 7.
33. Moore, *Fire and the Rose*, 10.

component of the feeling through the experience of attraction. Third, there is the word "another." I experience myself drawn to another person, and that feeling is completed when another is drawn to me. In this simple axiom, Moore highlights the mutual exchange of love at the heart of being human. Later, Moore would speak of the dialectic of self-love and self-gift.

Complementing Moore, Wilkie Au asserts that we can find the much-needed balance between self-love and self-gift and reach wholeness. He speaks about the balance between self-esteem and self-denial. All other loves limp along unless they are grounded in self-love. A person's self-acceptance is the beginning of their way to another, so we must all embrace the humanity freely gifted to us and embrace ourselves.

Self-rejection is a constant temptation for us. We doubt and disparage ourselves by emphasizing our real or imaginary shortcomings. We say: I need to be more intelligent; I need to be more good-looking; I need to be more popular, prosperous, and talented.[34] However, Au makes the point: "It is futile to conduct an inventory of ourselves, claiming some parts as good and discarding others as undesirable. Psychologically speaking, healthy self-acceptance cannot be based on denial and projection. Maturity will elude us as long as we try to disown unattractive parts of ourselves and project them onto others."[35] Alternatively, focusing on ourselves without the other in mind shortcuts the growth process. If self-realization means self-fulfillment in the selfish sense of satisfying only one's wishes, then it is antihuman. Such fulfillment is a lie and is in denial of the intersubjective nature of human living. Likewise, if self-denial means denial or sacrifice of the true self and its radical exigences, then it, too, must be rejected. Similarly, in chapter 1, I wrote about the imperatives within human consciousness that Lonergan identified. These imperatives are: be attentive, be intelligent, be reasonable, be responsible, and be in love. These imperatives map out the process of self-transcendence. Self-transcendence incorporates both authentic self-realization and genuine self-denial. The self is not sacrificed but realized through authentic living. At the same time, the self, in its striving for meaning, truth, and goodness, rejects any self-centered living. The self reaches out to others.[36] These imperatives are centrally about discovering the "myself" part of Moore's axiom and reaching up to Moore's "for another." The

34. Au, *By Way*, 27–28.
35. Au, *By Way*, 28.
36. Conn, *Desiring Self*, 35.

difficulty in human living is getting the creative tension right between self-love and self-gift.

MOORE AND NARCISSISM

Moore goes on to describe Becker's claim of humanity's narcissism. Narcissism has two different meanings. First, there is a natural and healthy narcissism of the infant seeking nurturance from the mother through demanding to be fed and provided for. Becker recognizes the importance of innate narcissism for the creation of self-esteem. The Neo-Freudian school of psychology speaks to the importance of loving warmth and empathic interactions from parents, providing a sense of worthiness for the infant. These supportive acts help us form positive intrapsychic images of ourselves and significant others, the worthy feelings associated with these images, and the capacity for action in an environment guided by these images.[37]

Margaret Mahler, who would become important in Moore's psychological insights, maintains that the child's ability to develop psychological identity and autonomous functioning depends on support from the parents. This form of narcissism that is part of the infant's life is one where differentiation between the infant's self and the external world has yet to occur. It is narcissism without Narcissus, a state of being without any self-knowledge. The emergence of reflective awareness begins at a stage that Erik Erickson calls affective "autonomy." He contrasts autonomy with feelings of shame and doubt, such that if autonomy is not received, we feel bad about feeling good at having personal autonomy.

Second, there is the distortion of narcissistic self-absorption, which has three aspects: personal, cultural, and religious. Narcissistic self-absorption is the condition where we have failed to move beyond ourselves, our needs, and our wants, seeing the world as a reflection of ourselves and deciding there are no other questions beyond the ones that directly relate to ourselves, our comfort, and our security. A narcissistic self-absorption becomes the foundation for creating a culture that focuses on pursuing an egocentric contentment above everything else: a culture of immediate gratification and competitive individualism. Such self-absorption radiates profound despair and resignation, egoism, and indifference and gives rise to the dispositions and assertions of those without

---

37. Conn, *Desiring Self*, 62.

religious faith.[38] In Becker's view, this derived kind of narcissism, gives rise to anxiety and the threat of death and mortality. Moore weighs into the issue with great intensity and novelty. Self-absorption is a condition bubbling away under the surface of all our thinking and valuing from early infancy, and it amounts to "a radical insecurity in ourselves."[39] We seek to establish security by discovering our significance.

MOORE, SELF-ABSORPTION, AND GOD

At another level, natural self-absorption comes from an awareness of ourselves living in the in-between of finiteness and infiniteness. Agreeing with Becker, Moore asserts that self-absorption is the continual and never successful attempt to deal with our unknowingness about our origin. Our unknowingness pressures us to search for something more or, alternatively, makes us pretend to ourselves that we are of our own making.[40]

Moore, reflecting on Becker, brings together three insights. First, there is the insight that the denial of death is a denial of a dependency on a mystery beyond our grasp. Second, there is the insight that self-absorption is a pursuit of meaningfulness through a dialogue with an unknown origin. Third, there is the insight that the experience of self-absorption reaches completion in being significant for another.

If we coalesce these insights, our self-absorption ultimately finds meaning and release in knowing that each person is significant for the unknown reality of our origin.[41] While many believe their relationship with God does not begin until there is a connection of faith, Moore postulates that a psychic-organic relationship with God is hinted at in an unrecognized anxiety about our origin and goal.[42] While Becker postulates that the denial of death originates out of an uneasiness with our creaturehood, Moore states that religion speaks to that uneasiness. We ask: Does the ultimate reality honestly care about me? Are we, who have love affairs through which we find our significance, also ultimately significant? Is all of our risking, loving, and investing in projects and people pointing to

---

38. Gallagher, *Struggles of Faith*, 87.
39. Moore, *Fire and the Rose*, 12.
40. Moore, *Fire and the Rose*, 13.
41. Moore, *Fire and the Rose*, 13.
42. Moore, *Fire and the Rose*, 14.

something, or is all this effort based on denial, one big "extraordinary human side-step from the way of the universe?"[43] Is human awareness, when it finds its fulfillment in loving another, actually resonating faintly with an origin that behaves infinitely and constitutively as human love behaves? The question of whether one is significant might be the human question, but the question of whether one is ultimately significant is the religious question. The answer to religion is a wholehearted "yes" to our ultimate significance.

Suppose the answer to our ultimate significance leads us into the presence of God. In that case, our human story goes beyond defining our humanity by saying, "to be myself for another." The making of ourselves comes from a bliss-giving "yes," and our life is not merely what we do with ourselves but an unfolding Mystery and miracle that has God as our fulfillment. "Who" we are becomes "why" we are, breaking mystically into our hearts.[44] What we make of ourselves could be imagined as a swift and wild river of desire, running out to the unknown and yearning to be heard from that mysterious Beloved. To believe in God means that our hunger for meaning and personal significance and the realization that we are not of our own making come together in an inseparable union.[45] Becker suggests we suppress our sense of dependence since our understanding of dependence only points to our frailty and creatureliness, something we try to escape through immortality projects. For Moore, the sense of dependence and the desire for meaning move us toward *a dependence for meaning*, and we learn this form of dependence when we fall in love.[46] Dependency without love cripples the person. Dependence and love are more radical than we could ever know: the mind and the heart are one, and the fire and the rose are one.[47]

Thus, Moore reframes a relationship between self-awareness, self-absorption, personal significance, and ultimate significance. The more self-aware we become, the more we engage in passionate self-absorption and find a conviction fundamental to the human race. The conviction we discover is that our anxiety and self-concern about our origin and

---

43. Moore, *Fire and the Rose*, 15.
44. Moore, *Fire and the Rose*, 17.
45. Moore, *Fire and the Rose*, 18.
46. Moore, *Fire and the Rose*, 19.
47. Moore, *Fire and the Rose*, 20.

destiny and, with it, as to whether we ultimately matter is grounded in "the unknown origin and shaper of our being."[48]

Genuine religion becomes the believed-in answer of the "unknown Other" to the question: Am I ultimately valuable in your eyes? Therefore, there is a link between self-absorption and finding my ultimate significance. When we realize that "to be myself for another" answers the question of identity as other-directed and achieving personhood through the quality of love, then another question emerges: why am I? We find the answer to why in God. While we are usually inclined to hear the answer to the "who" question of identity in personal relationships, the answer to the "why" question of direction is a greater need in our lives.[49] Moore names the "why" question as our pre-religious orientation toward God, and the question exists in us before religious conversion and surrender to God happens. Before we even notice God's love for us, which causes us to love God, these questions arising from self-absorption and the need for significance are bubbling away in the human heart from infancy. Thus, Moore establishes the connection between self-love and self-gift.

MOORE AND OUR PRE-RELIGIOUS AWARENESS

For Moore, Becker is correct to speak of our misguided efforts to deny our creatureliness and, thus, by denial, overlooking that there is much to indicate that we are not the center of the universe. We mistakenly consider successful those people who can best live with the lie that they are the center of the universe. But when we deny our creatureliness, we dodge our relationship with the all-embracing Mystery. The ultimate Mystery is not a threat to our self-making. The lie disguises the truthful insight that our sense of worth driving us forward has its ultimate moorings in the Mystery that gives us existence. The Mystery of God is the secret answer to that mistaken lie. The lie prevents us from seeing "an erotic dependence [desire-shaped] on the unknown Other who knows us, an erotic dependence which is pre-religious, conscious at the deeper level and the shaping of all, we think and do."[50] Therefore, religious conversion does not mean so much a start in our relationship with God, but rather, religious conversion releases us from the erroneous assertion that we are

---

48. Moore, *Fire and the Rose*, 25.
49. Moore, *Fire and the Rose*, 30–31.
50. Moore, *Fire and the Rose*, 34.

on our own, and the release it brings is something all of us crave. It leads us to admit that the One who loves us loves us as self-aware people. We are God-questioning beings. If we don't articulate the question (Why am I here?), and if we do not come to its solution in God throughout the length, breadth, and depth of human experience, we shall never hear the Word of God.

MOORE AND SOCIAL POLITICS

Approaching life from a pre-religious awareness has the power to revolutionize how we approach everything, even politics. The widespread ineffectiveness of organized religion today is its failure to speak to politics from a pre-religious God-awareness. There is always a danger that the teachings we impart concerning the reality of God are not hitting the mark since, often, teachings are not rooted enough in a more profound and universal human experience. Recognizing the human experience of significance leads to the religious experience of ultimate significance. Religious faith comes from hearing God's "yes" in our search for ultimate significance. The hunger for God's approval is built into the human heart, and we cannot eliminate it. Nothing can stop it, even if people try to shut up religion. For Moore, it is no wonder that the mystics take their pre-religious orientation as their primary reference point. In the mystic's mind, the union between God and us comes first, and this union helps explain why the meaning of human union between people is so important.

Moore states that a proper relationship to politics begins by acknowledging our orientation to the Mystery as built into an integral dimension of human experience.[51] In social problems, for example the ever-widening gulf between rich and poor, Friedrich Hegel argues that the root desire for exploiters is to feel more significant than those they exploit. Exploiters of others employ self-serving strategies toward exploitation. They admit only as much significance in them to call another their slave. The enslaved person has no sense of their importance or power; therefore, they feel weakened in their ability to get things done. To redress personal significance and the power imbalance, exploiters must come to acknowledge that power and love must combine.[52] If love combines with power, then we are always thinking in terms of ourselves

---

51. Moore, *Fire and the Rose*, 30.
52. Moore, *Fire and the Rose*, 46.

and others. There is no dichotomy between the dual focus on oneself and others since to be and feel uniquely significant is the need to find self-acceptance from another. In the early stages of life, our significance is received *from* others outside ourselves, especially our parents, which makes us dependent on them. In later life, we need to be significant *to* another and, thus, other-fulfilled.[53]

MOORE AND GUILT

The lack of personal significance can help define the origins of personal guilt. Guilt is any counter-pull to the positive pull, and the positive pull is to be myself for another. One cannot cease to be oneself; therefore, as the interior positive pull continues and we remain out of harmony with it, the pull makes us unhappy. At its worst, felt guilt can influence us to become withdrawn into an isolated selfhood, especially in adult life. Self-rejection comes from isolation, and isolation comes from cutting ourselves from our primary concern, "to be myself for another."[54] It becomes a state of affective impotence in ourselves; radical guilt becomes a sense of unhappy un-lovableness.

In one way or another, guilt stems from a sense of having failed to love. Infantile guilt occurs when we are not afforded the significance that we desire due to the reaction we get from disappointing the expectations of others, and this lack issues emotional impotence. Adult guilt is the sense of failing another person directly. Adult guilt occurs when we cannot afford another the significance they require. Further, the person we have failed becomes strangely unattractive. It is not that we dislike them, but rather, that we have failed them, and then, because of our failure, we find them ugly. Moore states: "We tend to think and speak ill of people whom we are failing."[55] We observe the phenomenon occurring in politics, racial matters, sexual relationships, and in how we speak about those who have fallen into hard times. Our failure toward others becomes the powerhouse for resentment, which leads to a failure to connect, the projection of dislike on another, the conclusion that others are alien to us, and moral condemnations toward what others might find pleasurable.[56]

---

53. Moore, *Fire and the Rose*, 40.
54. Moore, *Fire and the Rose*, 66.
55. Moore, *Fire and the Rose*, 61.
56. Moore, *Fire and the Rose*, 61.

MOORE, THE DENIAL OF CREATURELINESS, AND ORIGINAL SIN

Moore links the theological idea of sin and, specifically, the Catholic doctrine of original sin to the denial of death and the denial of our creatureliness. Original sin is a doctrine whose proper understanding intrigued Moore for many years. I will speak to Moore's understanding of the doctrine of original sin more thoroughly in chapter 5. But for now, let me say this. Moore states that original sin points to a condition "produced by the withdrawing of the self from its primordial leanings towards ultimate mystery into an absolutely isolated selfhood."[57]

First, the rejection of our creatureliness and its accompanying denial of death leads to our withdrawal into an isolated self-awareness concerning the Mystery from which we draw all our sense of meaning and purpose. Second, our withdrawal from others and our disposition to fail others comes from an isolated self-awareness, which becomes an isolated identity. Original sin, then, becomes "a universal socialized withdrawal of man from the mystery (of God)" and "a socialized truncation of human life, the systemic reduction of the child mystery to the brain or world of man's own making."[58]

All sin flows from this distorted base. If sin is bound up with isolation, Moore asserts that the "empty person" becomes the norm in a culture that denies death. The result is self-disesteem, which becomes the root of all human evil. More broadly, people prioritize consumerism out of the conviction that they are worth it, and yet, at the same time, distorted consumerism implicitly states we are worthless unless we use a particular product. Moore also notes that as believers in God, we must also be careful about using terms that amount to a self-deprecating attitude or unworthiness before God so as not to solidify disesteem. Disesteem becomes a deep root of self-negation; more profound than the guilt we sense when we have done wrong. Moore states: "Feeling worthless, leads to feeling inadequate, acting worthless leads to feeling downright inadequate."[59]

Therefore, Moore's understanding of sin takes account of self-isolation. Sin is feeling, thinking, valuing, and acting within an isolated horizon. While it is easier to see sin as an attack on something positive,

---

57. Moore, *Fire and the Rose*, 67.
58. Moore, *Fire and the Rose*, 67.
59. Moore, *Fire and the Rose*, 69.

Moore's understanding of sin sees it as a disengagement from God and others. Sin is the closing up of the self. Therefore, the essence of sin is far worse than all that moral condemnations convey. There are no words for the desire "to be absolutely-myself-for-myself-alone, absolutely isolated."[60] Yet this is the consequence of the denial of our creatureliness, a heightening of autonomy, a search for personal significance on our terms, and engagements that aim to prove one is meaningful through one's immortality projects. Sin, therefore, does not make sense since no one can account for that "inner decision to be for [me] only."[61] If guilt springs from willed isolation, freedom emerges when we move from our willed isolation into love with God the Divine Lover, whose forgiveness dissolves guilt, overcomes isolation, and enables us to become lovable again. I will explore the link between the weakening of desire and original sin in chapter 6 and the significance of Jesus for original sin in chapter 7.

MOORE, THE DENIAL OF CREATUREHOOD, AND CONSCIOUSNESS

When the tension between finite and infinite is lost, Moore states that the human spirit can

> become split off from, and ineffectual toward, the passions and urges of the animal nature in which it is incarnate. It is a language that bespeaks, again, a failure of integration between the finite and the infinite components of the self. When the decision for finitude has not been able to penetrate the psyche and integrate its finite and infinite elements, the self in its identification with infinite possibility sees in the essential determinants of finite, an enemy, an alien power that debunks and humiliates the aspirations of the spirit. These essential determinants are concentrated in sexuality and death . . . sex and death [become] the hidden partners that betray all beauty and meaning.[62]

Similarly, overreaching our finitude brings a depressive cycle and despair at the project of human existence. In the manic phase, the person spurs ahead, ignoring their bodiliness, since one believes anything is

---

60. Moore, *Fire and the Rose*, 69.
61. Moore, *Fire and the Rose*, 72.
62. Hughes and Moore, "Hamlet," 194–95.

possible. Yet the manic stage is a stuckness in the "seductive infinite."[63] In this realm, death feels like a barrier or boundary to life and becomes a fundamental horizon as all-powerful; therefore, death threatens us. Moore states that since "the self has not conquered death by embracing it in the form of its own limited actuality, death continues to conquer the self by draining value and purpose from life. Death as the specter of meaninglessness rules over the kingdom of infinite possibility."[64]

Drawing on Alice Miller and her first book, *The Drama of the Gifted Child*, to be discussed in chapter 5, Moore asserts:

> Our denial and hatred of death, our dismissal of the elderly, and our adoration of adolescence are indicative of our fear of finitude. Our refusal to accept mortality and our wildly confused attitudes towards sexuality betray the loss of our feeling of finality, of our fulfillment in fully conscious loving. It is a culture that resembles in many ways the gifted child, whose grandiose and narcissistic expectations are unknowingly sustained by a refusal to separate from its oceanic source (the mother).[65]

Correspondingly, a distorted understanding of death presents a cover story aligned with a distorted culture that coalesces being complete self-governing and freedom, no longer seeing ourselves as creatures of God but coming fully into our own, where freedom and creaturehood are radical different alternatives. Yet, this misguided way of affirming freedom is a *"disguised dependence"* analogous to the relationship between the brilliant child to adult disguised dependence, where the child thinks they can live and thrive without parents.

For Moore and Hughes, the result is a culture defined by relentlessly collapsing the third and fourth levels of consciousness into the second. The result is truth reduced to shimmering significance and morality reduced to whatever seems good at the time. Also, the result is a culture in love with infinite possibilities. It is because our culture, arrested in a state of thinking that it can do anything, finds it difficult to progress beyond the stage of brilliance. Our culture remains rich in creativity and technical achievement but without an orientation to complete goodness.[66] Our task for responsible growth is to discover our creaturehood and, in

---

63. Hughes and Moore, "Hamlet," 195.
64. Hughes and Moore, "Hamlet," 195.
65. Hughes and Moore, "Hamlet," 199.
66. Hughes and Moore, "Hamlet," 200.

that discovery, realize that finiteness and death are not the themes of bad dreams but the very habitat of our freedom.[67]

When a distorted cultural and social milieu successfully dominates and imprisons our minds and hearts, there are all kinds of utopian views, whether humanistic, social, or political, that distance death from each of us. For some, especially in the field of the cryogenics of the body, death is simply a disease that will be beaten by technological medicine. Death is already, through popular culture, a morbid fascination, degenerating to voyeurism "when death-dealing violence becomes so integral to what has come to be regarded as entertainment, as thrillers in pulp literature, the terror movie (and) TV crime series. If such titillation should turn to disgust and begin to touch on real questions about human fate, it can be assured in the commercial break that in the real world populated by the beautiful and successful, no one ever dies."[68]

For many, disposing of God leads to disposing of death. Suppose Nietzsche, Marx, and Freud have disposed of "God" in the modern mind. In that case, death becomes a more intense matter for reflection, since with "nothing and no one to receive one's last breath, culture is bereft of its traditional ways of coping with death, let alone celebrating it with a final rite of passage. A passing into nothingness hardly inspires any confident ritual expression!"[69] Despite the promises of utopian visions and earthly paradises, death remains on the horizon of awareness.

The assertion that death is external to human existence and, therefore, not intrinsic to being human prevents us from possessing a wholesome view of death. Moore suggests that as soon as we speak to the reality of death, we tend to put it at a distance, similar to some obscure issue for discussion that must not allow our feelings to get in the way and, thus, we fail to understand how personal to us death is. We are engaging in rationalization based on a false idea of objectivity. As soon as we unhelpfully put death at a distance, it can quickly become something over there, impersonal, and disengaged from our lives. Our distancing strategy implicitly postulates death in terms of limitation only, ourselves as located solely in time and space and the product of a particular culture or society.

The same unhelpful "objectifying" of death pushes it into the beyond of God and into the realm of God whom we judge as remote, impersonal, and belonging to a no man's land, beyond our experience.

67. Hughes and Moore, "Hamlet," 200.
68. Kelly, *Touching on the Infinite*, 50.
69. Kelly, *Touching on the Infinite*, 51–52.

We end up with a distorted notion of God battling a Mystery that we disown in death, and this cycle gives rise to ever-diminishing returns for understanding our human existence. Our distorted idea of God comes from our guilt and the deformed position of isolation. The reality of guilt points to how we have created a closed world through self-assertion. Our real guilt brings with it the judgment that, since we spoil the world, death is our self-inflicted punishment that equalizes our failure for the distorted world we have created. Death compensates for what we have destroyed.[70] Moore states: "We have a self that has contracted a debt to God which it had to have paid for it, a debt whose enormity is suggested uniquely in terms of the greatness of the person offended."[71] For Moore, the paradox is that when we are robbed of death as belonging to us and as our Mystery, we are no longer fully ourselves.

In light of our denial of death, Moore meditates on the mystery of death. Rather than keeping death at a distance, Moore seeks a way for us to embrace our death. Moore asks: Is it possible then to embrace our death? Can we become active agents toward our end?[72] The truth is that death is a part of our constitutive makeup as humans. It might be, as Hamlet spoke, "the undiscovered country, from whose bourn no traveler returns," however equally, it is part of us.[73]

To break through the denial of our creaturehood will require a more alluring language. We must seek a more "poetic consciousness" to appreciate death's reality.[74] Moore's poetic consciousness speaks to the need to discover a set of authentic feelings and images regarding death. Poetic consciousness is grounded in an undifferentiated awareness that gives us a sense of what death means from our emotions before concepts and ideas. Symbols, rituals, myths, and drama capture the importance of feeling the truth of reality. Moore speaks to the helpfulness of this kind of consciousness: "It is rich yet confused, an intense undifferentiated awareness. Man speaks primitively, immediately, at the level where matter and spirit are wedded in him. At this level, he can express his whole sense of personal identity in terms of a journey over the sea, or into a dark forest. He can be wholly engaged in this expression."[75] As suggested in

70. Moore, "Reflexions on Death II," 21–22.
71. Moore, "Reflexions on Death II," 24.
72. Moore, "Reflexions on Death I," 376.
73. Moore, "Reflexions on Death I," 378.
74. Moore, "Reflexions on Death I," 378.
75. Moore, "Reflexions on Death I," 378.

chapter 2, there exists an intimacy between the poet and the sensible world from which poetic imagery emerges so that the poet's imagery may help humanity come to terms with the intimacy of death. This imagery indicates a real response to death from the depths of consciousness, real but primitive."[76]

Through the vector of religious faith, we discover the ultimate Mystery communicating itself to us in and through love. Moore states:

> I regard faith as something that makes God *real*. Now to get into relation with God first conceived is to bring into being a special religious self for this purpose, a modality of the ego or self-constructed self. In terms of these two surface conceptions, of God and of myself, I try to put right, to reverse, the initial lie at the center of my being.... [The self] is strangled in its own toils and can only be released by a sort of interior landslide. When *so* released, it exists and is confronted with a God in such a way that it cannot disassociate its newfound selfhood from God. In short, self and God belong for the first time to a world of *fact*. The language of "conversion" is, suddenly, immediate and real.[77]

When we embrace death in the here and now, it becomes intimate to us since death is our mystery belonging to us, not beyond us but within us, and witnessing not the remoteness of God but a closing of the gap between God and ourselves.[78] Religious belief contradicts what we feel and think about death when we assert death to be a form of punishment. Death is not something that God requires because we have spoiled the world. It is not up to us to bridge the gap between ourselves and God. It is up to God to reveal that there is no distance between God and ourselves, and this religious affirmation comes out of conversion. In the Christian tradition, Jesus reveals God to humanity and reveals to us what being human is. Christ is the primary revelation of what love is, and his redemption is the ultimate revelation of God's love. In chapter 8, I will explore Moore's understanding of Christ, the significance of his redemption, and what his redemption tells us about death.

---

76. Moore, "Reflexions on Death I," 378.
77. Moore, "Reflexions on Death I," 380–81.
78. Moore, "Reflexions on Death II," 14.

DUNNE COMPLEMENTING MOORE

I want to now bring into dialogue with Moore the insights of Tad Dunne on death. Dunne, in response to the death of Matty Ventresca at the age of nine, wrote a book titled *We Love You Matty: Meeting Death with Faith*. Dunne explores our attitudes and beliefs around death. The first area concerns our mistaken beliefs about death. The second area involves our image of God in relation to death. Both these areas have significance for Moore.

Dunne and Attitudes about Death

Dunne proposes three incorrect attitudes about our mortality: first, the ideal is to live forever; second, everyone will experience the end of their bodies as their souls pass on; and third, another life is coming after this one. The first mistaken attitude, the ideal of living forever, is a jaundiced view that lurks in everyone.[79] The film *Groundhog Day* tells the story of a man who wakes up every day to start the same day with the same meetings with people and events to attend. The sameness of each day gives him the possibility of changing his response each day for the better and overcoming his mistakes. On the positive side, it is a story about being offered a chance to improve one's character. On the negative side, it fails to capture that the events of any one day have meaning in themselves. Dunne states: "The realm of meaning is very real. It may not be geographical; you can't travel there. Nor is it any narrow period of time. You can't take a timeout from meaningful living. This is the realm. I believe, that ancient religion spoke of when they spoke of immortality."[80]

Dunne affirms the importance of ourselves as meaning-makers. Moore's appropriation of the importance of personal significance and our dependency on meaning complements Dunne's insight that no matter what men and women everywhere hope, life carries a meaning that death cannot abolish. Following Lonergan's imperatives of consciousness, a meaningful life takes responsibility and involves love commitments. It means following through on one's ideals and promises. Dunne states: "The only way to find meaning in life is to make a difference . . . in

---

79. Dunne, *We Love You*, 9.
80. Dunne, *We Love You*, 10.

the life we share with others."[81] Moore states the same truth through his axiom: to be myself for another.

The same can be said of the relationship between freedom and a meaningful life. When it comes to living a meaningful life, most people would affirm that some measure of freedom is needed. Freedom can mean freedom from restraint or freedom to be a better human being. The former is an external freedom. The latter is an interior freedom. A meaningful life is based on internal freedom. Freedom from exterior barriers is a social good to pursue in society and may even help to generate a more expansive interior freedom. But without interior freedom, the absence of exterior barriers will come to nothing. Dunne asserts. "The people who are truly free not only live in countries where rights are protected, they live *in themselves* and are responsible for the choices they make."[82] Dunne affirms that "death is necessary for true freedom because, without it, we would not be serious about defining the selves we hope to become. Without death, the very question of the meaning of our lives would never come up. Death may stand at the far end of our lives, but it casts a long shadow. It is present in every moment of our lives calling out again and again, 'What will you be?'"[83]

Often, when someone we love dies, consolation is not to be found in the belief that someone has migrated to a better place. But our real and more profound consolation is to be found in "every good work that came from their mouths, every genuine engagement, every kind of deed. We discount whether or not their contributions were to our benefit; we focus instead on the deeper judgment that their contributions were good [in] themselves."[84] Here, again, Moore's hypothesis to be oneself for another is the criterion by which to define our lives as free and responsible.

The second mistaken attitude is that another life is coming after our current life.[85] The problem with this attitude is that it can potentially rob the event of death of its power and meaning. It tends to "depict death as just a check valve through which people squirt into another, happier chamber."[86] We tend to depict the afterlife through several naïve descriptions even when we become adults, which is why some adolescents lose

---

81. Dunne, *We Love You*, 10.
82. Dunne, *We Love You*, 10.
83. Dunne, *We Love You*, 11.
84. Dunne, *We Love You*, 12.
85. Dunne, *We Love You*, 13.
86. Dunne, *We Love You*, 13.

their religious faith. As the naïve descriptions of their childhood are broken, we are left in adolescence feeling that we have lost our religious faith without the power of narrative to get a handle on the Mystery. All this is happening while life continues to bear down on people. In an adult faith, the desire for a fuller life necessarily turns to God in the dark "without the thin presentations of words and pictures."[87] Talking about death may not be as easy as saying it is a doorway to the afterlife, but that is no reason for people to stop praying, loving, and hoping. In my mind, Moore's analysis of the disciples' experience after the crucifixion felt by them as the death of God and desolation of desire gives us a template for understanding that we cannot simply assuage our grief in the certainty of an afterlife. There is a need to acknowledge the darkness of our grief with the light of the resurrection, which will require turning to God in prayer.

The third mistaken attitude is that everyone will experience the death of their bodies as their soul passes on.[88] The difficulty with this attitude is that no one has ever experienced death. Even though everyone dies, the moment of death is nothing anyone ever experiences. If human knowledge depends on how we interpret experience, then any reliable understanding of the experience of death is minimal. Much of this mistaken attitude springs from needing assurance and comfort in the face of a frightful unknown. The danger of imagining a soul escaping from the body makes it too easy to excuse ourselves from making a total surrender and act of faith. While we may affirm the belief that death is not the end, our religion itself requires an act of faith. Suppose we accept that the whole of ourselves genuinely dies. In that case, we are more likely to remember and acknowledge the importance of our absolute dependence on God and his free choice of us, not to abandon us in death, but to accept us into his loving embrace. Again, Moore acknowledges the importance of our dependence for meaning.

Dunne and Images of God in Death

Dunne's second concern is our image of God in death, again essential to Moore. People often connect death and the idea of God. Dunne suggests that if people connect death and God, then a closer look at death should

---

87. Dunne, *We Love You*, 16.
88. Dunne, *We Love You*, 17.

tell us something more intimate about God.[89] The Mystery and ultimate reason for death is found somehow in God's loving care for us, yet few people think of death as part of God's providence. We look toward images to help us appreciate the identity of God. Such images and ideas include a creator of a world that will end, a maker of the world, a God who snatches individuals from their family and friends, an all-powerful God, a God who watches us from a distance, a judging God, a punishing God, and a forgiving God. I want to address two of these images: God as all-powerful and God as remote and distant.

The first image is God the all-powerful. God doesn't simply create life and hold it all powerfully in existence. God creates life so we can improve and struggle for life with his help. In Dunne's understanding, "God works best against odds, it seems. Human life is meant to be a struggle, not a perpetual escape from struggle. God's wisdom is to design the human condition to involve putting things together and repairing what's broken. We create, we rest. We rest, there's trouble. We fix the problem or redeem the situation, we rest. Trouble again. By the time we're old, we are weary of rest."[90] The image of God as all-powerful, refusing to let anyone approach God unless stripped of every possession, betrays God as liking us but under the condition that we don't want anything else. It portrays God as ultimately fully responsible for everything. While it may be true to say that God is fully responsible for the universe, it is also true to say that God calls us to cooperate with him in making our lives, our world, and our universe more meaningful. God calls us to create new meanings that will offset and transform the distorting influences on our lives.

Moore holds a deep and abiding conviction for what Lonergan calls the Mysterious Law of the Cross. Moore states: "When the psyche begins to sense the ultimate Mystery as love and not as power, everything changes. The guilt and anxiety, in every person's link with the Mystery which constitutes us, is being dispelled."[91] Again, Moore affirms: "[A] new human consciousness comes from the deepest regions of people where love has set us free from guilt."[92]

The second image is of God as remote and at a distance. People have depicted God as a divine watchmaker who winds up the universe and counts down to the final hour. This image betrays life in terms of time

---

89. Dunne, *We Love You*, 52.
90. Dunne, *We Love You*, 69.
91. Moore, *Fire and the Rose*, 92.
92. Moore, *Fire and the Rose*, 95.

and calendar days while suggesting that God is unconnected to human living. We live out our days, month by month, year by year, till we reach our end. We begin to understand time as our enemy. However, as Dunne affirms: "It is important not to name time as our enemy, lest we overlook what really threatens human life. Time can be a framework for love and care. Our schedules, appointments, and dates are the only way we know how to make our benevolence work. They are the means by which we stay connected to each other. They can give us the opportunity to rely on others in our needs and to allow others to rely on us."[93] He goes on to affirm that time is not our enemy since

> God's idea of time was to make it possible for us to collaborate with the divine. Time is the divine room to make mistakes as we grope our way through life. Time tilts the odds to our side that we will find God and allow God to work in us. With human life in particular, God seems to loathe acting independently of us. There is no unquestionable miracle, recorded by any religion, that God has ever performed without time-consuming human cooperation. In other words, it seems that God wants to build life with us on earth, not just for us on some land beyond.[94]

Moore would agree with Dunne. Time is not the enemy, and God is not remote. Each of us is ultimately significant, and this affirmation urges us to affirm the significance of others, and their ultimate significance in the eyes of God for the building of creation. At best, the all-powerful image of God helps us realize that we are not God. However, our ultimate meaning and value discovered in a relationship requires an appreciation that the truth "I am absolute" is true, but only in the sense that the dream of myself is the dream of others. It is only in the truth that the other receives from us their affirmation and discovery of worth that we can say that each of us is unique and non-derivative.[95]

---

93. Dunne, *We Love You*, 71.
94. Dunne, *We Love You*, 70–72.
95. Moore, *Fire and the Rose*, 52.

5

Moore and the Psychology of Ego and Self

INTRODUCTION

In the brief biography, I mentioned that Moore underwent psychoanalysis in the 1950s following a personal crisis. After that event, he progressively spoke about self-discovery and couched self-knowledge in terms of knowing our conscious and "unconscious" selves. Moore also began using the terms *ego* and *self* to speak about the human person's relationship with God and others. He explored Sigmund Freud and Carl Jung's contributions to personal growth. These new experiences paved the way for developing religious insights into theology and spirituality, grounded in psychological thinkers and practitioners.

From the outset, I admit to the complexity of unpacking the meaning of the terms *ego* and *self* and their application to Christian theology. One of the reasons for the complexity is the assortment of terms and the different meanings of each term as various people employ them. There are many terms: "I" and ego, self, Self, person and subject, and the "me." Getting to a precise definition and differentiating one from the other remains an extensive study. I will attempt to present an understanding of their meaning so that I can better explain how Moore appropriates each term to explore our relationship with God and others. The task will require understanding the thoughts of Freud, the Neo-Freudian school, and Jung.

EARLY PRECURSORS OF EGO

Let us begin with Freud and the Neo-Freudian school of thought. My aim is not to be comprehensive in my treatment of Freud's personality structures. I want to identify several terms and insights that have a place in Freud's and, later, the Neo-Freudian school's understanding of personality. These include the ego, id, and superego, the centrality of anxiety, the Oedipal complex, the process of oneness and separation, and the mirroring function of the mother. All these terms become commonplace for Moore. Philosophically trained, Moore had an intuition about the complexity surrounding the term *ego* as early as the 1950s. After he had undergone psychoanalysis, he stated: "It becomes clear that the term 'ego,' worse 'the ego,' has to be avoided. If I had set myself to think [of] a concept designed to confuse, one could hardly have done better. It tries to mean indifferently, the person from without and the person from within. I [ego] am the source of my actions, and his ego is the source of his actions. Further, it confused consciousness and self-awareness."[1] What he thought about ego as a term back then, he would abandon for the wholehearted use of ego, ego state, and ego consciousness in the 1980s and onwards. However, the terms required much intellectual effort to clarify their meanings.

Understanding the meaning of "ego" is complex since the word took on several meanings through the influence of philosophical and psychological contexts. From Immanuel Kant's (1724–1804) "transcendental ego" to Johann Gottlieb Fichte's (1762–1814) focus on the *Ich* or Ego, the language of ego was already in the zeitgeist when Freud began to use it. Briefly, philosophers before Freud were concerned with questions to do with a theory of knowledge, and their use of ego was in the context of affirming with certainty what we can and cannot know about the world of objects and God. Kant distinguished between *phenomena* or sensory experiences (impressions, sights, sounds, feelings, and imaginings) and *noumena* or things in themselves (something outside the mind that gives rise to impressions in the mind), concluding that the mind cannot know reality. While Kant did not deny the existence of objects outside the thinking subject, he affirmed the impossibility of reaching any knowledge of them. He concluded that we cannot know *noumena* and that what we know has only a subjective existence. In other words, the mind looks at phenomena or sense impressions, imposes on these

---

1. Moore, "God Suffered," 134–35.

impressions qualities already present in the structure of the mind, qualities of space and time, and pronounces on the objects that it sees from looking at or understanding them. His arguments for the existence of God, who is not sensible, are based on moral duty. For Kant, the mind does not understand and is not intelligent or reasonable in the sense discussed in chapter 1, according to Lonergan's activities of consciousness.

Fichte admired Kant enormously; however, he parted company with Kant's conclusions about knowledge and the knower's reliance on sense impressions. Fichte focused on human interiority, concentrating his attention on the inner life of the mind or the mind's thinking rather than the objects of the external world. He went beyond Kant's theory of human reason. He made the mind into an aspect of an absolute, all-encompassing Mind, which later Friedrich Hegel would call the Absolute Spirit, underlying all reality. To paraphrase Fichte's thought: "Who am I? I am an absolute idealist: a thinking substance that is part of a transcendental Ego (an absolute divine all-encompassing Mind, which reveals itself through the activities of my mind)."[2] My very brief excursion into German philosophical thought indicates that the category of "ego" had been in the intellectual culture since the eighteenth century.

EGO PSYCHOLOGY

Walter Conn judges that the terms *ego*, which is central to ego psychology, and *self*, which is central to the psychology of self, diverge into several different meanings that are variously considered conscious and unconscious within the one discipline of psychology. Conn notes that the ego is often spoken as a first-person reality (similar to the way we say "I") and used in a third-person manner (similar to the way we use "person") to represent a subjective reality (similar to the way we use "self").[3] Thus, the meaning of "ego" is complex to negotiate, and its meaning depends significantly on what one means by consciousness. Ego is the Latin for the word "I" which has a first-person experiential meaning, yet ego has been used to indicate it has a third-person hypothetical meaning. To add greater complexity, ego is also a popular word in current ordinary language, especially when discussing someone having a big ego, being egotistic, or, even more positively, the importance of affirming one's ego.

2. Fellows of Woodstock, "Realm of Desire," 84.
3. Conn, *Desiring Self*, 42.

Conn presents a courageous effort to clear the conceptual decks around the term *ego*.

FREUD, NEO-FREUDIANS, AND EGO

Freud's theory of psychic functioning is very complex, and a complete study of it is beyond the scope of this book.[4] Freud was not primarily a theorist. He was a practitioner, and the terms he used derived their descriptive power from their ability to better help his patients overcome the debilitating effects of mental illness. Since Moore favored the use of ego in his theological writings, examining what Freud meant by the term is essential.

In brief, Freud has a tripartite model of psychic functioning: the ego, the id, and the superego. An ego is a group of psychic functions or patterns rather than an entity or central player in personality formation. It represents a cluster of perceptual and cognitive processes, including memory, problem-solving, reality testing, inference-making, and self-regulated strivings that are conscious and in touch with reality. The ego also expresses specific defense mechanisms that mediate between the primitive instinctual demands of the id, the social parental inhibitions and prohibitions of the superego, and our knowledge of the context of the world in which we live. It serves an executive function, always adaptive so as to maintain psychic balance between the three parts of the mind. For Freud, the ego functions consciously to organize the person in their response to the context of their lives.

According to Freud, the ego is hypothetical since we have no direct experience of it, yet it is central to an understanding of personality. Freud's understanding of the ego develops through several phases and over some time. In the first phase, the ego is part of the organism whose presence interferes with passages of prohibitive instinctual energies.[5] It is postulated hypothetically in the light of blockages that Freud observed in his patients. The ego serves to repress or erect a defense against ideas considered to be unacceptable in polite society. In the second phase, Freud postulated that the ego has the function of repression and sublimation in correspondence with the reality principle, especially toward

---

4. Meissner, *Freud and Psychoanalysis*, 162–86.

5. Meissner, *Freud and Psychoanalysis*, 157.

sexual instincts emerging from the id.⁶ In this phase, the reality principle has greater prominence in Freud's understanding of the ego. The reality principle overarches one's behavior such that the child discovers what is possible in its environment and accommodates to that reality for fear of punishment. It brings us back to an ordered existence in which we are not the center. In the third phase, the ego is a structural entity, though relatively weak, resulting from pressure applied by the id, the superego, and the reality principle.⁷ The idea of ego develops into a fourth and different stage through the writings of Heinz Hartmann and Anna Freud. Both emphasize the ego's autonomy and renewing capacity over other personality parts.⁸

Freud also postulates the id and the superego. The "id" of the mind is a primitive and instinctual element of raw energy demanding immediate satisfaction. Some of our demanding raw energy would not be acceptable in polite society. Freud regards the id as the unruly component of the psyche. It is entirely self-contained, isolated from the world, and bent on achieving its aims. The governing device for the id is the pleasure principle or gratification, and restraining the single-minded id is a significant part of the ego's function, always trying to balance the pleasure principle with the reality principle. Similar to the ego, the id should be used only as the descriptor for a system of actions and behaviors and not as an entity in itself.

The superego is that part of the mind associated with ethical and moral conduct and is responsible for self-imposed standards of behavior. It is the interior of the experienced exterior code, a kind of "conscience," according to the governing social norms of a society, punishing transgressions with feelings of guilt. It develops in response to punishments and rewards meted out by significant persons, especially parents, toward children, which results in the child becoming inculcated with the moral code of a community. The superego is viewed as being concerned with the ideal within living.

---

6. Meissner, *Freud and Psychoanalysis*, 158.
7. Meissner, *Freud and Psychoanalysis*, 159.
8. Meissner, *Freud and Psychoanalysis*, 161.

FREUD AND THE OEDIPUS COMPLEX

Moore uses Freud's Oedipus complex to understand the formation of sexual identity.[9] What is Freud's understanding of the Oedipal complex?[10] The theory is an attempt to explain the emergence of childhood sexual identity. It describes the path of sexual development in the child who detaches himself from the parent and becomes a member of society on their terms. Freud judges, in part, the problem of neurotics to be an inability to achieve the needed separation between themselves and their parents, often resulting in an inability to transfer their instinctual energy to another person outside the family unit. The child's separation is vital to human development. Freud's genius is that the Oedipus complex places each child within the context of a family and history. The person's history has a unique psychic reality and, when uncovered through psychoanalysis, can be used to help build a road towards more healthy living.

Freud bases the Oedipal theory on his childhood experiences of falling in love with his mother and the ensuing jealousy of his father. In the classical interpretation of Freud's theory, the various elements of sexual identity in the child converge around the age of five or six in a genital-directed organization. Before the genital orientation, the oral and anal stages of sexuality predominate until they are subsumed into a genital stage. At this age, the aim of all the child's desires becomes genital intercourse with the parent of the opposite sex. In contrast, the parent of the same sex (the father for boys and the mother for girls) assumes in the mind of the child the characterization of a dangerous and feared rival. A boy wants to remove the threat posed by his rival father by castrating the father, assuming his father's role, and presuming that his father will punish him in a like manner for having feelings toward the mother. It is only because of the threat of castration by the father that the child's Oedipal ambitions are renounced. The superego is the heir of the Oedipus complex to account for the internalization of parental values that accompany the resolution of the child's struggle and hold infantile sexuality in check. Childhood sexuality becomes organized in the Oedipus complex, and that organization becomes the underlying structure for the rest of the person's life. The whole application of the complex, with the castration

---

9. Moore, *Let This Mind*, 72–74.
10. Meissner, *Freud and Psychoanalysis*, 105–11.

aspect, has proved challenging to resolve for girls, and the model is undergoing significant revision.[11]

OTHER NEO-FREUDIAN THINKERS

For other Neo-Freudian thinkers, for example Erik Erickson, the ego also has an unconscious function, safeguarding our coherent existence by screening and synthesizing all the impressions, emotions, memories, and impulses that try to enter our thoughts and demand our actions.[12] It is as if the ego filters what the body feels and senses without our knowledge. Were it not for the ego, these thoughts would tear us apart if left unsorted and unmanaged under the ego's slowly grown and reliably watchful screening system. Alternatively, Erickson distinguishes the unconscious ego from the conscious "I" or the live and numinous center of awareness.[13] At this stage in the development of thought, psychologists had not yet clearly understood the distinction between conscious and unconscious, except to presume the conscious was equivalent to knowledge and the unconscious as a aspect of the mind that operated out of sight and in the dark recesses of the psyche.

Briefly, I want to mention Herbert Fingarette, who also works from an understanding of ego as an unconscious organizing principle toward meaning and integration.[14] Moore mentions the work of Fingarette positively.[15] When a client comes to therapy because they are both unhappy and find no meaning in their unhappiness, the therapist addresses the lack of meaning and unhappiness since the task of personal integration may not be the same as the task of adjustment to the unhappiness. Fingarette specifies a structural meaning to anxiety as the breakdown of the drive toward meaning.

Fingarette distinguishes two general kinds of anxiety. In the previous chapter, I examined the effect on each personality when the anxiety of meaninglessness occurs in the face of our creatureliness and the subsequent disordered reaction known as the denial of death. Neurotic anxiety occurs when the ego falters in a typical environment. Normal anxiety

---

11. Meissner, *Freud and Psychoanalysis*, 110.
12. Conn, *Desiring Self*, 63–64.
13. Conn, *Desiring Self*, 42.
14. Conn, *Desiring Self*, 44–45.
15. Moore, *Let This Mind*, 11.

occurs when the ego fails in the face of universal human events such as illness, catastrophe, and death. Whether neurotic or normal, anxiety is a uniquely provocative threat to the ego, a threat that disrupts central ego integrity. Anxiety is ego disorganization and ego disintegration. When the drive for meaning functions properly, it is called ego. The ego is the unconscious drive toward integration, and anxiety is the failure of the ego to achieve meaning. It is no wonder that certain Neo-Freudians, for example Erickson, speak of ego identity as essential to human development. In conclusion, going forward in psychological theory is an ego, which has a neutral function as a unifying drive toward meaning in the personality. The ego is the drive toward integration, organization, and meaning. Some posit the ego as conscious, but name the conscious function the "I" and others posit the ego as unconscious. Anxiety arises out of the failure of the ego to achieve its purpose, and the results are disintegration, disorganization, and meaninglessness.

Finally, I will mention two other Neo-Freudian developmental thinkers who had a significant influence on Moore and who used both the language of ego and of the self: Margaret Mahler (1897–1985)[16] and Alice Miller (1923–2010). Mahler is one of the first developmental psychologists to explore the lives of children suffering from both neurotic and psychotic difficulties. While Freud's focus for those suffering from neurosis is in terms of instinctual drives focused inward, giving rise to narcissism and self-absorption, Mahler judges neurosis to be a failure in the basic formation of the self and the accompanying confusion around one's identity and purpose.

Critical to Mahler's investigations of mental illness is both the environment and the relationship between mother and child. The mother provides the infant's immature ego with a crucial mirroring role or frame of reference. The infant emerges from their state of primary narcissism (what Moore calls oceanic consciousness) into a stage of separation from the mother. The child will want the mother to be in eyesight during the risky process of separation. The infant needs the mother to be predictable, stable, and at ease with the child as the child separates, which the mother provides in her demeanor, acting like an auxiliary ego to the infant. The child breaks out of what Mahler calls their autistic shell into the environment, and this breakthrough becomes the beginning of the child's sensing their differentiation from the mother. Suppose the mother

---

16. Mitchell and Black, *Freud and Beyond*, 43–48.

is unpredictable, unstable, anxious, or even hostile during the breakthrough period. In that case, the child's new frame of reference is stifled, and eventually, the child's independence is less likely. If the mother is only functionally available but emotionally detached, the child will not negotiate their development milestone well. The risk is always that the mother will read or interpret future progressive developments of the child as regressive and react with impatience or unavailability, precipitating an anxious fear of abandonment in the infant child who does not yet possess the psychic capacities to function as an independent agent. Thus, a complex interplay exists between a child's physical and cognitive maturation, psychological evolution, and the need for critical formation by the maternal partner.

Mahler's central insight is that, from a very early age, there is a tension in the baby between oneness and separateness. Moore uses the distinction often.[17] The tension represents two pulls within the individual: in one direction, the oceanic pull to oneness with the mother and, in the opposite direction, the not-yet formed pull, growing into a separate individual, a sense of myself and yourself being two different and independent individuals. The differentiation through separation is the first form of the ego. Through our life cycle, several crises drive growth and, each time, establish a new ego form, if transitioned well, potentially able to mature the ego with a new understanding and a new felt awareness of the tension between oneness and separateness. While Freud conceived of these two pulls as contradictory, inviting an either/or of either feeling safe or coming to terms with the complex reality of human existence, Mahler asserts that the tension is creative. Mahler traces the non-differentiated state of autism and symbiosis to what she calls the first instance of the infant's psychological birth in the process of separation and individuation.[18] The process results in a subjective sense of bodily and psychological identity and autonomous functioning. Although the process heightens a struggle within the child between the longing for independence (separation) and a desire for attachment (oneness), Mahler maintains that a strong early attachment between infant and mother supports autonomous exploration.

Moore posits that the psychological tension between oneness and separation is lifelong and applies to one's relationship to and desire for God. Moore states: "Thus the growth of the person is the progressive

---

17. Moore, *Jesus the Liberator*, 15–24.
18 Conn, *Desiring Self*, 60.

liberation of desire. It is the process whereby desire finds very deeply its subject, whereby desire comes to be in one who can say, ever more deeply and wholly, 'I want.' The process comes from the first cry of the infant's desire to the final liberation of desire in union with God. We move from the oceanic unknowing bliss to oneness with the mare pacific ('tranquil sea'), as Catherine of Siena calls the Godhead."[19]

Now, let us focus on Alice Miller. Miller outlines her development theory in her three books, *For Your Own Good*, *The Drama of the Gifted Child*, and *Thou Shalt Not Be Aware*.[20] The central insight is that the child's proper development requires them to see themselves in the mother. The child negotiating separation needs to be able to return to the mother. The balance between going away and returning to the mother's loving and secure gaze is essential. Each time the child separates, they enjoy themselves without getting lost in the mirror-to-mirror experience. Enjoying oneself indicates a natural form of narcissism. Now, if the mother hesitates, becomes overanxious, or stops the child's separation, the self in the child is crushed. Miller asserts that we become prisoners to how we are parented. The child cannot grow physically without sufficient narcissistic satisfaction to initiate a proper love of self, thus becoming psychically unhealthy due to insufficient mirror needs in the mother and father. The overall result is that the child feels shame rather than positive self-love since the child prioritizes their fundamental duty as fulfilling the expectations of the mother rather than personal autonomy. Therefore, we do not enter the first ego phase well, which makes us reluctant to grow emotionally beyond it.

THE INSIGHTS OF JUNG

What about the self? Again, Moore uses the word *self* extensively in his theology. It would seem that ego psychologists transition to the term *self* as the primary term for describing human personality. The history of the development of the notion of the self is complex, admitting various shades and forms. Ronald Fairburn postulates the self as a personal ego equivalent to the subjective sense of conscious "I" with an object-seeking life drive. D. W. Winnicott posits the emergence of the concrete self that may or may not be helpful to the person and depends on the quality of the mother's

---

19. Moore, *Jesus the Liberator*, 17.
20. See Lombardo, "Some Observations," 1–3; Miller, "Feeling Child," 1–10.

care from birth. Edith Jacobson puts forward a developmental understanding of the self, based on the objects in the child's environment and whether they are perceived as good or bad. Otto Kernberg also posits a self in development according to its self-object differentiation and the internalization of the good and bad mother. These psychologists do not drop the notion of ego altogether. They give greater prominence to the self.

More importantly, Moore turns to the insights of Carl Jung, who also uses the terms *ego* and *selfhood*. Again, I shall present a partial understanding of Jung's thought. However, I want to mention several insights that Moore adopts that have a place in Jung's thinking about human personality. These include ego and self, the self, individuation, the persona, the shadow, contrasexual personality, and archetypal images.

Ego and Self

In chapter 1, I spoke about Lonergan's understanding of consciousness that distinguishes psychic and intentional consciousness. Jung's understanding does not account for Lonergan's distinction within consciousness. For Jung, the psyche alone is central to consciousness in its conscious and unconscious manifestations. However, Jung is still concerned with articulating a path to wholeness. The path to wholeness means ownership of the psyche and its products. The ego is a set of performances through which we feel at home with ourselves (homeostatic state) and through which we know ourselves to be competent, able to understand, pass judgments, and make decisions. But, again, for Jung, the ego remains a set of activities entirely in the psyche oriented toward organization, meaning, and an integration of the personality. For Jung, the ego is located in the psyche as the center of consciousness.[21] Thus, Jung's ego differs radically from Freud's and is equivalent to what we mean when we speak of the "I." In another system of thought, Jung's ego might be named the "self," but not so for Jung, since in contrast to Jung's quite ordinary meaning of ego is his rather extraordinary definition of self. The self is the subject of the total psyche, both conscious and unconscious. The self is an ideal personality hinted at in the dream symbolism of a mandala. To achieve the self is to successfully own and negotiate all psychic products, including negotiating what is awkward, unknown, and malicious within us.

---

21. Doran, "Jungian II," 416–17.

Individuation and Ego

Jung also speaks of the process of individuation as vital to the person's life. The successful negotiation of conscious and unconscious products of the psyche leads to individuation.[22] Individuation is discovering, exploring, and attending to our psychic life in all its complexity. Through psychic exploration, one becomes a person of meaning and can live a fully human existence. Individuation means becoming a unique individual and one's true self. When a person is on the path of individuation, ego transcendence begins. When the ego is well established, enabling the person to have a realistic sense of one's area of competence in the world, the person grows in individuation. Such growth comes from a solid base, namely, a self-esteeming ego. If the ego refuses to negotiate with its unconscious products, the individual will not grow. We can understand why Moore discusses maturity as ownership and progress of our conscious and unconscious lives.

The Ego-Persona and Individuation

For Jung, closely connected with a well-developed ego and growth is the persona.[23] The persona is our public face and is the social side of the ego. It is the outer mask that we wear before others. Its development depends on the kind of social recognition we have received from others and what we have had to do to secure the esteem of others and, consequently, our self-esteem. It is easy for the ego to identify with the persona, particularly if parents have not provided the child with the inner spiritual sustenance to enable them to be relatively well-centered in their capacities. The common element in all forms of ego and persona identification is that one tends to identify oneself in terms of who one is to others and for others. In the long run, the identification of ego and persona is not helpful to growth. Nor is it helpful to receive our identity solely from our social role.

Despite the possibility of identification between ego and persona, the differentiation of the ego and the persona is one of our life tasks in individuation. The network of one's external relations with others and the recognition granted to us by significant others are critical in forming

---

22. Doran, "Jungian II," 416–17.
23. Doran, "Jungian II," 417–20.

one's ego. However, the differentiation of ego from persona points to the insight that we are far more than our societal role. The differentiation of ego from persona means not that one abandons one's social role but ceases to identify with one's social role. In other words, our identity is a far more extensive and richer story of experiences, feelings, insights, judgments, decisions, and religious commitments than simply the social role allotted to us by others. Who we are, or our identity, is far more than what we do, our behavior, or how we perform the social role expected by significant others.

Breaking ego-persona identification can be very difficult.[24] Jung's experience of individuation in his own life story involved an extremely painful course of events that led him to dissolve his ego-persona, in his case, the identification assumed from his association with the Freudian circle and from Freud's projections upon him. The ego-persona identification would have prevented him from developing his way. What can develop from the identification is a form of self-alienation and is certainly not the sort of individuation needed for complete human existence. Instead, ego-persona identification can lapse into a form of collective consciousness, which can assume far more disordered and bizarre forms in a broader social and cultural milieu.

The Shadow and Ego

For Jung, the emergence of the shadow also exists.[25] The shadow represents the aspects of our being that are awkward, undifferentiated, and even malicious, the dimension that ego consciousness does not want to admit belonging to ourselves. If the persona is the face we show our social group, the shadow is the face we hide. If the persona is the face we wish, the shadow is also an aspect of who we are. To achieve individuation, we must negotiate a differentiation between ego and persona and take ownership of our shadow. In the face of our refusal to own the shadow, the ego cannot achieve transcendence. We repress those parts of ourselves because they conflict with how we wish to be. It is the negative side of our personality only from the standpoint of the ego.

Yet, hidden from ego consciousness, the shadow has a deeper connection with the forces of our psychic depths. In part, the shadow comes about due to ideals planted within us. Each of us has a desired self-image

---

24. Doran, "Jungian II," 422–26.
25. Au, *Urgings of the Heart*, 25.

planted deep within us from infancy, and we conform to parental ideals to gain approval. It is similar to Freud's superego. We are taught specific values and judged to be good when we conform to them and bad when we do not. The more we hide the shadow, the more it becomes an inferior sub-personality that has its own life with goals and values that contradict the desired self-image acquired from parents. Although Jung never intended the shadow to get a "bad" reputation, it only seems bad because it houses all the unacceptable and inferior parts of us.

Reclaiming what has been lost in the shadow is essential to our inner journey. Jung asserts that the shadow is more like a treasure hidden in a field and a potential source of richness unavailable to us as long as it is buried.[26] Ultimately, we can only grow in wholeness by becoming aware of and accepting our multidimensional selves, including the shadow. Conversely, the longer the products of the shadow are repressed, the more hostile they become.

One of the main reasons why we do not recognize the existence of our own shadow is because of projection. We project onto others what is already present in ourselves but fail to see or attend to in ourselves. When we have a strong negative or positive reaction to someone else, that person may carry an aspect of our shadow. People we fiercely criticize, whom we cannot stand to be around, who irritate or upset us, and whom we consider our enemy may be carrying aspects of ourselves that we detest. For example, suppose we see someone behaving selfishly and have repressed our selfish tendencies so that we regard ourselves as never selfish. In that case, we may feel more judgmental toward that person than if we had accepted our selfishness. Conversely, people we idealize may carry positive traits we are blind to in ourselves.

To begin to know our shadow requires us to notice our reactions to others, whether in our behavior, the tone of our voice, Freudian slips, humor, or the symbolism of our dreams.[27] Our encounter with and negotiation of the shadow marks a beginning in coming to terms with our unconscious. The proper negotiation of the shadow is the beginning of the shift from the ego as the center of our personality to the self as the center of our personality and from a state of rift between the ego and the totality of our psyche to a condition of wholeness. With Jung, Moore

---

26. Au, *Urgings of the Heart*, 39–41.
27. Au, *Urgings of the Heart*, 33–35.

held the conviction that to be whole, we must address our conscious and unconscious and come to terms with our shadow.[28]

Contrasexuality

Jung insists that we all bear in our psychic repertoire an image of the opposite sex, who is at the same time the carrier of our contrasexual makeup.[29] Contrasexuality is one of Jung's most complex theories, and I cannot explore all its dimensions. It will become a key concept for Moore in helping him understand how we can best achieve a creative relationship with people of the opposite sex.

First, the man's psychic makeup is constituted by the archetypal image of femininity or anima, and the woman's psychic makeup is constituted by the archetypal image of masculinity or animus, which helps each to negotiate their relations with people of the opposite sex. Jung views each person as a balance of masculinity (animus) and femininity (anima) and his insight requires that we think of men not exclusively masculine and women not exclusively feminine.

Second, for men, the anima (for women, the animus) helps them approach and interact with women through being in touch with their "inner woman" or what Jung calls his femininity. The reverse holds for women; in her case, it requires her to negotiate her animus when interacting with men.

Third, both anima and animus have a primordial pre-experiential reference point and a post-experiential reference point. As pre-experiential, Jung conceives these archetypes as originating in the psyche as unconscious, and in some sense genetic and organic, before encountering other humans as historical beings.[30] We are born with a contrasexual makeup. The pre-experiential reference point affirms the existence of an archetype with its innate pattern of behavior, resulting from endless repetition by other humans and passed down through heredity. However, a post-experiential reference point for these archetypes also exists. In this case, our personal history comes into play in which we are influenced by significant others and dominant cultural symbols. It is usually noticed through our projections so that men and women become conscious of

---

28. Moore, *Fire and the Rose*, 57–65.
29. Doran, "Jungian II," 426–27.
30. O'Connor, *Understanding Jung*, 129, 131.

their inner image through contact with other people and the kind of projections they place on them regarding how they should behave toward them.

Fourth, regarding the content of the anima and animus, these projections can become stereotyped with society's view of masculinity and femininity so that we become convinced that men should behave predominately in one way and women in another. We become confused when men or women do not behave in these expected ways. Western cultures, for example, have described characteristic anima behavior through qualities like compassion and being people of sympathy and care. In contrast, animus behavior has been judged as being protective, strong, and powerful.

Fifth, it is also the case that both the inner anima and animus have negative and positive aspects or faces.[31] For example, for some men, the anima often reflects their mother as caring and nurturing. In contrast, for other men, the anima might be a plaything image, a vessel of hidden wisdom, or even an emasculating power that they must resist with all their will. Therefore, for men, their anima must be negotiated when they meet women in their lives if they desire healthy relationships with women in the external world. For the women, the animus may reflect their protective father. For other women, it can also be a violent and dominating image. It must also be negotiated with men she meets in the external world. Problems arise when the projected inner image onto the external person does not always match who is standing before them. We can imagine a man projecting onto a woman his inner anima as an emasculating power and, consequently, treating the person before him, who may not be emasculating, as somebody to control out of fear of his being emasculated. In this case, the projection distorts our understanding of the real person on whom we have projected our inner image with its associated fearful feelings. This factor becomes a source of conflict between men and women. When the projected image is destructive, the psyche can be a potent force for harm against another.[32] If this is the case, it becomes crucial for men and women to appropriate their image and feelings with intelligence and responsibility so as to reorient the destructive images of anima and animus within. It also becomes essential to appropriate one's

---

31. O'Connor, *Understanding Jung*, 132.
32. O'Connor, *Understanding Jung*, 134–35.

projections honestly so that any mismatching between inner and outer realities, which will only lead to confusion, does not happen.

Sixth, the anima and animus accommodate the persona so that if a person has developed their persona, their anima or animus is probably the least developed. With this in mind, we must appropriate our inner image, whether anima or animus, and the various persona or faces we project onto our social world. Both efforts at appropriation aim to uncover any lack of intelligent and responsible living and orient ourselves towards greater authenticity.

Archetypes

Lastly, the emergence of other archetypal images exists within the human psyche.[33] Anima and animus are archetypal. However, there are other energy centers within the psyche. An archetypal image is a cluster of primordial energy in the psyche around an image that reveals its existence and potency in dream symbolism, especially in the mandala. These archetypes can motivate us toward a particular course of action and can be dangerous if not interpreted responsibly. They can become dangerous if the ego submerges itself in the imaginal undertow of the archetype or when the ego inflates itself to the level of the image rather than negotiating its significance intelligently and responsibly. The optimal time to negotiate their significance is when the process of individuation has reached the point of ego-persona differentiation when we have achieved a withdrawal from the projections of the shadow and a sufficient negotiation of our contrasexual opposites. Therefore, these archetypal images must be negotiated. Otherwise, one is sure to lose one's way in the process of individuation.

ARCHETYPES, SYMBOLS, AND GOD

According to Doran, at one point in his life, Jung has a dream in which he found himself in India, where he enters the Council Hall of Akbar the Great. The sultan's hall makes a deep impression on Jung. In the dream, Jung interprets the center of the hall as the sultan, the highest authority, giving out his orders to everyone. Jung is in the large hall with his father, with galleries and bridges leading to a basin-shaped center. For Jung, the

---

33. Doran, "Jungian II," 425.

dream represents a mandala, a symbol of the integrated self as both the center and totality of the personality. The sultan is the lord of the world. In the dream, Jung's father, who is a church minister, tells him that there is even a higher authority than the sultan at the top of the flight of stairs located at a stop that no longer corresponds to something in the created world. He is being pointed toward a higher authority, even greater than the sultan, the incomprehensible Mystery of God, to whom he is invited to surrender in adoration. In his dream, Jung is reluctant to take the final step of surrender.

Doran concludes: "There is a fascination with the wholeness of the mandala, of the self, [and] of nature, that prevents him from granting that the mandala is not self-enclosed. There is a small door that opens from the center of the self through the mystery of suffering onto the incomprehensibility of a God in relation to whom we have to adopt the final posture of Job himself. But something in me," says Jung, "was defiant and determined not to be a dumb fish."[34] For the Christian, contrary to Jung, the deep center is not just our natural self. We are not self-enclosed within a natural universe. We are called to participate in a power that is the source and final end of the natural world. We are constituted through grace in such a manner that God dwells in our innermost being, and we come to know the incomprehensible mystery only by God's grace.

MOORE, PSYCHOLOGY, AND CONSCIOUSNESS

Now, we turn to Moore. In chapter 1, I demonstrated Moore's indebtedness to Lonergan for shifting one's focus to the importance of consciousness, as a basis for a better understanding of self-awareness. It turns out that when we understand consciousness, we are better able to navigate such terms as *ego*, *self*, *"I,"* and *me*. The very brief exploration into ego psychology leads Conn to conclude that, for Freud and Neo-Freudian thinkers, the ego is often an unconscious inner organizer of experience that we become aware of when it is working but of which we are never aware in itself.[35] Even as an unconscious organizer, we speak about it in an objective sense rather than a subjective manner. It is equivalent to saying, "I have an ego," but I am an "I." It was Erickson who distinguished between the ego and the "I." Thus, the ego is part of the unconscious self,

---

34. Doran, "Jungian II," 441.
35. Conn, *Desiring Self*, 43.

while the subjective "I" is the conscious side of the ego. We are truly conscious only to the extent that we can say "I" and mean it. A person may make the affirmation, "I am a human being," and their use of "I" reflects a subjective reality as to where they are standing in their lives. The "I" is the center of awareness, our sense of being alive.

However, the "I" is different but related to the "me." Conn turns to Lonergan for a richer understanding of the "I" and a more precise grasp of its nature. In chapter 1, I spoke of human consciousness as consciousness-in and consciousness-of. Consciousness-in is consciousness as a subjective experience. The reality of consciousness-in is known not by its being an object of inquiry but through its being *in act*.[36] It is constitutive of who we are. It is our conscious self-presence and what Moore calls self-awareness. Conn affirms that the "I" is "an understanding of consciousness as the self's constitutive presence to itself."[37]

However, when the self performs the acts or operations of noticing, understanding, judging, and deciding, the self is also present to itself. Such operations both intend objects but also render conscious the operating self. The operations make both the intended object present to the self and, at the same time and in the same act, the operations make the person an "I" or make the person present to itself. For example, I could be totally absorbed and lost in watching a film, in which case the self that becomes absorbed and does the losing is the self-as-subject, and the self that is lost and, therefore, not reflectively an object of inquiry is the self-as-object. This means that the "I" has a presence to itself in two ways: as a subject intending and as an object of inquiry. Conn concludes that consciousness-in is the "I" present to itself as subject, operating, and conscious (Moore's self-awareness). At the same time, consciousness-of is the "me" present to the "I" as an object of deliberate inquiry or reflexive knowing (Moore's reflective self-awareness).[38] Interpreting Moore, the "I" is our self-awareness, and the "me" is our reflective self-awareness.

Lonergan's notion of consciousness is crucial. The "I" exists because I experience myself as a subject, and "the self is brought into being as an "I" by the very consciousness that reveals it to itself."[39] Both this understanding of consciousness and its relationship to the "I" become the basis for speaking about self-transcendence, something that both Lonergan

---

36. Conn, *Desiring Self*, 48.
37. Conn, *Desiring Self*, 48.
38. Conn, *Desiring Self*, 49.
39. Conn, *Desiring Self*, 50.

and Moore affirm about persons. The "I" is the dynamic principle of transcendence. To go beyond ourselves in self-transcendence requires a strong self. The strong self is grounded in an "I" that participates in a drive to know, value, and love rooted in our entire being. When we do not affirm the "I" or our self-presence to consciousness and instead propose that we only experience ourselves as a series of passing states, then, Conn concludes, there remains "a truncated and thus distorted self, a self [that is] capable of aspiring to nothing more than one form or another of shallow individualism, the perfect pawn to be manipulated in a consumer society."[40]

THE "ME" AND THE "I"

What about the "me"? Conn characterizes the "me" as the self-as-object. The "me" is the self as known or everything we know about ourselves borne from a desire to know. Coming to know the different aspects of ourselves by making ourselves an object of inquiry, we must be mindful that we come to know the self in two distinct ways.

First, we come to know the self by means of naming aspects of our life that are vital to us. These may include our physical body, our home, our clothes, our family, those who give us recognition, and those who do not give us recognition, as well as our emotional, cognitional, and volitional capacities and many more aspects. Second, we come to know ourselves in our psychic reality. Our psychic realities are our feelings and our felt responses or reactions to many aspects of our world. We have perceptions of these things which can be congruent with reality or very much incongruent with reality. The self is real, but it is made up of both externally identifiable dimensions and the psychic dimensions or aspects of "me."[41]

Second, in terms of the important project of making ourselves or the process of self-creation, there is an ongoing constitution of the self through personal experiences, discoveries, decisions, and deeds. Conn asserts that the "ongoing historical constitution of the self-as-object through meaning and value occurs because its dialectical counter-pole, the 'I,' the center of conscious subjectivity, is a radical, self-creating drive

---

40. Conn, *Desiring Self*, 52.
41. Conn, *Desiring Self*, 55.

for integrating meaning and value in self-transcendence."[42] The historical insights from Freud to Jung and our present-day uncovers a greater prominence given to the self, both in "desiring *to be a self* and *to move beyond the self* in relationship."[43] The self is dynamic, embodied, and bipolar, that is, a creative tension between the "I" or self-as-subject and "me" or self-as-object."[44]

Moore highly values self-awareness, or what we have called the "I" or the self-as-subject. For a person to stand up and claim their rightful place in their group, in the church, in society, and the world, there must exist a measure of self-awareness. He states that "it is the basis of all human communication and thus is of inestimable importance and value for our self-understanding."[45] Meanwhile, the term "self-awareness" in the popular imagination is very different. It has come to mean a person who has a profound knowledge of themselves and what they are about, someone who does not act out of routine alone but with purpose. The self-aware person is thoughtful, someone who does not go along with the masses and who has moved beyond any collective consciousness that does just what everyone else is doing. Since they are self-aware, they are more likely to be authentic in their judgments and decisions. In the popular mind, self-awareness is a combination of self-presence and self-knowledge. Our popular meaning compresses the self as subject and the self as object of inquiry.

While this may be the popular meaning of self-awareness, Moore distinguishes between self-awareness and reflective self-awareness. We can only have real knowledge about ourselves (through reflective self-awareness) because we are conscious and self-present (self-awareness). Moore describes the self-as-subject through a simple phrase: "The self aware is self-aware."[46] He calls self-presence a dialogue with oneself, which is going on all the time until we stop, change gears, and become reflectively self-aware. Thus, for Moore, "self-awareness precedes and presupposes self-reflection (knowledge about myself).... [T]o limit self-awareness to reflective awareness is to say that 'myself' is absent from my normal awareness as is Iceland or the 'Titanic', and has to be recalled to

---

42. Conn, *Desiring Self*, 56.
43. Conn, *Desiring Self*, 70.
44. Conn, *Desiring Self*, 70.
45. Moore, *Inner Loneliness*, 9.
46. Moore, *Inner Loneliness*, 8.

consciousness just as they do. This makes me a stranger to myself, *and thus*, makes all others strangers to me."[47]

Self-awareness is not looking at myself. It is more a *being with* myself and "this being-with myself, which I expose to others and which I recognize in others: this being with myself that is my primary act of existing and that is my primary motive for living, my driving force, is a highly convinced and emotionally charged being-with. It is in fact self-love."[48] Nevertheless, the key to authentic living requires a grasp of our conscious and unconscious lives, self-presence, and self-knowledge. Moore states that "we live in an age where spiritual health and growth demands the conscious appropriation of our psychic drives, in which no freedom worth the name is attainable without this appropriation."[49]

MOORE, EGO CONSCIOUSNESS, AND CONVERSION

In his writings, Moore has no hesitation in speaking about conversion and ego as interrelated. He talks about ego forms as changing and assuming different shapes in childhood, adolescence, and adulthood.[50] He is convinced that both our psychic life, which is largely unnoticed, and our day-to-day dealings with people and situations are distinct yet related aspects of the self. The ego forms and the ego habits that they give rise to are more or less unnoticed and unattended to in daily living. For the ego forms to be noticed and understood requires a heightened consciousness or a determined and focused effort at self-discovery.[51]

Each ego form in the person will be plunged into a crisis throughout the course of life, whether through falling in love, undergoing a religious conversion, or suffering bereavement. The crisis amounts to a form of death. Moore asserts that the fact of "death threatens the meaningfulness of the world as viewed from the standpoint of the ego and begins no longer to do so once there has been some dying of ego."[52] However, Moore distinguishes between dying to ego and dying to sin. Both could be an opportunity or, if not accepted, an impediment to growth. Each person

---

47. Moore, *Inner Loneliness*, 9.
48. Moore, *Inner Loneliness*, 10.
49. Moore and Maguire, *Dreamer*, 65.
50. Moore, "Forming and Transforming," 165.
51. Moore, *Crucified Is No Stranger*, 95–116.
52. Moore, "Forming and Transforming," 171.

inhabits an ego form that serves to keep their lives predictable and in a homeostatic balance given all the complexity of their external environment. When a person is dying to ego or "ego consciousness," they reach a point in their lives where growth requires the ego form, which currently organizes meaning in their lives but, in the face of crisis, can no longer do its job, to be transcended. Through its encounter with the elements present in the crisis, the ego moves out of its homeostatic condition and integrates into another homeostatic ego form, and in that new state, will feel more at home, that is, less prone to fear and anxiety.

Dying to sin is different. Sin already implies a maladjustment to the true direction and purpose of life. Sin implies that we have stopped growing and are protective of our world without reference to others. Sin indicates that we are living in isolation from others, emotionally and spiritually. It can also be the case that if we are paralyzed in an early ego form and refuse to move beyond it, our ego fixation can eventually bring about a condition of sin since it is a distortion of the person through not achieving who they are meant to be. Obviously, Moore has in mind the importance of the early ego form of childhood narcissism that gives way to adult self-giving in the normal course of events. If the child remains fixated on their primary narcissism, then when the child becomes an adult, the adult person will be paralyzed and never become a person for others. As Moore asserts, in proper growth, self-love gives way to self-gift, although he is not so naïve to think that such growth is an easy process given the sinful structures all around us.

Conversion can be a helpful process both in the dying of ego and the dying to sin. Moore speaks to the conversion experience of the disciples as an example of moving from ego death to liberation. The gospel account of the crucifixion of Jesus is a record of psychic transformation where the disciples, in their guilt, confusion, and shame, following the death of Jesus, undergo, in and through the resurrection, an ego transformation. I will reflect more on ego transformation in chapter 7. When we refuse to grow, we are espousing that the ego is absolute. Thus, Moore speaks about the illusion of the "ego is for keeps" as a consequence of sin, when what is required is nothing more than a complete ego crisis followed by ego transformation.[53]

---

53. Moore, "Forming and Transforming," 182.

MOORE, SELF, AND TRUE SELF

The other term that Moore is at home with is *self*. He calls the movement from animal consciousness to human consciousness "the newly emergent self."[54] Moore recognizes the distinction between a love *of* self and a love *for* self or selfishness, the former being a natural narcissism and the latter being a distorted narcissism.[55] The distinction is grounded in another important difference: the self as a gift for others from the self against others.[56] Moore explains that when we wake to the once unnoticed evil that we may have perpetrated, we realize that we have been denying, suppressing, or even destroying our true selves. Since the true self is the center of our life, it follows that the true self becomes a victim of what we now know as sin.[57] Through sin, we victimize our true selves.

Finally, there is the one true self that Moore comes upon through Tolle's conversion experience spoken of in chapter 3. When Tolle was contemplating suicide, he uttered in frustration that he could no longer live with himself. This frustration and disgust set him on a path to work out what it could mean. He concluded that surely it did not mean that there were two selves within him, one self who expressed frustration and despair, his current state, and the other self that experienced disgust. Therefore, he concludes that maybe only one of them is real, and the other is an illusion.[58] Moore relates his own experience of what he calls "twoing," or thinking about himself as two selves. Again, Tolle's experience and the conviction of Saint Augustine that God dwells in the soul in a way that is more intimate toward us than we are to ourselves, leads Moore to the conclusion that the self into which the dying of ego and the dying of sin is invited is "the self that is one in all."[59] His religious faith leads him to conclude that, for there to be a dying of ego and dying to sin, each of us must come under the guidance of the Holy Spirit and the presence of the unknown mystery, the Abba Father of Jesus. Jesus comes to embody the self in all of us.[60] Our true self is reached by the grace of God and within the context of mystical consciousness.

---

54. Moore, "New Life," 154.
55. Moore, *Inner Loneliness*, 47–49.
56. Moore, "Our Love Is Crucified," 27–28.
57. Moore, *Crucified Is No Stranger*, 75.
58. Moore, *Body of Christ*, 24.
59. Moore, *Jesus the Liberator*, 14.
60. Moore, *Jesus the Liberator*, 9.

Apart from our true self, Moore asserts that Jesus is the "symbol of the true self."[61] In this affirmation, Moore is using Jung's understanding of the self as the most ideal person that we can become. Even though the ideal is located in the person of Jesus, "our best self is a lover, is generous, finds peace in the other, lives in the limitless universe, is self-transcending."[62] Jesus is the True Self and the psyche's essential life.[63] Moore adds that only the Holy Spirit makes Jesus the transforming symbol of our innermost life, the inward shape of our motivation.[64] To grow consciously and unconsciously, we need to be pointed to that spacious territory of ourselves that lies in "the shadow of the ego" in order to experience its coming together in Jesus. We need to appreciate the manner by which we suppress goodness within and understand how we are inflicting harm on our true selves.[65] The rejection of our true self is the rejection of Jesus. Only by meeting God in the Jesus symbol can any rejection of our true self arrive at a point that "makes the unbearable truth of ourselves bearable through the power of love."[66] What empowers the symbol of Jesus within our psyche is nothing more than the grace of God, the historical goodness of Jesus, and the psyche's deepest power to project the symbol of the true self of Jesus into the drama of our self-crucifixion.[67] These elements are fused by the power of the Holy Spirit so that Jesus becomes a "transpersonal symbol of the crucified whole."[68]

SUMMING UP

In dialogue with Lonergan and Conn, we have a clearer control of meaning around ego and self, "I" and "me," true self and True Self. The word *ego* denotes a principle of organization and integration within consciousness, giving rise to various ego forms. Ego consciousness is a way of acknowledging that the ego as an organizing principle exists and operates. Thus, we can speak about ego forms in a homeostatic state or

---

61. Moore, *Crucified Is No Stranger*, 75.
62. Moore, *Crucified Is No Stranger*, 95.
63. Moore, *Contagion of Jesus*, 19; *Crucified Is No Stranger*, 19–20.
64. Moore, *Contagion of Jesus*, 20.
65. Moore, *Contagion of Jesus*, 21.
66. Moore, *Contagion of Jesus*, 27.
67. Moore, *Crucified Is No Stranger*, 51.
68. Moore, *Contagion of Jesus*, 28.

ego states in a process of change, reaching a new integration. The ego is a third-person way of speaking about the "I." If the ego form changes, the "I" changes. When we speak of "I" we are denoting our self-affirmation of existence and worth, as well as the self-as-subject or self-presence or self-awareness. The "I" is my existential orientation to life. To know ourselves, we need to objectify the "I" and we do so by asking the question, "Who am I?" The "me" is the specific and detailed articulation of the "I" and our way of affirming self-knowledge. While the "I" gives an affirmation to the subject's existence, the "me" particularized that affirmation: I prefer red and not blue, that's "me;" I prefer Italian food to Asian food, that's "me;" I believe that God is real and not simply a product of wishful thing, that's "me."

For Jung, the self is the totality of the psyche. He reduces the person's interior to the psyche. Against Jung, the self is the total of my being: organism, psychic consciousness, and intentional consciousness, three interpenetrating and interrelating realities, each distinct yet one identity in the self. For Moore, the self is the whole of the "I" affirming and developing, and there is only one self, not two selves. Therefore, the self is a larger way of speaking about the human person, which incorporates the organism, psyche, and the human spirit. Nor is the self to be understood in terms of a discontinuous objectification of episodes of my past or simply equivalent to my ability to objectify others. Jean-Paul Sartre characterizes this objectification as the "stare" by which we objectify the other and negate their subjectivity. The true self does not objectify the other through a stare nor negate their subjectivity.[69] The true self "has its being in love," and love serves to loosen the grip that the "continually objectifying self wants to exercise on my life [and the life of the other]."[70] Contrary to Sartre, who posits objectification and freedom as coterminous, Moore concludes that only by situating the self in a world of love can there be any hope of becoming free.[71]

Moore brings to the foreground the importance of the bodily dimension of the self, not so much as organic but as the self-embodied and as a vehicle of communication with others. Through Alice Miller, Moore can appreciate that violence visited on children "is stored in the body, the cells and the neurons and their connections. No matter how much we deny, redefine or push from our memories the hurtful and damaging

---

69. Moore, "Reflections on the Thought," 148.
70. Moore, "Reflections on the Thought," 148.
71. Moore, "Reflections on the Thought," 148.

feelings of powerlessness and diminished human dignity we experienced in childhood at the hands of adults, the body does not forget."[72] If we falsify or negate any aspect of the self, we can never understand ourselves fully. Only through an acceptance of "our body of death" can we achieve authenticity.[73]

The True Self is a symbol of my life in God, participating with God's grace to communicate the love of God and the love of neighbor. For Moore, Jesus is the ultimate symbol in the psyche of the True Self; only in the case of Jesus are we dealing with a historical figure, made glorious in the resurrection, and not an archetype (in similar manner that anima or animus are archetypal) inherited through our genetic makeup.

What the Neo-Freudians call the unconscious ego is really our conscious organizing principle but, as yet, unattended to and unobjectified. What psychologists call the conscious ego is our organizing principle, as objectified and known to the self. This approach leaves the unconscious as the strictly organic dimension of our person. From chapter 1, we saw that Moore affirmed the technique of focusing as a means of paying attention to our body so as to identify feelings, especially disturbing feelings. The organic dimension is every aspect of ourselves that works cooperatively to maintain our organic integrity yet also has a profound connection to the psyche. Most especially, the neural manifolds send messages via the nervous system and these messages register as psychic representations in the form of images, feelings, symbols, and memories. These presentations become the starting point for intentional consciousness. There is, therefore, a relationship between our body and our feelings, and there is a sense that we do not just have a body; rather, we are a body.

MOORE, BECOMING AUTHENTIC, AND MAHLER

Let us turn now to Moore's appropriation of Margaret Mahler's work. I will speak about Mahler's influence on Moore's grammar of desire in the next chapter, but at this point, it is important to note that Mahler's insights help Moore understand the progressive growth of the self. Earlier in the chapter, I unpacked the basics of Mahler's understanding of human infant development. A crisis can be a moment of danger or opportunity, regression or progression. However, if the early developmental

---

72. Lombardo, "Some Observations," 1.

73. Moore, "Reflections on the Thought," 150–51.

stage is not negotiated well, then a feeling bad about ourselves comes into consciousness and puts all kinds of blockages before us when a "fateful decision" has to be made later in life.[74] Feeling bad about ourselves causes hesitancy in making good decisions. The version of ego in childhood is, after all, the first form of ego, and there will always be subsequent pressures for change on subsequent ego forms. As indicated, each crisis event, usually painful, will call for a death to the current ego form and a new integration of the self.

Moore affirms two constitutive forces in a person's whole life: the force towards oneness and the force towards separateness. Moore couches the emergence of separateness from oneness as a point of crisis in our lives. In the beginning, the sense of oneness for the child is experienced in an undifferentiated union with the mother in the womb up to about 12 months until separation happens. For Freud, the reality principle comes forward early in our development. The reality principle helps us to come to terms with the harsh fact that we cannot have a felt sense of oneness any longer and must adjust ourselves to being separate individuals. By contrast, Moore judges the force and desire for oneness as critical to our spiritual development and lasting the length of our lifespan. Therefore, for him, it is not a matter of either one force or the other but the creative tension between them throughout our entire lives.[75] The tension gives rise to a new "me." The new subject especially happens in the experience of falling in love. Falling in love brings about a new "me" and the new "me" seeks union with the one desired. The person is aware of being one's own separate identity (separateness) yet seeks union with another person (oneness). The person seeking the union is also aware that a new "me" is operating. Moore puts the matter perfectly, using the language of desire: "The desire whereby I am drawn to another is partly constitutive of who I am. To be drawn to another [union] is to become more [my person in separateness]."[76]

Further, the tension of oneness and separateness is heading towards our total transformation, initiated by the mystery of God and finding its fulfillment when the finite becomes one with the infinite. Moore asserts that we are purposed to move from being separate, independent people to being a self-in-mystery, a self in the Mystery of God.[77] So, while our

74. Moore, *Let This Mind*, 71.
75. Moore, *Jesus the Liberator*, 16.
76. Moore, *Jesus the Liberator*, 18.
77. Moore, *Jesus the Liberator*, 19.

finiteness accentuates ourselves as separate and independent, the force towards oneness keeps calling us, and the call felt as dark and unknown, is ultimately the Mystery of God, calling us to experience rebirth out of death. Moore concludes that if the Mystery appears untrustworthy, capricious, and cruel, it is most unlikely that the person will respond positively to this particular invitation to oneness. If the Mystery appears trustworthy, then the person is more likely to undergo the dark crisis of death with religious hope, confident that the mystery one trusts waits on the other side. Whether we like it or not, each crisis will seem like a swallowing up by death. If this occurs, then it will be safe to assume that our physical death is the climax of a lifelong process of other deaths to ego. If real desire wants to grow in us, then we must welcome death to ego and death to sin throughout our lives, and these points of crisis become a prelude to death as a final liberating movement. Death becomes a passageway into a fuller liberation.[78]

Pondering authentic development in terms of the tension between oneness and separateness, we observe an important stage in our affective development. If the situation of development is not negotiated better, our felt sense of being ourselves becomes less than an ecstatic sense of being alive.[79] It hinders growth in the child through the loss of feeling good about themselves, and the loss of feeling good about themselves touches on the child's very sense of existence. The felt loss affects growth in awareness. Later and providently, we may be able to open ourselves to the healing grace of God. Inasmuch as we do this, healing will have to address the "radical uncertainty" about our goodness.[80]

In the interpersonal zone, the chronic experience of not feeling good about ourselves "starts the habit of seeing one's life is not entirely satisfactory and looking to others for reassurance."[81] Thus, it is a habit that starts with a stifled separation from the mother and extends to others. Moore asserts: "Not knowing ourselves apart from others is our trouble, to remedy which we look to others."[82] The "look to others" amounts to rating ourselves through the eyes of others or measuring ourselves by the manner by which others react to us. This unhelpful habit seriously discounts our true worth, which is "our experience of ourselves

---

78. Moore, *Jesus the Liberator*, 22.
79. Moore, *Let This Mind*, 72.
80. Moore, *Let This Mind*, 72.
81. Moore, *Let This Mind*, 72.
82. Moore, *Let This Mind*, 72.

as God's desired."[83] If there occurs a serious discounting of our esteem, then what follows is repression of all that is in us, a felt self-rejection, and disesteem in the first steps of our personhood when we are meant to feel ecstatic about ourselves. We repress our passionate nature and our desire to live. Moore concludes that, ultimately, evil arises out of self-doubt and self-hatred. This disordered process is not what God intends for us. God intends for us to become self-aware and to come to a stage of selfhood where there exists "a joy in being myself, there is a love for others in being wholly myself, of which the (normally) borrowed selfhood can give no idea. That discovery, of self as luminous, is of the spirit."[84]

Deep within the psyche, there forms what Ormerod calls "a felt rejection of our own nature, a radical disvaluing of self, a feeling bad about being what we are."[85] Feeling terribly wrong, we may seek pathways that we feel and think will return us to the untroubled womb and away from feeling bad, whereas the path to growth is always away from the womb and toward death and rebirth. Moore connects a radical feeling bad about ourselves and feeling bad about what we are with the mythic story of Adam and Eve. By eating the fruit of the tree, they reject their creaturely status, either by wanting to return to a primordial oneness with God or by rejecting those aspects of themselves that point back to animal consciousness rather than integrating it. The lack of feeling of self-worth creates a "wobble." It creates an original disesteem, which Moore affirms is the distorted foundation for original sin. I will unpack Moore's insights into original sin in the next chapter.

MOORE, BECOMING AUTHENTIC, AND MILLER

Let's now turn to Moore's appropriation of Alice Miller's work. Earlier, I briefly unpacked Miller's understanding of proper development. It is interesting to note that Miller was very concerned to expose the damage and dangers of sexual abuse toward children in their home setting. In 1997, the mother of Moore's nephews and niece, Jini Fiennes, had her novel *Blood Ties* published posthumously under her maiden name, Jennifer Lash. It is a fictional story of a couple who adopt a boy in his childhood, who subsequently receives little to no emotional support from

---

83. Moore, *Let This Mind*, 74.
84. Moore, *Let This Mind*, 75.
85. Ormerod, *Grace and Disgrace*, 155.

them and who is then thrust into the world as an adult to confront his problems. Undoubtedly, it is based on Jini Fiennes's own abuse experience at the hands of her father.

Miller is centrally concerned about the impact of abuse on a child. Following Miller, Moore affirms that the child's proper development requires the child to see themselves in the mother. The child who is negotiating separation needs to be able to return to the mother and know they will be accepted by the mother, even though they are seeking separation from the mother.[86] The balance between going away and coming back to the loving and secure gaze is essential. Each time the child separates, they enjoy themselves without getting lost in the mirror-mirror experience.

Now, if the mother hesitates, becomes overanxious, or stops the child's separation, the child's self is crushed. As Moore notes, the "prime disorder in self-love is the repression of the self in the name of a parent identity that the child cannot afford to do without, and the disorder infects all the person's relationships."[87] Moore, commenting on Miller's insight, states that Miller demonstrates "our worst vice," namely, that "we do unto others what long before we could do nothing about it was done unto us."[88] We become persons according to the manner by which we are parented. The child grows physically but without sufficient narcissistic satisfaction, and thus, a proper love of self does not develop. Similar to the foundations of a well-built house on which other structures are built, the foundations of personal growth need to be right for other stages to progress. If these fundamentals are not right from our early growth, we could find ourselves returning to these places constantly throughout our lives, seeking healing.[89]

MOORE, EGO STATES AND THE TRUE SELF

Moore presents further observations of his own regarding the insights of Mahler and Miller. First, the dynamic tension between oneness and separation is the developmental side of our self, situated within the broader tension of finite and infinite within human existence. If the former developmental dynamic is not negotiated well, the state of "not feeling good

---

86. Moore, *Jesus the Liberator*, 5.
87. Moore, *Jesus the Liberator*, 5.
88. Moore, *Jesus the Liberator*, 5.
89. Moore, *Jesus the Liberator*, 6.

about ourselves" or "feeling bad about being who we are" gives rise to a felt rejection of our creaturely status. These negative feelings can easily work against the activities of consciousness that direct us to proper judgments of truth and judgments of value. The result is observed in overreaching or overcompensating in our lives. Miller's insight that we have to beware of the gifted child with their grandiose expectations is a manifestation of overcompensation.

Second, Moore observes that a development stage not properly integrated ends up trapping the person in an ego phase, that is, they become an "ego-still-having-to-be-built-up," and it is the ego as "compulsively self-securing that makes to seem quite unreal the journey of transformation."[90] Turning to the disciples of Jesus, Moore states that the resurrection of Jesus transforms them by grace and reverses in them an inherited tendency "to deny to this transformation any reality, to identify ego with reality."[91] In the experience of the disciples, as forgiven, Jesus reveals to them that only in the fullness of ego death will they find a final transformation.

Third, for Moore, sin is grounded in our self-hatred and alienation from the true self. At the same time, sin follows a paralyzed ego form that cannot move forward through transformation. Moore affirms Jesus as the True Self. This affirmation means that sin is our rejection of Jesus. Sin is a rejection of the true self, and the full theological description of our denial of the true self is "a certain will to non-being."[92] In chapter 7, I will unpack further Moore's understanding of the significance of Jesus for sin.

Fourth, Moore offers insights regarding Freud's Oedipus crisis and its relationship to ego states. In the Oedipal crisis, the child establishes its own sexual identity. The male child's love for the mother, which emerges after separation, finds a challenge in another claim of the mother's love, the father. The child responds by being confused since the message, at the level of feeling and psyche, is that the hedonism of being in love with the mother is not permitted.[93] If this is the message felt, then the sense of being good and worthy is further diminished. The deficit is offset by the establishment of a neophyte sexual identity and the capacity to move from attachment to the mother to attachment with another.

---

90. Moore, *Jesus the Liberator*, 6.
91. Moore, *Jesus the Liberator*, 7.
92. Moore, *Jesus the Liberator*, 12.
93. Moore, *Let This Mind*, 80.

A New Awareness

At the same time, what happens in the process of sexual identity formation is the repression of our contrasexual aspect; for boys, the repression of femininity, and for girls, the repression of masculinity. The danger of repression shows up later in life when the child becomes an adult and exhibits distorted attitudes about their sexuality and toward the opposite sex. I will explore such distorted attitudes to sexuality more deeply in chapter 12. Again, the danger is that the "not feeling good about myself" which may come to pass, gives rise to felt disesteem. Social roles and cultural orientations conspire to reinforce disesteem by promoting overreaching in the males and submissiveness in the females. Even in Western societies where women have broken out of the submissive role, they are encouraged to "have it all" and so are offered the possibility of all possibilities. This attitude is yet another example of overreaching within social groups, promoting freedom and choice above everything else. The temptation in cultures of modernity is to adhere to a sustained imaginative eclipse of Divine being and replace it with a sustained imagining of the self as the source of all meaning and values. This grandiose imagining fills one's consciousness and, therefore, feels quite compelling and irresistible to the ego state. As indicated in chapter 1, Moore states that an exaggerated self-assertion by people causes in them a rejection of God's order for the universe.

Moore proposes that our only rescue from a distorted perspective, that is, an ego-state that refuses to change, is the response of religious faith. Religious faith is born of religious love, and religious love comes about because the love of God is poured into our hearts by the gift of the Holy Spirit (Rom 5:5). We are always and everywhere loved by God since God does not make junk. While no feeling is bad, it is only by appropriating our feelings thoughtfully and intelligently, especially the more negative and dark feelings of our hearts, that we can help overcome a distortion in our judgments of truth and value. God's valuing of us restores our damaged self-esteem. God's grace can work directly in our hearts to restore a proper sense of esteem. God's grace is also at work in our parents or significant others, mediated through their patience and care, especially through these moments of developmental crisis.

MOORE, FREUD, AND CONTEMPLATION

Moore posits a vital link between the importance of contemplation to human living, the proper interaction between Freud's reality and pleasure principles, and trustfulness between mother and child in early development and trust in God. Freud's immediate contribution is the idea that the pleasure principle must accommodate the reality principle. The reality principle is an order not of our making and of which we are not the center. We approach order with an element of "intellectual passivity, I mean of passivity for the sake of integrity and freedom, a surrender to truth."[94] We do not create reality. We interpret reality, participate in reality, and contribute to changing the world. The order God has created is not confrontational or violent. It is created by God, and through our knowing of it and participation in it, it is meant to give us the deepest satisfaction. If this is the case, Freud's pleasure principle and the reality principle are less radically different than he makes them out to be. Moore insists on the need to be open to receive the order of the universe. Each act of openness is contemplative by nature since contemplation is an act of receiving. Therefore, mystical experience is not a regression back to the oceanic consciousness of infancy but a return to oneness without the loss of adult development. Moore states: "A totally difference picture of the human being begins to appear: *as emerging out of unconsciousness* [oceanic oneness] *on a trajectory which is the progressive translation of symbiosis into conscious union.*"[95]

What Freud had not noticed, and what philosophy and science had overlooked in the preceding centuries, is that the mind is not simply a "pattern maker." Moore explains: "*In other words, the mystery of mind as mirror to an order not of its making was not felt.*"[96] From the perspective of the mind as "pattern maker," the universe became passive to our conception of it, and we began to mold the universe according to the shape we wanted it to have. Consequently, humanity did not go on to ask whether our pattern corresponded to *the* (my italics) pattern that God had put into creation. Humanity came to see the universe as chaotic, heartless, and dead, and human beings as the only source of pattern and order. Moore asserts the stance taken amounts to a sickness of the

---

94. Moore, "Psychoanalysis and Religious Experience," 401.
95. Moore, "Psychoanalysis and Religious Experience," 401.
96. Moore, "Psychoanalysis and Religious Experience," 402.

intellect, resulting in the discounting of the act of judgment within human consciousness.[97]

Moore asserts that contemplation is "feeling in touch with what is ultimately real, with what reality is. Thus, feeling seeks to come into its radical exercise, and emotional development is the journey toward this blissful state. But because we have ignored this yearned-for release of feeling in contemplative participation in the divine order, we have isolated emotional development from the true trajectory of desire, from our total intentionality."[98] He insists that our desire points toward the fullness of desire with God.

One insight of Freudian psychology, especially through the insights of Mahler and Miller, is the importance of the trust between mother and infant as the infant negotiates the tension between oneness and autonomy. The trusting bond becomes the foundation for our ultimate surrender to God. Such trust implicitly signals that reality and the order of the universe is trustworthy and intelligible. Reality is not confrontational. It is the trusting bond between mother and infant that paves the way for an appreciation of order and for the realization that emotional freedom is a total consent to God's order.[99]

MOORE AND JUNG

What about Moore's appreciation of Jung? First, I have already noted Moore's differentiation between self-awareness and reflective self-awareness. Using Conn's terminology, the differentiation in the two modes of self-awareness is the difference between the "I" and "me." The "I" and "me" are in a dialectical relationship, and living within the dialectic tension potentially reveals self-knowledge. Affirming Lonergan, Moore states: "Lonergan said he never understood Jung until he realizes that 'what he calls the unconscious, I called the conscious but not attended'—perhaps even, not attendable—to."[100] The ego and the self are conscious but only sometimes attended to or objectified but not without a sustained effort of self-discovery.

---

97. Moore, "Psychoanalysis and Religious Experience," 403.
98. Moore, "Psychoanalysis and Religious Experience," 403.
99. Moore, "Psychoanalysis and Religious Experience," 405.
100. Moore, "Are We Getting," 63.

First, there is one trajectory that Moore and Jung agree on, namely, the importance of access to our psychic depths and the need to be an archaeologist of the psyche. Access to the unconscious comes from listening to our body since our body is our connectedness to everyone and everything and is a bridge to the symbols, images, and memories stored in our psychic depths.[101] The task of appropriating the symbols that emerge in the psyche is a task that both Jung and Moore affirm as vital if the person is to know what they are valuing and deciding and why they are valuing and deciding in any specific way. For Moore, only human intentionality as potentially intelligent, reasonable, responsible, and loving can give us an adequate meaning and evaluation of feelings and symbols. To attempt to negotiate the symbols from simply their absorption by the ego can lead to disaster. Moore is right to say that we must work with both our conscious and "unconscious" products. If we are to be transformed, Moore asserts the need for psychological conversion, as well as religious, moral, and intellectual conversion.

For Jung, the reason for appropriating our psychic depths is to get closer to the regulating principle of integration and individuation within the psyche, the self. However, for Jung, the self, though never empirically verifiable because it is the totality, is only detected in certain symbols of the mandala. Jung's compression of the self within the boundaries of the psyche does not take into consideration the activities of intentional consciousness. By contrast, for Moore, it is the task of the human spirit to discover our psychic depths, what he calls self-awareness and reflective self-awareness as two important modalities of consciousness. The human spirit is constituted by the activities of noticing, understanding, judging, deliberating on values, and loving. Without the human spirit, we would never come to terms with our psychic depths. Without the human spirit, we would never know the ego forms. With the human spirit, we discover the existence of the shadow and its products. While Jung compresses the person to their organic and psychic dimensions, Moore, following Lonergan, is more inclined to affirm the triple dimensions of organism, psyche, and human spirit.

Second, Moore speaks about the importance of Jung's idea of reconciling the contrasexual opposites. In the context of arousal between a man and a woman, Moore names two ingredients that bring them both together. The first ingredient is the arousal of desire awakened in us by

---

101. Moore, "Are We Getting," 64.

the other person and consisting of intense physical pleasure. The self draws sexual pleasure into its intense desire for attention. The second ingredient is the experience of arousal, which "arises from the world of dreams."[102] The centers for these arousals are the anima and animus hidden deep within us. Moore states: "Deep within me and sometimes clothing my feeling of her in a dream, there is the 'partner.' She is of my substance. She is me, but a 'me' I hardly dare to avow. At the thought of her, I feel something like guilt, the guilt of 'having it both ways:' for she is *both* myself *and* another. She is a mirror of myself and not a straight prosaic mirror like the one I shave in front of but one of deep mystery in which I can appear wonderful to myself."[103] Moore goes on to explain the role of the contrasexual anima in the male. He asserts: "She is there so that through her I can experience the woman's desire for me and so enlarge my feeling for her. The intentionality of the inner partner is not narcissistic but relational. Through the inner partner or soul, we have an absolutely overmastering desire to live both our desire for the other and the other's desire for us."[104]

Moore postulates that, after the fall of Adam and Eve, the emerging self-awareness in both Adam and Eve causes a diminishment of attention away from the other and toward themselves, with a subsequent felt strangeness of the other. But, says Moore, "If I were as vividly in touch with the woman life in myself as I am with my male desire, I would not see a 'stranger' in the woman I desire."[105] For Moore, the "inner woman" of Adam prompts him to cry out, "Bone of my bone, flesh of my flesh." This insight, which is heavily influenced by Jung's reconciliation of the contrasexual opposites, explains to Moore why there is an incest taboo. Incest is a symbol of returning to the primordial union where there was "bone of my bone and flesh of my flesh," and away from the needed journey towards self-awareness and beyond to the other as they are and not as I imagine them to be. The only kind of union between the self-aware person and another always lies forward and not back to the primordial union.

Third, Moore affirms the importance of recognizing, negotiating, and seeking to remove the projections of the shadow. He uses the notion of the shadow to understand guilt. Guilt is "the shadow of joyous infant eros, of the child 'grasping at kisses and toys' (T. S. Eliot)," and in infantile

---

102. Moore, "Original Sin, Sex," 90.
103. Moore, "Original Sin, Sex," 90.
104. Moore, "Original Sin, Sex," 91.
105. Moore, "Original Sin, Sex," 92.

guilt, what gets hidden in the shadow is the child originally and totally at home with feeling good about themselves, now stymied and made to feel they have not measured up to the expectations of their parents.[106] Infantile guilt changes into adult guilt, a failure to go out to others in love.[107] The first movement within the condition of adult guilt is separating myself from others. What gets hidden in the shadows is that we are primed to be ourselves for another. The second movement within adult guilt is a form of dislike for the other, caricaturing the other, or making the person look ugly. What gets hidden in the shadow is the goodness of the other. Both these movements complexify the shadow. Coming to grips with our shadow requires us to step back and realize what we are doing when we fail others.[108]

Fourth, for Moore and going beyond Jung, there is the shadow that we cast onto God. We project onto God an ugliness or dislike to the extent that "I received from it no reassurance, to the extent that my life in this world seems merely the plaything of blind forces, to the extent that I'm not comfortable with my life the way it is given me, beyond my control, with my body or my sex or my sexuality or any of the other innumerable things which go to form the given me, the me I cannot do a thing about."[109] Any false projection onto God goes against all that constitutes our lives and puts into the shadow a most important truth for human living: we are "self-aware, self-fascinated, questing, questioning-beings" with an "in-love-ness with the all-powerful mystery."[110]

Fifth, for Moore, the process of "psychic self-discovery" is vital for the Christian and the life of the church.[111] Moore insists that "we live in an age where spiritual health and growth demands the conscious appropriation of our psychic drives, in which no freedom worth the name is attainable, without this appropriation."[112] He understands the task of the Christian to be an archeologist of their past and buried life. Coming to terms with our buried life means coming to terms with the symbols and memories buried deep in the human psyche whose discovery alone will enable us to "pass into consciousness from a state of sleep to a

106. Moore, *Fire and the Rose*, 38.
107. Moore, *Fire and the Rose*, 38.
108. Moore, *Fire and the Rose*, 62.
109. Moore, *Fire and the Rose*, 65.
110. Moore, *Fire and the Rose*, 65.
111. Moore and Maguire, *Dreamer*, 23.
112. Moore and Maguire, *Dreamer*, 65.

state of being awake, and to know in this latter, the meaning of spiritual wakefulness."[113] What we have buried is what we have relegated to the shadow but what needs to be brought into the light and negotiated intelligently and responsibly. The buried life is what most psychologists call the "unconscious" self.

Sixth, similar to Jung, Moore affirms a connection between the process of individuation and the transcending self. Individuation brings "a person into full responsibility for his or her desire. Individuation is the emergence of a self that owns all desire as opposed to normal consciousness that is desire's slave."[114] By normal consciousness, Moore is alluding to our ego consciousness, especially in its refusal to grow or not let go of its current ego form in the face of crisis. Similarly, Moore adheres to a distinction between the ego and "the deeper center of consciousness," which Jung called the self.[115] For Moore, the deeper center of consciousness is the indwelling of God, the ground of being, and our coming to know this ground requires both the grace of God and a successful negotiation of the finite and the infinite, the relative and the absolute (Kierkegaard) or what Eric Voegelin calls living in the metaxy.[116] Moore's deeper center, open to the grace of God, stands in contrast with Jung's self, which is purely natural.

---

113. Moore and Maguire, *Dreamer*, 27.
114. Moore, *Contagion of Jesus*, 133.
115. Moore, *Contagion of Jesus*, 11.
116. Moore, *Contagion of Jesus*, 11.

6

Moore, the Grammar of Desire, and Girard

INTRODUCTION

There is no doubt that Moore considered desire one of the most significant categories for understanding our relationship with God, with others, and toward ourselves. Moore's use of desire is more than just a term by which to gain some interior perspective. For Michael Gallagher, Moore's appropriation of desire is "an ocean of energy, the realm of crucial acceptance or refusal of ultimate love."[1] Moore is the theologian of desire. This chapter will explore Moore's understanding of desire, the influence of René Girard, the weakening of desire, and the way the notion of desire shapes his theology.

DESIRE

I want to begin the chapter with other authors who have accepted the category of desire as important for understanding our lives and, compare their understanding to Moore's idea of desire. Dunne states:

> We experience desires. First, as psychological events. But their origins are buried in sub-psychological events and their effects extend beyond our psyches to the larger society and the yet unborn progeny. Furthermore, the history we inherit and the

---

1. Gallagher, "Contexts and Horizons," 59.

> history we make are always entangled in sinful desires and yet graced by a doubly self-giving God. So, if we are to understand desire in its fullest context, we should take into account a number of perspectives: cosmological, psychological, theology of history, theology of grace, biblical hermeneutics, and Trinitarian theology.... Let us begin with a partial definition that sets desire in its cosmological historical and sin-fraught contexts: desire is our experience of the burgeoning character of the universe in the throes of [an] uncertain birth.[2]

Dunne affirms that the universe is constituted by a series of interrelated and layered plateaus from the physical, to chemical, to psychological, to intellectual, to reasonable, to responsible, to the affective and loving that mold communities and direct history.[3] Through all the layers from down upward,

> there are events that instigate changes, raising the odds that a higher level of controls will emerge, and there are events that consolidate changes and so preserve any higher level of controls that happen to emerge. Within the human arena desires are part of the great hierarchy of events that instigate change. Desires are the drivers of specifically human evolutionary processes insofar as they help make us what we become. But they are also the experienceable part of a continuous creation going on in the universe.[4]

Our human nature has a say over who we are going to be, and we experience the desire to be as an inner pull that directs

> our own nature through our intelligence, wisdom, and love and particularly through our desire to do what is intelligent wise and loving. We experience desires first as many instinctual events in reaction to our perceptions, or to organic functioning much as animals do. But our minds measure the costs in our hearts, where the wisdom of following these instincts so that instinctual desires can be transformed into responsible or irresponsible desires.[5]

Happily, there is more to the dynamics of history than good and bad desires. There is also the gift of God's grace. Therefore, there are three fundamental tasks regarding desires. First, there is the intellectual task of understanding specific desires. Second, there is the task in the moral

2. Dunne, "Desire," 1.
3. Dunne, "Desire," 1–2.
4. Dunne, "Desire," 2.
5. Dunne, "Desire," 2.

realm to either allow or suppress desires since not all desires are for good objects. Third, there is a task of recognizing that in our desire for the truly good, we must take into account that our hearts are also entangled in a sinful heritage. Humanity's sinful heritage causes us to fall short of what a truly life-giving alternative might be. Our sinful heritage prevents us from carrying out what we consider to be the best option. The sinful heritage provides too little assurance that our actions will be effective unaided by divine assistance. Given this sinful heritage, we suffer from blindness, impotence, and despair and all these need the healing grace of God.[6]

Glenn Hughes affirms that each human being is always a "being-with" or relating to the rest of the cosmos, to persons, and other subjects. As we develop, Hughes states:

> Genuine freedom—freedom of attention, of reflection, of choice—comes to play its part in my individual drama. So, it dawns on me somewhere along the way that it is up to me to set about shaping myself [and] that my story is not just established, not just *fated* but also self-directed. . . . How does it happen, this freedom? . . . Already as an infant, an illumination [unlike the experience sensed by any animal that is merely animal] is pressing in me toward insights: a desire to understand and know things. This desire even in the infant is already an inchoate *notion* of reality, of being. From the beginning, I want the kind of discovery that the apprehension of meaning is. . . . A human being is a highly complex multitude of situated desires so many of which fulfilling the trajectory of sensory and emotional aims, bring us into communion with the truly beautiful and the truly sublime! Still, it is the desire to understand—the longing that both leads to understanding and constantly follows from me to seek more understanding—that is [a] distinctively *human* desire that unfolds together with our other desires to become personal and human history. . . . The desire to understand and know, and then to knowingly love—the highest design of all knowing the ultimate purpose of knowing—is human. Its presence is personhood. Its fulfillment in its incrementality is realizing of spirit.[7]

Philip Sheldrake speaks to the notion of desire to better understand Christian spirituality. He notes that where love has been allowed a role in Christian spirituality, it was predominately considered as spiritual, disinterested, and universal love (agape) rather than an engaged, passionate,

---

6. Dunne, "Desire," 3–4.
7. Hughes, "On Desire," 1–3.

and particular love (eros). He states: "Yet, desire has a particular association with eros-love. It is best understood as our most honest experience of ourselves, in all our complexity and depth as we relate to people and things around us. Desire is not the same as instincts, but actually involves a reflective element. Desire associated with our capacity to love truly. This proves itself in focused attention and equality of dedication that is deeper than duty or willpower."[8] For Sheldrake, a key teacher of the spirituality of desire was Ignatius of Loyola. Ignatius speaks of desire in relation to prayer and discernment in everyday life. His decisions are formed around a gradual process of learning how to focus his desire on choosing well. The spirituality of desire became a quest for spiritual freedom and away from displaced or superficial desires and disordered attachments that imprison us. Authentic human desires that center our attention on God and our surrender to God are "an invitation to acknowledge our immediate sense of need, but also as a starting point for a gradual unfolding of what we are most deeply concerned about."[9]

Each of these authors presents desire around five key dimensions. First, there is the desire to know, to affirm what is truly worthwhile, and to love knowingly. By discovering meaning and being meaning makers we are more able to discern what God asks of us and who we are to become in relation to others and the world. Second, there is the desire for authenticity, to be ourselves or our true selves, in response to the question: What kind of person do I want to be? Third, there is the desire for transcendence. The highest form of transcendence is being in love. The experience of love transforms us as no other experience can. Fourth, there is the acknowledgment that desires can go astray, and blindness, impotence, and despair can bear down on us and take us away from personhood. We become inattentive, unintelligent, unreasonable, irresponsible, and unloving. Fifth, God never abandons us to our inordinate desires but, through grace, heals us and helps us discover again our desire for God and a life of love toward others.

MOORE'S GRAMMAR OF DESIRE

Moore located desire in its most fundamental manifestation, long before we may desire this or that object. Desire is the condition of "just wanting"

---

8. Sheldrake, "Desire," 231.
9. Sheldrake, "Desire," 232.

or "wanting-I-do-not-know what."[10] It is Freud who first discovers the positive aspect of "just wanting." In his early works, "libido" is associated with sexual energy, and unfortunately, till today, many people still think of sexuality when they hear the word *libido*. But, toward the end of his life, Freud thinks of libido more in terms of life energy. Desire as just wanting is like an unseen undercurrent that draws out the human spirit. Just wanting is desire in its undifferentiated state and, for Moore, is "the dream of myself."[11]

As the dream of myself, desire is "a feeling good that wants to go on feeling good and looks for things to feel good about."[12] This felt sense of desire is very clear in the oceanic consciousness of the infant, which Moore affirms is a bundle of pleasurableness at birth or "a huge sea of delight, the ocean dream of self."[13] Therefore, the condition of desiring is not some response to a feeling of emptiness. It is not just wanting because one is without something. Desire is not emptiness seeking fullness. Rather, it is a feeling of fullness that seeks to keep on feeling good by going out to something or someone. Moore states that we go from "everything" to this particular thing. Indeed, it is more accurate to say that "I am a fullness."[14] Therefore, "I am" before one can say that one wants anything.[15]

Desire and the One I Desire

For Moore, one of the most fundamental experiences of desire is the desire between two people. First, a person comes into our environment, and we make them the object of our desire, and simultaneously, our feeling good about ourselves awakens in the very act of desiring them and becomes even stronger in their desire for us. In turn, one feels good and seeks to *be* good for someone else.[16]

Second, to be is to be good, and consciously, to be is to be desirable. All of our lives, we have been wanting to be desired by the one we desire. Just wanting stems from the implicit certainty that we are desirable.

---

10. Moore, *Let This Mind*, 5.
11. Moore, *Let This Mind*, 15.
12. Moore, *Let This Mind*, 5.
13. Moore, *Let This Mind*, 6.
14. Moore, *Let This Mind*, 5.
15. Moore, *Let This Mind*, 15.
16. Moore, *Let This Mind*, 6.

A New Awareness

Our implicit certainty of being desirable flows out of our self-awareness. Most especially, "I want this good feeling to be exercised in my being desired by that person. I look to the cause of my desire for the exercising of the good feeling in which my desire is grounded."[17] There is nothing more satisfying than to be desired by the one you desire and, thus, to be attractive to them. Through being desired by the other, my "desirability-propensity" is activated.[18] When one feels one's desirability, one has been actuated by another.[19]

Third, yet another way of expressing the actuation of our desirability is in one's relationship with God. While being desired by another actuates a profound sense of being desirable, being desired by God actuates one's very being moment by moment. God's desire for us expresses not only who and what we are but also "why" we are. God fully desires us, and in God's desire of us, we are fully awakened in our desirability, which prompts in each of us, when awakened, the desire to go out and desire another.

Self-Awareness, Feelings, and Desire

If self-awareness is self-presence, then we can say that "I am for myself" through self-awareness. In self-awareness, I am "selfing myself."[20] The state of "I am for myself" is an act of self-affirmation. Self-affirmation is the self-belief that one has in oneself. It amounts to being unable to not believe in oneself.[21] This belief in ourselves is our fundamental sense of ourselves. If this is the case, its opposite, disesteem, is not allowing the fundamental sense of ourselves to emerge. Therapy is grounded in the assumption that a good sense of ourselves is already there, needing to be coaxed out of us; otherwise, why would the therapist or the client bother? Through disesteem, the fundamental sense of ourselves as good, desirable, self-awareness, and self-affirming gets buried. The movement in desire is from an awakening sense of being desirable, which one picks up through desiring another, to a complete sense of being desirable,

---

17. Moore, *Let This Mind*, 6.
18. Moore, *Let This Mind*, 8.
19. Moore, *Let This Mind*, 8–9.
20. Moore, *Let This Mind*, 13.
21. Moore, *Let This Mind*, 13.

which one can affirm through being desired by the one whom we desire.[22] Moore's shorthand for such a movement is to say that being desired makes one desire-enabled. Since "I am" before wanting any particular object at all, there exists a prior affective presence to oneself, which could be described as a basic love for oneself, grounding all other objects one may come to desire.[23]

Through the recognition of desire, our desirability, and our mutual awakening to desire, feelings are the most important locus for telling us who we are. The problem of disordered narcissism, not to be confused with the natural narcissism of infants, is that we have acquired an internal image of ourselves "to the displacement of our spontaneous first-hand feeling response to what happens around us."[24] Disordered narcissistic people generally become fixated on their self-image and do not pay attention to the "self of feeling."[25] Often, the imaged self is suppressing the actual feeling self. Moore turns the insight into an axiom: the self feeling is the self felt.[26] You may not be what you imagine yourself to be, but you are what you are feeling. As discovered in chapter 1, the technique of focusing is allowing our body to tell us who we are through attuning ourselves to our feelings, and so it is opposite to "a self-image imposing itself on me imperviously to my own immediate primitive self-feeling."[27]

Being attuned to our feelings is also important to the whole of intentional consciousness. Moore turns to what he calls "the perfection of consciousness."[28] Following Lonergan, he grasps that intentional consciousness answers the question, What am I doing when I am knowing and what am I doing when I am choosing? We begin with an image and, through questions, move toward intelligence and then verify in judgment what we have understood, weighing up the evidence of our sense experience.[29] However, more importantly, Moore states that the judgment that something ought to be done about what one has learned involves

---

22. Moore, *Let This Mind*, 14.
23. Moore, *Let This Mind*, 15.
24. Moore, *Let This Mind*, 17.
25. Moore, *Let This Mind*, 18.
26. Moore, *Let This Mind*, 18.
27. Moore, *Let This Mind*, 18.
28. Moore, "New Life," 148.
29. Moore, "New Life," 151.

not just the *world of sensation* in which not so much of myself is involved... but *the world of feeling* in which the whole of myself is involved, which *is* the whole of myself becoming aware. So, while the cognitive part of the process moves from the sensed apple to the sensed apple via a sweep of intelligence, the full process moves from the primitive feeling of being alive [to] the desire to live more fully, via the whole process of learning what is going on in the world, to that direction of this feeling to the needs of the world which we know by the noble name of conscience.[30]

Moore is saying that coming to know and to value is imbued with feeling. We feel assured when a correct intellectual insight and moral insight emerge. A felt and firm grasp of reality leads to the more important issue of acting based on reality. Conscience moves us in the direction of doing the truth based on what is true and real and so, feeling at peace. This orientation is the whole thrust of consciousness in the process of realizing or perfecting itself to the full. Indeed, doing the truth reaches its apex in self-gift. Through grace, desire finds its way to the highest levels of consciousness where "joy is in self-gift" and where we discover that our original protean desire is nothing more than a hunger for the Creator.[31] Therefore, the motive for desire is never to be found in feelings of emptiness, rather, it emerges from a sense of being worthy, great, special, and unique. It is the wholly positive sense of ourselves that motivates our desire, stretching it to receive "in awesome joy, the creative act in which all being takes its origin."[32]

Desire, Power, and God

In the process of mutual desiring between people, there is power at work. When I desire another person, I come under their power. When the other person desires me in return they come under my power. Moore affirms that power is a life force, not a possession, whose interest is to unite people. The power we experience is the beauty and the goodness of the other person and when the other person comes under my power, then they experience my beauty and goodness. In the act of mutual giving and receiving, a single surrender happens, and both people are awakened to the sense of being conscious participants in a mystery that

---

30. Moore, "New Life," 151.
31. Moore, "New Life," 152.
32. Moore, "New Life," 152.

is drawing them through their feelings of self and their feelings of the other. Intimacy is born.[33] Moore calls our mutual sharing in each other's power and the intimacy that it generates "intersubjective." Intimacy is both communal and personal. It does not just happen. It is a skill and virtue that has to be developed.

God is at work in this pull toward another. Intimacy reflects a divine pull toward each other, and as such, "it is at once the opening of our *desire* to God and God's *point of entry* into us; our way of opening, God's way of entering."[34] Therefore, our desire for God springs from a sense of our worthiness and not from a sense of our worthlessness. Moore states, "A sense of worthlessness makes God unbelievable; a sense of human greatness is the threshold of belief. This threshold is that special sense of human greatness, which is had in the experience of our larger intersubjective life. We sense this intersubjective life when we understand human intimacy as a glimpse or foretaste of universal human unity."[35] Since God is at work in the pull toward one another, universal human unity is grounded in the Mystery of God. Therefore, the pull of desire for one another connects us to the power of a mystery beyond our mind's grasp but able to communicate with us through love.

Desire, Arousal, and Interdependence

The perennial philosophy of the past started with the faculty of the will or the appetite of conscious beings as desirous for the good in general. From a universal perspective, philosophy then moved to a particular perspective and philosophers placed the emphasis on the objects of desire. Thus, perennial philosophy claimed that the universal motivates each of us towards a particular object. Moore understands desiring differently. Every particular desire is implicitly a state of desiring all goodness so that one's desire for any particular object is myself with an opportunity to expand endlessly. When we are aroused by another person, we are awakened to a fullness of life, more so than was there before. Arousal puts me into the other person's power. However, it does not stay there. The other must come under my power. The dynamic becomes: the one I desire desires me and creates a relationship of interdependence between us. In the state

33. Moore, *Let This Mind*, 21–22.
34. Moore, *Let This Mind*, 25.
35. Moore, *Let This Mind*, 25.

of interdependence, we feel affirmed and we appropriate our goodness. The feeling for our goodness is our self-acceptance and the feeling the other has in their goodness is their self-acceptance.

Each of us has a role to play. At the arousal stage, there is only dependence on the power of the other to allure me. This basic arousal stage accounts for people defining desire as something or someone being drawn to someone by the allure of another. What remains hidden in the definition is that something or someone being drawn to another is drawn due to their fundamental goodness. One's desire for another person has another subject besides the other's allure over me, namely, her being a subject to whom I am attracted due to her fundamental goodness and me being her object of desire due to my fundamental goodness. This dynamic becomes a source of hope and anchors the goodness of each person.[36] Moore affirms: "Hope is desire in the skilled hands of God," and desire as hope impels us towards all goodness, toward the absolute good, God who is the cause of desire from the very beginning. It is as if God is barracking us on, which is a barracking for all goodness and for the good itself without leaving behind any particular good. In any particular good, one has sensed and touched goodness itself.[37]

Desire Is Love Trying to Happen

Now, we come to a phrase most linked to Moore and his grammar of desire. Desire is love trying to happen.[38] If, for example, rather than accepting the desire of the other responding to my desire, I reject it for whatever reason, the intentionality of desire fails, and love doesn't happen. In other words, love is not decided upon. The will becomes atrophied in a dead end and the true directionality of desire does not reach its end. The desire remains truncated in the image of being attracted to someone.[39] Moore's final insight regarding the perfection of consciousness has to do with answering the question: When am I most myself? Cryptically, Moore suggests if to be conscious is to be and to be more conscious is to be more, then to be most conscious is to be totally in love. Each of us is most

---

36. Moore, *Let This Mind*, 27–28.
37. Moore, *Let This Mind*, 29.
38. Moore, *Let This Mind*, 30.
39. Moore, *Let This Mind*, 34.

ourselves when we love and are loved.[40] Love is "being as movement" or "desire as decided for." Love is desire decided for. God actualizes our being through a movement of love, and this actualization is equivalent to what Saint Ignatius called "the consolation without a cause."[41]

Desire and Our Awakening to God

In chapter 3, I spoke about Moore's insight that we awaken to God in two ways and gave particular emphasis to contemplation as our direct awakening to God. I want to speak to our indirect awakening to God. In my desiring of another, my desirability is awakened indirectly, through directly perceiving the one whom I desire, desiring me. We become more drawn to one another, and the reason why we want the other to be drawn to us is that our awakening sense of being desirable wants to be completed by our being desired. Through the exchange, we experience an indirect awakening to God since "the mysterious energy that flows between persons, is what opens us to God."[42] Thus, human love carries at its center Divine love.

Desire and Self-love

Moore does not shy away from expressing the importance of self-love and its relationship to desire as a fundamental quality of being human. He asserts that self-love is not love *for* self but love *of* self. The love of self is the love with which I am myself in the world. The awakening of self-love is an increase in the sense of my significance. But the significance is significance for someone and that someone must be the unique person who is making me feel significant, by their desiring of me. The desire for another person issues a new feeling of my significance that he or she has awakened, and the feeling awakened is the feeling of significance for that person. Moore concludes that "self-love properly understood as creative of community reveals its roots in the mystery of existence."[43]

---

40. Moore, "New Life," 152.
41. Moore, "New Life," 153.
42. Moore, *Let This Mind*, 25.
43. Moore, "Self-Love," 32–33.

A New Awareness

Summing Up

In brief, I would sum up Moore's grammar of desire in these five points. First, created by desire, I am desirable. It is a basic truth whose meaning is only sometimes, but rarely immediately, evident. Second, as I feel desirable, I begin to desire, and desiring comes from my pleasure in myself, my feeling good about myself that wants to extend to another. Third, since it is out of being desirability that one desires another, the other causes desire in me, and to cause desire is to arouse my desirableness. Fourth, it is my desirableness, thus aroused, that makes me want to be desired by that other. To be desired by the one that I desire is truly a wonderful exchange. Fifth, the nerve center of human relationships is arousal. I am aroused by another's awakening of desirability in me through their desiring of me. The key to intimacy is that by desiring another, I come to acknowledge my desirability by another desiring me.[44]

ROY INTERPRETING MOORE

Louis Roy unpacks Moore's phenomenology of desire. First, we feel ambivalent about describing human existence from the perspective of desire. Commonly, we think of desire as dangerous and thus capable of being taken to excess and leading us to our downfall. We fear that at the end of all of our desires, we may end up with false disappointments so great as to leave us defeated by our very desires. Our experience teaches us that not all desires lead to our happiness. Over a lifetime, our desires wax and wane, becoming more important and then less important, causing us to consider whether they are really helpful to human growth. Yet, on the other hand, we know that without the fullness of desire, our knowing, valuing, deliberating, and taking action will only feel paper-thin. With desire, we feel enthralled by the energy and motive force of life.[45]

Second, because of the ambivalence we have around desire, Roy describes two camps of thinking about desire most commonly expressed. In the first camp, desire is fundamentally rooted in dissatisfaction, and so is a sign of some lack or emptiness that needs filling. However, metaphorically, as we fill the hole, the water is getting away and so there can be no long-lasting satisfaction. One's emptiness is felt as a state of suffering,

---

44. Moore, *Let This Mind*, 44–45.
45. Roy, *Embracing*, xiii.

a false conviction from the beginning that there is something wrong with us and there is something wrong with being a human being. The feeling that there is something wrong can easily develop into disesteem, self-hatred, apathy, and self-pity. At this point, we feel ourselves identifying with several mistaken affirmations: I am not worth it, I cannot accomplish much at all, and I am not worth saving. All desire comes to be seen as an attempt to assuage unmet emptiness. In the second camp, desire begins from the stirrings of an abundance or fullness first felt as an infant. We are born into the world full of life and joined to an oceanic consciousness with our mother. Our mother is there for us, and the pleasure we feel because of this felt oneness allows us to explore, grow, and be happy.

Third, Freud postulated the libidinal energy of the unconscious. Inasmuch as people often perceive libidinal energy as sexual, it is not solely sexual but a source of deep satisfaction and a creative force for other pursuits in human living. In the form of sexual energy, libido is the same as desire seeking union with others. This energy does not prevent desire from being raised to a higher integration or purpose. This energy can be directed toward committed and fruitful interpersonal relationships. Sexual libido can put us in the direction of intimacy, conversation, closeness, belonging, and friendship. The purpose of desire is to enhance self-love, self-affirmation, self-recognition, and self-acceptance. As I desire the one who desires me, I feel the attraction of the beauty and goodness of the other. Our mutual desire bolsters esteem and heads toward love for one another.

Fourth, desire and happiness are also interrelated. Roy presents us with some key insights into happiness to complement Moore's insight that being enabled to desire is the basis of happiness.[46] In the Hebrew Scriptures, we do not find happiness as a direct theme. However, God's promise to his people, their election as God's precious possession, and the covenant to stand by them, are meant to increase their happiness. Happiness is one side of the coin, while obedience to God's way is the other side of the coin. In Christian Scriptures, happiness is grounded in becoming a son or daughter of God through the life, death, and resurrection of Jesus (Rom 8:16–17). Through the light of faith and the empowerment of the Holy Spirit, the Christian is healed and enabled to put into practice the values of Jesus.

There are at least three levels to an understanding of happiness. For many, happiness is equivalent only to feeling pleasure and not feeling pain.

---

46. Roy, *Embracing*, 18–20.

Pleasure has more to do with biological vitality. We can measure our happiness by being attentive to pleasure and pain through the body. Here, happiness becomes equated with material comfort, security, and self-preservation. Happiness becomes a means to protect ourselves from the fear of death. Roy suggests that the first level of pleasure as happiness does not express the full range of the human experience, since pleasure is fleeting.

Alternatively, happiness is more enduring. While the pleasure-seeking person may never arrive at long-lasting happiness, the happy person has found a way to integrate pleasure into a range of other activities. At this second level, happiness becomes equivalent to enduring joy, permanent peace, and the fruit of a good ethical orientation. We may increase our pleasures, but we may be unable to fulfill our desire for happiness, especially if our search for happiness amounts to a search for power, control over others, superiority, and dominance. Happiness and living a good and honest life are coterminous.

At a third level, the highest level of happiness is called beatitude or blessedness. Beatitude is a fullness felt as joy or perfect peace or feeling good. This fullness and feeling good about ourselves and others can even accept the dissatisfaction and sufferings of life in an effort to grow in love, even to the point of enduring a maturing suffering. While pleasure is subordinate to happiness and can be integrated into a happy life, happiness is subordinate to beatitude. Love alone is absolute.

RENÉ GIRARD, DESIRE, AND MIMETIC THEORY

I want to unpack the influence of René Girard's phenomenology of desire on Moore. To do so, I will briefly explain some of the key insights Girard proposes and, therefore, what Moore finds most illuminating. In terms of cultural anthropology, René Girard has extensively explored the roots of violence and its relationship to religion, though it is difficult to pinpoint his writings as belonging to any one body of literature since he covers literary theory, cultural studies, anthropology, scriptural exegesis, and psychology.[47] There is much debate as to whether his writings represent a systematic theory or are simply a number of key guiding insights for understanding the perpetuation of violence in our world.[48]

---

47. Kirwan, *Discovering Girard*, 91–93.
48. Kirwan, *Girard and Theology*, 6–9.

First, Girard's writings are concerned with the nature and mechanism of desire. Girard's mechanism is summed up in this axiom: *we desire according to the desire of another*.[49] Girard departs from the Freudian notion that, as individuals, desires wait to be triggered by some enticing object. For Girard, there is no inherent quality in objects that directly attract us. Every object prior to our attraction to it has some significance within a community, and it is this significance in the community that makes it desirable to us. Therefore, Girard asserts that people form their desires according to the object being desired by another. Our subjectivity, which includes our freedom, is profoundly social and relational.[50]

Second, desire as intersubjective can be triangular: the respondent, the model, and the desired object are the three points of the triangle.[51] Desire is "mimetic" since it is based on imitation. Mimesis means that our desire is evoked in us by those from whom we "borrow" our desires (models, mentors, or mediators).[52] Indeed, we often imitate others without being fully aware that we are imitating, which also helps explain why it is that rivalry is so common. Without rivalry, desire itself can languish. It explains why people might find no significance in an object until it is appreciated by another, giving it a new meaning for them. Further, this intersubjective dimension moves desires from an instinctual base to human interiority. The intrinsic goodness of mimetic desire is that it liberates humans from instinct. It is distinguished from instinct or "appetite" since, while instinct is biologically determined toward the direction of sociality, sexuality, and self-preservation, desire is open to development.[53]

DESIRE AND RIVALRY

Normally, the structure of mimetic desire can lead to good relationships and actions without obstacles or rivalry and pacific.[54] However, when two persons desire the same object, rivalry may ensue. Girard states:

---

49. Girard, *Girard Reader*, 9–10.
50. Girard, *I See*, 137n2.
51. Webb, *Self Between*, 92.
52. Alison, *Joy of Being Wrong*, 10.
53. Kirwan, *Girard and Theology*, 50.
54. Alison, *Joy of Being Wrong*, 13; Girard, *I See*, 13. For example, Jesus invites us to imitate his desire for the Father. There is a difference between ordinary imitation and discipleship.

> Our first task is to define the rival's position within the system to which he belongs, in relation to both subject and object. The rival desires the same object as the subject and to assert the primacy of the rival can lead to just one conclusion. Rivalry does not arise because of the fortuitous convergence of two desires on a single object; rather the subject desires the object because the rival desires it. In desiring an object, the rival alerts the subject of the desirability of the object. The rival then serves as a model for the subject, not only in regard to such secondary matters as style and opinions but also, and more essentially, in regard to desires.[55]

According to Girard, rivalry can escalate to the point of violence through scandal. In possessive or acquisitive mimetic desire, one person imitates the desire of another for a specific object.[56] Rivalry ensues when both the model and respondent attempt to appropriate the same object. The model becomes both a guide (by wanting it) and an obstacle to the attaining of desire (by keeping it for themselves). The desire of the model increases and intensifies as he or she notices the desire of the respondent. The intensified desire reaches where the originally desired object loses much of its attraction and becomes secondary in importance to the model and the respondent. The rivals become more and more fascinated with each other as rivals. The respondent's desire, which is first focused on the object, shifts toward the model. The model arrives at a situation of double bind: imitate me and do not imitate me.[57] The model is both model/rival for the object and model/obstacle against acquiring the object, and therefore, a state of scandal arises.[58] The consequences are that rivals become locked in a gravitational field of attraction generated by their competition, and often violence ensues. Even if the respondent were to triumph over the model, it would not be long before the former respondent, on becoming the new model, would find another rival to be a new respondent. The more these rivalries intensify, the more the roles of model, object desired, and respondent become interchangeable at the heart of a conflict.[59]

Through this intense rivalry, the fascination that each rival has for the other makes differences disappear and each comes to possess equal amounts of envy, jealousy, and hatred. Rivals are transformed into

---

55. Girard, *Violence and the Sacred*, 145.
56. Alison, *Joy of Being Wrong*, 12.
57. Girard et al., *Things Hidden*, 291.
58. Girard, *Violence and the Sacred*, 147, 161.
59. Kirwan, *Discovering Girard*, 41.

mimetic doubles, mirroring each other's emotions and actions. The assertion of the difference between respondent becoming rival and model becoming obstacle is illusory. The loss of differences fosters even more mimetic rivalry. Desire becomes fixated on wanting to be the other. Not only do we desire what people do, how they appear, or what object they seek, but we are also moved by a stronger pull: *the desire to be*. As competition grows, the prestige of the model grows because possession of the object seems, from the respondent's perspective, to have invested the model with self-sufficiency or a greater being or some special quality that the imitating respondent lacks or feels to be lacking and finds desirable. Mimetic desire in the respondent now becomes the *desire to be another*.

In the experience, the respondent recognizes in himself an extreme weakness. It is this weakness that he wants to escape through acquiring the illusory self-sufficiency of the model. The respondent is ashamed of his life. In despair at not being self-sufficient, he searches for this self-sufficiency against everything that threatens his life and everything that thwarts his mind.[60] Girard calls this "metaphysical desire" or "primordial desire."[61] The model that evokes my desire possesses a fullness of being that I lack. Girard notes that the romantic cult of individuality or originality serves to make clear what really is at issue, namely, that through mimesis, the respondent does not seek an object of desire but the mode of existence of the model.

Metaphysical desire is the foundation for the desire of all other objects. The objects are a means to greater being and self-sufficiency.[62] We want what people have because we feel it makes us into what they are. The object is a means to an end. Yet the simplest and most popular tactic for denying our desire to possess the being of another is to attribute the source of the desire to the attractive power of objects. In this way, we can claim that the desire is our own and can discard it when we want to, without having to admit that dependency, envy, or imitation have anything to do with it. To admit dependency is to admit an inequality between ourselves as respondents and the model.

---

60. Girard, *Deceit, Desire*, 282.
61. Webb, *Worldviews and Mind*, 83.
62. Webb, *Worldviews and Mind*, 79–80.

DESIRE, RIVALRY, AND GOD

This same primordial desire can apply to a distorted desire to be godlike. Religion presents the Divine as inaccessible and impenetrable.[63] Religiously, the desire for God can become a desire to acquire the object and identity of the model, in this case, God. This desire emerges out of a sense of ontological incompleteness revealed in the dynamics of mimetic desire. The felt sense of ontological incompleteness is at the heart of our denial of death, as presented in chapter 4. To desire or obey the Divine is to turn to the source of all power, the ultimate Owner of all that is desirable.

Girard's simple assertion is that violence reflects a distorted manifestation of the sacred in archaic societies. Humans can model themselves on God so as to become like God, in order to acquire what God has and is. One strives to have the power of the Divine since one is ashamed of one's lack of being. Violent opposition toward others is the signifier of the desire for divine self-sufficiency. If all desire and desiring is primarily primordial desire, that is, seeking to overcome the felt lack of fullness of being, religion could easily gravitate to becoming masochistically structured. This is the kind of religion that is unrelated to any genuine experience of the transcendent ground in unconditional love but rather comes about due to unconscious, disordered human processes.

DESIRE, SCAPEGOATING, AND RELIGION

For Girard, a distorted feeling of religious awe has its origins in scapegoating. Religion is born in an effort to preserve the unity and peace brought about in society by the killing of the scapegoat. Indeed, for Girard, an act of collective murder against the victim is foundational to all human culture.[64] Since mimetic desire becomes mimetic rivalry, a situation of all in rivalry against all ensues and becomes the formula for social disharmony and long-term breakdown.[65] Girard proposes that social chaos in a group comes to an end when the larger group chooses a victim(s) or scapegoat(s).[66] This choosing begins in an arbitrary gesture directed against the potential scapegoat who is viewed as being responsible for

---

63. Girard, *Violence and the Sacred*, 148.
64. Kirwan, *Discovering Girard*, 54.
65. Kirwan, *Discovering Girard*, 44–46.
66. Girard, *I See*, 154–60.

the collapse of order. The situation in the group is transformed from all against all (open-ended rivalry) to all against one (blame focused on the scapegoat).[67] By choosing a scapegoat, the rivalrous groups now have a victim. The victim turned enemy can come from within or from without the society; if from within the group, the victim is expelled; if from outside the group, a "holy war" is declared, or the victim is murdered.[68] The victim, chosen on the basis of not being able to retaliate or take vengeance on the rivals, is subsequently sacrificed and becomes the bringer of unity to the group. The mechanism of scapegoating is allowed to occur and recur only because the group represses the true intent of this mechanism. Those who scapegoat never believe themselves to be murdering or expelling innocent victims.[69] Finally, it may even be the case that the perpetrators of violence pronounce the victim as God-like since, through their actions and the scapegoat's death, the group is united.[70]

This myth of bringing order out of rivalry in societies continues in post-religious societies. Girard explores the fundamental role of scapegoating in society and culture once religious rites and rituals are no longer widely accepted. As long as rites, whether secular or religious, are able to preserve the distinction between the "good" violence sanctioned and the "bad" violence of a community engulfed in mimetic chaos, then the community remains relatively stable. But when the rituals and myths of the community begin to lose their effectiveness and no longer insulate the community from violence, the community descends into a "sacrificial crisis." The erosion of the distinction between pure and impure violence means that purification and the return of peace is no longer possible, and impure, contagious, reciprocal violence spreads throughout the community. Whole groups turn on each other.[71] Girard asserts: "Inevitably the eroding of the sacrificial system seems to result in the emergence of reciprocal violence. Neighbors who had previously discharged their mutual aggressions on a third party, joining others in the sacrifice of an 'outside' victim, now turn to [sacrifice] one another."[72]

For Girard, there is only one way by which a society perceives that a distorted culture is founded on the lie of peace through scapegoating.

67. Kirwan, *Discovering Girard*, 49.
68. Kirwan, *Discovering Girard*, 52.
69. Girard, *Girard Reader*, 97–117.
70. Kirwan, *Girard and Theology*, 26.
71. Kirwan, *Girard and Theology*, 22–23.
72. Girard, *Violence and the Sacred*, 43.

It requires that a community gives rise to a slow and long discovery that victims can be innocent.[73] This affirmation directly opposes the view that there are no innocents, an affirmation that underpins an approach to conflict which makes little to no distinction between civilians and combatants. According to Girard, in the Judeo-Christian tradition, there emerges the revelation that there are innocents in any conflict and that God is on the side of the victim. In his later writings, Girard gravitated more and more towards Christianity, properly understood as the revelation of Jesus Christ as a victim who is on the side of victims to expose the true intent of the scapegoat mechanism.[74] Christ reveals the role that victimization and scapegoating play in society and he shows us the way of nonviolence. Little by little, Girard affirms that the Judeo-Christian revelation of the Divine understands God on the side of the victim and distinguishes completely from the violence of the gods. God reveals God's very being by revealing what we do when we sacralize violence.[75] This new revelation emerges as a new form of self-giving mimesis incarnated in Christ and passed on through the Spirit to the Christian community.

MOORE APPROPRIATING GIRARD

How does Moore appropriate Girard? First, Moore is wholly appreciative of the insights of Girard. There is finally an alternative to individualism, and that alternative is inter-individualism and a recognition of the importance of intersubjectivity. This emphasis fits well with Moore's assertion that desire reaches its best expression when two people mutually enhance one another. Desire is a force working in us that comes about from being put in each other's way as models "in which to recognize our desire, whether as rival or as encouragement."[76] An interdividual existence means that our desire involves us "in each other in the pursuit of security and happiness. . . . Sex is the most dramatic way in which people become interested in each other long before they have time to develop interests that they share. . . . I see myself in the other, and thus excited, I come to see the other is fascinating."[77] For Moore, the big lie is to say

---

73. Girard, *I See*, xvii–xviii.
74. Girard, *I See*, xviii–xix.
75. Williams, *Girard Reader*, 117–88.
76. Moore, *Contagion of Jesus*, 21.
77. Moore, *Contagion of Jesus*, 21.

that we are desire's subject; in other words, to use an image, we are the horse pulling the cart of desire. The truth is that we are subject, in the quite other sense of being subject, *to* desire, and we are being subject *to* it since we desire to be desired by the one that we desire. Desire is the horse pulling the cart of the subject.

Second, when one understands the model as awakening the respondent to be against the model, then desire becomes synonymous with rivalry. Our desired autonomy becomes a priority out of our confrontation with the model. Moore calls this the "self-against."[78] This self-against prevails because there is "something in our life that makes the easier way look like the *only* way, *the* way so that conventional wisdom can see conflict normative for social theory."[79] The underlying and fundamental problem is that we do not easily have a positive regard for ourselves. With this in mind, Moore proposes that when one is slighted, rather than fight back or even imitate the model, one ought get in touch with the radical wounding, a wounding that denies creativity and gives the go-ahead for rivalry. We then come to touch our original happiness that is desired, of which the denial is once again mirrored in this current offense. Somewhere in the past, the child comes into a world full of ecstasy, "only to be systematically disappointed at the real world."[80] What follows is sulking over the offense and the denial-to-me of ecstasy. As adults, each time one is offended, and the model mirrors our hostility, leading to the respondent buying into the hostility of the model, the offense persuades us to affirm a belief that we are not a gift. The temptation when the offense occurs is to go into the self-against mode and we deny the graced invitation to the reverse.

Third, Moore prefers to focus on creative and encouraging models. Creative and encouraging models invite us not to have more but to be more loving and life-giving. The encouraging model "invites into life, into participation, into being loved, and loving."[81] The encouraging model brings out the self as a gift and if one is a gift, one is given to others. Further, the problem of rivalry goes back to the problem of a lack of self-acceptance. Moore comes back to the importance of self-acceptance and self-love. He states: "If I like myself in a situation in which I am expected to imitate the other's enmity and the other gets the message, reads my smile, then what

---

78. Moore, *Contagion of Jesus*, 28.
79. Moore, *Contagion of Jesus*, 28.
80. Moore, *Contagion of Jesus*, 29.
81. Moore, *Contagion of Jesus*, 28.

is happening is the reversal of [rival-laden] mimesis; my creative pro-life modeling is displacing the other's provocative modeling."[82]

Fourth, for Moore, Jesus is the supreme and creative model. I will explore Jesus as the supreme model more extensively in the next chapter. At this point, Moore links our original open-ended desire, desire denied, and rivalry. Now, if rivalry grows out of a denial of our desired original happiness or ecstasy, then "original ecstasy is looking for something like Jesus."[83] Rivalry is the symptom of the underlying cause of ecstasy denied. Our appropriation of this original ecstasy comes to us indirectly, that is, through being desired by the one we desire who activates our desirability. One can trust being attractive to another since one is made in the image and likeness of God and this affirmation grounds a proper self-love. When one is moving toward another in attraction and love, one is actualizing the self-as-gift. The self-as-gift is the true self. If the former is the true self, then the self-against, the mode of rivalry, envy, and malice, is the ego or ego form as refusing to grow. There is potentially an enormous generosity waiting to be demonstrated, the self-as-gift, grounded in our being created in the image and likeness of God. This person becomes an enabling model, as distinct from the competitive model. Jesus is the enabling model par excellence. Moore affirms: "Jesus tests out his imaging of God all the way into the dark heart of our political inertia, to be crucified, to be returned to us, yielded up to us by the death we inflict on victims to preserve our social role, and in this new fullness to repeat his offer of peace. The risen victim is the indisputably unique model for the limitless generosity in us that, until thus empowered is helpless."[84] In Jesus, one sees all that one is meant to be and never allowed oneself to be.

MOORE, JESUS, AND SCAPEGOATING

There is no doubt that Moore appropriates the category of scapegoat and applies it to Jesus. I will examine this more extensively in chapter 7. Moore speaks of an experience that he had in the 1960s when he gave an address to the BBC. In an effort on the program to get the listeners thinking, he states: "Christianity is not a teaching on brotherly love. It is a statement of

---

82. Moore, *Contagion of Jesus*, 28.
83. Moore, *Contagion of Jesus*, 29.
84. Moore, *Contagion of Jesus*, 30–31.

something God does with brotherly hate."[85] The statement received a great deal of negative feedback from his listeners. For Moore, looking back, the statement makes far more sense given the insights of Girard. Girard is saying that distorted desire leads to conflict and beyond this to many victims "so that it is only in this victim [Jesus], revealing God as [the] victim, that he [man] can find its model for imitation."[86] Where there are victims, there has been scapegoating.

Moore speaks to the pervasiveness of scapegoating in our world:

> Now, scapegoating is the worldwide and world-old way whereby we contain this violence in us. The whole tribe focuses on one person to take it out on and this brings them together. In the ancient world, the King was the scapegoat and had to be slaughtered to hold the tribe together. Slowly people learn to cool it, and the time interval between crowning and sacrifice became longer and longer. But there are many other forms of scapegoating to take. We in this country have lived for a record number of years without war, without any official Enemy, but the process is everywhere. Politics are full of it and never more than now. Families are seldom without it—the one member everyone tends to take it out on.[87]

MOORE, SELF AS GIFT, AND SACRIFICE

Overall, Moore is wary of using the word *sacrifice* when talking about a love that "costs no less than everything (Eliot)." He has observed how sacrifice has been used incorrectly as a word of praise for a mode of oppression where the victim ends up without self-acceptance and self-love. Sacrifice can be used as a cover for having power over others. Moore uses the word *sacrifice* sparingly and prefers the term *self-as-gift*. Moore suggests:

> Actually, it is very easy to see how the total mistake about the sacrifice of the Cross arose. It comes from John's description of Jesus as the *sacrificial lamb*. Thus, the believer who contemplates the crucifix tends to see double. On the one hand, a man [that is done] to death by wicked men, on the other, a human sacrifice that by reason of the theological status of the victim is acceptable to God. Now what has to be said is that the assumption of the

---

85. Moore, *Contagion of Jesus*, 37.
86. Moore, *Contagion of Jesus*, 27.
87. Moore, *Contagion of Jesus*, 32.

role of sacrificial lamb by [himself] Jesus is *strictly and exclusively his own*, embodying his deliberate assumption of the role of the scapegoat victim which is the basis of human sacrifice, for which animal sacrifice is the substitute or dramatic euphemism. The moment the role of lamb is imposed on Jesus, the primitive attachment to sacrifice [as] violent, as bloodletting takes over and then we get the ghastly notion of the unbloody sacrifice, as the real bloody is sacrifice drained of blood for liturgical purposes.[88]

In this passage, Moore makes several points. The first is that Jesus accepts his cross freely and that is what makes his freedom so scary to us. The second is Moore's sensitivity toward the manner by which preachers and theologians have depicted the death of Jesus as sacrificial over the years. This portrayal has often put the Father of Jesus forward as the One demanding the sacrifice of his Son, and Moore is keen to correct this mistaken understanding. The third is that a distorted religious culture has interpreted sacrifice as the forfeiting of self in daily living when clearly Moore could not countenance a disordered sense of self-denial. Moore's grammar of desire points toward an ever-expanding self-formation. To forfeit the self is equivalent to lauding disesteem and self-rejection. Because we cannot give what we do not have, self-donation (self-as-gift) cannot happen before there is self-possession (self-love). I will explore this insight more extensively in the next chapter on the significance of Jesus for the believer.

But probably, the most compelling reason for Moore's aversion to the use of the term *sacrifice* is that Girard himself thinks of sacrifice predominately in the distorted form of scapegoating. Girard wants, above all, to avoid what he calls "sacraficalism."[89] However, in correspondence entered between Raymund Schwager and René Girard on August 19, 1979, there is a distinction placed by Schwager to Girard, namely that sacrifice can be understood in two ways. There is the sacrifice of the perpetrators, in this case of a violent mob, for whom sacrifice is a transfer of their collective violence onto a victim. But there is also the sacrifice of the victim as ready to accept the transfer of violence, ready to bear the sins and the human lies, but at the same time not sharing his enemy's viewpoints. The biblical texts highlight both aspects of sacrifice. I will examine in the next chapter what it means to say that the death of Jesus is a sacrifice.

---

88. Moore, *Contagion of Jesus*, 28–29.
89. Girard, "Girard-Schwager Correspondence," 95 (Aug 18, 1980).

IS ALL DESIRE MIMETIC?

There is no doubt that Moore appropriates wholeheartedly the insights of Girard, especially when Girard presents a theory around desire that brings out its intersubjective nature. This intersubjective element fits well with Moore's understanding of desire as reaching its full potential when the one I desire desires me, and so releases my desirability. However, other scholars cannot accept the basic premise offered by Girard, namely, that all desire is mimetic. To do so would be equivalent to saying that we are all imitating the desires of others.

One scholar who parts company with Girard is Neil Ormerod. Ormerod affirms aspects of mimetic theory as true, such as when parents catch their children fighting over toys. The fact that a child (the model) desires a toy immediately makes the toy more desirable for the other child (respondent), thus laying the ground of desire between respondent and object. In rivalry, the respondent and the model become competitors within the same field of action often due to their proximity to one another. The respondent then becomes a mimetic rival, with whom one competes, always seeking the prized object for their possession. Since rivalry can reach a pitch within a society to the point of destroying it, it is resolved that a single victim, the scapegoat, signaled out as the cause of the rivalry. One way of talking about Girard's category of desire is in terms of "elicited desire." Here, the desire for an object is accounted for by way of desire being elicited from us through our contact with another person. However, even if we can posit elicited desire, Ormerod argues: "The favorite example of children competing for a toy works well with a particular object of desire, but less well for higher level goods. One cannot compete in the same way over a common desire for justice or truth. They cannot be possessed exclusively like a toy."[90]

The prospect that Girard is drawing attention to elicited desire leads Ormerod to question what Girard would say about Lonergan's natural or innate desire discussed in chapter 1. Natural desire is the desire for meaning, truth, and goodness, and ultimately a desire for God. It originates in the desire to question.[91] Ormerod states: "The questioning drives all our science, mathematics, scholarship, philosophy and theology. Its proper object is being itself, with the desire to know constituting a 'notion of being' within consciousness. Lonergan refers to the desire to know as

---

90. Ormerod, "Desire and the Origins," 5.
91. Ormerod, "Is All Desire," 253.

'detached and disinterested' to distinguish it from the various other desires/attachments which create a polyphony within consciousness."[92] When we become aware of desire, we speak of being conscious of it, first in the desire to notice, then in the desire to understand, third in the desire for a judgment of the truth, and fourth, in the desire for a judgment of value. It is from value, from worth that the humans make their best choice.

Our innate desire can indeed be rendered ineffective through bias and distortion, including the distortion of rivalry, but it is also true that innate desire predates any imitation of others. Through bias, instead of seeking the path of self-transcendence, which is the natural orientation of the self, one instead seeks the path of a descending and deficient transcendence. Therefore, there is no doubt that the path away from self-transcendence can lead to rivalry and violence. There is also no doubt that positive mentors can help us to seek the path of self-transcendence and away from the path of perdition. We may be set on the path of rediscovering the desire to know, value and love by learning about it from another and admiring its achievements in another. However, we discover the orientation of self-transcendence by finding it in ourselves and in our desire for what is true, what is good, and what is beautiful rather than by imitating another person. Therefore, self-transcendence is an intelligent and responsible set of activities innate within human consciousness.

Ormerod suggests a number of indicators for this innate desire. First, the clue to this innate desire lies in Girard's own performative desire to know and to value. He states:

> First, there is the extensive familiarity Girard developed in relation to literature, identifying a significant *set* of *data* to draw upon. Out of that familiarity, there emerged a particular *insight into the data*, the role of my memetic desire in relationships. This was an interesting and important insight, but did stand up to judgment. Girard expanded the range of data to take up materials from a broader base, materials from primal religions and cultures. He found further and further confirmation of his insight in the broader range of data. Having found this further *empirical data to ground his judgment*, he then acted to publish his wide-ranging insight into mimetic scapegoating and the origins of religion and culture. He took *responsibility* for making his insight grounded in judgment more widely known and understood.[93]

92. Ormerod, "Is All Desire," 253.
93. Ormerod, "René Girard," 5–6.

The acts within consciousness that Girard performs are not imitated. They are, at their best, an example of an autonomous process of acts where one act follows another from noticing to understanding to judgment to deliberating. Ormerod is telling us that when we are attentive to our own performance, we can identify the innate desire to know and value. Insight is not mimetic.[94] When we are not attentive to our performance, we might miss the errors in what we affirm and the error when we over-determine meaning. For example, Rudolf Giuliani, in an address to journalists, proclaimed to them there is no truth. If we follow his performance, he is saying: "The only truth is that there is no truth; remember that!" On the one hand, he is asserting truth, and, on the other hand, he is negating truth. Therefore, his assertion to those journalists is a massive contradiction based on his performance.

Second, Ormerod suggests that we compare the notion of *homo imitator* to the more traditional notion of humans as rational animals with an intellectual and spiritual soul not reducible to the brain. This comparison helps us distinguish between an empirical and a teleological view of the human person. The teleological view affirms that we are rational and are meant to be intelligent, reasonable, responsible, and in love. Teleologically, we are oriented toward truth, goodness, and objectivity. However, this is not to discount wholeheartedly Girard's mimetic theory outright. Ormerod concludes:

> The mimetic quality becomes even more overpowering, inasmuch as we fail to be attentive, intelligent, reasonable, and responsible in negotiating our desires. Girard is right to say that many of our desires are not original or autonomous but mimetically derived. Inasmuch as we fail to objectify that and deal with them responsibly, they will inevitably [with the inevitability of moral impotence] result in conflict and scapegoating; however, we can also recognize the fact and deal with it responsibly, in whom we choose to imitate and why we choose to imitate them.[95]

Then, there is the question of God. How does the respondent stand in regard to God? Is it a relationship grounded in mimetic rivalry "with a resolution in the obliteration of distinction through absorption into the divine?"[96] Is our relationship to God simply destined to be another

---

94. Ormerod, "René Girard," 7.
95. Ormerod, "René Girard," 8.
96. Ormerod, "Desire and the Origins," 5.

form of primordial desire grounded in the desire for self-sufficiency? Is the insufficiency we feel that brings on a sickness to be read metaphysically or is it an empirical fact that arises from our proneness to sin? Or is the deficiency felt by us in the gulf between the finite and the infinite authentically overcome through union with the Divine, a union enabled by God's unconditional love and a union that fulfills our desire without the obliteration of our identity?[97] These insights require us to proceed slowly in adopting Girard without critique.

THE WEAKENING OF DESIRE AND ORIGINAL SIN

Finally, I want to turn to a number of insights by Moore about the weakening of desire. Moore speaks to the weakening of desire through the doctrine of original sin and personal sin. I will leave personal sin to chapters 7 and 8 and focus now on original sin.

First, for the most part of Moore's life and thought, the meaning of original sin is uppermost in his thinking. If, at our best, we desire to trust life, want to know the truth, value goodness, and love unconditionally, then original sin is a weakening of that desire.[98] Thus, there emerges the task of coming to terms with our enmeshment in a sinful heritage, which may lead us into further blindness, impotence, and despair.

Original sin is inertia woven into the human condition. This inertia causes us to be inattentive, unintelligent, unreasonable, irresponsible, and unloving. Original sin operates below the level of personal sin. At one point, Moore calls it Lonergan's "flight from understanding."[99] It is a pervasive refusal to understand through resistance to change and a new life.[100] This pervasive refusal is far more radical than the patterns of sin which may follow. Long before personal sin tightens its habitual grasp on us, original sin is already at work. It is echoed in the assertion there is something very wrong with us, with the mistaken idea of ourselves as a mistake, and the assertion that we were not wanted apart from what our mother and father may have needed of us as part of their hopes and fears. Original sin is the doctrine of our universal cut-off-ness from the source of all well-being.

    97. Ormerod, "Desire and the Origins," 5–6.
    98. Moore, *Jesus the Liberator*, 5.
    99. Moore, "Communication," 56.
    100. Moore, *Let This Mind*, 90.

Second, original sin gives rise to the pain of felt self-rejection. Moore states: "I began to see an unconscious refusal, a failure of man to come to some great meeting place, stopping short. And though this route is unconscious, it is a very powerful, a refusal powered by a nameless and pervasive fear. . . . A refusal so powerful, so influential of all behavior, so unreachable in its roots, that even the fear that powers it seldom goes by that name."[101] This fear issues in the sense that our desire cannot be trusted.[102] One's feeling bad about oneself or feeling bad about feeling good is the origin of our undoing and is present long before we have engaged with it in action. Eventually, personal sin develops even more into a reluctance to grow, to open the mind, and may even be aided by the mechanism of repression, blocking needed images for emotional and moral insight.

Moore also speaks of original sin as consciousness shaped and trapped by fear, guilt, and self-punishment. He states that "original sin is our anti-desire on the analogy of anti-matter. It is our original resistance to the tendency of desire to bring us together. It is anti-desire, that is, the root of unloving."[103] While in later life, we may distinguish between sins and mistakes, original sin "is at the deepest level, where the distinction has not yet risen, it is an original resistance that is indistinguishably stupid and malicious."[104] Using the language of Freud, Moore proposes that original sin is our death wish. Moore's specific use of the term *death wish* has in mind the nuclear arms race and the attitude of Mutually Assured Destruction that gives rise to this race, and the tragic plight of hunger in the world, including, and more personally, "your own unaccountable behavior" and "arrested development."[105]

THE BIRTH OF SELF-AWARENESS AND ORIGINAL SIN

Moore proposes an understanding of original sin in terms of the development of human consciousness from animal consciousness to the traumatic birth of self-awareness. Animality carries an original hedonism. It concerns itself with procreation, security, and nourishment. In animal consciousness, awareness is only at a sensitive level. With

---

101. Moore, *Crucified Is No Stranger*, x.
102. Moore, *Let This Mind*, 83.
103. Moore, *Contagion of Jesus*, 131.
104. Moore, *Let This Mind*, 114.
105. Moore, *Let This Mind*, 114.

the development of human consciousness comes self-awareness and the possibility of reflective consciousness. This massive and explosive development generates a crisis and any crisis renders growth less than automatic and assuredly dramatic. This crisis signals a shift happening in consciousness from an undifferentiated state of being, by which we experience a felt oneness with everything else, to life as experienced, understood, and evaluated and, as such, life in our hands, of our own making, and to which we are accountable. He states: "There is a sense that life, which yesterday was everywhere in everything, is now in our hands. . . . There is a sense of enormous disproportion between the all-encompassing mystery enshrined in a 'forest of symbols,' and its conduct 'in our hands.'"[106] Although we are an animal species, in and through our birth into self-awareness, we experience something that shatters any continuity between animal and human psychic life.

THE MYTH OF THE FALL AND ORIGINAL SIN

For Moore, understanding original sin means grasping the importance of myth, especially, the myth of Adam and Eve from the book of Genesis. The Adam and Eve myth in the life of the church has been understood over the centuries as a form of the "myth of the golden era."[107] The myth of the golden age invariably postulates that things were better at the beginning before a dark tragedy visited society. It is usually couched in the form of a narrative that describes human origins as an original blessedness and harmony between the group. The theme of a golden era arises out of "a profound sense of nostalgia, a sense of longing for the way things were."[108] Long before the trauma in the shift from animal to human consciousness and before the need to work things out intelligently, rationally, and responsibly, life is experienced more simply. Life is experienced akin to Freud's oceanic consciousness, enjoyed by the baby within the womb of the mother, completely one with the mother, and without any feeling or thought of a personal separate identity. After the trauma, there arise the difficulties of understanding the truth and, doing the truth and being accountable for one's actions.

---

106. Moore, *Let This Mind*, 78.
107. Ormerod, *Grace and Disgrace*, 145.
108. Ormerod, *Grace and Disgrace*, 145.

The idea that such stories are mythic narratives does not take away from their truth value. Myth is a type of communication that differs significantly from rational and evaluative consciousness. Myth touches on our imagination and employs symbols. It, therefore, contains a symbolization of truths. We are dealing with truth at an elementary level of meaning. The symbols employed are dense with feeling and they have the potential to carry a multiplicity of meanings. They are placed in the narrative to motivate and energize our feelings. Feelings orient us toward values, including the ultimate value of the Mystery of God. They also can disturb, frighten, and obscure our thinking. Symbols require, therefore, a subsequent stage of attention, questioning, and judgment so that we can get a hold of their full meaning. The myth of the golden age carries a before-and-after narrative telling. The after is usually associated with a moral struggle. In the face of this moral struggle comes "an implicit awareness of the divine, the source of all moral being. The development of moral consciousness brings with it the first taste of the transcendent, the implicit horizon of all our deciding."[109]

Moore judges the story of Adam and Eve as vital to our understanding of the shift from animal consciousness to human consciousness. However, with regard to church teaching, instead of understanding the story within the context of all its mythic power and truth and as a narrative that speaks to the trauma felt in the birth of self-awareness, Moore states:

> Traditional theology has taken the story literally in the important and fatal particular that *before* the crucial event, the couple is self-aware and God-conscious beings. Thus, the way was effectively blocked again seeing the Fall as the birth of our consciousness and the beginning of our God-awareness as we lost the pre-conscious primordial union to which we are now drawn as conscious beings. In other words, the revelatory mirror to our condition was rendered opaque by monkish thinkers. And it has taken the eventful century since Darwin for us to realize that not to believe in original sin is not to believe in evolution; for it is never to have appropriated emotionally, the traumatic implications of apes becoming self-aware.[110]

---

109. Ormerod, *Grace and Disgrace*, 152.
110. Moore, "Original Sin, Sex," 88.

DEVELOPMENTAL TRAUMA AND ORIGINAL SIN

The myth of Adam and Eve will speak to us more profoundly if we can find an analogy for it in our individual development. Moore proposes an analogy in the crises of development visited on children and presented through the insights of Sigmund Freud, Margaret Mahler, and Alice Miller. The first crisis, explored by Mahler and Miller, is the separation crisis between the child and the mother. The second crisis is Freud's Oedipal crisis through which the child comes to sexual identity. I spoke about the content of each of these crises in the previous chapter. The point is that each of these events requires the individual to break through to a new level of consciousness.

In the separation crisis, we cannot remain in the state of oceanic consciousness. Only through our separation from the mother, even as we wish to return to her for reassurance, do we end up growing. In the Oedipal crisis, explored originally by Freud, each of us must come to our sexual identity. Sexual identity is clearly a complex issue and biology is not enough to determine it. One of the clear differences between ourselves and the animal world is the question: With whom will we mate? In the animal world, there is no incest taboo, and mating is often on the basis of instinct. With the breakthrough of human consciousness and the birth of self-awareness, incest becomes an issue. Moore states that "in primitive societies, the strongest of all the taboos is on incest, sexual relations with sibling or parent or son or daughter.... The existence of a strong prohibition means the existence of a strong temptation."[111] Removing the incestuous union is one way of promoting a venturing forth into the more threatening world of intimacy beyond the family circle.

Nor can we remain undifferentiated sexually. Each of these crises can be either poorly negotiated or well negotiated. Each crisis opens up the possibility of a new horizon, new questions, new insights, new values, and decisions for growth.[112] However, when the crisis is poorly negotiated, we come across the wounding of disesteem and self-rejection in our being, creating an inertia in the human condition. Due to inertia, we "get the feel and shape of the human condition as one of less than full aliveness and of consequent concentration upon itself. By far the most

---

111. Moore, *Inner Loneliness*, 51.
112. Moore, *Let This Mind*, 79–80.

dramatic way of presenting this condition is to see it in the trauma of self-awareness.... From this trauma, we are still trying to recover."[113]

THE MYTH OF ADAM AND EVE REVISITED

Moore proposes an interpretation of the mythic story of the fall of Adam and Eve in a new light. Man is alone in the garden. God creates woman, and man cries out, "At last, this is bone of my bone, flesh of my flesh." Moore interprets life in the garden as "an immemorial rhythm . . . rudely interrupted by a drama."[114] God issues a command to both man and woman not to eat the fruit of the tree of the knowledge of good and evil. The serpent claims that God has placed this prohibition on them only because God is envious, and that an envious God knows full well that by eating the fruit, they will also be like gods. They do eat the fruit and find it delightful and their eyes are open to the sexual novelty of shame, prompting them to hide from the Mystery now felt by them to be menacing and threatening. The command to not eat the fruit symbolizes the anomaly of our lives and the direction it could take when placed in our doubtful hands.

For Moore, what happens in the garden, when Adam and Eve eat the fruit and hear the voice of God calling them, is what Moore calls their "first focus" in the socio-drama as well as their resistance to the free forming of a new focus. The new focus would have brought them back to the time they spent with God in the garden, suggestive of a felt awakening of their being desirable and, in this case, absolutely desired by God; sadly, the result is a resistance "to the spirit of life that would lead us out into a fuller existence and to the hedonism which makes for the mutual surrender of man and woman."[115]

Suppose original sin is the first denial of our desirableness. In that case, the first denial of wanting to go out to others, to be good for others, and to feel good about ourselves, then "previous to this first denial is the profound change in feeling that invites the denial, the ambivalence of our sense of being good."[116] If one does not feel good about oneself, one ends

---

113. Moore, *Let This Mind*, 80.
114. Moore, *Let This Mind*, 78.
115. Moore, *Let This Mind*, 80.
116. Moore, *Let This Mind*, 81.

up not doing what is good. Not feeling good about oneself is the origin of the sin of not doing what is good.[117]

Moore's novel way of understanding the origins of original sin parts company with a more traditional Christian view, which emphasizes pride or arrogance. In Moore's view, original sin comes from feeling bad about feeling good. As far as God is concerned, Adam and Eve remained totally desirable as the desired ones of God. God still intended man and woman to be one. Their feelings and desire for one another are not bad but good as far as God is concerned. They still belong to the whole human family.[118] However, due to original sin, the mindset of humankind is different. Humans begin to view themselves as not very desirable, the prospect of a fuller life as only illusory, an increase in conflict between the sexes as normal; and these distorted and false convictions give rise to persons grasped by biases and afraid to change.[119] Humankind has even been persuaded that no changes are possible because of original sin, which ends up being "the belief that human nature cannot change."[120] Thus, the distorting voice of original sin keeps saying there will always be war, slavery, hostility, envy, and division.

In the mythic story of the fall, the serpent seeks to explain God's forbidding of the fruit: eating the fruit they would be like God or gods and have the knowledge of good and evil. According to the serpent, God issues the prohibition out of envy. Complementing Moore's insights, John Jacob Raub proposes that the couple's eating of the fruit with the hope of becoming god-like opens the way for adopting a completely alien standard for themselves as creatures. The new status of being god-like determines they measure up to a new standard of being a seat of judgment and criticism, a standard afforded to them by the full knowledge of good and evil. The standard implicitly carries the rider that self-judgment and self-criticism are inevitable.[121] The desire for godlikeness hides the couple's felt self-rejection of their humanity and limitedness. The standard of self-judgment contributes to their shame of nakedness. Shame comes from the realization that they are not a god. It is as if Adam is saying to God: In my nakedness, I can see that I am not like the gods. I might even say that I am separated from the gods. I am, therefore, weak, bad, imperfect,

---

117. Moore, *Let This Mind*, 83.
118. Moore, *Let This Mind*, 84.
119. Moore, *Let This Mind*, 85.
120. Moore, *Let This Mind*, 85.
121. Raub, *Who Told*, 9.

wrong, and unsuccessful. I am not what I should be. Because I feel shame for not being who I should be (god-like), I feel guilt. I am afraid and so I have hidden myself.[122]

Further, self-criticism gives rise to a neurotic guilt for not being the supreme human being, for not being god-like. The guilt one carries for not being the supreme human will lead to behavioral guilt and existential guilt. Our identity can become guilt-based, coloring all our dealings with people, projects, and purposes.[123] Guilt gives rise to a felt sense of being "split off" from God and is another manifestation of original sin.[124] The guilt can also give rise to false ideas that we project onto God. We project onto God envy, jealousy, and rivalry. We project onto others the punishment we feel ought to be our lot for not measuring up. We project onto the task of building society, a verdict of rivalry, division, and alienation as the norm. Powering shame and guilt, our projections render false ideas about the real God, people, and society.[125] Ironically, one's dependence on the true God will be the pathway to freedom.[126]

If shame gives way to guilt, then guilt gives way to judgment, fear, and punishment. We judge others by writing them off. We write people off according to the strict polarity of good and bad, right and wrong, should and should not be, rewardable and punishable.[127] We tie our judgment to what we have learned negatively about others and from the people who taught us. When these people become "our gods," judging becomes part of our security, and it ties us to them. No matter how painful or destructive that bond may be, we don't want to undo it. Fear comes from the feeling of being punished or abandoned by these voices whom we have internalized.[128] We fear having to face things apart from them. Adam says to God: "I was afraid." Adam sees himself as guilty and fears that God will only see him as guilty. When we fear God, we make God into an idol.[129] Our fear declared that God's forgiveness is not for us. For the sake of our security, we would rather live in guilt and fear, than live in the freedom of God.

122. Raub, *Who Told*, 10–12.
123. Raub, *Who Told*, 21.
124. Raub, *Who Told*, 21.
125. Raub, *Who Told*, 22.
126. Raub, *Who Told*, 14.
127. Raub, *Who Told*, 23.
128. Raub, *Who Told*, 24.
129. Raub, *Who Told*, 29.

A New Awareness

By contrast, the traditional view of original sin is very different. Prior to the fall, Adam and Eve are considered self-aware and God-conscious beings. The fall, then, becomes their rejection deliberately of God due to their sin of pride. Alternatively, Moore understands the fall in another way. Prior to the fall, there exists a primordial union between the couple and God, similar to the union between child and mother in the period of oceanic consciousness. Adam and Eve walk in the garden together with God, as if there exists an unbreakable union. In other words, the distinction between God and themselves had not yet been grasped. After the fall, they are God-conscious for the first time, distinct in themselves. The undifferentiated felt union of the couple in their pre-fall condition has been lost through self-awareness and the mounting sense that life is in their hands. However, this lost felt union causes the desire for its return, back to the felt experience of being one with the whole. But they cannot go back. The trauma of this change causes them now to experience God, who originally desires them into being, as a threat. The birth of our self-awareness and the knowledge of good and evil bring a collapse to the felt experience of their true nature as "God-originated, God-directed, and God-destined beings."[130] We cannot go back to the time before self-awareness. We must look forward.

Lastly, after the fall, Adam and Eve feel the power of death. It is not that Adam and Eve would not have died prior to the fall; rather, their understanding of death has changed. It is no longer death as a natural process but death as destruction and dissolution. This view of death causes a negative kind of self-absorption brought on by the threat and fear of death. It causes us to weaken our desire by becoming an isolated self and reorienting our desire into self-absorption. Turned to ourselves, we are weak "in that which lies beyond ourselves. We are fallen into ourselves. Lacking heaven, we fall into the hell of our separateness."[131] The beginning of self-awareness and the experience of death could have been different. Self-awareness could have brought a widening of possibilities under the direction of God. But instead, under the influence of original sin and the fear of death, we lapse into a lack of self-transcendence. Rather than experiencing enhancement, we experience diminishment.[132]

---

130. Moore, *Let This Mind*, 90.
131. Moore, "New Life," 157.
132. Moore, *Crucified Is No Stranger*, 69–70.

7

Moore and the Person of Jesus I

INTRODUCTION

For well over fifty years, Moore wrote about the person of Jesus, his life and ministry, his message, the significance of the cross and resurrection, his redemption, the meaning of salvation through Jesus, our liberation of desire in Jesus, the impact of Jesus on the disciples, and the call to follow him today. As I mentioned in chapter 2, Moore describes himself as a monk obsessed with the crucified Jesus. This chapter will map out Moore's thought development toward his understanding of the significance of Jesus risen for us today.

EARLY EXPLORATIONS: THE HISTORICAL JESUS

If one reads the kind of theology Moore wrote in the 1940s to 1950s and compares it to his writings in the 1960s, one immediately notices a chasm of difference. His theological reflection of the earlier period is densely philosophical and often turgid in style. Before the 1960s, Moore offered diverse insights on the Trinity, redemption, and Jesus' self-knowledge. Post-1960, the reader notices Moore turning away from dogmatic concerns to more biblical ones. A reason for the shift is the kind of people Moore is meeting. By the 1960s, Moore met a different set of Christian believers, lay men and women in parishes, who were intelligent yet unsophisticated in the art of theologizing. The Second Vatican Council has happened, and in its wake, the biblical, liturgical, and catechetical movements have all been given a new lease of life and a new focus.

In matters of Christology, various trajectories are taking theologians away from a preoccupation on dogmatic issues concerning Christ to historical issues concerning Jesus of Nazareth. Scholars had already proposed the first iteration in the quest for the historical Jesus with Hermann Reimarus in the mid-eighteenth century, and another group of biblical theologians initiated a second quest in the early 1950s. Loewe assesses the results of the old quest in these words:

> What emerged from the Old Quest was the recognition that when the New Testament submitted to historical scrutiny, the resulting historical image of Jesus differs from the gospel portraits of Jesus as the Christ. That difference, in turn, appears to be a dichotomy. From Reimarus's failed Davidic Messiah to Schweitzer's mistaken apocalyptic preacher, from Bauer's denial of Jesus's existence to Wrede's claim that Jesus is unknowable by historical methods, the contrast between what is thought to be known of Jesus historically and now is regarded by traditional Christian faith seemed no less than a contradiction ... The Old Quest, it seemed, left Christians stuck with Kahler's dichotomy between the historical Jesus and the Christ of faith.[1]

In the later period of the Old Quest, there are a variety of positions regarding the Jesus of history. For different reasons, the biblical scholar Rudolph Bultmann and the dogmatician Karl Barth, also affirmed the quest for the historical Jesus as impossible. This position largely prevailed till 1953 when a new generation of scholars took a second tilt at the question, and this became known as the New Quest for the historical Jesus. Ernst Käsemann proposes that the quest is legitimate since, he argued, there is some historical basis for the Christian faith. Not only is the quest legitimate, but it is also necessary to dispel thoughts that the Christ of faith is mythological and to assert a continuity between the Jesus who walked Galilee and the Christ who sits at the Father's right hand. The new quest receives a more decisive impetus due to the new knowledge in historical research. Regarding the Catholic approach, theologians could not sidestep that even the Creed presents several indicators of historicity: he was born of the Virgin Mary, suffered under Pontius Pilate, crucified, and buried.

---

1. Loewe, *Introduction*, 32.

JESUS AND HIS MESSAGE

In this context, we can better appreciate where Moore is standing. In the 1960s, Moore began to focus on the person of Jesus as a historical figure. Moore is intrigued by the questions: What did his listeners experience when they heard his words and saw his actions? What was the dent in their worldview created by Jesus? These questions implicitly reveal Moore's approach to Jesus, namely, that we can only understand Jesus and his mission from the perspective of his collision with the world.[2] Confrontation and collision become Moore's keywords when speaking about how Jesus would have come across to his listeners. It may be only coincidental, but at the same time, Italian film director Paolo Pasolini wrote and directed *The Gospel According to Matthew*, which depicted a very confrontational Jesus. To emphasize the confrontational stance by Jesus, Moore recalls being a seaman on the HMS Rodney and hearing one of his mates say to him: "God couldn't have sent his son. It just isn't that kind of world."[3]

For Moore, Jesus does not move around Galilee, speaking in low and docile tones. Jesus' approach to his mission and ministry is incomprehensible to those in the gospel who listen to him. He notes: "[Jesus] was asking God what no man had ever asked of him, that he would change the nature of things, that he would vindicate him in the assertion that the reign of God was not an idea, but a fact and the fact that knew no bounds, no distinctions between the political world in which some men strive to realize the idea and the spiritual realm in which others pursue it."[4]

Again, what Moore longs for is some account of the confrontation between Jesus and those on the receiving end of his words. Jesus is a revolutionary in a broad sense. To say he is a revolutionary is to assert a an acknowledged difference without separation between the political and the spiritual. The dichotomy between religious and political did not exist for his listeners. Jesus did not set out expressly to be a threat to the established order. But the new world, coming in his person, his teaching, and relationships, would not have come if only they had followed his teaching alone. It is something that is coming whether they follow it or not. The new world could not fit into their old ways of thinking. Primarily, Jesus stays in the shade about himself and his identity, so the

---

2. Moore, "Search for the Beginning," 81.
3. Moore, "Search for the Beginning," 82.
4. Moore, "Search for the Beginning," 86.

people conclude from their own spiritual resources he is the King Messiah. He leaves it to his listeners to make of him, whomever they could. Jesus speaks the language of the kingdom or the reign of God, which is inflammatory to his listeners. Moore states that to force upon people something more than what they understand humanness to be is to provoke in them a reaction. Their reaction's inadequacy to the whole must be a collision against that part of Jesus, which is all they see.[5] Surprisingly, it is the kingdom that would come through his total failure.

Therefore, Moore concludes:

> The gospel documents are a head-on collision between the human and the truly divinely human in which man is knocked silly into the glory, the Resurrection. There is only one way to the kingdom: it is the way taken by all good men who protest at the pettiness, the greed, the fear, the slavery by which we live. The cross and the Resurrection live at the end of that way, and the only thing that distinguishes the Christian is how far he can see and is prepared to go.[6]

The contentious aspect of the words of Jesus reveals the shocking truth that the kingdom has come, and the world seems unchanged. Jesus does not come to his trial because he is a troublemaker. Jesus becomes the way for his detractors to formalize a conflict unique in human history, a conflict due to their whole existence, and a view of sin that equates with falling short of the kingdom.[7] Life meets an obstacle in us, and in that rejection, it explodes into the resurrection, where death gives way to life.[8] Our discovery of the reality of Christ will not be found in our "fitting in" with the world but in our ability to "be centered" in the new world of Jesus.

THE CROSS, HIS DEATH, AND RESURRECTION

For Moore, Jesus' option to go up to Jerusalem demands an epiphany at the crossroads of life unhedged by the protective screen of culture. Therefore, the birth of religious faith is unaccountable solely in terms of ordinary psychological terms. While the church as the community of faith grows to a level of being able to express dogmatic truths about Jesus,

---

5. Moore, *No Exit*, 88.
6. Moore, *No Exit*, 103.
7. Moore, *No Exit*, 130.
8. Moore, *No Exit*, 106.

Moore's concern is to demonstrate that the dogma does not prevent the believer from the human workout of understanding what gave birth to it.[9] It is just as important to affirm "Jesus died for us" as it is to understand why this event occurred.[10] To know why people clamored for his death is to begin to understand why his death is redemptive. This human workout is essential for today's believer, that is, the human workout of naming historically what helps and leads Jesus to Jerusalem for the Passover. In Jesus, what it means to be fully human is happening for the first time, and his person and message call for a new single-mindedness.[11] In Jesus, human life is being restored to its original meaning and a new pattern of relationships. In Jesus, someone unique enters our lives in an unprecedented way and into the religious history of humankind. Jesus is the fulfillment of all the religious ideas humankind has ever had.[12]

At this stage of his Christological thinking, Moore already appreciates the uniqueness of the cross. The cross becomes a fascination for him throughout his life as that "event that evades all our categories and confuses all our human values, reducing to common dumbness all the sons of men."[13] It might be said that Jesus' message about the kingdom is confrontational and leads to his death while not "asking for" death. It seeks death as the place of its "working out." Moore affirms that "his love of men takes the shape of death."[14] Jesus puts death at the center of the kingdom, a human polity that one entered only by personally dying.[15]

The old religious world dies in the crucifixion, and the new one is born.[16] The old religion gives way to a new revelation. The new revelation finds the apostles preaching not so much a Jesus of goodness but Jesus as someone badly treated through the actions of mistaken people. They preach about a crucified Jesus and the resurrection as the outlandish event that got Christianity off the ground. Indeed, "no prophet in his wildest moments could have dreamt of such a counterblast as was Calvary."[17] The significance of the crucifixion is immense, for it

---

9. Moore, "Search for the Beginning," 88.
10. Moore, *No Exit*, 10.
11. Moore, "Search for the Beginning," 89–90.
12. Moore, *No Exit*, 9.
13. Moore, *No Exit*, 33.
14. Moore, *No Exit*, 24.
15. Moore, *No Exit*, 91.
16. Moore, *No Exit*, 74.
17. Moore, *No Exit*, 74.

reaches out into and makes its painful demand of, the furthest and most intimate recesses of the mind, where ancient fears demand the erection of symbols for their pacification, where morality desperately prefers a paternalistic to a free and fraternal norm, where we flee from the searing pain of shame at failing our brother to the comparatively tolerable guilt at displeasing Father or Mother. It hunts out man in his hiding place, where he wants to remain a child, and dreads the freedom of an uncharted universe. It threatens this fearful man with the dissolution of all his values.[18]

Further, the crucifixion shatters our homage to the false cage we erect for God. It brings us to a world beyond morality, an eschatological world, that is, an anticipation of the end of our tidy moral world and its small ways.[19] It is no wonder that sinners are horrified by the crucifixion since the cross dismantles "the sin in us, the oldest in us, the respectability of us, the moral tidiness of us that are shocked by God's statement, God's tearing down of all that we erect to honor him and keep ourselves in order."[20] The crucifixion is a call to a dangerous way of life. The problem with previous reflections concerning Jesus that Moore and his contemporaries face is not the unbelievability of the cross but an understanding of the cross as some super-sacrilege. For Moore, we need to recapture the unbelievability of the cross so that "kings may stand speechless before him" (Is 52:15). So, at his crucifixion, the world could only react in an obverse manner to the new and utterly strange truth of the gospel. His crucifixion and death make Jesus the mysterious Messiah he really is. For, if there is a choice between the image of a warrior-king and a suffering servant, Jesus chooses the latter.

Moore also appreciates the depth and significance of the resurrection as integral to our understanding of the crucifixion. In former Christological writings, the resurrection was a proof of Jesus' divinity; for Moore, in his resurrection, he is, through his body, "in" the new Israel, not King over against the new Israel. Only under the sway of the Holy Spirit do we come to appreciate the full significance of his messiahship, which is a messiahship in the form of a servant-slave. The Victim of the kingdom becomes its life. In the resurrection, the dead One is revealed as alive, through the outpouring of the Holy Spirit. The only way forward is

18. Moore, *No Exit*, 74.
19. Moore, *No Exit*, 75.
20. Moore, *No Exit*, 76.

for the Victim to come into the disciples, to become one with them, and to become their life. Moore states that, in the resurrection, "the Christian knows but one taste; further the victim that is his meat and drink; for the risen Christ; for the new society which is the body of Christ; for the Spirit given without measure; for the kingdom which makes of him, the believer, its witness, its victim, and its life."[21]

JESUS AND AN INVERTED PERSPECTIVE

By inverted, I mean understanding the person of Jesus by being attentive to his listeners and their response to him. Using the word "inverted," Moore expresses one of the chief concerns for his understanding of Jesus that would become part of his thought throughout his life. The concern is: While we hear of Jesus from his chroniclers, set out in a historical context, and while we hear his teachings and see his miracles, we do not hear who Jesus is in relation to his listeners. We hear little from their inner world or about Jesus' impact on them. The writings of the Gospels slant toward the task of winning over the hearers of Jesus' words but rarely present us with the interiority of his listeners. Moore states: "And thus we have side-by-side the unreported news of his actual self-presentation at the receiving end simply by reason of the nonexistence of such records and the seeming [non-reportability] of it by reason of its peculiar nature. . . . And when you have an extraordinary event [and its] only chronicling is by those who believe in it, the effect on them must be to forget just how extraordinary it is."[22] The characters of the gospel, such as the Jews, Pharisees, and zealots, are presented in a way that has them falling short of the mysterious new humanity of Jesus. However, in portraying the Jewish leaders as perverse and willfully blinded men who should have known better, we blur the quality of breathtaking newness that is the essence of Christianity. The effect is that these figures, thus portrayed, are not historical; instead, they are personifications of theological attitudes. They are the "judgment on history."[23]

No less is the case for the evangelists. They also should not be taken on face value. He asserts: "Only insofar as I can enter empathetically into the lives of those to whom the news was given, people with whom I know I share the primordial limitations of death-bound man can I get a real, as

21. Moore, *No Exit*, 95.
22. Moore, *No Exit*, 22.
23. Moore, *No Exit*, 24.

opposed to a notional idea of the break with [the] immemorial human custom that Jesus is and makes."[24] Moore hopes to better appreciate the significance of Jesus by entering the minds and hearts of the listeners. He states: "May it not be that through this distancing of time, the 'unconscious and exposed' side of the author will be the more evident to us and put us more deeply in touch with the influence under which he is writing?"[25] He is following an insight about literature in general: so many times, a person takes more from his source material into himself that others can see but that he himself may not see.

A final comment needs to be made about Moore's first attempt to present a new approach to the person of Jesus. I believe that his choice for the title of his first book is not accidental. *No Exit* is the same title given to a play by the existentialist Jean-Paul Sartre. Sartre's play deals with the central idea of being objectified by another through a cold stare. He recalls the unpleasantness of being stared out as a defeated French people after the invasion and takeover of Paris by the German army in 1940. Sartre takes a role in the underground French resistance for the duration of the occupation.

The play depicts three people trapped together in a room: a military deserter accused of being a coward, a cruel lesbian, and a flirtatious gold-digger. Each exercises cruel judgment on the other, and each person desires to escape the other's pitiless eyes. In the famous last scene, with the line "hell is other people," Sartre is saying that in death, our freedom goes, and we are entombed in other people's memory of us and unable to fend off any inaccurate interpretation.[26] In life, we rob others of their subjectivity and evaluate ourselves through the eyes of those who stare at us. When stared at by the other, one becomes ashamed of one's freedom. Every aspect of human life is influenced for good and bad by this intersubjective principle at work. Life is either being controlled or controlling the other. Everything else is in vain including the power of love.

By contrast, Moore presents the gospels as good news that we cannot escape. There is no exit for us. The heart longs for it, and God is determined to offer it for our salvation. Jesus is without the stare of judgment, honoring the subjectivity of all he meets, who rules as King Messiah through being the Suffering Servant, and whose mission to present the kingdom cost him no less than everything.

24. Moore, *No Exit*, 26.
25. Moore, "Notes and Comments," 174.
26. Bakewell, *At the Existentialist*, 213.

INVERTED SOTERIOLOGY

Moore's next meaningful plunge into the saving person of Jesus focuses on the significance of the crucifixion, this time in his classic work, *The Crucified Jesus Is No Stranger*. Again, he does not pretend that his theological insights are comprehensive. They are "a series of hints, not a system of theology to be taken over, lock, stock, and barrel."[27] Many of Moore's religious, social, cultural, and psychological terms, discussed in chapters 4, 5, and 6, including an understanding of ego, self, the True Self, the shadow, and the unconscious, take prominence throughout his soteriological insights. He shows a debt to Freud, Jung, and Becker.

From the outset, Moore's writings on the cross's significance arise from his conversion experience. It is the experience of Vespers in the Roman church on the Feast of the Sacred Heart, 1959. The writings are also based on some spiritual insights gained by Moore while working through the Exercises of Ignatius in the role of spiritual director.

The human condition is the starting place for Moore's understanding of the cross. Thus, Moore calls this kind of Christology, an inverted soteriology. Necessarily, any appreciation of the crucifixion must account for who Jesus is in relation to us and in relation to sin. Jesus represents the True Self and the crucifixion becomes the central drama of man's refusal of his true self.[28] We engage in a refusal of our true self in favor of the insatiable needs of the distorted ego. The believer's experience is that of someone who willfully seeks to destroy his true self, concretely manifested in the man on the cross. The symbol of the cross transforms evil into sin; before the cross, we are faced with evil at its most intense moment, and the evil we face is none other than the evil of our sinfulness. From this inverted perspective, we discover that the cross is not primarily life's crucifixion of us, as when Jesus urges us to pick up our cross and follow him, nor is the cross equivalent to when we face some crisis and are encouraged to bear our suffering patiently. Still, instead, the cross is our crucifixion of life. Therefore, the origin of evil within us equates to the self-discovery that each of us is a crucifier.

William Loewe states that, for Moore, the first moment of our encounter with the crucified is when our encounter

---

27. Moore, *Crucified Is No Stranger*, xii.
28. Moore, *Crucified Is No Stranger*, x.

unmasks and reverses my ordinary awareness of evil as a power vaguely diffused throughout the world outside me and afflicting me in various ways. In contemplating the Victim on the cross in his true sinlessness and real innocence, there stands exposed the inauthenticity of my usual self-image as an innocent victim of life's general unfairness and of the stupidity and malice of others, with the mix of self-pity, resentment, and apathetic resignation which such a self-image permits me. And I react: thus exposed, stripped of the protective mask I have crafted to excuse my mediocre compromise with life. I lash out at the innocence that judges me. I take my place among the Christ-killers; evil is transformed into sin.[29]

The encounter with Christ unmasks our sham and reveals the distance between what we are and what we could be, between ourselves as we are and the true humanity revealed in Jesus. Thus, an awareness emerges as to just how much we crucify our true selves in our efforts to flee life.[30] In the crucifixion of Jesus, we show up as crucifiers since there is no evil in the crucified One. In the encounter with the sinless one, the evil in the crucifier becomes an act and does not remain any longer an atmosphere or mood. In Jesus' crucified body, we see for the first time our evil as conscious and personal. Evil becomes explicit in the destruction of Jesus but, ultimately, finds resolution in the forgiveness of God, of which, again, the crucifixion is a symbol. By God's action, sin is transformed into sorrow and forgiveness. When he discovers sorrow and forgiveness, the sinner finds the true self he rejected and crucified as his own.

GOD'S VIEWPOINT IN JESUS CRUCIFIED

In the whole drama of the crucifixion, it is also essential to see things from God's side and to state what God is doing and not simply what we are doing. God is loving us without condition. Only in our acceptance of God's love can we appreciate God's viewpoint for the first time and the truth about ourselves. What we come to affirm is that, in the crucifixion, God is convincing us of his unconditional love. We cannot experience ourselves as accepted by God in love until God's love meets us in our evil. The crucifixion and death of Jesus, "authorized" by God, declares God's

---

29. Loewe, "Encountering the Crucified God," 219.
30. Loewe, "Encountering the Crucified God," 220.

love for us simply because God accepts us at our worst.[31] God reveals us to ourselves as the ones who crucify the sinless One so that we can experience God's love and acceptance. The cross is a meeting between God and us far beyond our rational grasp and "is made known to mystics in those moments of irresponsible love that subvert all normal values."[32] God is no naïve optimist. God is a realist, asking us to face the chaos of our evil.[33] Yet, God allows us to glimpse our true selves in the person and teaching of Jesus. But his true self is separated from us, and we find ourselves being the crucifier of the One without whom we cannot become authentic. The depth of our evil is such that the Self crucified is God's Self, the Self-for-God nailed on the cross by our organized ego.[34]

In our acceptance of the cross, Christ's torments are God's sign of his taking to himself our evil for the greater good. When we hear in the Scriptures that God made Christ into sin, this phrase expresses just how God uses sin. Christ is in the space of sin, and the mystery of the Incarnation is the mystery of God, who comes among us and loves us beyond the limits of our ego-organized potential. God touches us in the innermost region of our soul, where only God and nothing else can touch us. The meeting between ourselves as sinners and God's love has us naming how excessive God is towards us and how far God is willing to go for our transformation since nothing can separate us from the love of God. Sin comes into Christ by his absorption of the evil inflicted upon him. Still, ultimately, sin becomes forgiven due to God's love, which reveals sin's ultimate meaning in forgiveness. We understand what sin is through an experience of forgiveness, the occasion for God's demonstration of love, and this understanding of sin and forgiveness would never have been obtained without Christ.

In the person of Jesus and the characters present at Calvary, we witness the drama and resolution of our inner turmoil. On the one hand, humanity is willing "to act out, in a uniquely total way, our desire for the good and the true and the holy personal not to be there." On the other hand, there is Jesus, the sinless One destroyed because he *is* without evil. Only by the Spirit can the murder of Jesus be understood as God's saving way and God's loving acceptance of us. Through God's acceptance and Jesus' empathetic self-identification with our plight, we discover our

---

31. Moore, *Crucified Is No Stranger*, 3.
32. Moore, *Crucified Is No Stranger*, 4–5.
33. Moore, *Crucified Is No Stranger*, 5.
34. Moore, *Crucified Is No Stranger*, 7.

evil for the first time, and again, for the first time, we discover the love that overpowers all evil.[35] Only love can reveal the goodness of God to us, even in our pernicious desire to extinguish our being. Thus, Moore affirms that, in the crucifixion, evil becomes sin, and sin becomes sorrow and forgiveness. In forgiveness, we know our identity for the first time, and, with a passion, we cling to this figure on the cross, which brings about a transfiguration of evil with love. For Moore, the cross reveals a "God, we cannot get at, short of evil and who, therefore, in some way wants us through evil. . . . The Cross of Jesus is appropriately placed as the foundation of the created universe."[36]

BECKER, FREUD, AND SOTERIOLOGY

Moore returns to the themes of personal significance and its opposite, feelings of disesteem and self-rejection. Sin is the refusal in each of us to come to some excellent meeting place powered by a nameless and fearful unconscious. Hiding in the unconscious is a fear of existence powered by our fear of death, which causes a distorted idea of death to rule us. In that fear, we are refusing the fullness of life. Following Becker, Moore states that we are "the conscious animal, the animal who, knowing his total contingency turns from it in fear and builds the idolatrous image of himself. The root of all evil, says Becker, is the necessary attempt of man to deny his creaturehood."[37] Our egotistic self-importance is manifested in opting for independence over interdependence, leading us to see death wrongly. We see death as the end of our earthly life, the end to our significant projects.

It was Becker who came to the insight that humankind has a secret, and the secret is that we crave personal significance but wrongly think that attaining it requires independence and isolation from others. When we distance ourselves from God, our desire for independence leads to a denial of our creaturehood. In the beginning, the first sin committed indicates a rebellion against God, a denial of our creaturehood, and, with it, a distorted understanding of death.

A perverse disesteem is a manifestation of what Freud calls the death wish. The death wish is a will-not-to-be creatures and dependent

---

35. Moore, "Language of Love," 89.
36. Moore, *Crucified Is No Stranger*, 17.
37. Moore, *Crucified Is No Stranger*, xi.

for meaning on God. The death wish indicates our wish to dismiss and reject the call to an ever-greater identity of selfhood. Moore states that evil "is operative in us as the denial about contingency through fear and as the cognate fascination with ourselves."[38] Put another way: "My hold on reality impedes my quest and your quest for life. My self-expression is impeded by my hold on reality. My hold on life is my unfreedom, a stranglehold. Can I release it?" Ultimately, our controlling hold on reality is a hold on a false view of reality and a refusal to change. From this perspective, evil, manifest in the death wish, is not only a false understanding of ourselves, but it also becomes "a death wish, [turned to a] necessity to justify itself by removing the very grounds for requiring of us a more intensely personal life. We are filled with resentment in the presence of someone exceptionally good. We passionately protect our mediocrity. The inertia of fear is impossible to overcome without an extraordinary new birth of love in us."[39] In another way, Moore proposes that so pervasive is our self-hatred that we think of ourselves as slobs, with a perverse self-distrust and a suppression of the lover within.[40]

Even the Mosaic law cannot undo sin within us. The Mosaic law is grounded in the mistaken assumption that evil results from disobeying a direct law.[41] However, the disobedience of the law is a mere shadow of the first disobedience, the refusal to accept our finiteness. The law allows sin to maintain "its diffuse and not fully enfleshed condition in us."[42] Even if we were to obey the law, it would not be equivalent to restoring obedience to God in Christ. Living the law would not bring about the ability to live the in-between of finitude and infinitude.

Only through the obedient One, who is crucified by evil, is this original disobedience unmasked for the first time, allowing us to accept what alone can prevail over the disorder in ourselves, namely, God's love. For Moore, the cross is not so much the motive for believing in God's love. It is the process made visible dramatically in the flesh, whereby our self-hatred reaches its climax of realization, avowal, confession, and surrender. Our self-hatred is not only the obstacle to our acceptance of God's love. It is also the medium in which God's love is revealed in Jesus and transforms us. God does not just give us a reason not to hate ourselves.

38. Moore, *Crucified Is No Stranger*, 35.
39. Moore, *Crucified Is No Stranger*, 13.
40. Moore, "Language of Love," 84.
41. Moore, *Crucified Is No Stranger*, 10.
42. Moore, *Crucified Is No Stranger*, 10.

He transforms our self-hatred through the cross. Moore asserts: "In the mystery of Jesus, contemplated in faith, [the] sinful man plunges murderously, desperately, hopefully—who knows?—into the self with which he has ever been at odds, and [there, it] is accepted [by God], there finds identity and freedom."[43]

MOORE, JUNG, AND SOTERIOLOGY

In chapter 5, I discussed Moore's use of the category of "the self" gained from his appropriation of Jung. He is well aware of the limitations of Jung's language and ideas. For Jung, "the Self" is of our own making alone. The Self is "the obscurely perceived totality of a person's life [which is] a reality able to become conscious and to be a source of psychic energy far in excess of and more far-reaching than the self, of which we are readily and inescapably conscious, and which we call ego. My life is so much more than me."[44] For Moore, the distance between the conscious ego and the total Self in God's world is the fruit of a wise movement of the self through "silent contemplation, in humility, and then the indefinable benefits which the wise confer on the less aware."[45]

In other words, contrary to Jung, we need God's grace and the revelation of God in Jesus. Jesus alone is the True Self. Moore adds his own personal note: "I recognize myself in the total context of this mystery, as the sinner brought to consciousness and sorrow as the crucifier of the self that is not 'my best self' or 'my full potential,' or any other pretentious euphemism, but is symbolized most truly by a sinless man crucified on a hill for whose crucifixion I gladly accept liability within the mystery of God is all-encompassing love."[46]

Jesus is the totality of the Self. Only the Holy Spirit reveals to us Jesus as the transforming symbol for the emergence of our innermost self. To cooperate in the making of our true self, we need self-knowledge. We need to know about the spacious country of ourselves that lies in the shadow of the ego to experience coming together with Jesus. We need a vivid sense of our impatient and fearful ego riding roughshod over that

---

43. Moore, *Crucified Is No Stranger*, 38.
44. Moore, *Crucified Is No Stranger*, 19.
45. Moore, *Crucified Is No Stranger*, 11.
46. Moore, *Crucified Is No Stranger*, 11.

fine country, crucifying Jesus. We need to experience Christ within, as our fountain of life.[47]

In self-discovery, one first finds the state of not being one's true self. In not being one's true self, we crucify Jesus. Because we are crucifying Jesus, God responds by flooding us with love. We are forced to admit that we hate that which will lead us to the fullness of life. In our evil destruction of the true self, we demonstrate a hatred of ourselves and a hatred for the wholeness we know ourselves to be. We hate ourselves as free, as free from evil, and free from sin.[48] We are always running away. It becomes an endless cycle of "fear of man for himself, the endless flight of man from himself, and the endless crucifixion of man by himself."[49] Moore states that it requires "something immense . . . to make and empower the symbol of the crucified in the citadel of the soul. That 'something' is the historically reported goodness of Jesus, combined with the psyche's deepest power to project in symbol its drama of self-crucifixion. These two components fused in the power of the Holy Spirit, the Spirit of wholeness."[50] Moore is not saying that Jesus is only some archetype of the psyche, as Jung proposes the Self to be. Someone must hang on the cross and that someone is the historical man without sin, Jesus.

THE CROSS: PERSONAL AND ULTIMATE SIGNIFICANCE

In chapter 4, I present Moore's definition of the human being as "to be myself for another." The axiom points to a natural or pre-religious love affair with God. It is an orientation that answers the question: Am I significant? If the answer is "yes," it prompts a second question: Am I ultimately significant? If this orientation constitutes my true humanity, evil indicates a resistance against personal and ultimate significance. We push away others and opt for an isolated self. A perverse disesteem arises by pushing away or denying others the relatedness that will fulfill us. Further, our guilt at failing others causes us to cast a shadow over people, viewing them as ugly, repulsive, and to be feared. Through the cross, we

---

47. Moore, *Crucified Is No Stranger*, 20.
48. Moore, *Crucified Is No Stranger*, 24.
49. Moore, *Crucified Is No Stranger*, 25.
50. Moore, *Crucified Is No Stranger*, 27.

are exposed for who we are, and once we admit what we have become, our admission can turn to sorrow, and sorrow becomes forgiveness.

The cross transmutes fear into hate, hate into sorrow and forgiveness, evil into sin, and sin into sorrow and forgiveness.[51] Jesus "makes the unbearable truth of ourselves bearable, through the power of love."[52] We begin to see the sins of our past as expressions of fear. It is the fear of that center in God where there is no fear, for there is no darkness in God. In that new place, we are suddenly aware that fear is the heart of sin. Moore affirms that "the heart of man is converted by seeing that his violence is directed to himself; to himself dramatized in the symbol of Jesus crucified, where he (man) appears as most unlovable and most hated and in sorrow and pardon, most loved."[53] Similarly, only in the Spirit can we recognize our hunger for ultimate meaningfulness in the person of Jesus. Jesus is the embodiment of our desire for ultimate significance. Since we lose sight of the need for ultimate significance, we lose sight of Jesus and the capacity to see him as the reflection of our deeper life, feelings, and aspirations.

THE CROSS DESTROYS OUR DEATH

Evil arises out of our distorted understanding of death and causes the death of Jesus so that we might protect our distorted view of death. Jesus is the unbearable life, personhood, identity, and freedom beating on our comfortable existence and our "choice of death." Without Jesus, we cannot find sorrow and forgiveness. Without sorrow and forgiveness, we can never understand death and fear. Without a fundamental understanding of death and a befriending of our fear, we can never come to our true selves and, thus, remain locked into a distorted ego.

Through the crucifixion, a new understanding of death emerges. Our immortality projects, our need to constitute reality on our terms, and our willful independence are all manifestations of our fear of death. Death becomes the penalty of sin.[54] From the ego's mistaken perspective, our death ends our significance and meaning. Death brings to an end our ego operations. Alternatively, the reification of death reflects the centrality of the ego and its refusal to grow. Sin confers on death its old

---

51. Moore, *Crucified Is No Stranger*, 21–22.
52. Moore, *Crucified Is No Stranger*, 27.
53. Moore, *Crucified Is No Stranger*, 17.
54. Moore, *Crucified Is No Stranger*, 56.

symbolism. Sin is the constituting of our reality as the only reality in which death has the ultimate victory. Our sin makes death the ruler.

For Jesus, death is "a return to the Father." Viewed from the transformed ego, death is a doorway. Moore states that "in acknowledging ourselves as sinners, we find our identity in the man our sin has crucified and in him know death as the Father's embrace."[55] The death of Jesus is not simply the death of a holy man, for in that description, the symbolism of death is not broken open. Instead, the Christian proclamation is the destruction of our old view of death: "Dying you destroyed *our* death." Moore asserts: "Jesus goes to the Father, in our experience of him as victim, which is our experience of ourselves as forgiven and cut loose from our self-made world."[56] For Jesus, death is a consummation, a clearing of death's distorted cultural meaning and the full flowering of the Victim in his power to absorb and transform our evil. His death is joyful in our world and glorious in the Father's house, but the way from a culturally limited existence to the Father is only through forgiveness. Jesus' obedience unto death is not obedience unto our understanding of death. It is obedience as a gift to the heavenly Father.

SORROW AND FORGIVENESS

Moore offers some final insights on sorrow and forgiveness. He states:

> My past evil is seen as my suppression of the self, of the true center, that is now awakening. Not you, my friend, and not God but my true self is the Victim of what I now know as sin. I hurt you, yes. I failed God, yes. But more radically than this and by a secret action that is the mystery of evil at its core, I [am] rendered unable for you, unabundant towards you and impervious to the voice of the Spirit, and of life, that center, that heart, whence alone human goodness can come.[57]

Due to this disabling, the heart becomes encased and suppressed. The heart is the evil person's Victim. Jesus is also the Victim and the true self "of which we allow evil in us to neglect, ignore and crush. He is the heart that I have refused to myself, to you, to God."[58]

---

55. Moore, *Crucified Is No Stranger*, 57.
56. Moore, *Crucified Is No Stranger*, 61.
57. Moore, *Crucified Is No Stranger*, 75–76.
58. Moore, *Crucified Is No Stranger*, 76.

A New Awareness

Again, the passage from evil and sin to self-discovery, leading to sorrow and forgiveness, requires the grace of God. First, sorrow comes to its full stature only when the offender has said they are sorry. The acceptance of sorrow brings about a new intimacy. Sorrow is more about the present and not about the past. It is an awakening, enlargement, and new promise of the future without forgetting the past. It is an expression of the person becoming. The unconscious past becomes the conscious present. Since an inward betrayal has happened, an inward healing is needed. Sorrow is the sign of healing and the pang of new birth. Through sorrow, the person becomes in Christ what he destroys in Christ. A mature sorrow becomes the awareness of a life one has made unavailable to oneself and one's neighbor. The self that one destroys is the self that one neglects. Sorrow is the hinge between piercing the heart of Christ and compunction for our own heart.[59]

The sorrow for sin can be felt as both shame and guilt. Sorrow is felt as shame. Shame is what we feel when we fail to live in the tension between the finite and the infinite. Shame comes from accepting the tension but, for whatever reason, feeling that we have failed in that task. The sorrow for sin can also be felt as guilt. Guilt arises when we have determined that the tension is not for us. We prefer to live as isolated, pushing others or God away and going alone. In as much as the felt sense of the chasm is put aside willfully, there is a denial in our participation in the Mystery of God. In sin, the person is saying the known is enough, or what is here and who we are now is enough. It amounts to a denial of desire.

Second, God's forgiveness is a transformation of our consciousness. Part of the problem in seeking forgiveness is linking forgiveness to payment. We think to ourselves that to forgive our neighbor first requires some payment to be made by them to us. As long as we do not see ourselves in God's debt, we will not see the need for forgiveness. If the ego is the center of our lives, then the sense of ourselves as autonomous and needing payment has priority, and God's forgiveness has no place. But if the center of our lives shifts from the ego and our center is placed in the spiritual universe that declares its need for God's pardon and the preposterousness of exacting payment from others, then forgiveness ensues.

Every day people seek the forgiveness of God, but the God they seek forgiveness of is the God of Freud's superego. The kind of forgiveness the superego seeks encourages a revulsion at ourselves and arises

---

59. Moore, *Crucified Is No Stranger*, 79.

from a context in which we are the center of attention. Alternatively, the true forgiveness of God touches the sin of self-importance, not the self-importance of the sinner. The sin of self-importance serves to bolster our failing self-esteem.

In forgiveness, the sin of self-importance is dissolved. Grace gets in and liberates the captive heart, inviting us to experience ourselves in a new context and contemplate the destructive things we are doing to secure our self-esteem. In the new context of grace, one's meanness becomes an awareness of "something I am doing to myself."[60] A new awareness happens in which our freedom is awakened to our responsibility to exist. We begin to be able to think of ourselves, even in our meanness, as touched by God, who is the living center of all being. Moore asserts: "The very idea of forgiveness is experienced as the bridge between the human meanness normally interpreted in an ego-centered way and the transcendent center."[61] Indeed, by opening to God and yielding our basic stance concerning others, we break down the regular and distorted system of disesteem and self-denigration that we live by. To be forgiven is to be set free.[62]

EGO CONSCIOUSNESS AND SIN

Moore distinguishes between our present ego-consciousness and the need for its transformation to a new stage. If the ego is in a state of homeostasis to regulate meaning in our lives, it will not quickly transform even when transformation is needed. Its natural inclination is to remain in a steady state. What becomes even more problematic is the distorted social and cultural milieu that resists transformation. If we are to move from inauthenticity to authenticity, there comes a stage when we have to grow out of our current ego state and accept change. With regard to our ego-state, Moore states that "sin tries to keep it in place."[63]

However, more than a change to the habitual attitudes and behaviors of the ego is required. We need an ascetical approach to life. Dying to ego is dying to sin and the current form of ego consciousness. Sin is

---

60. Moore, *Crucified Is No Stranger*, 87.
61. Moore, *Crucified Is No Stranger*, 87.
62. Moore, *Crucified Is No Stranger*, 90.
63. Moore, *Jesus the Liberator*, 32.

the resistance that prevents the challenge from revealing itself.[64] Moore asserts: "A sinful situation is without fear except in the unconscious. It is characterized by a huge complacency, a triumphant assertion of the status quo that is unaware of its vulgarity and banality."[65] In the transformation process, there are two kinds of fear at work. The first fear arises from our tenacious insecurity by the early ego to move beyond its boundaries. This fear is a natural insecurity and is part of our being human. The second fear emerges from a fixation on the present ego and an attitude that signals the collapse of the chasm between the finite and the infinite. Sin is the absence of that felt chasm and the fixation on the current ego. Sin deadens the nerve of the chasm between the finite and the infinite.

TRANSFORMATION AND SUFFERING

Each of us suffers whenever we move from our current ego consciousness to a new one. Suffering is recognizing our finitude in the presence of the infinite. It is natural and normal to suffer the process of ego transformation. But there is another kind of suffering: the suffering that follows when we have deadened the nerve of pain, which makes us hesitant before ego transformation. It is the suffering of sin. We do not feel it because we have killed it off through sin. We have brought suffering onto ourselves by holding on to a present ego or ego state in the face of needed change and fuller development.

Jesus undergoes suffering because of our sin and our refusal to undergo needed change. Only in Jesus can we undergo the suffering required due to our refusal to transform. The appeal of Jesus from the cross is for sufferers to see themselves as victims of their self-rejection, hatred, and malice.[66] For Moore, "Jesus, [the] sufferer of the infinite, suffers empathetically with that in us which, because of sin, is unable to suffer and it is the awareness of being suffered with where sin prevents us from suffering that causes sin to fall away."[67] Jesus is the "suffering inherent in living out the self's true being, which is being-in-oneness in a way that questions all the defensive barriers between people, all the role-based relationships that institutionalize the normality and permanence of ego

---

64. Moore, *Jesus the Liberator*, 32.
65. Moore, *Jesus the Liberator*, 34–35.
66. Moore, *Jesus the Liberator*, 24.
67. Moore, *Jesus the Liberator*, 36.

as a way of being."⁶⁸ The awareness of Jesus suffering with us awakens the nerve, and sin's deadening is dissolved.

JESUS, INCOMPLETENESS, AND EGO CONSCIOUSNESS

To speak of Jesus as sinless affirms his total self-possession in freedom. He is free of a fixated ego and free to transform humanly. Jesus, in his humanity, undergoes ego transformation at all the needed points of growth in his life. Each transformation is akin to speaking about a death that he dies every day. Living well in the in-between chasm of the finite and the infinite gives us a sense of contingency and incompleteness, and sin exploits the felt radical uncertainty of incompleteness. One alternative is to bid for certainty, autonomy, and becoming the captain of one's ship.

Jesus' sense of incompleteness did not lapse into the unfreedom of willful autonomy. He chooses to remain incomplete, trusting in his heavenly Father. He grows beyond the felt insecurity of incompleteness.⁶⁹ The disciples, therefore, experience in their encounter with Jesus "the self uniquely free in oneness," expressed in Jesus' Abba experience.⁷⁰ It is both a growth toward his true self and a convergence of oneness and separateness. In chapter 4, I spoke of the tension between oneness and separation that grounds our psychological growth. Jesus' earthly life witnesses to the self whose separateness is identical to his oneness.⁷¹ Each of us has to negotiate the convergence of oneness and separateness to realize our true selves. While the true self is desired but dreaded by us since it involves multiple changes to our ego state, the disciples experience in Jesus one who has a profound oneness with the Mystery of God, even in the face of contingency and the incompleteness of death.

The kingdom message of Jesus (realized in his person, teaching, relationships, and miracles) speaks to the eschatological convergence of the tension between finite and infinite, when God will be luminous in everything. For Jesus, the crucifixion becomes the moment when all our desires and fears are put onto his shoulders: our desire for authenticity and our fear of transforming. In this respect, Jesus is the Victim. His

---

68. Moore, *Jesus the Liberator*, 37.
69. Moore, *Jesus the Liberator*, 41–43.
70. Moore, *Jesus the Liberator*, 47.
71. Moore, "Jesus, the Liberator," 9.

death on the cross is the death that sin intends and the non-being that sin is.⁷² The cross is the revelation of sin "as the denial of contingency through fear."⁷³ In Jesus, the drama of our self-rejection works out, the drama of our refusal to embrace our creaturehood and negotiate the tension of oneness and separateness. Thus, on the cross, Jesus is "made into sin." He becomes "the self that we have to destroy in our fear of the ultimate mystery that we desire."⁷⁴ We can now see how sin leads to death, to non-being, and our self-undoing, to our refusal to live within the tension, and to the refusal to undergo ego transformation. In Jesus crucified, sin reveals itself as a denial of who we are, that is, a person rejecting the true self in favor of the survival of some socially learned self, with a will to non-being.⁷⁵

JESUS AND THE LIBERATION OF DESIRE

Moore's second imaginative entry into soteriology is *Jesus the Liberator of Desire*. Moore continues exploring what it means to say that Jesus saves us, only this time by means of the language of desire. For Moore, the best place to start is with the disciples. For the disciples, the ministry of Jesus causes an awakening of desire within them. As Jesus mentors the disciples on the importance of ego transformation, his teaching and example profoundly affect them. His authentic ego consciousness loosens the hearts of his disciples, who live a half-life, partly closed and partly opened to his person and teaching. One example of closedness is their insistence that he should not suffer even, as he set his face towards Jerusalem. Their insistence comes from radical insecurity.

The crucifixion becomes the paramount psychological crisis for the disciples. They observe that Jesus surrenders freely to his oncoming brutal ordeal and his surrender horrifies them. The disciples feel the suffering of letting him down and they feel let down by him. At this point of their lives, they are living half a life and participating in an evasion of transformation. When he dies, the disciples are flung into death themselves and experience the death of God. They undergo the desolation of desire and suffer confusion through denial, betrayal, and loss.

---

72. Moore, "Jesus, the Liberator," 10.
73. Moore, "Jesus, the Liberator," 35.
74. Moore, "Jesus, the Liberator," 11.
75. Moore, "Jesus, the Liberator," 12.

In the resurrection, their dark night and feelings of dissolution are met by the healing and transformation of love imparted by the risen Jesus. In the resurrection, the disciples are taken out of a "psychological dead land" into a true "ego-shedding life" when Jesus reveals his final glory as "who we are and who we are to be."[76] Now, the disciples are in a transformed state of being. They have transformed desire. The disciples who were made to suffer Jesus' death, now know its consummating sequel and can embrace, in the death of ego and a daily dying to self, the death that lies ahead of us. Therefore, to believe in Jesus is to be in love with him and allow his death to be in us as a form of death to the ego. In his risen life, to live is to act as though death, previously thought of as destruction and extinction on the part of humankind, has been left behind. In his risen life, the disciples experience the liberation of desire. Moore speaks to that desire as "the desire to look upon the face of the beloved, the desire to know, which knows nothing of that split between mind and heart of which our culture is dying."[77]

For Moore, the resurrection breakthrough comes when we hear the crucified saying to each of us: "I'm still with you, you don't have to be afraid anymore, can't you see that its only fear that makes you put me on the Cross."[78] The healing aspect of the resurrection is forgiveness imparted to the disciples for having let him down and denied him. Their transformation helps them to understand why they let him down, namely, so that Jesus could bring them to a fullness of ego-death and transformation.[79]

SIN IN US AND JESUS WITHOUT SIN

In contrast to living in the full knowledge of what is the case, sin is a preference to live in a state of "non-being," rather than in a celebration of being.[80] On the cross, the true self, reflected in the suffering, death, obedience, and love of Jesus, becomes the target of our will to non-being.[81] We mistakenly think that we are living reality, but we are living an unreal reality. Reality finds its center in God.

---

76. Moore, *Jesus the Liberator*, 49.
77. Moore, *Jesus the Liberator*, 58.
78. Moore, "What God Has Joined," 171.
79. Moore, "Jesus, the Liberator," 7.
80. Moore, "Jesus, the Liberator," 10.
81. Moore, "Jesus, the Liberator," 11.

About intimacy with God, sin is our fear of the ultimate intimacy, which, in the true self, we desire. Apart from conversion, we are likely to miss a true understanding of sin. The key to Jesus' self-identification with suffering humanity is his unique intimacy with the Father. The cross attracts Jesus to itself as the mode and place of his consummation because of his intimacy and oneness with the Father. Through his intimacy, Jesus is in love with life, and the cross is the destiny of a man of oneness in a broken world.

Regarding self-rejection, sin is grounded in a "fundamental self-rejection that is the human canker," which gives rise to relationships of domination.[82] Sin is saying no, that is, "saying no . . . to the thing in me that wants to say yes. It is my feeling of myself as being good."[83]

Concerning the fear of change, sin is our refusal "to understand, to see the way the world really is, because we have to change, and we are scared to change."[84] Sin is a fear-filled flight from understanding and from what is the case.[85] For Moore, the refusal that proceeds and prevents understanding is more radical than the refusal that presupposes understanding. It grounds the belief that human nature cannot be changed.

About growth, sin is a resistance to growth, a reluctance to change, and a refusal to live more adequately, and our interior resistance prevents understanding.[86] When that growth requires shedding ego states, sin is the refusal to grow into a new intelligent and responsible ego state.[87] In the unavoidable first shaping of our journey from childhood to adult life, whether through the process of separation from our mother or the formation of sexual identity, sin regards those frontiers as the final shape of our person. We refuse to grow and take on new shapes, acting out the attitude of self-negation. We engage in repression and sexual estrangement.

About freedom, Moore understands "living by the flesh" as Paul's way of signaling that we can be trapped in the first stages of consciousness and, thereby, confine ourselves to a half-life.[88] We mistake half-life for freedom. To achieve the fullness of life is to die to our various ego states. Refusing to die to our ego states nods us toward the direction of an

---

82. Moore, "Jesus, the Liberator," 13.
83. Moore, *Let This Mind*, 81.
84. Moore, *Let This Mind*, 83.
85. Moore, *Let This Mind*, 85.
86. Moore, *Let This Mind*, 90.
87. Moore, "Jesus, the Liberator," 8.
88. Moore, *Let This Mind*, 100.

utterly self-determined life. There, we alone are the masters of our destinies and the captains of our ships.[89] Subsequently, we end up with a distorted idea of freedom, mistakenly thinking that our thrust for freedom and our drive for life is freedom through independence. By contrast, true freedom is found only in interdependence. Our unfreedom reveals itself in our "self-crucifixion" through self-worship. It is "an act of self-worship that sets the limitless miracle of man's life on a pedestal where it becomes limited, a possession, an asset."[90] If this is the case, concupiscence is not equivalent to having spontaneity, as was often thought to be the case. Therefore, we should not think of overcoming it by crushing the natural spontaneity of infants and adults. Instead, concupiscence is our spontaneity out of phase with freedom.[91] In unfreedom, God is not the center of our existence, so sin becomes the unreality of God or "the unreality of the real to the unreal."[92] To achieve true freedom requires us to answer the question: Who is God asking us to become?

About death, sin has a part to play in our distorted understanding of death. Moore assumes that Adam and Eve would have come to the end of their mortal life as all humans come to physical death even if they had not rebelled against God. For many, the phrase "death is the consequence of sin" mistakenly indicates that Adam and Eve would have lived without death had it not been for their rebellion. A better understanding of "death as the consequence of sin" requires distinguishing between death as meaningless and death as meaningful. Death as meaningless is a consequence of sin. Sin intends and renders a distorted meaning of death, namely, as extinction, dissolution, and annihilation. In other words, we mistakenly assert that in death, all meaningfulness and significance are lost to us, and there is no recourse to anything else. Moore also introduces the difference between the power of death and the fact of death.[93] The fact of death is part of the ordering of the universe according to God's wisdom. But the power of death over us creates fear and anxiety. Death has a power over us. The power of death clouds our minds and hearts as to what death is. Fear often causes us to lapse into self-absorption tied to the fear of self-extinction. Thus, sin facilitates the creation of a cover story and the story is that there exists a realm of the dead outside God.

89. Moore, *Let This Mind*, 130.
90. Moore, *Crucified Is No Stranger*, 51.
91. Moore, *Crucified Is No Stranger*, 44.
92. Moore, *Crucified Is No Stranger*, 33.
93. Moore, *Crucified Is No Stranger*, 55.

About our greatness and not unconnected to death, sin causes us to repress our greatness. We choose to stay with the known and familiar and build walls around ourselves. We choose to deny death by repressing and banishing it. We treat as unimportant death as our limit. We know that "the rejected status of death is the sign of our wretchedness, of our lawlessness, of our incapacity to feel that we cannot deal with."[94]

If what Moore has said is a truthful statement of sin, then we can better understand Jesus' inner being without sin. Moore describes the psychology of Jesus that might help us understand the One who redeemed us and freely chose to die for us and to die on account of our sins. For Moore, one of the most critical ways to appreciate the person of Jesus is through the title Jesus the Guiltless One or Sinless One. To call Jesus guiltless is to call him sinless or without sin. As previously mentioned, we can only understand what it means to call Jesus sinless when we truly know what sin is. To appreciate the horror of sin, we need to experience sorrow and forgiveness, which God freely gifts. Religious conversion allows us to grasp for the first time God's immense love for us, God's self-acceptance of us, the experience of sorrow and forgiveness, and, simultaneously, the depth of lostness that is sin. Then, we realize the depth of evil that humankind can reach and the link between the rejection of our true self and a state of non-being. Only then can we begin to appreciate what it means to call Jesus the Guiltless and Sinless One.

Jesus the Sinless One lives in the celebration of being. He enjoys a deep intimacy with his Abba God. Jesus undergoes the shedding of ego states throughout his life. He is prepared to live in the incompleteness of being human. The dynamic of oneness and separateness finds convergence in Jesus, living in oneness with the Father, yet in his human incompleteness with trust. He lives with a freedom that is simultaneously an obedience to the Father. He is convinced that death is a return to the Father, but not without having to trust when the darkness of his suffering overcomes him. There is no self-rejection in Jesus: self-love becomes self-gift.

JESUS: SELF-LOVE BECOME SELF-GIFT

To further understand the psychological dynamics of this freely chosen death by Jesus, Moore turns to the importance of self-love becoming

---

94. Moore, *Let This Mind*, 128.

self-gift. Self-love is the natural state of the child who wants to live and be. Unrepressed self-love "presents itself to the other without fear and asks for relationship, seeks to combine, to work with, and then generates security. Somewhere along the path of growth, we are pressured to disavow ourselves from self-love and erect control in its place. This amounts to control of our feeling good about ourselves and keeping our feelings toward others in check."[95] Alternatively, self-love is "repressed, unacknowledged, unshared, generates insecurity, a certain unease, a need to have everything and [every person] my own way."[96] Insecurity seeks power over others, hiding one's self-love from others and ourselves, pressuring us to retreat into ourselves, and, sadly, feeling cut off and isolated. The isolated self seeks to control others, and the need to dominate becomes compulsive, coming from an "unconscious" mind. There is a nonalignment in our self-love before there is a felt sense of failing others. The split within self-love between unlimited desire and control hampers its proper direction toward self-gift.

Concerning Jesus, Moore states that there is no split in his self-love, such that his self-love becomes self-gift, and both are entirely aligned.[97] For Jesus, the dichotomy between the God of desire and the God of controlling one's desires is a faulty dichotomy. In Jesus, the God of desire is totally to be trusted.[98] His complete trust in the Father means he does not have anxieties about survival. He is comfortable with his sexuality and at ease among women. He moves toward death as if it were his destiny. It is as if he says to his disciples: "I will not make you happy on your terms, but I can restore your dread of death from the condition in which you must forget it to the condition where you have nothing to hold you, but the everlasting arm in whose embrace is eternal happiness."[99] On the cross, Jesus' death reveals our fear of Jesus. It is the fear of one who is genuinely free since he takes on "a death that I dare not die."[100] It is the death of someone who has reached the pinnacle of self-gift, but from a perspective of death far different from our own. Jesus crucified is the man we dare not be, in the death we dare not die, with an understanding of death we dare not entertain due to our entrapment in sin.

95. Moore, *Inner Loneliness*, 47.
96. Moore, *Inner Loneliness*, 47.
97. Moore, *Inner Loneliness*, 50.
98. Moore, *Inner Loneliness*, 83.
99. Moore, *Inner Loneliness*, 99.
100. Moore, *Crucified Is No Stranger*, 71.

A New Awareness

THE FREEDOM OF JESUS

Moore's penetration into the reality of sin helps us appreciate that sinlessness is not simply keeping or not keeping laws. Our freedom goes far deeper than simply keeping rules. Freedom occurs at a depth where we confront the ultimate mystery, which is the place for an unimpeded intimacy with God. At this depth, there is no guilt, holding back, or rendering God fearsome and threatening. God and the believer flourish in ultimate companionship with the mystery and in the "total grateful and joyful acceptance of one another's being from the mystery."[101] In that place of Mystery, the one approaching God experiences a consciousness of self as beloved of the Mystery and the Mystery as "un-shadowed love and beauty."[102] It is a meeting place where the will of God would be fulfilled and would never be imposed, coerced, or forced, not even forced to a terrible death. The liberated self would be open to others in an inconceivably complete way. The self would be free of any un-self-worth. No one who met the liberated person would feel rejected, pigeonholed, stereotyped, or any other form of guilt projection. The believer would come to see "no other meaning" in his life than the inauguration of a new guilt-free fellowship of men and women on earth.[103]

Moore wants to construct a psychology of Jesus as free from sin. Moore states: "Jesus our true self, totally liberated from . . . cancer that eats away the self."[104] Jesus comes to the depth of unimpeded intimacy with God. He is the beloved Son of the Father. His intimacy with the Father means a friendship with all. Where sin needs outcasts, Jesus had no outcasts. Where sin causes humankind to project a dichotomy between God's infinite power over and against God's weakness, God's weakness is found in Jesus. Where guilt and sin in the disciples project different kinds of false images onto God, after the resurrection, God is encountered, not as power, but as love. The human psyche is the "home of eros, of guilt and of all the marvelous and conflicting movements shaped by these two forces, encountered the Absolute as love."[105] The risen Jesus is humanity's complete sight of who God is.

---

101. Moore, *Fire and the Rose*, 78.
102. Moore, *Fire and the Rose*, 78.
103. Moore, *Fire and the Rose*, 78.
104. Moore, *Fire and the Rose*, 77.
105. Moore, *Fire and the Rose*, 91.

JESUS: BEING IN THE FORM OF GOD

Moore turns to Saint Paul's Letter to the Philippians 2:6 and presents another understanding of the phrase "being in the form of God." Again, he aims to recover the unique moral-psychological shape of Jesus. The primary meaning of "being in the form of God" has nothing to do with the equality of the Son to the Father as two persons in the Godhead of the Trinity. Paul's intention is not to descend from the Godhead to the Word made flesh but to understand Jesus' descent into the horror of his death. The free acceptance of suffering and the taking to himself of sin is the form of God. Moore states: "It was because death was not necessary for Jesus as it is for us that he was able to choose it out of love for us in a unique act of solidarity."[106]

The affirmation that the passion was undertaken freely and chosen by Jesus is essential to understanding redemption. The memory of Jesus, whose horrible death was chosen freely by him, is not simply a memory. It is a "dangerous memory."[107] To be ready for death is to be living our earthly life to the full. Jesus lives his earthly life to the full and so befriends death and chooses that "depth in all of us, which we consigned to oblivion and confront therefore as an alien but inescapable fate."[108]

What has to happen for us to embrace the dangerous memory? Moore proposes a twofold process. First, the Spirit has to awaken our natural desires that we have denied, repressed, and forgotten. The process that the Spirit helps bring about is the awakening of forgotten desire. Second, the Spirit teaches us "to lose those desires in the huge movement of God into all that exists. We are to become, first honest, then cosmic."[109] Moore proposes an imaginative visualization of the cosmic. We would be standing "on this promontory of the infinite silence, our consciousness not covered with the immemorially created membrane, our desires stretched to the full and thus brushed by that final dissolution wherein it will be one with the love that pulsates in all the universe."[110] What we do know is that the meaning of death in Jesus' consciousness would be very different, since it would be coming from a person being free from any sense of the meaninglessness of death. While some may look upon Jesus'

---

106. Moore, *Let This Mind*, 126.
107. Moore, *Let This Mind*, 126.
108. Moore, *Let This Mind*, 129.
109. Moore, *Let This Mind*, 127.
110. Moore, *Let This Mind*, 127.

suffering and death and pronounce a heartless universe, in the presence of love, Jesus on the cross, who willingly enters the depth of ourselves that we have alienated, opens our eyes to a new universe.[111]

Our exploration into Moore's understanding of the meaning and significance of Jesus for us will continue in chapter 8 focusing on the meaning and significance of the doctrine of redemption in Jesus.

---

111. Moore, *Let This Mind*, 129.

8

Moore and the Person of Jesus II

INTRODUCTION

In this chapter, I will continue to unpack Moore's understanding of the meaning and significance of Jesus, especially with regard to the meaning of our redemption through Jesus. I will also examine Moore's response to disputes within Christology regarding the meaning of the resurrection and the empty tomb, the relationship between conversion to Jesus and church dogma, and whether we can say that the crucifixion indicates that God suffers.

LONERGAN AND REDEMPTION

Moore does not give a comprehensive theology of redemption in Christ. His insights are more corrections to mistaken views around what it means to say that Christ redeemed us. He does express caution towards the terms *satisfaction*, *vicarious satisfaction*, and *sacrifice* when speaking about the saving death of Jesus. Lonergan's understanding of redemption can be found in his *De Verbo Incarnato* (Theses 15–17) and the more mature work, *Supplementum de Redemption*, which are now both available and translated into English in the one volume *Redemption*. Moore uses positively a term important to Lonergan's theology of redemption, the Mysterious Law of the Cross. To understand the meaning of the term and Moore's reception of it requires an understanding of redemption from Lonergan's perspective. Lonergan's theology of redemption is elegant but complex, and my study cannot do justice to all its major or minor insights. I am relying on a study of Lonergan's theology of redemption by Mark Miller, who asks: Why the passion? I will now summarize Miller's salient insights about Lonergan's theology.

First, redemption is a mystery.[1] We know it exists, but we do not understand completely what redemption is or how it exists. Any theology of redemption is our attempt to understand the mystery. If redemption itself is a mystery, it remains a truth of our Christian faith which we will not completely understand in this earthly life. Originally, one of the meanings of the word *mystery* denoted a "secret plan" or "hidden plan" made by a wise king. In this case, God intends a particular order for creation, and God has a plan for the realization of creation when God will be in all things. For the Christian, redemption is made possible because of the actions of Christ. God's plan included redemption through the life, death, and resurrection of Jesus. Christ's intervention to bring about the plan of God is a movement or process which brings reconciliation and heals the rupture of sin. The end of redemption is full communion with God. The end of redemption is made possible since divine wisdom orders all creation.[2] Finally, redemption is a mystery since it is God's response to the problem of evil, and evil is unintelligible, even unintelligible to God.

Second, we may ask: Was it necessary that God in Christ suffer and die? For Lonergan, it was neither absolutely necessary nor hypothetically necessary (against Saint Anselm) that God in Christ should suffer and die. Lonergan states that it was fitting. Fittingness points to the fact that, while the way of redemption was not the only way, it was the wisest way chosen by God in his infinite wisdom to bring humankind to communion with God.[3]

Third, redemption comes about because of sin and on account of sin. Sin alienates us from God and each other. Paul states that "the wages of sin is death" (Rom 6:23). Prior to the crucifixion, death is the consequence of sin. In the crucifixion, death becomes the means of salvation. As noted in the previous chapter, we must establish two realities about death. Our idea of death before the redemption is distorted by sin. Jesus' understanding of death is opposite to our own and has not become distorted by sin. After redemption, sin remains, and the consequences

---

1. Miller, "Why the Passion?," 164–67.
2. Miller, "Why the Passion?," 164–68.
3. Miller, "Why the Passion?," 169–71.

of further sins remain, but in Christ, there are steps toward a transformation from a distorted idea of death, and toward a pathway to life.[4]

Fourth, in Thesis 15 of his treatise on redemption, Lonergan tries to come to grips with several biblical elements that become part and parcel of any unified theology of redemption:[5] the notion of a price paid (1 Cor 6:20; Mark 10:45); the idea of vicarious suffering and death (Rom 5:6–10); propitiation and expiation (Rom 3:25); the meaning of sacrifice (Heb 9:28); the meaning of meritorious obedience when applied to Christ (Rom 5:19); the risen Lord's power (Phil 3:10); and Christ the eternal priest's intercession (Heb 4:14–16). Navigating all these elements becomes crucial so as to avoid any mistaken understanding of the significance of the suffering and death of Christ so that we can intelligently work out what it means to say Christ redeems us.

The idea of redemption can be understood in two ways.[6] Firstly, redemption is taken from an analogy of a business transaction. Redemption is a transaction involving a payment. Secondly, redemption is taken from the analogy of being delivered from a terrible fate, for example, deliverance from one's enemies, so as to live in a state of social tranquility. Redemption is our liberation in Christ. We are delivered from sin so as to live in personal holiness. Lonergan is wary of understanding redemption as a price paid. The meaning of a price paid is still valid, but only in a very minimal way. The minimal way is when the term matches with "giving his life."[7] By "giving his life," we can observe the price for our redemption. Overall, the problem with the term *payment* is that it may lead to the misunderstanding that God demanded a price to be paid for the dishonoring of divine justice brought about by sin. The understanding that payment was demanded by God puts aside an important ingredient in the mystery of redemption, namely, the giving of Jesus' life is free, an insight that Moore emphasizes in the term "a dangerous memory." Christ's whole self, his life, his suffering, and his death were all freely given and not demanded.[8]

In the end, Christ dies for sinners *despite* their sins (there is a killing of Christ), but equally, Christ dies for sinners *because* of their sins (there is an act of redemption by Christ). If Christ dies for sins despite their

4. Miller, "Why the Passion?," 181.
5. Miller, "Why the Passion?," 175.
6. Miller, "Why the Passion?," 180–82.
7. Miller, "Why the Passion?," 186–87.
8. Miller, "Why the Passion?," 183–88.

sin, then we can say that Christ freely embraced the sins of humanity. Therefore, there cannot be any hint that Christ's action to remove sin was a matter of placating God or appeasing the anger of God. If this is the case, propitiation and expiation have nothing to do with appeasing an angry God. From the biblical account, these terms speak Christ's action on sin, not Christ's action toward God.[9]

Fifth, the action of Christ can be called a sacrifice or sacrificial.[10] Again, the word *sacrifice* is difficult to understand precisely and can be very easily misunderstood. As indicated in the previous chapter, Moore is suspicious of the term only because it has acquired a distorted meaning in the minds of many people. Sacrifice can mean appeasing the gods. By contrast, in the biblical account, sacrifice is about operating on sin, not on God. The sacrifice of Christ affects the remission of sin and acts on behalf of sinners. It is a permanent sacrifice. It cleanses consciences, removes sin once and for all, and is uniquely done by Christ, who is both the priest and Lamb of sacrifice.[11]

Sixth, the actions of Christ in the redemption are grounded in meritorious obedience.[12] Obedience is a response to a command. It is a command about something that moves another by reason and will. But a command is not a demand. Christ is obedient to the Father, who sends him on a mission. Christ's acts were acts of perfect obedience and perfect freedom. The Father does not coerce the Son. The Father works through the Son's knowledge and choice. Between the Father and the Son, there is perfect intimacy and perfect unity. In Christ, love and obedience are paired. The redemption, then, is not just that Christ suffers and dies but that he does so through his obedience and love.[13]

Seventh, Christ's mediating of redemption does not end with his death on the cross. The redemption continues in the resurrection and into eternal life. Christ's death is the death of the one who will be raised in his risen body. Yet, Christ is a source of sanctification, intercession, and our eternal priest.[14]

---

9. Miller, "Why the Passion?," 190–94.
10. Miller, "Why the Passion?," 193–97.
11. Miller, "Why the Passion?," 195–96.
12. Miller, "Why the Passion?," 197–201.
13. Miller, "Why the Passion?," 198.
14. Miller, "Why the Passion?," 201–4.

Eighth, Lonergan uses the term *satisfaction* to understand better the inner workings of redemption.[15] He admits that it is not a comprehensive term, but it is a most fruitful and fitting means for understanding redemption. The term *satisfaction* is part of the official teaching of the Church and Lonergan makes this clear in Thesis 16 in his work, *The Incarnate Word*. Lonergan calls the suffering and death of Christ a vicarious satisfaction. Vicarious means "on behalf of another" and not as a substitution for another. Substitution carries the misunderstanding that what was done by Christ meant that humanity had no part to play and continues to remain passive. Vicarious action carries the understanding of offering an apology for sinners and on account of sin, but with sinners having their part to play. Again, vicarious suffering is not demanded of Jesus or a condition for the forgiveness of God. It is neither a need nor a motive for redemption.

Satisfaction is an analogical term and an overarching way of bringing various elements of redemption together, including the price paid, sacrifice, meritorious obedience, the passion undergone for us, and for our sins. By his blood and passion, Christ satisfies divine justice and the Father's majesty. It is a proportionate action responding to divine justice on account of our sins. The process of satisfaction is grounded in God's "wise plan." The wise plan of God has to do with the ordering of the universe. The ordering of the universe is such that there are consequences to sin. Again, Christ's satisfaction is not necessary, either supernaturally or hypothetically. Christ's satisfaction is fitting, appropriate, and prudent.

Thus, satisfaction is completely different from satispassion.[16] Satispassion posits that the cross is a punishment that Christ bore in our place (substitutionary) and, therefore, linked to a payment to God or the devil. Satispassion is based on a juridical understanding of the redemption. In its juridical meaning, through sin, God's honor is disregarded, and what follows is a demand for punishment or paying a debt. The punishment is death. The Father commands the Son to take our place since only the Son can do for us what needs to be done toward the Father since the Son is the Father's equal and we are not. The obedience of the Son brings about payment of the debt. The emphasis is on punishment as a debt paid by the Son. It becomes the basis for a penal substitutionary theory.

---

15. Miller, "Why the Passion?," 205–6.
16. Miller, "Why the Passion?," 206–9.

The substitution theory does not adequately express the meaning of the redemption of Christ. The trouble with a substitutionary view is that if God were to demand punishment, then love and forgiveness would be conditional. If the devil were to demand a debt to be paid, then God would not be omnipotent. Further, the consequence of satispassion or the imitation of it in our lives offers the possibility of justifying an imposition of suffering towards the weak by the powerful. It could become an encouragement for the sufferer to meekly accept and resign themselves to their sufferings even when that suffering is being unjustly perpetrated on the victim. It falsely presents an image of God as just and who gives sinners only the suffering sinners deserve. It also reduces Christ's work to payment of a debt intended to appease the Father's wrath.[17]

Saint Anselm first introduces the term *satisfaction*.[18] For Anselm, satisfaction is not a debt of punishment but a debt of obedience and love. His understanding of redemption may be summarized in this way: everything comes from God, and everything should go back to God. Sin short-circuits our return to God by offending the divine majesty. Humans cannot pay back the debt for the offense. A savior God-man alone can do this. Christ offers his life and infinite worth to God the Father. Christ does not suffer the punishment of sin as we do since Christ is sinless. He offers God a satisfactory gift, which is his life. In the end, it is not that Christ suffers enough to pay back the debt to God but that Christ *does* enough. God is satisfied by Christ's offering of his life, not by the punishment endured, but because of his love and obedience. Humans then are to cooperate with Christ by repentance, sorrow, and forgiving others.

The problem with Anselm's theory is that it still couches redemption in terms of an exchange or transaction. It seems to make divine love subordinate to divine justice. Needing a debt to be paid seems to make God's attitude toward us to be one of pity. The stress on God's honor and a debt needing to be paid seems to make salvation conditional on the debt paid before forgiveness can be given. There is a kind of "necessity" for the God-man to offer to pay the debt. Further, God redeems humanity, and humanity remains passive in the whole exchange.[19]

Despite the imperfection of the analogy of satisfaction, Lonergan retains it since satisfaction aligns with the idea that Christ dies on

---

17. Miller, "Why the Passion?," 207–9.
18. Miller, "Why the Passion?," 209–12.
19. Miller, "Why the Passion?," 210–11.

account of sin.[20] He contextualizes the term within an understanding of punishment due to divine justice and friendship by God toward humankind. On the one hand, one could say that God did "punish" the Son for the sins of humankind since God sets up the order in the universe in a manner that allows consequences for sin. On the other hand, we must keep in mind that the order of the universe that God establishes by God's will is such that God directly wills good alone. God does not will sin, even though he permits it. Even the language of "God indirectly willing moral evil" is imprecise. To speak of God "indirectly" willing moral evil falls short of the complete saving attitude of God.

To understand this more clearly, we must start with sin itself. There are two kinds of sin.[21] The first is "basic sin" or our original fault. The second is each and every moral fault subsequent to our original fault. As a consequence of the latter, punishment or the penalty for sin becomes what we are forced to suffer due to our offense. However, the evil of penalty is not a form of retribution for the wrong we have done. The evil of penalty is a deprivation or suppression of some good that would normally have been there where it not for our sinful choice. Thus, in the order of the universe, even if we affirm that sin has consequences, the rightful meaning of the "wrath of God" (Rom 1:18) carries the meaning that there are consequences to sin and not the meaning that God's fierce anger bears upon us. The punishment of sin is not directly willed or inflicted by God. It is a consequence of the fault since offenses have consequences. The direct cause of Christ's suffering is the action of the actors involved. The indirect cause is the way God has ordered the universe.

Further, God directly wills Christ's unconditional love in the passion, even in the face of evil. What we must keep in mind is that the punishments endured by Christ are not forced, imposed, or inflicted by the Father. Christ freely chooses these punishments and offers himself freely in redemption for all. Thus, there is a distinction to be made between punishment inflicted in the context of retribution and punishment taken on in the case of satisfaction.[22]

This suggests two ways to understand satisfaction. Satisfaction can be linked to retributive justice.[23] In the normal course of events between an offender and an offended, conflict gives rise to fault. The fault creates

20. Miller, "Why the Passion?," 212.
21. Miller, "Why the Passion?," 214–15.
22. Miller, "Why the Passion?," 213–17.
23. Miller, "Why the Passion?," 218.

an offense against the offended. The fault also has a damaging effect on the offender (penalty or punishment). The offender gives payment for the fault or offense. The payment or punishment matches the fault. The debt is paid, and justice has been served. Alternatively, the process of satisfaction can also arise when a person offers an offended party something that they value as much as or more than the offense or fault against the offended party, something that pleases the offended as much or more than the hated offense.

If satisfaction is offered, it does not mean that therefore it is imposed. No imposition implies no retributive justice. Even when satisfaction is offered, the offender must still be prepared to undergo punishment as a consequence of the fault, even if sorrow (by the offender) and forgiveness for the fault (by the offended) have been expressed. Even if the offended party grants forgiveness, we cannot speak of forgiveness as being necessary. In the case of Christ, satisfaction is offered justly by someone who is not the guilty party. Christ offers satisfaction out of love, obedience, and divine justice.[24]

The satisfaction that Christ offers is vicarious.[25] Vicarious satisfaction acknowledges that healing can be achieved by someone other than the person who does the offense. The offender may even despise or reject such satisfaction and remain unrepentant. Therefore, there needs to be in the one offering satisfaction, a twofold friendship. First, there needs to be a friendship between the offender and the one making satisfaction. Second, there needs to be a friendship between the one making satisfaction and the one offended.[26] Vicarious satisfaction is based on the union of two wills by love: the will of the offender and the will of the one making satisfaction. The offender and the one making satisfaction are united in love, such that the one making satisfaction is sharing the offender's sufferings. The offender notices that the one making satisfaction suffers, even though they are without punishment, and sees themselves (the offender) as the cause of the suffering. They feel pain for the one making satisfaction on their behalf. The pain of the one making satisfaction is interior, and it leads to knowledge, love, detestation of sin, and sorrow. The offender acknowledges that the one making the satisfaction has a deep love for the offender, as well as a love for the one offended, a knowledge

---

24. Miller, "Why the Passion?," 218–22.
25. Miller, "Why the Passion?," 223–24.
26. Miller, "Why the Passion?," 224–25.

that the offender's fault is offensive, a detestation of the offender's fault, and a sorrow for the offense. That certainly is the ideal.

However, the reality may be that the sinner or offender may be unrepentant. In that case, satisfaction needs to be moved by charity on the part of the one offering it. The offender may not be sorry for their offense. They may not even wish for the friendship of the one making satisfaction. They may even be their enemy. Charity alone would draw out love from the unfriendly offender with the goal of reconciliation. In the natural order, friendship proceeds satisfaction. In the divine order, charity precedes friendship so that the one making satisfaction (Christ) brings out a similar love in the offender (sinners). Divine order satisfaction is based on the love of charity for the one offended and, love for the one satisfied (the heavenly Father), and love in the heart of the one doing the satisfaction (the Son). Divine charity moves the heart and mind of the offender to love the one who has made satisfaction and divine charity moves the one making satisfaction to sorrow and detestation for the sin committed. Only from charity can the process of satisfaction start, especially when there is no love from the offender towards the one making satisfaction and the offender towards the one who has been offended.[27]

Christ's satisfaction takes on the punishment of the sinner so as to express multiple realities: the love of the Father, the knowledge that human faults have consequences and are an offense against God, detestation of these faults, sorrow for the offenses, and the charitable love of humanity. Christ shows both his love of God the Father and humanity. In the cross, he takes on and satisfies the requirements of divine justice. He does not earn divine forgiveness since divine forgiveness is there from the outset through the divine initiative that flows from eternal love. The divine initiative works to reconcile human beings to God, to draw out love from sinners, and to move them to make friends with Christ and the Father. Christ's satisfaction for us is only made possible due to divine friendship. In coming to detest our sins and be sorry for them, we come to a new union of friendship with God.

Finally, we may have a part to play in the suffering caused by others. We can also be called on to participate by means of our vicarious suffering (our satisfaction) for the sins of others, and such participation is only possible because of Christ's satisfaction and the gift of grace. Our vicarious satisfaction is only analogous to Christ's satisfaction since only

---

27. Miller, "Why the Passion?," 223–26.

the satisfaction of Christ is perfect. Meanwhile, our satisfaction is never perfect, and so punishment is never taken on by us with the same simple freedom that Christ has taken it on. It becomes clear that a transformation is happening through satisfaction such that good is offered for evil. Evil may be permitted, but good comes of it. God's love is not earned by satisfaction; it is freely given. Christ's satisfaction expresses a perfect knowledge of and perfect love of God and humanity while, at the same time, Christ's passion expresses God's hatred of sin.[28]

Ninth, in Thesis 17 of *De Verbo Incarnato*, Lonergan incorporates a number of elements to bring together an understanding of what he calls the Mysterious Law of the Cross. The Law of the Cross cannot be understood apart from the adoption by Lonergan of the analogy of satisfaction. Satisfaction and the Law of the Cross are the interlinked principles of Lonergan's theology of redemption. The Law of the Cross is a fitting way to explain how Christ brings sinful humanity to God and how Christ builds the kingdom from humanity wounded individually and socially by sin.[29] It is called a "law" in the sense of being a process or change of the kind that a craftsman would use. As "law," it is not an absolute necessity flowing from some logical analysis. As "law," it is not conditional and necessary, as are the laws of nature. The Law of the Cross has a fittingness, goodness, and effectiveness and a universal process that does not flow from an arbitrary will of power but from divine authority and wisdom. Redemption is predicated on humanity being brought back to God, who is our end through grace. Only by the Holy Spirit can Christians recognize and follow the fittingness of the Law of the Cross. From a state marked by sin, alienation, disorder, and division, Christ brings healing through wisdom and charity, a restored relationship with God for humanity, the possibility of reconciliation between people, and a renewed order in the universe by overcoming evil with good.

There are three stages to transformation.[30] First, the evil of fault gives way to punishment. Second, the evil of punishment is voluntarily transformed. Third, the Father blesses this transformation with another good. For Christ, the sins of humanity lead to his sufferings. By his loving and obedient acceptance of our punishment, Christ transforms the sufferings of punishment for our sins into a moral good. This is the

---

28. Miller, "Why the Passion?," 227–31.
29. Miller, "Why the Passion?," 243–44.
30. Miller, "Why the Passion?," 250.

satisfaction, teaching, expression, revelation, and communication of God's wisdom and glory.

As God heals sinners, we observe the free acceptance of Christ to convert evil to good. We observe that his suffering and death are transformed from the mere consequences of sin to a means of new life. Christ died for us and for our sins. He put up with evil so that it does not act as a blotter but transforms our evil situation into a situation where good flourishes. The cycle of decline brought about by evil is not only stopped in Christ's act, it is reversed. The action of Christ is also an act in which the Father and the Holy Spirit are involved. There is no hint that the sufferings of Christ act like some kind of safety mechanism to hold back the anger of God, since it is the plan of God from the beginning to reconcile us to Himself. Christ did not earn the Father's love beacause of his sufferings. Our redemption was the divine intention of God's wisdom and love from the beginning.

The Law of the Cross becomes a precept, an example, and a promise.[31] As a precept, the law is imperative for our life in all its dimensions, that is, physically, morally, and spiritually. As an example, the law shows that the deeds of Christ match his words. As a promise, the law reveals in the resurrection the Father's blessing of his Son's meritorious choice when he gives his life without reserve, and the resurrection becomes the Father's final word to Christ's death and inspires hope.[32]

MOORE AND LONERGAN ON REDEMPTION

What are Moore's points of intersection and complementarity with Lonergan when it comes to a theology of redemption? First, in 1953, Moore published the second article of a twofold reflection on death. In the second article, Moore speaks about the theology of redemption and its needed correctives.[33] At this stage in his theological career, Moore's concern is to highlight how our misunderstanding of death and our projection of death into "a kind of no-man's-land beyond experience," which causes us to fail to "appropriate"[34] our death, pushes the mystery of death and its solution onto God. Pushing the solution to the problem

---

31. Miller, "Why the Passion?," 255–56.
32. Miller, "Why the Passion?," 237–58.
33. Moore, "Reflexions on Death II," 14–24.
34. Moore, "Reflexions on Death II," 21.

of death onto God has the consequence of alienating our human existence, resolving the reality of death in some beyond, and turning the mystery of God into "the reality that is beyond us," a reality that is "unfelt, impersonal 'mystery.'"[35]

Again, Moore points out that he is not about to provide an exhaustive account of the doctrine of redemption "but only to indicate . . . an important corrective for our way of thinking about it."[36] He begins with the ransom texts in the Gospels (Matt 20:28; Mark 10:45). If ransom denotes paying a debt, Moore asks to whom is the debt paid, God or the devil, echoing a perspective first taken up by the early fathers of the church when reflecting on these texts. Moore is clear about the end or term of redemption. It is God and not the devil. Moore's central starting point for correcting an understanding of redemption can be summed up in these words: "Christ gave himself for love and out of love . . . The Redemption is not only a work of love; it is the primary revelation of what love *is*."[37]

Moore states that redemption has nothing to do with retribution or "satisfaction" for the sins of humankind. By "satisfaction," I believe that Moore is alluding to the notion of penal substitution. Our misunderstanding of death and our distorted understanding of the mystery of God as beyond us gives rise to the idea that redemption is about retribution. Moore affirms that the claim of a price needing to be paid is distorted. The claim is made *relative* by Christ, such that when it lays hold of Christ, "our engagement with the world reaches its full intensity yet loses its poisonous fascination."[38] When it lays hold of Christ, the world and human existence are no longer an empty void but a location filled "with a presence which draws as love draws: it becomes the medium in which we apprehend Christ's work, whose 'satisfaction' at our level opens out onto the simple love in which he meets the Father."[39] Christ's joining of us to the Father through his satisfaction does not have a scintilla of legal overtone to it but is "a new dimension where God is known not merely through his ordinances but in himself, as love."[40] God's hidden and mysterious plan is revealed in Christ: the Spirit is poured over us, and we become his sons

---

35. Moore, "Reflexions on Death II," 14.
36. Moore, "Reflexions on Death II," 14.
37. Moore, "Reflexions on Death II," 19.
38. Moore, "Reflexions on Death II," 20.
39. Moore, "Reflexions on Death II," 20.
40. Moore, "Reflexions on Death II," 20.

and daughters and are enabled to call God, Father. Moore is quite happy to use the language of satisfaction when speaking of the actions of Christ. However, to say that Christ offers satisfaction does not go far enough in capturing or expressing his 'motive' since it does not capture well enough the motive of love and the motive that God will be all in all.

The truth is that while God permits these consequences out of wisdom and love, God's motive for accepting the suffering and obedience of Christ is not because the Father deems Christ's act as making up for an offense against him. Rather, God does all that is possible to provide a solution to the problem of sin and evil. God's mysterious plan is a plan of love. Christ's satisfaction is freely given, not imposed or coerced, and is part of God's hidden plan of love from all time and proportionate to divine justice. The satisfaction of Christ is grounded in Christ's love for the Father and friendship for us. Christ's satisfaction is not responding to a need in the Father for retribution, nor is it motivated by a wish to appease the Father.

Moore expounds on Anselm's theory of satisfaction and its unhelpful rendering by countless preachers. He is clear on this point:

> Christ's doing for us what we could not do for ourselves takes on another sense, a real sense. It ceases to mean some kind of transaction done for us somewhere in the background. It no longer involves our being told that over and above our experience of ourselves, we have a self that has contracted a debt to God, which it had to have paid for it, a debt whose enormity is suggested uniquely in terms of the greatness of the person defended. . . . Indeed, the Redemption *is* situated beyond our experience of ourselves, but we can learn progressively, by meditating on our death to understand the inadequacies of this experience: so that as this understanding develops, and we find that with it we can penetrate further into the great scriptural and liturgical statements of the Redemption, we see that it is our real life (so ill-known by us) that is engaged by this mystery and not a kind of [theological and legal] personality.[41]

Toward the later years of his life, Moore still struggles with the term *satisfaction*. My hunch is that too many people still hold to a distorted view of satisfaction, and Moore's hesitancy comes from considering a true understanding of satisfaction too difficult for people to appropriate. Perhaps he is speaking to a particular generation of believers when

---

41. Moore, "Reflexions on Death II," 24.

he writes: "Now we have an unusually vivid example of God's mind outstripping ours in the way we have been taught to understand how Christ saved us, by his death. By that death, we were told he paid the debt incurred by the sin of Adam. This explanation, called 'vicarious satisfaction,' once preferred by theologians, has God implementing our miserable ideas of offense, debt, and punishment, the rules of the game under the reign of sin."[42]

Similarly, Moore does not evade the complexity of the word *punishment*. Simply speaking, punishment is any lack of physical, moral, or spiritual good that is forced, imposed, or inflicted. The punishment for sin gives rise to a mistaken view of death, which causes fear and anxiety, a punishment permitted by God as an element of an ordered universe God has created. From such a perspective, the psychology of death is dominated by guilt. Mistakenly, we think that since death and our failure are interrelated, there is no way of remedying the situation. The only answer to the problem of remedy is paying some debt.[43]

Nor is the death of Christ to be understood as Christ's way of changing God's mind after punishing us with death. We are unable to gain a proper understanding of redemption as long as we view death as a punishment required by God. Death is part and parcel of being finite and mortal. Moore states that "the more death ceases to be, in our thought, 'what God requires,' the more we can see, in and beyond Christ's death, the fulfillment of God's real 'requirement,' which is love."[44] If we want to know the true meaning of death and thus move away from the notion of death being God's way of punishing us, we have no other place to look than Golgotha and the cross. Moore affirms that it is the aliveness of Christ that contributes to his death since

> he was so much more alive than other men: and men dread and fear a fullness of life in someone, and the fear turns to hatred. And so, the crucifixion was the conflict between life and the fear of life, between human truth and the human lie. It had to be. Put Jesus and other men side-by-side, and you get the Cross. The next thing to notice is this. This death, which men inflicted on Jesus, was what his whole being asked for. For this fully alive man saw death as his consummation. The more alive, the more awake a man is, the more he sees death *right ahead*. Whereas

---

42. Moore, *Contagion of Jesus*, 28.
43. Moore, "Reflexions on Death II," 22.
44. Moore, "Reflexions on Death II," 21.

we who are only half-alive, see it out of the corner of our eye, Christ's, or death right ahead of him as his fulfillment, . . . men, in crucifying our Lord fulfilled him. Underlying this savage conflict, there was a sort of unity between his desire and theirs. Calvary is a tempestuous love affair between Christ and man.[45]

In my presentation of Lonergan's theology of redemption, I note his striving for a unified view on the subject. As I indicated, any unified view would have to incorporate a number of notions: paying the price and ransom; vicarious suffering and death; meritorious obedience; the power of the risen Lord; the eternal priest who intercedes for us; deliverance from sin and evil; propitiation and expiation; satisfaction; sacrifice; sorrow for sins; the forgiveness of and for sins; the wrath of God; divine justice, divine wisdom, and divine friendship; charity; overcoming evil with good; and transforming evil into good. Moore does not deal with each of these notions systematically, nor is it his intention to attain a unified and systematic view of redemption. However, he makes a significant contribution to the theology of redemption by examining several elements in need of correction.

MOORE AND THE MYSTERIOUS LAW OF THE CROSS

There is a link between Moore and Lonergan's expression the Mysterious Law of the Cross. I suggest that Lonergan's theological understanding of redemption is constituted by two major elements: the theory of satisfaction, properly understood, and what he calls the Mysterious Law of the Cross. For Moore to take up the latter element without incorporating the former may be problematic. However, he does agree with Lonergan on his starting point. Namely, sin subjects us to death by making death the triumphant alien, the final unmeaning of our being, and, in many minds, an agent of an ambiguous God. Therefore, sin is taken away by Christ on the cross when he embraces our death out of love for us, who are its helpless subjects, so that our hearts can open to the unambiguously compassionate God. Moore states: "I have to see the drama of sin and death at the level of existential meaning rather than at the level of ontological for which death came only with sin."[46] Moore's emphasis is on the felt sense of meaninglessness in death, or existential death, that characterizes the penalty of sin.

---

45. Moore and Hurt, *Before the Deluge*, 21.
46. Moore, *Let This Mind*, 138.

A New Awareness

On another occasion, during a directed Ignatian retreat, Moore states:

> I have to rewrite Lonergan's law of the Cross. It starts off [as] 'sin leads to death.' But the only death produced by sin is that of Jesus. There and there alone sheer life . . . came up against the world in all its initial anti-life power, and this collision destroyed Jesus, drew all his blood from him. Faced with *that* death, faced with the result of the sin that is in me, I see my sin as [our] death wish, as that most profound turning of life against itself, which only the light of Golgotha makes clear.[47]

Another reference to Lonergan's Law of the Cross has Moore trying to answer questions concerning the self-knowledge of Jesus. Moore acknowledges that the use of the word *law* connotes a process, similar to any process that can be repeated to bear fruit, and he offers his example of what "law" could mean. His example is: "Without ordered self-love, there cannot be friendship."[48] Moore states that the new law of the cross transmutes the old law since the new law is constituted by the grace of the Holy Spirit, the resurrection fruit of the passion of Christ. He asserts: "The destiny of God's intimate as [the] victim is a divine order, a divine making-explicit of the human condition in all its mystery, in all its desperation, in all its perversity."[49] He also affirms that "the Law of the Cross inscribed in the soul of Jesus, wrote itself by an ominous contagion in the souls of his followers, to erupt into triumphant affirmation when they were brought from his death into his life."[50] The disciples understand the law and its deeper meaning only after the resurrection. Thus, in the resurrection, the disciples and all believers are brought from our distorted view of death through his death and into his life, that is, the new life of God.

Moore has no time for a theology of redemption, which predicates the efficacy of the death of Jesus simply due to "his unique status as divine." Rather, the efficacy of redemption is best understood in the changing effect on human beings as they encounter the crucified and risen Lord, following the template of change lived out in the experience of the disciples. Every act of faith, love, and hope arises from our encounter with the risen Lord. This encounter is the basis for any later affirmation

---

47. Moore, *Let This Mind*, 168.
48. Moore, *Jesus the Liberator*, 13.
49. Moore, *Jesus the Liberator*, 13.
50. Moore, *Jesus the Liberator*, 14.

made about his divine sonship. Redemption affirms that humanity can only be brought to humankind's proper end through the grace of the Holy Spirit, and it is only our encounter with the risen Lord that enables this affirmation of faith. In the power of his risen life, we recognize the meaning of redemption, acknowledge the fittingness of the cross as our means of redemption, and are enabled to follow Christ as his disciples. In the power of our encounter with Christ, we affirm God's wisdom and his hidden plan to overcome evil with good. In the Spirit of the Lord, we can take on vicarious suffering in our lives for the sake of overcoming evil with good. In the Spirit of the Lord, we have sorrow for our sins and open our hearts to the forgiveness of God. We recognize that although God creates order in the universe, the consequences of sin result in a mistaken view of death. Yet God's plan is always to redeem us in Christ. The cycle of decline is not only stopped in Christ. It is reversed so that human flourishing is possible. In the Spirit, we recognize a wise order and the gift of immeasurable love from God.

Moore's specific contribution to the theology of redemption is fourfold. First, as indicated in the previous chapter, Moore's contribution is to unpack the meaning of sin and evil that leads to death, including a distorted view of death itself. Second, it is to explore the psychology of Jesus that leads Christians to the claim that he is the guiltless and sinless one. Third, his contribution is to emphasize the freely chosen character of Jesus' acceptance of his passion, a freedom that creates a dangerous memory. Fourth, it is to emphasize the friendship of Jesus with the Father towards each one of us.

MOORE, REDEMPTION, AND GIRARD

I will now unpack the influence of Girard's categories on Moore's insights into the redemption. Moore wholeheartedly embraces the category of Jesus as the scapegoat.[51] Moore states:

> It seems that we cannot live as a society without scapegoating. Yet Jesus challenges it. The parable of the good Samaritan is so well-known that we forget what Jesus was saying in choosing as his hero the most despised figure there then was. He was challenging the whole way of thinking that needs scapegoats so powerful and all-pervasive as a system of scapegoating that it

---

51. Moore, *Contagion of Jesus*, 27–43. Chapter 3 is titled "Jesus—Our Scapegoat."

makes the scapegoat of the one who challenges it. This is an irony that any good novelist would give a fortune to have invented. Jesus says "You don't need to marginalize anyone to victimize anyone" and for saying this, he is himself victimized. He is lifted up on the very Cross that he says we don't have to put people on out of fear. God's Story is the best novel in the world. God's plan is the best plot.[52]

The category of scapegoating becomes important to Moore for understanding both the actions of Jesus and the opposing actions of the ones who put him to death in the context of the passion. Hence, scapegoating is linked to a false idea of sacrifice. Moore states that "God's attempt to *subvert* our deadly custom of having one die in place of all was taken to be the *implementation* of it, and the heavy irony of John, who has the High Priest, no less define the event, was missed."[53] Again, Moore affirms that Jesus' love and obedience lead him "to walk deliberately into the role of scapegoat on which our fallen world depends for its ordering, in order to set us free forever of this horror and make us lovers, not cannibals. He took the place of the Paschal Lamb, thus going to the human root of animal sacrifice in order to pull it up by the root. This involved psychological suffering that hardly bears thinking about."[54]

Jesus challenges the whole way of thinking that needs scapegoats. Yet, so pervasive is the whole system of scapegoating that it makes the one who challenges it, Jesus, into a scapegoat.[55] Moore sums up God's plan:

> God, in the person of his Son let himself be caught in the trap were all in and then he does the most outrageous thing of all. He becomes on his Cross, attractive to us, and this breaks the fundamental rule on which the whole system of scapegoating rests: the victim is supposed to stay victim, stay on the other side, stay excluded—that's what victimizing is for. [But instead] *this* scapegoat becomes the person we want to be. He comes to us with all his allure out of his death, [and] meets us by the lake. There is Jesus on the side of the excluded, inviting us across to that side! And so, he shines before us as God's alluring alternative to the way we live.[56]

---

52. Moore, *Contagion of Jesus*, 32.
53. Moore, *Contagion of Jesus*, 28.
54. Moore, *Contagion of Jesus*, 30.
55. Moore, *Contagion of Jesus*, 32.
56. Moore, *Contagion of Jesus*, 33.

Moore rightly asks the question: How does the willing scapegoat set people free of the need to survive at the expense of others as victims? How does the willing scapegoat set people free from the need to create victims?[57] Provocatively, Moore states:

> He does it by going to his death in a way that makes his own *followers*, its most immediate and shameful beneficiaries—siding with the enemy to save their own skins by deserting him, betraying him, denying him. It is these men who, shamefully spared the tortured death of Rome's victims by deserting their leader, are later shown him risen and all-forgiving, [without accusation], all-embracing, the nearest there can be to a realistic understanding about us being part of his body. Caiaphas, first prophetically and correctly, said that one man must die to save the people. The people that man most poignantly saved by dying alone were his *followers* to whom, totally demoralized through betraying him, he showed himself the new life for all of us.[58]

Moore appropriates Girard's scapegoat mechanism and links it to inauthentic religion. He states: "The self-against has played a vital role in religion."[59] Abraham is a figure halfway between the human blood sacrifice of archaic religion used to bring order to the community and the coming of Jesus inconceivably to all. In Abraham, the scapegoat becomes an animal and not a human. Even Israel's idea of Messiah embraces the self-against since it places those who accept the Messiah in one camp and those who do not in another camp.

Finally, Jesus is both the Lamb slaughtered and the Messiah, and through the resurrection, "the humanity of the victim is restored to our consciousness with the lamb as its metaphor."[60] With Jesus, we find someone who does not shun victimhood as part of the intrinsic idea of Messiah. On our part, to be saved is not to sweep aside somehow the dark places in which we hide. To be saved is to expose the lie. The lie is that we desire to be self-against and in rivalry. Jesus exposes our lie by revealing himself to be the self-as-gift crucified and all-embracing, leading us out of our lost and forgotten ecstasy into universal love. With the resurrection of Jesus, we do not have, simply, a good model but a model "done to death by all that is in us," who brings us together in the Spirit

---

57. Moore, *Contagion of Jesus*, 36.
58. Moore, *Contagion of Jesus*, 36.
59. Moore, *Contagion of Jesus*, 34.
60. Moore, *Contagion of Jesus*, 35.

and through the healing and forgiveness of the risen victim. Jesus models for us a "new way of being human as victim of the old way."[61]

In light of scapegoating, Moore struggles with the meaning of sacrifice when applied to Jesus. For Moore, the reason we miss or make a mistake about the true meaning of the sacrifice of Jesus on the cross is directly due to a mistaken understanding of the term *sacrificial Lamb* taken from the Jewish Passover tradition and applied to Jesus without remainder. There is confusion in the mind of the believer when the very person who is done to death by wicked men is also, by reason of being the victim, acceptable to God. What is important to remember is that the cross is not imposed on Jesus. The cross is not the torment of suffering and death demanded of Jesus, otherwise, such a meaning would attach to sacrifice the meaning of violence and bloodletting. Moore suggests: "What Jesus showed to his chosen ones was life free of our world, a world that death rules by fear and takes one victim to do for all, the world of Caiaphas. Those who saw him burned inwardly with his new life larger than death, as the Emmaus story makes clear."[62]

Ormerod suggests that there exist two discourses of sacrifice in the Christian biblical tradition. The first discourse of sacrifice is the darker side of sacrifice, of which Girard and Moore are most suspicious.[63] Scapegoating is the direct outcome of our darker propensities. Taking a historical-critical account of the Gospels, Jesus represents the stage of final purification for the religious society of Israel through his mission to the poor.[64] People experiencing poverty are the objects of sacrifice. They are thought about only as sinners and social outcasts. Religious leaders judge them to be far from the traditional customs and laws. Jesus appears as a subversive force to question the distorted practices of the community towards sinners and outcasts. From the beginning of his public ministry, Jesus sought out the victims of the social structures of sacrifice, aiming to restore the original charter of justice to the society of Israel.[65] Jesus' identification with the victims becomes the context for society's compulsive need to kill him. For the sake of its own survival and social cohesion, the community and its leaders turn their attention towards destroying him, making him the victim, the perfect victim, since there is every reason for

---

61. Moore, *Contagion of Jesus*, 36.
62. Moore, *Contagion of Jesus*, 29.
63. Ormerod, "Eucharist as Sacrifice," 46.
64. Ormerod, *Grace and Disgrace*, 167–68.
65. Ormerod, *Grace and Disgrace*, 168.

eliminating him. Yet, he was the most innocent of victims, the scapegoat victim. On the cross, the identification becomes complete and total as Jesus becomes the Victim, the pure sacrifice, uncovering the scapegoat mechanism for what it really is.

This reading of the sacrifice of Jesus fits well with the passion narrative: a sacrifice by unjust men for an evil purpose masked by a religious ideology. In the words of Caiaphas: "It is better that one man die for the nation than for the whole nation to be destroyed" (John 11:50).[66] Scapegoating, which survives on being hidden from view, falls into its own trap, and, according to Girard, violence reveals its own game in such a way that, through Jesus, its workings are compromised and exposed to the light. Rather than being, as claimed, an act to save the community, violence towards the innocent victim exposes itself as an act of evil and distorted self-preservation. The interests of some are being protected over the good of the whole for all the wrong reasons. Thus, we can recognize the countless ways that others become violently sacrificed on the altars of our disesteem and felt self-hatred, malice, anger, and apathy.[67]

However, there is a second discourse to sacrifice in the Christian Gospels: the true sacrifice of praise and thanksgiving. In chapter 6, I noted that Schwager, in conversation with Girard, suggests the same insight when reflecting on the book of Hebrews. Schwager's understanding of sacrifice can be located in Heb 5:7–10, where the priest, who is synonymous with sacrifice, is defined by prayer. The prayer rises to the heavenly Father when it speaks of the sacrifice of Christ. Psalms 50 and 119 already speak of the sacrifice of praise, and Hebrews picks up the same theme as well. The sacrifice of Christ is the prayer of one who is ready to bear the violence of others. This is Christianity's "non-sacrificial" definition of true sacrifice.[68] This action is a form of sacrifice that is not violent but rather an obedient handing over of one's life in love and service to God. Genuine obedience sacrifices the lower good for the sake of some higher good. We recognize it in the events of Jesus' passion.[69] Further, Jesus sums up in the Eucharist his whole mission to the lost sheep of Israel, the mission of healing and forgiveness, and the mission of loving and praying for one's enemies. Both at the Last Supper and on Calvary, Jesus embraces his

---

66. Ormerod, "Eucharist as Sacrifice," 47.
67. Ormerod, *Grace and Disgrace*, 171.
68. Girard, "Girard-Schwager Correspondence," 79–80 (Aug 19, 1979).
69. Ormerod, "Eucharist as Sacrifice," 48.

victimhood and offers it to God as a living sacrifice of praise, exposing sacrificial necessity as a sinful mechanism leading to victimization.

IMITATING JESUS: THE SELF-AS-GIFT

Given all that has been stated about scapegoating and the true meaning of sacrifice, how can we speak of Jesus as our model? How might we imitate the desire of Jesus in our lives? In chapter 6, I mention that Moore accepts Girard's insights around the relationship between model and respondent in terms of two opposed horizons of feeling and valuing: the self-against and the self-as-gift.[70] Moore picks up on the political ramifications of scapegoating Jesus as a normalizing of the self-against. However, by contrast, Jesus represents the self-as-gift within the embrace of his Father, reflecting the fullness of self-love and addressing at the same time a concrete political situation. We hear from the lips of Jesus the words: "They hated me without cause" (John 15:25). There are three types of people: those who rejected him (self-against), those who were his disciples (a mixture of self-against and self-as-gift), and those who would be transformed by the Spirit (fully self-as-gift). The disciple's encounter with the risen Lord shows that the only resolution to our plight of self-against is the recovery of our original ecstasy witnessed uniquely by Jesus, a recovery that goes beyond what we call morality.[71]

It seems that all the violent things that we live in fear of cause us to wrongfully project onto God an understanding of violence which mistakenly states that violence is the means by which God controls us. Our false projections claim that God permits, or worse encourages, violence so that we might be afraid and, in our fear, turn to God. Jesus reveals that nothing could be further from the truth. In Jesus, "God has let us use the violence of the world against him and he doesn't mind, he comes through to us as who he really is—God for us in love. . . . [God] is now with us against all the terrible things in the world that we feared he would use against us."[72]

Jesus, our first witness and model, becomes the divinely ordained solution to the problem of evil. Jesus does not use violence to promote his cause, either by fighting evil or by fleeing it. He chooses to enter the

---

70. Moore, "Our Love Is Crucified," 30–32.
71. Moore, *Contagion of Jesus*, 33.
72. Moore, *Contagion of Jesus*, 39.

darkness of evil freely and, while not eliminating the possibility of evil in the lives of people forever, shows his disciples that we can wrestle with our conscience in the darkest moments of our lives, trusting in God and confident that our identity continues. Evil is not destroyed or overcome through greater violence but by taking evil to oneself and returning good for evil. Evil is transformed through suffering and self-sacrificing love into a generous moment of conversion and forgiveness. On the one hand, Jesus' death denounces all sacrifice that amounts to any kind of victimization of others and victimization of the self.[73] On the other hand, the sacrifice of Jesus affirms that the life and action of God, who is love, is the source and end for discerning God's will.[74]

Following Jesus, the witness of the martyr is to act in a way that transforms the evil of the world by means of intelligence empowered by grace and hope. The life of grace for the martyr has affective, intellectual, moral, and religious dimensions. The martyr senses a felt urgency to take the path of suffering self-sacrificing love, and solidarity with victims. The martyr's witness is not simply meant to be for the martyr and martyr's community but for the whole human family. Intellectually, the martyr's thinking is manifested in an intelligent, reasonable, and responsible grasp of reality, truth, and value through the eyes of love. Morally, the martyr's actions are not so much an act of defiance as an act of courage and patient endurance. Religiously, the martyr's experience is measured by the standard of God's love for all and God's presence in our lives, creating in the martyr both sadness and joy: sadness over what opposes our life with God and joy in recognizing the life of God in themselves and others. The martyr's act of self-sacrifice is meant to persuade all, even the hearts and minds of those who kill the martyr so that the gift of grace offered and responded to leads each person towards reality and truth.

Further, if the church is an approximation of the reign of God brought about by the Spirit-filled risen Lord, then the church also must witness the healing of God towards all those who are abused. To not do so is to rob the abused child of their ecstasy, and the failure of the church is the failure to model Jesus dramatically.[75] This realization invites a new pathway for the Church: The Church's task is getting the triumph of life over death into non-mythic language, into the triumph of life in you and me, and hope into the region of fear between you and me.

73. Ormerod, "Eucharist as Sacrifice," 49.
74. Ormerod, *Grace and Disgrace*, 170.
75. Moore, *Contagion of Jesus*, 32.

A New Awareness

DESIRE AND DEATH IN JESUS

In chapter 7, I gave an account of Moore's understanding of desire and its relationship to Jesus, the liberator of desire. Throughout his writings, Moore demonstrates the urgency of uncovering what happens in our moral-psychological makeup when we undergo a profound change. Moore, therefore, turns to the transformation witnessed by the disciples. In Moore's mind, the transformation of the disciples might be a template for our growth. In this vein, he constructs a highly creative picture of the disciple's inner journey toward their surrender to Jesus.[76] Our story starts when Jesus is walking among them. They are originally drawn to his words, deeds, and quality of relationships. The desire of the disciples for Jesus is a response to his desire for them, and it awakens in the disciples a new desire for God. It is the lyrical stage of their story with Jesus. Their attraction toward Jesus can only be characterized inwardly as a profound awakening of desire, for they feel differently towards themselves, people, and God, the feeling that whatever happens, they are significant and worthwhile. Moore states that the disciples "had caught the contagion of a person free from sin: free, that is, from that cosmic loneliness which is *the* break on hope, on that central movement of desire that yearns for an infinite relationship. This uniquely liberated desire was focused on and crystallized in Jesus, who had awakened it. In a sense, it was *more* crystallized in him than it was present in them. Or rather, their experience of it was fullest in this crystallization in him."[77]

Then, something quite dramatic changes through the events of Jesus' arrest, persecution, and death. What follows is a crucial period of crisis when the disciples are thrown into darkness: Jesus is taken and crucified. He is cruelly taken by force and executed as a common criminal, and the turn of events brings on a second state of desire, which could only be described as the "desolation of desire." Desire in them undergoes a mortal rupture. The disciples feel themselves to be as good as the dead, accompanied by feelings of rootlessness, lack of direction, the experience of one's world caved in and shattered at its core, the sense that things cannot be the same, and the felt experience of failure and worthlessness. Their felt desolation is akin to the death of God, for the sense of God awakened by Jesus dies with his death.

---

76. Moore, *Fire and the Rose*, 80–89.
77. Moore, *Inner Loneliness*, 89.

Then, something quite new happens, not only to Jesus but to them as well. We enter a third stage of their story of desire, which might be called the transformation or "liberation of desire." Moore outlines the process in these words: "Still this desire, while feeling its infinity, was necessarily channeled into the finite Jesus, its awakener. At the climax of the story, the channel is destroyed to produce a death of ego in which everything is lost. With the risen Jesus, desire infinite becomes infinite in its exercise. Desire is liberated, and becomes itself. This is why the Risen One is invisible, [and] partakes of the invisibility of God known as the Spirit. Resurrection is the liberation of desire."[78] Jesus is risen, meets them, and speaks to them.

The encounter with the risen Jesus changes the way they feel and understand God, the way they see themselves, the way they see their world and destiny, and the way they understand evil, sin, guilt, death, and suffering. He awakes in them a liberation of their desire towards its end in God. The resurrection pulls the disciples beyond the limits of their lives with him before the cross. The risen Jesus meets the disciples in the place left empty by the death of God. The resurrection is not some once-off transformation. It is an event that draws the believer into an ongoing process of transformation. They experience healing completely and in a new way. They feel the opposite of their sense of being nothing, healed from their guilt and from the false image of God that is part of their shadow, both during Jesus' ministry and after his death. Just as Jesus awakens a new feeling for and understanding of God during his time with them on earth, now he makes God alive to them in the resurrection with an aliveness never felt before. In the resurrection, Jesus feels the infinite emptiness of death with "the Holy Spirit of the all originating."

Indeed, Moore suggests a connection between desire and an authentic understanding of death. We cannot make the connection since we neither remain in the conviction that desire is limitless nor do we have a firsthand experience of death. In the case of desire, we are created with desire, for desire is limitless, and we are intended for God. We have a desire for God, but we are held captive from our desire by anxiety, dread, and shame. Desire can only become unlimited when restored in Jesus.[79] Through Jesus, we appreciate that desire finds its fulfillment in our being for another's fulfillment. Desire is not the sign of an emptiness needing

---

78. Moore, "Jesus, the Liberator," 497.
79. Moore, "Death as the Delimiting," 51.

to be filled. As noted in chapter 6, we are born with limitless desire and we act as if desires are limited.[80] Jesus' ministry is the awakening of limitless desire in the hearts of the disciples, "unshackling the accretions of cultural accommodations."[81] Awakened, while it works for Jesus, it does not work for them without being "in consort with him." Thus, in the resurrection, their desire is transformed in consort with him through the outpouring of the Spirit.

In the case of death, our experience seems to indicate that death is like falling away from all the connections we acquired here on earth. Therefore, death as the dissolving of ties is a falling away of limits. In his death, they encounter their utter powerlessness. Christ transforms this disconnection brought on by his death in the resurrection. It is not death as extinction but "of a carrying to infinity of the loneliness in us."[82] His death brings the disciples "on the other side" where to "see" requires the quickening of the Spirit, carrying to infinity the loneliness in them.[83] In the resurrection, the disciples are "advanced to an emptiness that underlies life and is all of the next; an emptiness that must be entered willingly, with desire, for the Spirit to fill it with eternal life."[84] Through the resurrection experience, death is not an extinction but a resting in God, and from that rest in God, we are urged to go out to love others more intensely. In the falling away of limits in death and in the conviction that desire is limitless as God intended, we can appreciate the connection between desire and death.[85]

DESIRE TRANSFORMED AND THE DIVINITY OF JESUS

Moore asks: "What did it mean to experience this dynamic oneness of God and Jesus? It meant that Jesus no longer appeared as an extension of God such that each who experienced him would be confined within himself as one who saw and wondered: Jesus was now experienced as the extension of God . . . [and] the disciples came into a single common

---

80. Moore, "Death as the Delimiting," 52.
81. Moore, "Death as the Delimiting," 53.
82. Moore, *Inner Loneliness*, 94.
83. Moore, "Death as the Delimiting," 55.
84. Moore, "Death as the Delimiting," 56.
85. Moore, "Death as the Delimiting," 52.

consciousness."[86] The teaching and presence of the earthly Jesus initiates for the disciples an awakening of desire for God and one another. The resurrection of Jesus creates a transformation of desire within the disciples. This profound experience of transformation brings about psychologically a "displacement of divinity."[87] There is a displacement away from a false image of God, who led them more and more into feeling guilt, and who was remote and simply overpowering. It becomes a displacement of divinity toward Jesus, who liberates their desire. The presence of the risen Jesus causes that process of displacement to be complete; for now, God and divinity are fully alive in Jesus. These strictly monotheistic disciples are free to celebrate Jesus as an extension of God in the same breath. Following this perspective, Moore insists that the affirmation of Jesus' divinity in the subsequent Councils of the Church has its beginning in the experiences of the disciples: the path of awakening, desolation, and transformation of desire. The implication is that if this was the pathway to transformation endured by the disciples, then it is the template for our pathway to God and one another.

THE CROSS: DESIGN OR ACCIDENT?

For Moore, several exploratory insights bear on the significance of the person of Jesus. The first comes from a comment from a friend who is visiting him at Downside Abbey. Reflecting on the Catholic cult of suffering, especially on Good Friday, Moore's friend happens to say, "Why don't we recognize that the crucifixion was an accident?" The comment provokes Moore to reflect on the question, and he couches a subsequent article in terms of whether the cross is an outcome of "accident or design?" The cross as appeasement and the cross as ordained by God are often brought together. Again, Moore is wary of the old notion of the cross as appeasement. He states: "The only alternative to saying that the crucifixion was an accident is to say that it was 'ordained by God.' It is only as ordained by God that this horrible event could be presented to people as a divine affirmation that suffering is to be sought and espoused. Also, it is only as ordained by God that the crucifixion can be thought of as 'appeasing God' in some way."[88] Do we then accept that the crucifixion is an accident and

---

86. Moore, *Fire and the Rose*, 88–89.
87. Moore, *Fire and the Rose*, 89.
88. Moore, "Crucifixion: Accident?," 155.

so avoid the idea of God's need for appeasement? Or do we accept that the crucifixion is ordained, where the word *ordained* means "willed by God," and carry within this affirmation the idea that God wanted a blood sacrifice so as to be appeased? Here is Moore's response.

First, Moore sets out his understanding of the crucifixion. In thinking of the cross as an act of appeasement, we are engaging in a false projection of God and throwing "the image of my unknown and feared side onto the screen of another person."[89]

Second, there is a possibility that the crucifixion may be God's way of showing love to us by helping us learn something about ourselves that we never quite face, that is, our propensity to ignore, refuse, and put down the true self. God ordains or wills that we discover our dark secret. For Moore, the death of Jesus is the sacrifice to our anger, which destroys God, who is a threat to us and reveals the God of healing and forgiveness.

Third, Moore suggests that there is no better way to uncover the dark secret of our fear of God than Jesus, the ultimate human scapegoat. He states: "So the crucifixion is the ultimate act of scapegoating in which at last, it is possible for God-the-ultimately-scapegoated to 'reply' to all our anguish to reply, to the Nietzsche in all of us who more than we know it, rages at him, to reply in the person of our scapegoat-victim returned from the death we have inflicted on him."[90] Moore affirms: "The age-old 'Christian' idea of a 'mysterious' God brooding over the blood of his Son and, for reasons of his own that are a 'great mystery,' opening-up heaven to us in token of this bloodshed gives way to: God the scapegoat of a self-ignorant and turbulent humanity, revealing his scapegoated nature in the crucifixion of his Son or Word who risen from the dead shows us the love that in scapegoating him, we repel."[91]

Fourth, the "necessity" of Jesus' suffering is not a necessity found in God. If we can speak of necessity, then it is a necessity located in us. Moore asserts: "What is implanted in us by the word of the Cross is freedom from the victimizing that makes us an unloving collective."[92] The only way for victimization of others to stop is for Jesus to take the action that he did. In that very slim sense, the "necessity" of the cross is coming from us. Fifth, inasmuch as we do not truly understand the content of Christian freedom through the cross, we fail to be motivated to take the

---

89. Moore, "Crucifixion: Accident?," 157.
90. Moore, "Crucifixion: Accident?," 157.
91. Moore, "Crucifixion: Accident?," 157–58.
92. Moore, "Crucifixion: Accident?," 158.

risk that Jesus took and demands of us. The mind of Jesus that set him steadfastly towards Jerusalem is a mind that saw the world as God sees it, "the human world knit in love, as opposed to the human world knit by the torturous relationships that are only stabilized by scapegoating."[93]

Sixth, the crucifixion reveals the real God, who is not identified with power as we know it in our world, but rather, identified with the victims of distorted power. Moore states: "Thus, the demystification of the scapegoat, which is the demythologizing of sacrifice, is the disclosure of a God who has nothing in him of the forceful quality of earthly rule. And God's crowning dissimilarity with such power consists in this: that, unlike the power that imposes order on an existing chaos, this power has no pre-existing chaos to impose order on. Creation out of nothing becomes clear for the first time when the killing and Resurrection of the Son of God finally disidentifies God with power as we know it, such power figuring here only as the power that crucifies."[94]

Moore's way of answering the dilemma complements what traditional theism argues about the nature and purposes of God. God, in his wisdom, creates an ordered universe. God creates a universe where there is pain, suffering, and the possibility of evil. Pain and suffering are the consequences of being finite and creaturely. This kind of suffering is not a punishment imposed on humanity by God following the disobedience of Adam and Eve. Bodily parts wear out, and we physically suffer. Adam and Eve would have physically suffered even if they had not eaten the fruit. God detests evil, never desires evil, and works to bring about a solution to the problem of evil.

However, it must be said that suffering comes both out of being physically human and encountering evil. The problem of suffering tests the conviction that we have meaning. We may even question: If I feel bad, does that mean I am bad? Is there something wrong with me? Is there something wrong with being human? From these crises, there arise moral challenges about what we are doing to ourselves, others, and our world. Many respond to these moral challenges with virtue, hope, and courage. But then, there is the suffering of evil. Ormerod rightly argues that, in one sense, to speak of God permitting evil is wrongheaded since the question as to "why God permits evil sounds like God gives permission for evil to occur. In fact, God repudiates evil: God forbids evil. God

---

93. Moore, "Crucifixion: Accident?," 159.
94. Moore, "Crucifixion: Accident," 162.

creates us as intelligent, reasonable, and responsible, with the expectation that these imperatives will guide our actions."[95] Therefore, God's permission and repudiation of evil must be held together. The problem of evil "ups the ante" on God. To be the victim of another person's evil deeds becomes a severe moral challenge. We ask: "Is God's choice of this universe worth the history of human evil that continually threatens to engulf us, the horrendous evils we have witnessed, particularly in the last century, and with the current thread of irreversible human-caused climate change, with its disastrous consequences for future generations?"[96]

From the perspective of religious faith, what we can say is that God implements a divinely originated solution to the problem of evil through Jesus. Ormerod states:

> Evil may be a cause of suffering. . . . But there is another form of suffering that is not found in the lack of meaning, but in giving birth to new meaning. It is a suffering that absorbs evil, freely and willingly, making of it an opportunity for a gift of forgiveness and compassion for the sinner, who in the end is not just damaging the victims of sin, but mutilating the sinner's own humanity. Jesus' willingness to suffer can both expose evil for what it really is in all its banality and disarm it of its power over us. For the power of evil lies in its ability to evoke like for like to respond to evil, with further evil, an eye for an eye, or worse, and so there builds a spiral of violence and evil spinning out of control, destroying all who cross its path. Forgiveness and compassion break the spiraling of evil.[97]

MOORE AND THE KILLING OF JESUS

A second point of reflection about Jesus has to do with a novel Moore read many years before, in which a child asks the question: "Why did God kill Jesus?" The question mirrors a trajectory of thinking about the crucifixion that has God the Father demanding a bloody sacrifice of his Son to appease his anger. While we can appreciate that a child may ask the question, the question misses several insights about the death of Jesus and, as such, is the wrong question.

---

95. Ormerod, *Public God*, 167.
96. Ormerod, *Public God*, 168.
97. Ormerod, *Public God*, 170.

First, our human way of acting is often out of an instinct to survive, and that usually means surviving at the cost of someone else. Thus, society creates victims of history. Our bias towards exclusion comes from our distorted understanding of freedom due to our alienation from God, the source of freedom.[98] Through our desire for God, freedom is born. In Jesus, there is only freedom since his desire was completely focused on God. Moore asserts: "Desire, for him, is not trapped in the routines of survival and exclusion. . . . So, he presents himself to a world that is thus trapped as embodying the freedom the felt lack of which gnaws at people inside and seeks outlets and scapegoats. What we have all been the most done out of is God."[99]

While Jesus is free to love all in us, we are selective and in chains, and these chains make him a victim, which Jesus accepts freely. Moore continues:

> For his freedom, his way of perceiving and being in the world, grounded as it was in unrestricted desire made him the perfect victim. . . . [Jesus] shows to us an alternative humanity that we desire and dread, our desire for which provokes reactively in us the dread that we learn under the reign of death. Now, unless we see this execution as provoked by the freedom of the victim, as his freedom's necessary final self-expression in this world, we cannot see in their original saving unity, the two facts, that he died and that he was killed.[100]

Therefore, it is Jesus who holds together both the death inflicted by sinners and the death accepted on account of sin. Moore states: "*Before* his death, he *represents* this new humanity in life, in teaching. *Through* his death, he *inaugurates* the new humanity which now every time it obeys the strange command to celebrate his murder, and its issue is to know that it is free of the immemorial law of [creating victims], that in 'proclaiming the death of the Lord until he comes' it is proclaiming the end of sacrifice, except in the sense of that word, that is quite strange."[101]

Second, Moore finds the traditional formula of Jesus as simultaneously the priest, the altar, and the victim unhelpful. Rather, Jesus, who has the same freedom as God, is the target and victim of an unfree and godless world. In other words, our desire to create victims or dominate

---

98. Moore, "Why Did God," 16.
99. Moore, "Why Did God," 16.
100. Moore, "Why Did God," 17.
101. Moore, "Why Did God," 17.

others is the root of all evil. His free victimhood gives him insight into our unfree victim condition that makes us victimize others. In the extreme of his victimhood, which is his death on the cross, Jesus comes to his perfection as the free victim able to cut through the guilt, remorse, and conflicting emotions of all his victimizers to the victim within us. He brings that victim with us to himself and sets that victim free "from the immemorial implanted need to victimize."[102] In the resurrection, Jesus uproots from the victimizers their need to destroy their true self, who, thus, freed from that universal bondage, can spread in the world an end to the cycle of creating victims. The action of Jesus amounts to allowing the reign of God to displace the reign of death and the church to break down the gates of the underworld.[103]

Thus, we can say that the transformation or liberation of desire within us for God that creates our freedom is what we mean in the phrase "saved by his blood" (Eph 1:7). If we are to come to terms with these seemingly two opposed statements, namely, that we are "saved by his blood" and that God "did not spare his own Son but gave him up to benefit us all" (Rom 8:32), there exists only one resolution. Moore asserts: "The only resolution is found in experiencing the drama of victimization and captivation by the victim, revealing me to myself for the first time as victim behind my victimizing of him. It is nearly impossible to believe that God is using our liberation process to bring us into his/her love until we experience this happening, feel the divinity in our mutual liberating forgiveness."[104]

THE RESURRECTION AND THE EMPTY TOMB

Moore remains the monk obsessed with Jesus. Part of his obsession involves keeping up with the latest scholarship in Christology, especially with its emphasis on the historical Jesus and the birth of the early church. We find Moore both praising and criticizing Edward Schillebeeckx's treatment of the resurrection in the latter's book *Jesus, An Experiment in Christology*. Moore praises Schillebeeckx for shifting the focus in our understanding of Jesus to the centrality of the resurrection. It is also a shift from an objective center of interest to a more subjective center. It is

---

102. Moore, "Why Did God," 20.
103. Moore, "Why Did God," 20.
104. Moore, "Why Did God," 23.

a focus that shifts from questions such as who moved the stone and what became of the body, to questions like what was happening in the mind of the people who were saying the Lord had risen.

Moore is as much concerned about a psychological inquiry of the disciples as is Schillebeeckx. Where he parts company with Schillebeeckx is in the emphasis put on the question of whether the tomb was empty or not and a reduction of resurrection to the post-bereavement experience of the disciples. For Moore, to speak as though the empty tomb is the resurrection is totally to miss the point, just as to ask the question as to whether the physical remains of the body are still there or not is to miss the point. There is far more in the resurrection than simply the empty tomb.[105]

Moore states that the empty tomb is not the clue to the massively transformative presence that is the risen Jesus. But neither is the empty tomb simply a story from pious legend. Similar to Aquinas, Moore holds onto the empty tomb as fact while believing in the resurrection as God's mystery that cannot be witnessed or imagined.[106] The resurrection can only be understood and not imagined. Moore affirms: "There is no way to combine these two ideas, other than to say that the empty tomb is the *outside*, the historical deposit, the drama of what on the *inside* is ineffable."[107] Schillebeeckx concludes that the empty tomb is simply a post-resurrection holy site of ritual and remembrance by the continuing Christian community, who probably never encountered Jesus in his historical life but needed somewhere tangible to meet and pray.

Moore parts company with him on this point. He seeks to avoid the two extremes of objectivism and subjectivism. He knows that the resurrection tells us something far more about Jesus than we know of him in his public ministry: "The statement that Jesus is alive goes far beyond the statement that he is not dead, which could not be made were the bones still there, but the former statement does entail the latter. The statement that the Resurrection is 'not the resuscitation of a corpse,' though perfectly true has worked as another of those massive obfuscations."[108] Although the proclamation that Jesus is alive is more than saying that he is not dead, both proclamations require an empty tomb. Moore further makes the argument that thinking about the empty tomb is similar to talking about

---

105. Moore, "Forming and Transforming," 180.
106. Moore, *Contagion of Jesus*, 46.
107. Moore, *Contagion of Jesus*, 46.
108. Moore, "Resurrection," 266.

death. Is death the cessation of life, or is death the beginning of a new life? An answer to the former question is empirically based. An answer to the latter question is based on prayer and religious faith grounded in love. For Moore, the disciples need to come to the empty tomb as well as have the personal experience of the power of the risen Lord. What Moore calls the empirical and the spiritual are interdependent. He gives this reason: "Because the profound spiritual experience of death is of another order than the emotion engendered by corruption, the latter emotion will persist, however powerful the spiritual experience has been, even if it has been of the unique kind that I am predicting of the disciples of Jesus."[109]

In congruence with Schillebeeckx, Moore is content to call the resurrection a conversion experience for the disciples. However, he is not content to reduce the resurrection simply to a conversion experience. He notes that what makes Schillebeeckx adopt a reductionist position is the lack of a proper psychology.[110] In Moore's view, Schillebeeckx's psychological portrait of the disciples needs to go beyond "the shallower level of guilt and forgiveness" characteristic of bereavement.[111] It needs a psychological framework that owns "a deeper confusion of existence, the shame, what Eliot called the boredom, the horror, and the glory—the melting pot out of which the Spirit forges the ego and its transformation in the Resurrection encounter."[112]

Therefore, the consolation that the apostles feel after their time of grieving the death of Jesus cannot be adequately explained by a psychology of normal grief.[113] Rather, the psychological state of the disciples is grounded in the experience that "Jesus, after his death, 'took' the community with the ravishment of the eternal Spirit and became in their midst, a life-giving Spirit."[114] As an ineffable Mystery, the resurrection is "the realization of God's original intention for this mad being that we are, a realization that takes into his sweep, the last depth of our alienation and proneness to the nothing, whence we are drawn, and, with Easter, drawn all the way into infinite being. God forbid that we should think we can

---

109. Moore, "Empty Tomb," 242.
110. Moore, "Forming and Transforming," 180.
111. Moore, "Forming and Transforming," 180.
112. Moore, "Forming and Transforming," 180.
113. Moore, "Resurrection," 261.
114. Moore, "Forming and Transforming," 181.

imagine as a corpse in the hands of a divine mortician, the darkness that the light of Easter dissipates!"[115]

Moore agrees with Schillebeeckx's understanding of resurrection as a search for the risen Lord in the experiencing and believing community. At the same time, he also feels the need to take the meaning of the resurrection one step further. Moore states: "The Resurrection Kerygma says that he is now where all this—the teaching, the doing, the living, the total Jesus intentionality—was headed: with the infinite Godhead. It is a statement about Jesus now, about the present and enduring state of Jesus. And it is a statement of where death brought Jesus. And no psychic experience, of the reconciliation-with-the-past kind, is sufficient to ground it."[116] In the accounts of the resurrection stories, the disciples are telling us what it is like to have Jesus among them in this unique and new way. They were possessed totally by a new awareness of Jesus, and it did not occur to them to wonder how the body got from its dead condition to Jesus now.[117] For Moore, the reason why this bothers us so much is because we have so very little sense of utter newness of their experience of Jesus risen as they did. In the story of the empty tomb, the evangelists seek to convey the contrast between Jesus in his ministry and Jesus after the resurrection "because the sense of Jesus now is so overpowering."[118] One of the texts of Scripture that conveys the contrast is found in 1 Pet 3:19: "He was put to death in the flesh, but made alive in the Spirit."

Further, our distance from the original events precludes us from its startling strangeness. Moore proposes that we

> don't feel the now of Jesus because we don't feel ourselves as a *new* community, which is the same thing as feeling the now of Jesus. Jesus as the focus of the power of now, Jesus is what he has now become. So, if God hasn't yet made Jesus now for you, you find yourself trying to imagine him getting out of the tomb—"emerging." The fact is we have no image whatsoever of a glorified body. Father Aelred Watkin used to say that, as *we* have him under the appearance of bread and wine, he came to *them* under the appearances of hands and feet.[119]

---

115. Moore, *Contagion of Jesus*, 46–47.
116. Moore, "Experiencing the Resurrection," 48.
117. Moore, *Contagion of Jesus*, 48.
118. Moore, *Contagion of Jesus*, 48.
119. Moore, *Contagion of Jesus*, 48–49.

9

Moore and the Community of the Church I

INTRODUCTION

In the 1960s, Moore accepted an appointment to St. Mary's Liverpool parish as its parish priest for nine years. During this time, a new set of explorations emerged from his theological writings. In 1959, Pope John XXIII announced his intention to call together an Ecumenical Council. Between 1962 and 1965, the organizers arranged four separate sessions in St. Peter's Basilica. Sixteen documents emerged from the council fathers covering all aspects of Church life and the relationship between the church and non-Christian believers. From these years till his death in 2014, Moore maintained a healthy engagement with issues arising from being a member of the Catholic Church, and the challenges raised demanded religious, moral, intellectual, affective, and psychic conversion. Few of these issues are treated systematically by him. However, most become the subject of exploratory insights from someone who cared greatly that the church be a human community called into being by the risen Lord and transformed by the Holy Spirit.

Overall, one of the most important reasons for Moore speaking his thoughts on the church was to address the extraordinary changes that had come into society and in the minds of the faithful with the aim of presenting God as real. These cultural and social changes influenced the progressive lessening of Church authority and a diminishment of adherence to Church obedience from what it was before the 1960s. The societal changes also led to a new general doubt about the relevance of God and the church for the faithful and, more widely, in people throughout society. Moore's reflections on the church sought seek to address both situations.

EXPERIENCE IN THE LOCAL CHURCH

As a parish priest, Moore is in daily contact with the people of his parish. At that time, Church authorities communicate with a mindset that could be summed up as "pray, pay, and obey." Moore pivots the direction and purpose of the church towards speaking the truth and doing good. A person must know reality and truth in order to do the right thing.[1] He seeks a transformed Church that genuinely nourishes the faithful and no longer avoids the world surrounding it. He is well aware of the fortress or "siege" mentality that was part of the imagination of the church before the 1960s. Later, he would feel the same fortress mentality reemerge in the papacies of John Pope II and Benedict XVI.[2] In the 1960s, Moore made a bold statement regarding the church as a community: "We must therefore reverse the direction, starting with the people and where they are and end up with a new and authentic sign."[3] He used the metaphor of "dream" to express what it means to be a more authentic sign. While a scientific age had provided the context for ripping apart the dream of unity between society and the church, even this new age could not in Moore's mind destroy the dream of Jesus at the heart of the church.

THE CHURCH AND PERSONAL RENEWAL

If the church is to transform, personal renewal is essential. Moore refers to the example of the countless men and women in the history of the church who underwent conversion, similar to the pattern of transformation that we witness in the disciples of Jesus. Just as the disciples experienced a complete dissolution at the death of Jesus, by which they were emptied and then transformed through meeting the risen Lord, so moderns have to tread the same path. The dream is "to come to know and suffer in ourselves, that process of dissolution and recreation that we

---

1. Moore and Maguire, *Dreamer*, 11.
2. Moore, "2008 Blog," Sep 11, 2008.
3. Moore and Maguire, *Dreamer*, 18.

have hitherto been unable to contemplate only in the march of history."[4] The path of dissolution might mean letting go of aspects of the church's life that do not lead people to God and that no longer speak the gospel's message to people's hearts. The church cannot be content by the number of people coming to Sunday mass. A gathering of people does not make a community of faith.[5]

Personal renewal is not social conditioning or adaptation to a new social environment. The Christian believer has to appropriate the dream of the risen Lord through a process of dissolution and re-creation. Dissolution is a kind of death. Death is a metaphor for the process of ego death and the needed change for authentic living. However, it is not death realized by going back to the womb; rather, it is death as a new birth. When we are inhabiting a consciousness of death as a second womb, then each crisis sends us back to a safe place where we do not have to encounter problems, where we do not have to make decisions and face the prospect of failing, and where we don't have to take responsibility for ourselves (fundamentalism and restorationism). The womb we seek mirrors the womb before birth, where our mother makes the decisions for us and there was certainty. When we inhabit the consciousness of death as new birth, we live by an ethic of risk, are prepared to encounter whatever change is needed, and are ready to take responsibility for our lives. Moore states that the whole meaning of the sacramental system is to help us through our passage of death, and "it follows that if our sense of death as new birth is not touched, awakened by sacramental worship, then this worship is failing for its purpose."[6]

Moore is speaking about religious, moral, and psychological conversion. He states that "the dream personally and consciously appropriated is indispensable to becoming a real person."[7] If the past could be described as a "buried life,"[8] new life requires an acceptance of the new task of psychic self-discovery.[9] As he sees it, the challenge is to live within the rites of the church but simultaneously to live ever more deeply with ourselves.[10] Moore talks about psychic change as a passing "in con-

---

4. Moore and Maguire, *Dreamer*, 21.
5. Moore and Maguire, *Dreamer*, 25.
6. Moore, "In Water," 91.
7. Moore and Maguire, *Dreamer*, 21.
8. Moore and Maguire, *Dreamer*, 23.
9. Moore and Maguire, *Dreamer*, 23.
10. Moore and Maguire, *Dreamer*, 24.

sciousness from a state of sleep to a state of being awake, and to know in this latter the meaning of spiritual wakefulness."[11] He is advocating a "two-level awareness in people," an awareness of people's ability to reason and be intelligent and an awareness of our psychic depths. This two-level awareness requires an attentiveness to ourselves as both conscious and unconscious, where the "unconscious" is what is conscious but not attended to. We need a "partnership with our unconscious life implied in our very constitutions as persons."[12] Appropriating both the conscious and unconscious aspects of ourselves will bring us to a single new act of self-awareness and self-appropriation "able to breathe and to know our breathing as our natural being and life."[13] At this early stage of his thought, Moore already grasps the importance of reading the body as a clue to unattended images, feelings, and symbols within.[14] He is also aware that he has received a religious formation in a monastic culture dominated by an anti-body mentality. For Moore, the forgetfulness of the body and the unconscious can only drive a wedge between faith grounded in religious love and knowledge of faith through the doctrines.

Moore feels for the faithful in the church. In his judgment, many people of faith that he meets have minimal feelings for God and divine truth. The emphasis of the official church, especially in its teaching and pronouncements, is on holding the doctrines and not on the feeling for and surrender to God. What adds to the problem is a formal, encased liturgy rather than a liturgy that directs their groping lives. In sum, Moore uses expressions like the need for "psychological transformation," an awareness for "a profound revolution in the consciousness of modern man," a shift from thinking of ourselves as simply an "organized religion," a call to be "world-aware and self-aware," an acknowledgment that the past was characterized by a "catholic totalitarianism of our emotional life," and the urgent need to shed a "romantic vision of the Church" as well as viewing the church as "God's will on earth."[15] Although convinced about renewal, he is not naïve about change, especially by people in leadership positions in the church and the broader society. He refers to God's love as violent since it involves "the painful step forward, the

---

11. Moore and Maguire, *Dreamer*, 27.
12. Moore and Maguire, *Dreamer*, 80.
13. Moore and Maguire, *Dreamer*, 85.
14. Moore and Maguire, *Dreamer*, 91.
15. Moore and Maguire, *Dreamer*, 5–6.

painful rebirth, from the old man to the new." In the church, change beckons leaders to "read the signs of the times and reject old and outworn attitudes."[16]

THE CHURCH AND OUR IMAGE OF GOD

Central to personal renewal in the church is the image of God that powers a change in mind and heart. The church of the past favored order, tradition, and stability. The church of the future must be ready for challenge, revolution, and making something new without losing the truths of the past. The image of God that predominated in the church of the past was the image of the monarch, benevolent and loving but, ultimately, a ruler. The church's future will be motivated by a vision of God, who is profoundly mysterious when encountered and who gives all to his brethren.[17] What will be lost is a paternalistic Church. What will be gained is a Church associated with the joining of people in brotherhood and sisterhood rather than with their being ruled. Renewal is needed in the church since the battle is in the minds and hearts of the faithful and among the faithful. Yet insofar as each Christian succumbs to the power of love, they can commit to the power of love and take an active part in bringing other hearts to love.[18]

In her dialogue with atheists, a more authentic image of God is also essential for the church. Many atheists do not believe in God because of the problem of evil in the world, which is causing profound suffering to many people. Their refrain is: Why has God allowed so much wickedness to be perpetrated on his people (for example, the Jews in the Holocaust)? Moore responds: "The man who really believes in God is not the man whom God has protected from the shocks of life. It is the man who, abandoned by God has not surrendered to an inbuilt bitterness, has not allowed his heart to go, but has continued to say 'yes' to life." It is the church's responsibility not to tell such people that they ought to believe in God. Rather, "the only answer to the atheist is to love him."[19]

Images of God are communicated through sermons, prayer books, and pronouncements of the Church authorities. Moore is concerned that

---

16. Moore and Hurt, *Before the Deluge*, 14.
17. Moore and Hurt, *Before the Deluge*, 12–13.
18. Moore and Hurt, *Before the Deluge*, 32.
19. Moore and Hurt, *Before the Deluge*, 41.

the image of Christ is not touching the hearts of people. The problem is that our hearts have become numb to the power of God, and pronouncements by the Church authorities often only serve to point out failures when what is needed is the rebirth of love among the faithful and are reviving of charity in the deepest roots of the heart.[20]

The church's responsibility is to present a truthful image of God that reflects the concerns of contemporary people. For example, let us suppose that the concern for people is world poverty. If, for ancient societies, poverty consisted of an inability to cope with plague and hunger, poverty today consists of a growing sense of meaninglessness. Moore asserts: "Our poverty is the frightful shallowness that creeps into interpersonal relationships in the technological age. The big thing we have to learn about God is this: that when I don't love my brother it appears as something less than human."[21] The challenge, therefore, of the church is to present an image of God so moving that it leads us back to full recognition of the humanity of our brother and sister.

THE CHURCH AND DOCTRINES

Moore sees the need to relook at Christian doctrines, which found their birth in a classicist-oriented culture that tried to hold onto people's allegiances in a purely rational way, and especially after the reformation, with a polemical approach toward separated Christian churches but that did not always speak to the hearts of believers.[22] Later, Moore says:

> I think Christians of the future will be known not by a mass of dogmas, but by a simple, humble, joyful, full of hope YES to life. This is not to say that the dogmas will be bypassed. No, they will be better understood, centered in the simplicity of the Christ awakened heart, and of course, as we come to understand them in this way, and not as fix things in their own right, we find ourselves by differently related to those other Christians who have grown up with a different slant on the Christian dogma.[23]

Speaking in the mid-1960s, Moore is not content with the chasm between religious faith and religious knowledge within modern believers.

---

20. Moore and Hurt, *Before the Deluge*, 42–43.
21. Moore and Hurt, *Before the Deluge*, 44.
22. Moore and Maguire, *Dreamer*, 28.
23. Moore and Hurt, *Before the Deluge*, 34.

He finds that, for the most part, the laity need help to square what they are taught to believe with the language of a new cultural context.[24] Through adult faith education, Moore sees the need for the faithful to move from childhood to adulthood in their understanding of, appreciation for, and deepening of their faith.[25] Moore regrets the broader loss of the power of a myth-poetic language of faith brought on by the influences of a scientific and post-Enlightenment world.[26] Most significantly, he seeks a new appreciation for the person of Christ so that the people of God may hear the gospel's message in a way that touches their hearts. Thinking on the gospel text about new wineskins for new wine, he declares: "Really new ideas require a radically new mind. Christ knew this well. He knew it better than anyone else. What he was bringing was the newest thing ever, and so it made the maximum demand on the human heart to look at new ideas with new eyes."[27]

THE CHURCH AND SYMBOLIC LIFE

For Moore, the liturgy, sacraments, myth, and symbols need a rethink. He is not at ease with an attitude to the sacraments that emphasizes only the power of the sign adequately administered by the priest. This attitude resigns the faithful to losing the symbolic power of sacramental signs. The sacraments are understood to be signs that communicate the grace of God. The emphasis on sacraments properly administered comes from a Church living in a society penetrated with Christianity, such that one could not think of there ever not being a Church and it not ever being relevant. Now, Moore judges that the church lives in a society where "symbols having the force of divine reality" are no longer part of the wider society.[28] The catchcry is that the sacraments are "only a symbol." Moore is aware that people might know the sign's content and its cognitive meaning but have minimum feeling in the encounter between them and God through the signs. He states that the signs are "no longer *felt* to be *doing* their job . . . of releasing those deep drives which head

---

24. Moore and Maguire, *Dreamer*, 36.
25. Moore and Maguire, *Dreamer*, 57.
26. Moore and Maguire, *Dreamer*, 41.
27. Moore and Hurt, *Before the Deluge*, 11.
28. Moore and Maguire, *Dreamer*, 20.

towards a fuller life."[29] Yet, Moore is confident that the sacraments can still mean much to the faithful, even if they have passed from "man-in-the-village" to "man-in-the-world."[30] Again, the starting point is inner renewal through which the message captured in the narrative myths and stories of Christianity can rediscover.

Therefore, he addresses the importance of myth and symbolism within the faith community. Myth has the power to release a spiritual need within us.[31] Myth holds the two worlds of the conscious and the unconscious in a dynamic tension. For Moore, the difficulty for moderns is that the current Catholic myth has lost its power to straddle these two worlds, and "the feeling that it ought to work and doesn't is infecting the Christian body with a religious malaise whose symptoms are guilt, mutual accusations of betrayal, and a tendency to show to unbelievers the face of anger rather than encouragement."[32] Moore still believes profoundly in the importance of symbols for our lives since they "carry with them the invitation [by God] to receive at the deep level [the presence of God], an invitation which individuals can accept in different ways and with different thoroughness."[33] He is convinced that symbols can trigger a new awakening.

Moore judges that Christians were united to their faith and each other for centuries around a set of myths that had a powerful effect on their minds and hearts. Myths can hold us in the balance between our conscious and unconscious life, such that when one responds to the myth, a deep yearning wells up from our "unconscious self." They do not give us a direct account of our exterior world but, rather, an account of how human existence feels in our interior world. Therefore, Moore sees the importance of preaching as a way to ignite a feeling for God and a surrender to God. He urges a greater appreciation for the art of preaching and a departure from sermons dealing with sexual sin and dogmas.

Writing in the sixties and in a cultural milieu of upheaval both in the church and societies, Moore is concerned that the Christian myth has come to a point where its story has solidified into a doctrinal precision, but the feeling for it has gone. Whether it was, in the first place, a feeling for God that went missing, leading to a feeling behind the doctrine

---

29. Moore and Maguire, *Dreamer*, 41.
30. Moore and Maguire, *Dreamer*, 22.
31. Moore and Maguire, *Dreamer*, 40.
32. Moore and Maguire, *Dreamer*, 28.
33. Moore and Maguire, *Dreamer*, 42.

disappearing, or the other way around, the point for Moore is the importance of a mythopoetic retrieval of religious faith, as discussed in chapter 2. The Christian myth "is no longer felt to be doing (its) job of releasing those deep drivers which lead toward a fuller life."[34] The retrieval of the "unconscious" brings us into a larger world in which we are all rooted and in which we must learn to live.[35]

His reflections on symbols speak to the importance of the sacraments for the believer's life. However, even in sacraments, there must be a rethink. Moore asserts: "We should be prepared to pay any price for a real experience of Christ in the sacraments, such as the church today especially seeks. Doubtless, we are helped towards this by liturgical renewal. But the only way to have it is to be fully a man or a woman, to encounter the impossibilities and to suffer them creatively in the power of *the* Man."[36] Personal renewal in Christ will open us to a new perspective on the sacraments.

The sacraments must not be viewed as something that jealously holds people in the church and to the church, imposing a monolithic consciousness on the faithful. He gives the example of the sacrament of penance as an imposed "monolithic" consciousness. During Moore's time, the administration of the sacrament of penance was used, in his estimations, as a mechanism of control over Catholics who believed that receiving communion could never happen before confessing their sins. Or consider the Eucharist as so sacred that the host could not be chewed but would have to be swallowed whole. Or consider the sacrament of marriage, which carries specific responsibilities and obligations with the penalty of excommunication should the marriage partner choose to leave their spouse. These are all examples of sacraments becoming "monolithic" in character. They are hardly focused on revealing the dream of dissolution and recreation as a way towards the creative and inspiring obverse of life becoming fully conscious.[37] Rather than being offered signs that illuminate and fill consciousness with a feeling for God's love and a desire to surrender, people are socialized to accept the barrier between the sign and what is signified. For Moore, the church has arrived at a place in its history where the cognitive meaning of the sign is not enough. That may

---

34. Moore and Maguire, *Dreamer*, 41.
35. Moore and Maguire, *Dreamer*, 48.
36. Moore and Hurt, *Before the Deluge*, 16.
37. Moore and Maguire, *Dreamer*, 59.

have worked in the past where the life of the Church "identified with an outward culture that was thought to be universal."[38]

Moore proposes that the real purpose of myth and symbol is for us to appreciate "a deeper self, in which all the bearings can intersect a self, that is in terms of the ego, selfless, a self in which the world comes alive and makes its own sense, a self that is found only in being lost."[39] For a spiritually alive Church to grow in the modern world, we need to retrieve our symbols. The retrieval of symbols buried in the human psyche invites us "to become newly aware [of ourselves] as a rational man living in consort with his non-rational depths."[40] Symbols and myths are created to deepen our joy and point towards a larger world in which we are rooted and must learn to live. They are meant to relax the unconscious hold of the "catholic dream" with its narrowness, exclusivity, and encasement of the soul and release the believer on a new voyage of self-discovery and world enrichment.[41] The world's enrichment is grounded in an awareness of God's love for us, our love for ourselves, and flowing over into a love for others. Thus, the community of believers becomes a space where people are free to associate and feel each other in their depth, where the "we" of the community is a bridge between the believer and God. It is a place where we see others in ourselves, in the feeling of ourselves, that becomes the basis for relating to others instead of merely perceiving them. Moore is addressing a situation that he believes has given too much attention to the rational adherent to faith, while Christ speaking to "our buried and dreaming depth" has been lost, and thus, the powerful Mystery behind the sign has become trivialized and cut off.[42]

THE CHURCH AND THE CLERICAL PRIESTHOOD

Regarding clergy, religious, and the ordained life, Moore calls for a review of the meaning of celibacy, given the fact that in the 1960s, many religious were departing from their once-chosen vocation, a trend that progressively reached its pinnacle in the early 1970s.[43] He fears that the

---

38. Moore and Maguire, *Dreamer*, 44.
39. Moore and Maguire, *Dreamer*, 48.
40. Moore and Maguire, *Dreamer*, 28.
41. Moore and Maguire, *Dreamer*, 59.
42. Moore and Maguire, *Dreamer*, 43.
43. Moore and Maguire, *Dreamer*, 61.

socialization of clergy ties them more to the sign of the sacrament of priesthood and not to the human community. The sign is centered on the priest as a man set apart and ontologically changed through receiving the sacrament. Priests are spoken about as "other Christs" offering the sacrifice of Calvary on the altar at Mass. They are professional and given to the church. Within this context, they form a celibate clerical culture. They represent the "catholic dream," in a pre-Vatican II Catholic culture. Moore concludes that their celibate status is not equipping them to speak on sexual matters. Nor can they talk adequately about the challenges of marriage. They signal through their celibate status an attitude to sex as better off without it. Despite all these deficiencies, Moore still believes in a celibate priesthood. Celibacy is, first and foremost, a vocation centered on loving and tied to the human community. It should not be centered on being set apart from the community, giving rise to clericalism.

Priests, too, must appropriate their psychic lives if they are to live celibate commitment with joy. Celibate commitment cannot mean a denial of the sexual but must be wholly about genuine love. Moore concludes that for the celibate "to continue faithfully in the old way is to become sick with that sickness, which must result when life is denied."[44] He suggests that priests must find a new sexual awareness not plagued with suggestions that honoring one's sexuality can only be the "pull of the flesh." The priest must live with an ethic that awakens the body "to its beauty, to its strength, to its accuracy, in tenderness for one another, to its power to initiate and to sustain."[45]

If celibate men are to feel love more seriously, then, for Moore, they must also be more contemplative. Contemplation gives them the power to discern their relationships, not only with God but with other people. Discernment flowing from a reflective attitude is needed since celibate men cannot be locked out of the experience of love, as if they can remain untouched by human love and rely only on God's love. Love of one another exists to be suffered and transmuted into the love of God for both clergy and laity. One's love cannot remain in some encased isolation but necessarily implies altering another person's life. Linked to such an imperative is the importance of being in touch with one's body. Being out of touch with the body gives rise to a great deal of emphasis on preaching the evils of sexual sin. By doing so, priests have either become Manichean

---

44. Moore and Maguire, *Dreamer*, 71.
45. Moore and Maguire, *Dreamer*, 71.

and despise the body or Platonists asserting that real love is about the spiritual person divorced from their body. Moore sums up his thoughts poetically by saying: "We hardly suspect the bones and the precise tenderness the bones breathe."[46]

PRIESTHOOD, SEXUAL ABUSE, AND CELIBACY

As the years progressed, the church's life as exemplified through her clergy and vowed religious remained a source of concern for Moore. Moore was in Downside Abbey when allegations and guilty verdicts of sexual abuse by fellow priests who had worked at the Benedictine educational institutions of Downside School became public knowledge. These instances of sexual abuse were found to be the case also at Benedictine-run schools and abbeys like St. Benedict's Ealing, Buckfort Abbey, Ampleforth College, Belmont College, Douai Abbey, and Worth Abbey. The sexual abuse scandal hit the church in the early 1990s onward, and by the new millennium, Moore offered some comments. He states:

> Who shall say how to address the tragic condition of the church and its order represented by the revelations to which we are now becoming almost inured, of sexual abuse of the young by priests and members of religious orders? Only one thing is sure: that a profound conversion of the church has to take place. It is also sure that the promotion of this conversion is not by way of moral precept, by saying how people ought to live. What is required is some quite new deployment of imagination in the understanding of ourselves.[47]

He calls sexual abuse of children a great horror, creating a nightmare situation in which the whole church is united in a state of hatred at this misbehavior by clergy. For him, the wrongdoing was allowed to go on due to a cover-up behavior that amounted to "organized irresponsibility." Part of the reasons for the prevalence of sexual abuse, according to Moore, lies at the feet of the official church and its inadequate selection and formation of priestly candidates.

There are four people that Moore mentions whose writings had been formative for him on the subject of a renewed understanding of mandatory celibacy and, more broadly, sexuality, as a means to address

---

46. Moore and Maguire, *Dreamer*, 96.
47. Moore, "My Body for You," 203.

clerical abuse. These people were Marie Keenan, A. W. Richard Sipe, Eugen Drewermann, and Ute Ranke-Heinemann.[48] I am going to outline the insights of Keenan and Sipe.

Moore cites the work of the Irish Catholic sociologist Marie Keenan, who reflects on abuse within the Catholic Church in Ireland. With Keenan, he finds the formation of clergy inadequate in several aspects and these inadequacies feed into the problem of abuse. From Keenan's studies, first-hand interviews with priests reveal their confusion when asked to live among a community of people who are not celibate. They believed that the sacrament of ordination conferred on them the virtue of celibate chastity. This belief was articulated in a book by an Australian bishop, Julian Porteous, who until 2008 was rector of an Australian seminary in Sydney. Keenan quotes the book:

> A man once ordained is ontologically changed. He is a priest. Something mysterious happens. It is an action of grace, and something quite real.... The priesthood is not just the deputing of an individual to take on a particular role. It is more than a function; it is a radical reorienting of the whole reality of the person. He is changed at the level of his being.... Ordination is not just the power to exercise the priestly office in the Church; it is such a transformation of the person that a distinctly priestly character can be identified in him.[49]

This kind of perspective can mistakenly contribute to clericalism, an attitude of being set apart, and the view that priesthood is a primarily a permanent sacred calling, for the individual rather than a gift of service to the community. These mistaken notions feed into the problem of sexual abuse. The mentality can also encourage a dual model of church life where clergy are viewed as superior. It can contribute to feelings of desperation when the attitude comes up against the reality. Moore presents a needed point of recovery for the clergy, namely, "a massive process of re-education of the whole body about the body."[50] For himself, Moore later states in his blog: "Pushing 95, I have only to pray."[51] I will elaborate further on Moore's insights into sexuality in chapter 12.

Keenan's studies into sexual abuse by clergy, especially in Ireland, lead her to several conclusions as to why it has been so widespread. First,

48. Moore, "2012–2014 Blog," Sep 12, 2012.
49. Keenan, "Evidence to the Australian," 2.
50. Moore, "My Body for You," 204.
51. Moore, "2012–2014 Blog," Sep 12, 2012.

she identifies "the sexual underworld of 'normal' clergy" as the backdrop for sexual abuse.[52] Keenan believes that the sexual underworld of clergy and the unhealthy organizational culture in which the problems of sexuality arise are part of the context in which child sexual abuse by Catholic clergy becomes possible. To think that the grace of ordination will be all that is required is mistaken. The criteria for assessing fitting candidates for priesthood, the decision for mandatory celibacy by both the institution and the individual, and the ongoing monitoring and formation into celibacy are important.

Second, her research showed that perpetrators of abuse felt a diminished sense of authority and autonomy in the personal sphere that overshadowed much of their conscious awareness of their power as adult men and minsters in the church.[53] The research found them more concerned with obedience to their superiors and with those who had power over them, than with the power imbalance between themselves and laity including children.[54] Yet abuse toward children was less about gaining power over them and more about a misinterpretation of "friendship" with children, blindness to their power position, a preoccupation with rules, fear of church leaders with power over them, and an emotional immaturity and loneliness.[55] Without making excuses, these reflections on power and felt powerlessness, power without accountability, unsupervised, unsupported, and unchallenged all contribute to the problem of abuse.

Third, Keenan insists that abuse occurs due to an inadequate theology of sexuality and the absence of a relational sexual ethic. She insists that clergy are so focused on controlling the "sex act" that in cases of abuse, they do not think about the consequences of the "act" for the other person or even about the full significance of the age of the other person where the person is a minor.[56] For too many years within seminaries, celibacy was rarely spoken of in terms of a significant loss. It was mostly spoken about in terms of a personal and heroic sacrifice. This theology of sacrifice rose above all other considerations.[57] Yet, in her interviews with clergy, many abusers spoke of not being able to deal with the losses that mandatory celibacy required.

52. Keenan, "Sexual Abuse," 8.
53. Keenan, "Evidence to the Australian," 3.
54. Keenan, "Evidence to the Australian," 4.
55. Keenan, "Evidence to the Australian," 4.
56. Keenan, "Sexual Abuse," 9.
57. Keenan, "Evidence to the Australian," 6.

Fourth, the church's approach to scandal also is part of the problem of abuse. Church leaders believed that informing the laity of these matters was akin to giving scandal, and such scandal was to be avoided at all costs. Church leaders determined that the truth of human frailty must not scandalize the laity.[58] Fourth, clericalism contributes to the abuse. Clericalism is grounded in the idea that the clergy belong to an elite or "clerical club" who were set apart by ordination. For the laity, the clergy could do no wrong, and thus, children were not believed when they stepped forward. Keenan states, "For Catholic clergy, it led to the belief that children would never tell and that their families would not speak 'ill' of their clergy, giving some security to those abusive clergy that the stories would never be told."[59]

Fifth, clergy were schooled by an overdeveloped intellectual formation that did not equip them to make emphatic decisions. They lacked a relational approach to moral decision-making.[60] Little was said about the process of redirecting their generative strivings into more productive lives. Others found that the lack of emotional support contributed to heavy drinking, gambling or striving for power to compensate for the loss of support. Even abusers could not articulate the losses they endured through celibacy. Usually, they sought to deny sexual desires, control sexual expression and live emotionally lonely lives.[61]

The second person that Moore mentions in relation to insights into sexual abuse is the American psychotherapist A. W. Richard Sipe. According to Sipe:

> The epic consequences of the sexual abuse crisis by clergy have only begun to play out in the structure and culture of the Catholic Church. The impending restructuring will go to prove celibacy's inherent value and power. The real force of celibacy is going to be proven in the monumental outcome of celibacy betrayed . . . The exposure of the widespread failure of celibacy (especially in the criminal mode demonstrated in abuse of minors) by those who staked their power, validity and ministerial prestige on the perfection of perfect sexual abstinence has raised questions of gigantic proportions. Is celibacy a valid and efficacious mode of ministry? Is the Catholic Church's teaching

---

58. Keenan, "Sexual Abuse," 9.
59. Keenan, "Sexual Abuse," 9.
60. Keenan, "Sexual Abuse," 10.
61. Keenan, "Evidence to the Australian," 7.

about human sexuality true? These questions are of Copernican proportions, partially because the conclusion is apparent. The church's teaching about sex and marriage are wrongheaded and lack the scientific and commonsense justification to sustain them any longer . . . [In the words of one Catholic bishop, Geoffrey Robinson] "Sexual abuse of minors by a significant number of priests and religious together with the attempts of many church authorities to conceal the abuse constituted one of the ugliest stories ever to emerge from the Catholic Church. It is hard to imagine a more total contradiction of everything Jesus stood for, and it would be difficult to overestimate the pervasive and lasting harm it has done in the church."[62]

In Sipe's assessment, the problem of abuse is centered around a disordered narcissism:

> [The] veneer of holiness and altruism that cloaks the institution of the Roman Catholic Church covers a clerical culture infused by excessive narcissism. The institution is not what appears in its public pronouncements, ritual manifestations, and glorious vesture. I have seen how its self-serving elements have had a pervasive destructive influence in propagating toxic spirituality. Such a spirituality enables and fosters sexual assault on vulnerable children and adolescent minors while protecting and projecting an image of perfection and moral purity. The literature on narcissism, personal and cultural, is nearly epidemic. That ubiquity neither lessons its important for understanding human behavior nor its significance in the crisis of sexual abuse of minors by men publicly proclaimed to be celibate, so therefore sexually safe, nor can it be discounted as an element in a culture that selects, molds, produces and protects abusers, despite its protestations of selfless service to God and humanity.[63]

Sipe asserts that "the cause of abuse by men who sexually violate children and the vulnerable within a church context is that they are products of formation and inculcation into the clerical system. That system of abuse can be traced from top to bottom. If the culture did not operate in ways that tolerated secret sexual activity of superiors (including but not limited to child sexual abuse) and function as a web of mutually

---

62. Sipe, "Celibacy," 5–6.
63. Sipe et al., "Clerical Spirituality," 3–4.

supportive secret clerical liaison, sexual abuses of minors would find no place in the system."[64] Sipe speaks to the harm done:

> The harm done to the normal development of youngsters from the experience of sexual or physical assault by the trusted is incalculable. The psychological steps to mature loving relationships are sidetracked and, in many cases, destroyed. The self-absorption of men steeped in clerical culture is one element in their deficient empathy and disregard for the need of children to be protected. Innumerable bishops have given witness to their disregard for the rape and torture of children in favor of the primacy of the institution, its power, standing and reputation.[65]

Abuse happens within a system. Sipe assesses:

> Part of the process of introduction and survival in these ecclesiastical enclaves involves relinquishing to one or another of oneself to an all-male authority; a regulated, supposedly sexually abstinent group where conformity of mind and will are demanded and prized. These are "total institutions" which confer an alternative identity and security in exchange for sacrifice of the person . . . obedience that binds an individual even blindly to authority is the ultimate test of loyalty and proof that the individual can now justly assume institutional identity. There is little psychic distinction between self and institution, and thus one's value is subsumed by identification with the power, prestige and status of the church.[66]

Sipe is convinced that many studies of men in seminaries and religious houses reveal them to be psychosexually immature. At its core, the "blind obedience to authority, extolled and inculcated in clerics on every level of the institution, kills the development of spirituality. It distorts conscience because truth is subservient to the institutional mind that is dedicated primarily to self-preservation at all costs." He continues, "Any spirituality of reform must free itself from the institutional bonds of fear, shame and guilt that the narcissistically malignant institution instills with its control and the exercise of power. Only willful blindness and pathological denial can allow one to overlook the reality that the symptom of clerical abuse reveals a Roman Catholic Church as dysfunctional and corrupt sexually and financially as during the time of the Protestant

---

64. Sipe et al., "Clerical Spirituality," 4.
65. Sipe et al., "Clerical Spirituality," 5.
66. Sipe et al., "Clerical Spirituality," 6.

Reformation."⁶⁷ Once the practice of abuse starts, it becomes a disordered pattern in their lives. Not only are they immature, but they are also narcissistic and may become sociopathic in time.

The conclusion drawn by Sipe over the work of a lifetime is that only a small percentage of clergy live celibacy fruitfully, joyfully, intelligently, and lovingly. He estimates the rate of mature celibate clergy to be between 4 percent and 5 percent. Moore states: "Here were men saying what it was like to live among people of the parish, believing themselves to be endowed with a sacramentally conferred virtue of celibate chastity believed in by faith and not experienced as such as an exceptional human stance so that there would be a senseless gap between the priest's ordinary self-awareness as a sexual being and their weird asexuality."⁶⁸ I will explore Moore's ideas about a needed corrective through greater sexual awareness in chapter 12.

THE CHURCH AND PATRIARCHY

Before embarking on understanding Moore's thoughts on women and the church, I want to outline briefly the Roman Catholic teaching on womanhood, and I am choosing Susan Gray as my dialogue partner.⁶⁹ In the *Catechism of the Catholic Church* (CCC), the bishops state that man and woman possess an inalienable dignity that comes to them immediately from God the Creator. Furthermore, any form of sexual or racial discrimination by color, social conditions, language, or religion must be curbed or eradicated and is not part of God's design (CCC 1935). The fathers of the Second Vatican Council, especially in the document *Gaudium and Spes* (GS), note the increasing equal rights of women to men in society and the expanding of their roles into every workplace and social sphere outside the home.

Gray, following Catherine Clifford, asserts that the council presumed that women are self-conscious, self-determining, and full participants in both the life of the church and the larger society.⁷⁰ She notes that the council also recognized the high priority of the duties of wives and

---

67. Sipe et al., "Clerical Spirituality," 8–9.
68. Moore, "2012–2014 Blog," Sep 12, 2012.
69. Gray, "New Theology," 1–31.
70. Gray, "New Theology," 8.

mothers in the home (GS 52). Therefore, in the final analysis, women were seen as juggling the life of the home and their public life in society.

Pope John Paul II proposed the notion of complementarity between men and women. The idea of complementarity was intended to normalize two alternative sexual expressions for women: the single life and marriage within a heterosexual union. As such, the notion did not consider the expanding role of men within the family or the sharing of public and private functions for both sexes, each shaped by the ever-changing personal experiences in response to the context in which they live.[71] Pope Benedict XVI, following the thought of his predecessor, John Paul II, also spoke of the role of women both inside and outside the home, emphasizing a clear recognition of the woman's value through her maternal and family role compared to her public role.[72]

In John Paul II's document *Mulieris Dignitatem*, the theology of women is grounded in the female body, and her body "is the key to the full understanding of motherhood, which is the proper expression of the true nature of womanhood." Thus, the entire meaning of a woman's femininity comes from the

> self-discovery of her unique being . . . only to be found through the process of self-giving to others: her husband, her children, and God, thus her fulfillment is not self-nurtured. Discovery of her personhood is only found through her familial relationships and biological predisposition, regardless of the variety of relationships and experiences throughout her life and the meaning she derives from them as they relate to her whole being and existence—including but not limited to her professional life, her friendships, her successes and failures outside of the home.[73]

For Gray, the document is saying that the only way that a woman can discover the truth and move toward an authenticity of her unique being is by giving herself or by self-sacrifice in the family. Gray notes that the ideal "is unattainable for millions of women worldwide. Further, her authentic self-discovery can only be found within the confines of the traditional relationships of male-female marriage and with her children precisely because of her gender."[74] Gray concludes that the teaching of the church nods towards women's "doctrinal responsibility to fulfil her

---

71. Gray, "New Theology," 11.
72. Gray, "New Theology," 10.
73. Gray, "New Theology," 13.
74. Gray, "New Theology," 15.

matrimonial duty to both God or husband" and to live the two roles of wife and mother, prioritizing these two roles over the attainment of self-authenticity.[75] Gray assesses that the assertion represents a "narrow, classicist teaching about what constitutes authentic womanhood [and] excludes the many other facets of a woman's body, being, and relationships, including professional talents and skills, leadership roles, interpersonal competences and her spiritual depth."[76] While this teaching may have resonated with women before the Industrial Revolution, it fails to appreciate a complete understanding of womanhood for today. This brief history gives some context to appreciating Moore's insights concerning women in the church and the world.

Early in his theological writings, Moore raises the question and challenge of patriarchy within the church and the wider society. Patriarchy is a cultural and social distortion that prioritizes men's experiences by affirming that men are superior to women and that their interests, social goods, behaviors, and values are more important. Further, any distortion becomes institutionalized, such that inequality between men and women is set in place.

Through a basic historical typology of social and cultural orientation with regard to men and women, Moore divides society's treatment of women into three eras. The first era is characterized as the tribal society and its matriarchally empowered identity for women and men. The second era is a patriarchal society where men "conquer new domains of territory and spirit, and pay the price of having to work out their sexual identity [by themselves] instead of learning it from the mother-controlled tribe."[77] For Moore, the critical point in the second era is that growth is grounded in forming male and female identities based on "personal identity and not tribal solidarity."[78] Sadly, it is an era that finds its base in the dominance of men and the tendency to self-discovery by men alone. However, Moore believes that humankind is entering a third era in which there is "a new control by feminine wisdom far deeper and more universal than the old matriarchy combining the naturalness of the latter with the spirituality of the patriarchal age."[79] The third era replaces

---

75. Gray, "New Theology," 16.
76. Gray, "New Theology," 17.
77. Moore, *Inner Loneliness*, 55.
78. Moore, *Inner Loneliness*, 55.
79. Moore, *Inner Loneliness*, 55.

dominance by men with a friendship between men and women; a friendship prefigured in Jesus.[80]

In his more mature writings on Christian feminism, Moore draws on the insights of the Christian feminists Phyllis Trible and Tina Beattie,[81] who both address the limitations of a patriarchal culture in the church. He states: "Religious interpreters always cheat [on the point of gender roles] slipping between sex and gender in a 'heads-I-win-tails-you-lose way praising women to the sky as feminine and keeping them out of the sanctuary [of the liturgy] as female."[82] In Moore's mind, the cultural shaping of women, according to patriarchy, means that men are persons and women are places,[83] and to ask for a cultural shaping of women akin to men seems a long way off. The real social equality of men and women must find its starting point in a psychological self-discovery where equality is located in the soul's recesses and the reconciliation of anima and animus, masculine and feminine archetypes, within the psyches of men and women.[84] What Beattie is trying to communicate theologically, and, similarly, what Trible is communicating biblically, is a theory about women in the church "which follows from the revealed truth of God's transformation of humanity, known by supernatural faith, but which is grounded in woman's subjectivity. Such a theory would show the Christian fact as the death-blow to patriarchy, to the whole of ethology so far which is grounded in men's experience of women, not women's experience, certainly not women's experience of men. Tina wants tradition at its most emphatic combined with feminism at its more emphatic."[85]

For Moore, the resurrection must be the starting point for a new way of feeling, thinking, and valuing women in the church and in the broader society. To encounter Jesus risen after the nightmare and desolation of the cross is to be a witness with every fiber of one's being to the end of the reign of death as isolation and destruction. Moore sees patriarchy as having succumbed to the power of death. The transformation of the resurrection widens when we assess Jesus' deliberate stance with victims, especially women, as victims of male oppression. The

---

80. Moore, *Inner Loneliness*, 55.
81. Moore, *Contagion of Jesus*, 97–103.
82. Moore, *Contagion of Jesus*, 97.
83. Moore, *Contagion of Jesus*, 97.
84. Moore, *Contagion of Jesus*, 97.
85. Moore, *Contagion of Jesus*, 100.

resurrection strips us of all the vestiges of male dominance.[86] It issues a new age, a new creation, and a subsequent subversion of a distorted male-dominating culture.

Moore's conversations with Tina Beattie causes him to write again about women in the life of the church. The official church talks about women as complementary to men. Moore judges that the evaluation of complementarity is inadequate for, however "indispensable this makes her in the male mind, it does not make her a person, a subject, an 'other,' a self-wondering about herself." His language reflects Lonergan's influence and the importance of women's subjectivity and the shift from a culture that viewed women as objects of inquiry to a culture that must view women as subjects seeking personal meaning and value.

The designation of complementarity still renders women passive and, therefore, not persons.[87] It may have the positive effect of naming women who have been prominent in the Church tradition, but it places little store on their articulations, what they have to say about their bodies, and the messages and prophetic dreams that come from them about who God really is.[88] Moore views Beattie's theological concerns as grounded primarily in the revealed truth of God's transformation of humanity that acknowledges the centrality of women's subjectivity. He states that her theory would deal "a death blow to patriarchy [and] to the whole of theology . . . which is grounded in men's experience of women, not women's experience, certainly not women's experience of men."[89] Again, bringing these insights back to their relationship to the cross and resurrection, Moore equates Jesus on the cross as symbolically "reduced to a woman. The crucified is the one female subjectivity-laden symbol."[90]

Concerning the church and the proclamation of the Christian story, it should not be the case that women's subjectivity is championed solely by movements outside the church, which finally have their impact in new ways inside the church only many years later. The Christian story is "subversive of whatever culture it becomes articulated in, and consists of men and women saying things about men and women that are not automatically filtered through the assumptions of our culture."[91] Sadly,

86. Moore, *Contagion of Jesus*, 101.
87. Moore, *Contagion of Jesus*, 100.
88. Moore, *Contagion of Jesus*, 100.
89. Moore, *Contagion of Jesus*, 100.
90. Moore, *Contagion of Jesus*, 101.
91. Moore, *Contagion of Jesus*, 102.

Moore claims that the church's culture is wedded to a distortion based on male dominance, the only one it has known for a long time. While the Churches have been sensitive to feminine challenges in the broader society of late, challenges to do with work and politics, when it comes to the sacramental life of the church in its domain (and here, it would seem, Moore is addressing the ordination of women) the Church "clings anew to her assumption about women unaware that this assumption has nothing to do with the gospel and everything to do with my taught table manners."[92]

THE CHURCH AND THE WIDER SOCIETY

Moore offers social and philosophical insights into the church's relationship to the society and world in which it exists.[93] In the pre-modern relationship of the church to society, the order within the church connected the individual to their social environment with the whole of existence. In other words, what was to later become a distinction between the "sacred" and the "secular" already existed, but the dimensions of sacred and secular was experienced as an undifferentiated whole. The social order within the church was the locus of integrity for the individual in society. As far back as medieval society, institutions similar to the church were part of a unified belief and meaning system that linked people together. Since people were related to the social whole through their allegiance to the church, the rationality of belief was all that was needed to maintain people's commitment. People did not need a religious experience to ground their faith in God. Moore recognizes that this former cultural milieu is no longer the prevailing culture we live in today. The priority of the prevailing culture is towards the importance of the individual who shapes society. There has been a shift in society and culture. With the shift comes a distinction between sacred and secular, often with the secular claiming an absolute autonomy, rather than a relative autonomy, from the sacred. Therefore, in today's new situation, Moore's emphasis for renewal is on the self-discovery and transformation of the whole person.

For Moore, there are hopeful signs that the church is engaging positively with the broader society. From his perspective in the 1960s,

---

92. Moore, *Contagion of Jesus*, 102.
93. Moore and Maguire, *Dreamer*, 86.

he mentions the restarting of the worker-priest movement in France,[94] the spectacle of nuns joining in anti-racialist demonstrations,[95] the visit by the then Archbishop of Canterbury, Archbishop Ramsey, to the pope in Rome,[96] the address given by Pope John to the UNO, which Moore interprets as a symbol of the church listening intently and humbly to the world, the opening of the Second Vatican Council and the positivity of its decrees on religious freedom and interreligious dialogue,[97] He also believes that the church ought to be a counter-cultural sign, asking questions no one else wants to ask.

THE LEGACY OF THE SECOND VATICAN COUNCIL

More recently, the precise legacy of the Second Vatican Council became a source of debate within the church during the papacy of Benedict XVI when the church was celebrating the fiftieth anniversary of the council. During these celebrations, the divisions within the church were more clearly recognized. Prior to the debate, Moore suggests that Benedict XVI's attitude toward the council was very positive. He states: "Even the present Pope, who is, exceptionally for the office, a world-class theologian, can say that the true interpretation of the Council is to see it as reaffirming, deepening, confirming the church the way it has always been, and to see as *innovators* those theologians who insist that with the Council, the church underwent a sea change from the fortress church to the church in the world."[98] However, in his Christmas address to the Roman Curia on December 22, 2005, Pope Benedict spoke about problems in implementing the council arising from the fact that two contrary hermeneutics came face-to-face and quarreled with each other. He named those two hermeneutics as, on the one hand, a hermeneutic of discontinuity and rupture and, on the other hand, a hermeneutic of reform in continuity with the one church the Lord had given to his followers. The pope speaks of the church as a subject that increases in time and develops, yet always remains the same, the one subject of the journeying people of God. He

---

94. Moore and Hurt, *Before the Deluge*, 13.
95. Moore and Hurt, *Before the Deluge*, 13.
96. Moore and Hurt, *Before the Deluge*, 34.
97. Moore and Hurt, *Before the Deluge*, 23–24.
98. Moore, *Body of Christ*, 99.

also proposes that the hermeneutic of discontinuity risks splitting the pre-conciliar church from the post-conciliar church.

The context for the pope's latter comments is a book by Archbishop Agostino Marchetto titled *The Ecumenical Council Vatican II: A Counterpoint for Its History*. The book is an attack on an earlier set of volumes about the Second Vatican Council by Professor Giuseppe Alberigo and Professor Joseph A. Komonchak (editors) titled *A Brief History of Vatican II*. Alberigo uses the social science category of "event" to designate the momentousness of the council, which means some rupture or change from received norms and ways, delineating a "before" the council period and "after" the council period in the life of the church. Alberigo presents the council as a new beginning. He follows the Bologna approach to Church history, based on a historico-critical methodology. The book by Archbishop Marchetto turns the conversation into a polarization between those who view the council as a continuity with the traditions and teachings of the church and those who view the council as a discontinuity with the rules and teachings of the church. Pope Benedict XVI's address to the Roman Curia emphasizes that reform did not mean discontinuity but only change in a way that respects the continuity of principles in the life of the church.

For Moore, the issue is about the use of rhetoric leading to a phenomenon of polarization that portrays one group as bad and the other as good.[99] This formed perspective represents the "myth of dominance," even before a conversation has started.[100] From such a viewpoint, any hint of "new innovation" is interpreted as disruptive. "Disruptive interpreters" are judged to be "novelty pursuing people for novelty's sake." Innovators are assessed to be bent on pulling the interpretation of the documents their way, and the casualty is the word *new* deprived of "its implication of renewal and tradition-based growth and firmly associated with 'novelty.'"[101] In such a context, the "new" means something novel, invented, and disruptive.

From the point of view of authority, the controlling myth of dominance projects onto the "new," the interpretation that such newness can only disturb the life of the church. Moore speaks about his sadness in not hearing from the pope any encouragement towards a conversation or dialogue. He views the pope as siding with the Curia, while the Curia needs so

---

99. Moore, *Body of Christ*, 101.
100. Moore, *Body of Christ*, 101.
101. Moore, *Body of Christ*, 101.

much reform. For Moore, the actions of Marchetto, Riuni (Vicar General of Rome), and Benedict XVI tell the story of "resistance to reform kept up by those who represent the status quo.... It is of the nature of long-settled power."[102] Moore concludes that this situation only sends fear through the church, the impression that the pope is against reform and is resistant to the new. Moore's question is whether Benedict's theology has "taken on the immense task of integrating the birth and growth of historical consciousness into theology, which Lonergan saw ... as his life's work to restore."[103] According to Moore, the pope's German theological contemporaries state that the pope's theology lacked a "grappling with the implications of the demand made on theology by the development of historical consciousness."[104]

To be generous to Moore, prominent historians of the church assert that the council did change things in a new and startling way. Moore notes John O'Malley, a well-known theologian and historian on the Second Vatican Council, and his acceptance of the work of Alberigo.[105] O'Malley states:

> Change happens even in the church. Unless we admit that reality, the history of the church makes no sense and has no relevance and is reduced to a collection of more or less interesting stories as the church sails through the sea of history unaffected by it. Such a sailing is an expression of the historical mindset R. G. Collingwood identified many years ago as "substantialism," a notion that goes back to classical authors but still affects us. The church is not, however, a substance but a community of human beings living in time and space. The story of the Church, therefore, is the story of encounters with the other. In these encounters, both parties are affected. As the church converted the barbarians, the barbarians influenced the church. More important, change is inherent in the very concept of tradition, which is not an inert body of truths but an incarnated reality. The very transcendence of the message means it can be only imperfectly articulated by any given person or culture. Continuity is postulated, deeper than any discontinuity, yet certain continuities and shifts in emphasis seem equally postulated. The tradition is faithfully passed on only when it is rendered engaging and life-giving.[106]

---

102. Moore, *Body of Christ*, 102.
103. Moore, *Contagion of Jesus*, 69.
104. Moore, *Contagion of Jesus*, 69.
105. Moore, *Body of Christ*, 102.
106. O'Malley, "Vatican II," 58.

A New Awareness

Lonergan's insight into the difference between a classicist and empirical view of culture informs Moore's understanding of the dynamics behind the debate. I spoke about this distinction in chapter 2. Moore's appeal to historical consciousness presents a shift in the doing of theology away from prioritizing eternal truths to theology as grappling with revelation, a series of concrete historical events centering on the life, death, and resurrection of Jesus and resulting in the offer of salvation to all peoples.[107] Further, hermeneutics is concerned with questions of meaning and its transmission. Historical consciousness moves us away from taking texts and judging their meaning without reference to the context in which they were written. Historical consciousness moves us toward taking texts and considering their meaning with reference to the contexts in which they were written and how that context may differ from the present context. The contrast opens a meaning gap, raising questions about interpreting meaning from generation to generation.[108] Moore comes down on the side of discontinuity and change, the development of doctrine, historical consciousness, and an empirical notion of culture.

Ormerod also brings some light to the whole discussion. He asks whether there can be a way forward that allows the proponents of rupture and discontinuity to sit at the same table as the proponents of continuity. He suggests that one of the problems is the particular use of language in the debate. The contrasting metaphors of continuity and reform, on the one hand, and discontinuity, on the other, carry unintended problems. Here are some of Ormerod's helpful insights on the debate.

First, the metaphors of continuity and discontinuity are descriptive terms, while what is required for understanding the parameters of the debate are more explanatory terms.[109] Explanatory terms give rise to greater control of meaning, reducing the possibility of misinterpretation and lack of understanding. Second, large-scale social and cultural changes are highly complex.[110] Reducing the complexity to a single either/or metaphor is not helpful. Further, change cannot be measured with some scientific apparatus, in the manner of measuring temperature with a thermometer. The church is an intentional community brought together by a set of meanings and values its members share. These meanings and values cannot be measured only understood. The Second Vatican

---

107. Ormerod, *Introducing*, 30.
108. Ormerod, *Introducing*, 37.
109. Ormerod, "Vatican II," 611.
110. Ormerod, "Vatican II," 611.

Council took place within a complex historical setting, so what actually happened can only be assessed within a more extensive social and cultural change theory, providing a general account of "change." A general account of change can only come about through theology's dialogue with the human and social sciences.[111] Third, over the centuries, the church has tended to view novelty as only derived from its saving truth. Therefore, though it may not be intended, "rupture" is seen as departing from the saving truth.[112]

Ormerod proposes we use the categories of authenticity and inauthenticity and drop the categories of continuity and discontinuity.[113] The concern of Pope Benedict XVI is that the outcome of the council must not be seen to be promoting a watering down of doctrinal integrity. It must be said that Moore's lifework as a theologian and believer was to explore existential directions for crucial doctrines of the Catholic faith. Yet, as Moore and Ormerod both observe, the communication of these salvific meanings and values at the heart of the church to a post-scientific culture requires new symbols, new artistic expressions, a renewed focus on the interpretation of Scripture, and a new liturgical renewal. To do this, the Second Vatican Council promoted more effective communication between the church and the modern world.

Ormerod, therefore, suggests an entirely different approach to the continuity versus discontinuity debate. He turns to Bernard Lonergan and gives Lonergan's comprehensive account of the meaning of meaning, parts of which I outline in chapter 1. Lonergan starts with human interiority. If the world is mediated by meaning and motivated by value, then what kind of data of experience have people focused on to arrive at their specific meanings and values? Central to the emergence of meaning is the presence of conversion: religious, moral, intellectual, affective, and psychic. Further, an examination of the meaning of meaning maps out the various functions, stages, carriers, and realms of meaning.[114] In chapter 1, I examined the various functions of meaning. Lonergan specifies four functions of meaning: cognitive, constitutive, communicative, and effective. For Ormerod, the debate is centrally to do with one group choosing to prioritize certain functions of meaning over others.[115] Without delving

---

111. Ormerod, "Vatican II," 612.
112. Ormerod, "Vatican II," 613.
113. Ormerod, "Vatican II," 620.
114. Ormerod, "Vatican II," 626–27.
115. Ormerod, "Vatican II," 628.

too deeply into the topic, we usually associate meaning with the link between a word and the known object we are seeking to describe or explain. The most notable function of meaning is to orient us in an objective world.

Ormerod understands that the polarization in the debate between continuity and discontinuity is partly due to the priority of one function of meaning over another when what is required is a dialectical and creative tension of all functions of meaning. For Benedict XVI, there exists a prioritization for cognitive meaning. The cognitive function of meaning prioritizes the doctrines of the church. Cognitive meaning applied to doctrines seeks above all a precision in meaning. Moore prioritizes constitutive and communicative meaning.[116] In terms of constitutive meaning, Moore's turn to the subject, coupled with the turn to the body, is central to a new awareness of being Christian in today's world. In terms of communicative meaning, Moore's life project has been just as much about finding the right words to express faith as it has been about awakening consciousness from the staid formulae of the past, which no longer speak to people and, when spoken, bring on an immediate gazing of the mind.

THE CHURCH AND FEAR

We come now to several issues that Moore speaks passionately about and which have a bearing on order within the church. Moore understands himself as imbued with the spirit of the Second Vatican Council, which he sees as a revolutionary change in the life of the church. Speaking during the reign of John Pope II and Pope Benedict XVI, and on several occasions, he mentions a deep sadness that he judges exists within the life of the church in its current state. That sadness is the use of fear to control people. Moore finds evidence for fear in the number of theologians that were silenced during the papacy of Benedict XVI and during the papacy of John Paul II when Cardinal Ratzinger was head of the Congregation for the Divine Faith (CDF).[117]

Moore is concerned with demonstrating the many missteps of these papacies through silencing creative minds.[118] In several references, he cites a book by Matthew Fox, *The Pope's War: Why Ratzinger's Secret Crusade Has Imperiled the Church and How It Can Be Saved*. Fox's book documents

---

116. Ormerod, "Vatican II," 630.
117. Moore, "2012–2014 Blog," May 1, 2013.
118. Moore, "2012–2014 Blog," May 13, 2013.

the various condemnations against significant theologians. For example, liberation theologians Leonardo Boff and Jon Sobrino and Church leaders like Archbishop Oscar Romero and Bishop Pedro Casaldaliga, who were silenced or frowned upon by the official Church in Rome.[119] In Fox's view, the attack on liberation theology by the Congregation for the Divine Faith was a *quid pro quo* for the support that the *Solidarity* movement in Poland got from the CIA.[120] During the CELAM Conference in South America, Cardinal Ratzinger sent a delegation to push for the condemnation of liberation theology. Ratzinger's letter was headed off by another and different letter, this time of support by the Catholic theologian Karl Rahner.[121] In Fox's mind, Cardinal Ratzinger's Eurocentric perspective was incapable of grasping the originality of Latin American theology as a specific response to social injustice in a particular location. The same was true of the theology of Father Leonardo Boff. On May 9, 1985, he was silenced by the CDF. At the "colloquy," to which he was invited ostensibly to explain his theological views, Boff found that the meeting was simply a full-scale interrogation with a predetermined end.[122]

Finally, there is the case of Bishop Casaldaliga. Fox reports that Cardinal Ratzinger ordered him not to speak publicly or leave his diocese without explicit permission after an interrogation in Rome conducted by himself and Cardinal Bernadine Gantin, the then prefect of the Congregation for Bishops. According to Fox, there were five complaints against him. First, Casaldaliga refused to come to Rome on *ad limina* visits, which a bishop was required to make every five years to the Holy See. Casaldaliga told Fox that it cost a lot of money and that his poverty-stricken diocese could not justify the expenditure, and besides, no one in Rome listened to what he had to say about his people anyway. Second, he was criticized because his favorite writings were liberation theology. Third, he was criticized for traveling to Nicaragua to support his friend Miguel D'Escoto's hunger strike. Fourth, he helped create a mass that was centered on Indian and Black culture in Brazil. Fifth, Casaldaliga had referred to Archbishop Oscar Romero as a "martyr." When he refused to sign a statement saying he would back down from all these activities, he was silenced for three months.[123]

119. Fox, *Pope's War*, 11.
120. Fox, *Pope's War*, 23.
121. Fox, *Pope's War*, 27.
122. Fox, *Pope's War*, 41–43.
123. Fox, *Pope's War*, 56.

A New Awareness

Citing Father Donald Cozzens and Bishop Geoffrey Robinson, Moore points to several Church leaders and teachers who fear speaking about issues of tension within the church.[124] Moore asserts that "the *reason* why the unwillingness to speak out of faith is being felt in religious communities is that these are tied to the authority structure of the church in a way that your average Catholic is not, so we have to pursue an enquiry in the direction of this authority structure. How might fear come to be in the way authority feels itself vis-à-vis the church that it governs?"[125] For Moore, the use of the tool of fear is grounded in the official church's fear of losing power and not being in control of the church. He views the attitude as somewhat flawed, given that the Church in Rome does not control the church. Further, the imposition of fear from officials to religious leaders and from religious leaders to community members is very ugly. For Moore, the position does not pass on the vibrancy of the faith. Instead, it is maintaining a set of propositions "whose keeping in place is thought of as the essential mission of the authority. . . . There is a spiritual—certainly a spirited—and emotional investment in formulas as the test of faith which will characterize those in authority who feel their power threatened."[126]

The atmosphere of fear causes division in the Church community between those who subscribe to the old church and those who adhere to the new church. Moore lays the blame at the feet of the bishops of dioceses who did not vigorously pursue a comprehensive program of adult education of the faithful when they returned from Rome after the Second Vatican Council.[127] Further, the widening of Curial influence means that the church has become "more centralized in Rome than ever before in its history with modern instant communication facilitating this, an ironic sequel to a council that had tried to decentralize the Church."[128] Moore characterizes the officials who want to hang on to power as the ones who discount the council and declare it a council in which nothing of importance changed. It merely reaffirms what had always been, and this attitude to the council has become a mindset.

I will continue with Moore's theological understanding of the church in the next chapter.

---

124. Moore, *Body of Christ*, 96.
125. Moore, *Body of Christ*, 96.
126. Moore, *Body of Christ*, 97.
127. Moore, *Body of Christ*, 98.
128. Moore, *Body of Christ*, 99.

10

Moore and the Community of the Church II

INTRODUCTION

In this chapter, I will continue to explore Moore's ecclesiology. I will begin by exploring Moore's developing image of the church from the 1960s onward and arrive at the predominant image that informs his ecclesiology. Moore did not see himself as an ecclesiologist but was always interested and engaged in the life of the church and understood it to be a community that was an extension of the risen Lord and the sending of the Spirit.

THE CHURCH AS "BIPOLAR"

In the mid-1960s, and speaking to an audience of Catholics going through enormous changes in the church and the wider society, Moore starts to present some of his metaphors and images for the church. He aims to help Catholics transition from a former mode of being church to a new way. To help make the change, Moore speaks about the church as "unipolar" and "bipolar." He views the former era of high attendance to Mass and the sacraments, especially the sacrament of penance, as part of the "Unipolar" Church, ruled by a code and singular mentality that kept people together also by the fear of excommunication. It was a Church whose unity was aided by the fact that it shared much with the broader society. In the 1960s, the church finally woke to the reality that a sacred canopy no longer existed and had not done so for some time.

A New Awareness

Moore advocates a "Bipolar" Church. The "Bipolar" Church lives in tension. On one side of the polarity is the sign of the church as an instrument of salvation and the transforming power of the Holy Spirit. The sign is the source of the church's life. The sign points to the church's center in the life, death, and resurrection of Jesus and the sending of the Spirit. On the other side of the polarity is the church as a human community needing to do human things and not take them for granted. As a human community, the church needs to change in order to address a new social and cultural milieu.

In the "Bipolar" Church, religious experience and religious love will be of primary importance.[1] In Saint Paul's hymn to charity in 1 Cor 13, Paul "pushes out beyond all moral attitudes, however excellent. First, it takes you to the point where no moral attitude seems possible, were continued forgiveness of others is against reason, where a man is exposed to this bitter world in all its naked irrational strength, and it says 'even here, nay especially here, love survives'. Secondly, it makes us *see* the charity which pushes out beyond all moral attitudes pushes out also beyond the confines of this life."[2] The "bipolarity" brings into unity our surrender to God and a practical concern for one's neighbor, thus presenting the human face of the church. In the "Bipolar" Church, the members will be encouraged to "cultivate their inner ear."[3] The inner ear is a contemplative disposition that will allow prayer and poetry reading to aid in bringing believers' conscious and unconscious realities into harmony. At the same time, it will be a community of people characterized by a face-to-face meeting between believers where they know each other in depth.[4]

THE CHURCH, THE DREAM, AND LOVERS

Moore proposes the metaphor of a "dream" by which to imagine the church. The dream is

> the place of promise. In it a man's own deepest life stirs and peoples his imagination with figures who are really part of himself, bone of my bone flesh of my flesh. In the dream man meets the other, in whom, without any adjustment on his part, he

---

1. Moore and Maguire, *Dreamer*, 29.
2. Moore and Hurt, *Before the Deluge*, 30.
3. Moore and Maguire, *Dreamer*, 89.
4. Moore and Maguire, *Dreamer*, 25.

> meets himself in the dream. We extend into other people *as we are*. There is not there the waking check of discretion whereby a man withholds from the other a part of himself that the other could not hope to understand. The dream can suggest this total flow of people into each other, only because there is no real other. As the psychologists say, the dreamer plays all the roles.[5]

Moore's metaphor is based on his understanding of Jung and the anima or archetype of femininity (in men) and animus or archetype of masculinity (in women). Moore also calls the anima (and animus) the inner partner. I outlined this element of Jung's theory of the psyche in chapter 4. Just as men and women cannot be trapped in the dream of their sexual opposite by the archetype of their contrasexual "inner partner," the church cannot simply rely on some ideal image of itself accumulated over many years. The world has changed and so any hope for the future of the church will be discovered by negotiating our ideal of the church with the new situation; otherwise, we will become confused and cause more severe problems. The natural person standing before us is a metaphor for the changed world and the changed historical circumstances in which we find ourselves.

Moore uses the metaphor of dreams and lovers to articulate a new mode of awareness needed within the church. Just as a married couple finds their buried self in a situation of trust and a full acceptance of their conscious and unconscious lives, the church community will find itself through complete self-acceptance of its past in dialogue with the changed condition of the present. Just as a loving couple, after making love, speak so much truth to one another that otherwise they would keep to themselves, so love will generate for the church a new reality and a new openness where desire creates "the myth of the achieved human community."[6] Just as a couple find their fulfillment in love releasing the deeper self to interact with all parts of themselves, the church will achieve a community through the receiving and giving of love. Moore states: "A real awakening heads towards a condition where being alive, feeling ourselves alive and perceiving others comes to be felt as a single and indivisible faculty."[7]

---

5. Moore and Maguire, *Dreamer*, 46.
6. Moore and Maguire, *Dreamer*, 48.
7. Moore and Maguire, *Dreamer*, 55.

By contrast, the poor alternative is a model of Church that posits the primacy of correct behavior through moral bullying.[8] Moore then uses his knowledge of Jung to create a parallel with the church. Moral bullying amounts to imposing our dream (or inner partner) on another, just as a husband may want to impose his dream of a woman (his anima) on the real partner standing before him, telling her that she cannot be her historical and authentic self. Such an imposition would only cause disappointment in himself, by confusing his dream with the natural person, and, will cause alienation in his partner through not being accepted as she is with all her strengths and weaknesses.[9]

THE CHURCH, FRIENDSHIP, AND DISCIPLESHIP

For Moore, one of the most enduring images of the church that remains with him throughout his life is the church as a community of disciples and friends. No doubt the image gained purchase from living in a monastic community. These are his key insights.

First, Moore's whole approach to friendship is very practical. He had been formed in a monastic tradition that espoused excellent writings on friendship, including the treatise *Spiritual Friendship* by the medieval Cistercian monk Aelred of Rievaulx. Yet, the same formation discouraged "particular friends" within the monastery. In his reflections, Moore begins by saying that all our attempts to create, engage, and sustain friendship are to be facilitated by focusing. Focusing is a technique for becoming aware of one's embodiment to be more in tune with one's feelings. Feelings are a pre-apprehension of values. We must cultivate healthy feelings without being at the beck and call of every feeling we experience.

Second, when we speak of friendship, the elements of desire, attraction, and love come into focus. Without focusing, any love, including the love of friends, can become a do-goodism. However, focusing without attachment tends toward self-indulgence.[10] Desire is love trying to happen. Moore confesses that many times throughout his life, he did not respond to people who felt attracted to him and wanted friendship with him, preferring to remain inert. He assesses his response as a deliberate negative strategy to deny the messiness of desire, attraction, and love. His

---

8. Moore and Maguire, *Dreamer*, 55.
9. Moore and Maguire, *Dreamer*, 56.
10. Moore, *Contagion of Jesus*, 164.

notion of friendship means understanding and appreciating our feelings and mutual interests, the desire to spend time with one another, and, at a higher level, our desire to share confidences and help carry each other's sufferings.

Third, Moore is aware of the challenges when friends have fallen out.[11] He suggests that in the case of a falling out, it is essential that the parties try to de-obsess over what has happened and come back to some equilibrium within themselves. In the case of self-righteousness, there is again a deep problem requiring a practical solution. Self-righteousness is the attitude where one party needs to have the other party wrong so they can be right, usually out of fear and as a way of reinforcing a viewpoint.[12] Moore confesses that obsessive thinking following a falling out with a fellow believer and self-righteousness accompanying the need to be right is a constant source of difficulty for himself, and he admits to its pain. There are many layers to the problem of religious self-righteousness, especially for those who live within the shadow of death understood as annihilation or extinction. People do not like the bitter taste of having their faith threatened or trivialized. When their religious adherence is grounded in fear, threat, or anxiety, the believer, in the face of attack, can easily assume a position of self-righteousness.

By contrast, when religious awe arises, powered by spiritual love, the place that one speaks from, even when threatened, is the more profound desire for eternal life.[13] When focusing is practiced, the parties can better put Jesus imaginatively in the story, see Jesus taken to the crucifixion, see the disciples completely emptied, and then imagine Jesus returning in the resurrection with healing and forgiveness. This imaginative exercise helps both parties to relax in Jesus and, in that moment, melt the barriers of offense and self-righteousness.[14]

Fourth, Moore is familiar with the problem of fear within friendship. Moore asks: How do I feel about someone who has it all and somehow makes me feel without any goading or boasting toward me on their part that I don't have it all?[15] Moore draws from the interplay between Jesus and Peter in the light of Jesus' words about his approaching suffering and death. Peter refuses Jesus' declaration. In the lyrical period of

11. Moore, *Contagion of Jesus*, 164.
12. Moore, *Contagion of Jesus*, 166.
13. Moore, *Contagion of Jesus*, 166.
14. Moore, *Contagion of Jesus*, 167.
15. Moore, *Contagion of Jesus*, 168.

awakening to desire by the disciples, we find Peter both attracted to Jesus and repelled by him. Jesus' actions elicit an ambivalence in Peter. Even Peter's denial of Jesus following his arrest is grounded in a confused rage against Jesus, who brought things to a head by setting his face toward Jerusalem. One could easily see in the life of Peter the apostle, someone pulled from his trade, awakened to a new and hopeful desire for God, and then placed in circumstances he neither accepted, understood, nor wanted. Moore calls this "that deep ill-understood desire to be rid of someone loved but too big for you."[16] Reflecting on Peter, we can place ourselves into the hands of Jesus, who came back to Peter after the resurrection with forgiveness, freeing him from his wretched confusion so that he could restore the hearts and minds of the community of disciples.

Fifth, becoming a disciple of Jesus requires saying "No" to various other alternative paths in our lives so as to say "Yes" to the invitation of Jesus. Discipleship becomes an exercise in risk-taking.[17] If such a statement can be said more generally about discipleship, joining the community of disciples known as the church is nothing like obtaining membership in a football club. Joining the church as a disciple is risking one's life within the original risk of Jesus' cross and resurrection, and, in this mystery, finding a reward.[18] The original risk of discipleship is grounded in Jesus' "Yes" to the Father and his mission to bring about an alternative order in society that is opposed to our murder-driven world order. The risk of Jesus precipitates his death and is central to each eucharistic celebration which proclaims the Lord's death till he comes. For Moore, if Jesus is doing a pioneer action that disarms in love all our violence through his life and death, his disciples are entrusted to work for the kingdom as the faithful people of God.[19] To live as disciples in the community of the church, we must "learn to contemplate the figure on the Cross as drawing us and all things to himself, as the exemplar of life beyond the enslavement of having to vie with each other for the upper hand."[20] Through Jesus, discipleship can be an effective way beyond the "myth of dominance," which perpetuates the reign of death and sweeps away

---

16. Moore, *Contagion of Jesus*, 169.
17. Moore, *Contagion of Jesus*, 171.
18. Moore, *Contagion of Jesus*, 171.
19. Moore, *Contagion of Jesus*, 176.
20. Moore, *Contagion of Jesus*, 177.

the tender mercy of God, for whom not one sparrow falls to the ground without God knowing it.[21]

MOORE AND MARY, THE MOTHER OF THE CHURCH

Since one of Moore's strong images of the church is the community of disciples, he turns his attention to Mary, Mother of the Lord and Mother of the Church, to help him understand the meaning of discipleship and what kind of church we must be. He recognizes the universal need for proper mothering and fathering in our lives. The church as a mother, Mary's motherhood of Jesus, and our biological mothers are all crucial symbols for growth and transformation. However, Moore proposes that our psychological needs must be underpinned by intellectual rigor.[22] Again, Moore turns to the doctrine of original sin. Where did Mary stand? Moore asserts that Mary is the exception to the human flaw of original sin by the grace of God acting in her life and the life of her parents, and mediated by them toward her from birth. If grace is both healing and elevating, Mary requires no healing. She is a woman without envy. Grace sanctified her and prepared her for what was to come in the Annunciation and after. Mary's parents, no doubt, mediated the grace of God to her through her upbringing, and Mary built on this mediation through her listening to the Scriptures and prayer. While too many believers get bogged down at the level of biology and chromosomal development when contemplating the impregnation of Mary, Moore suggests another approach. For believers, the central question is more contemplative and circles around the text "Let it be done with me according to your word" (Luke 1:38).

Moore's appropriation of Jung's notion of the reconciliation of the opposites of masculine and feminine within the human psyche becomes an essential element for a spirituality that acts as a corrective to other spiritualities that have been too male-oriented. Reconciliation is already present in the humanity of Jesus, and its presence in the life of Jesus has a great deal to do with the maternal influence of Mary, his mother. Similar to her Son, Mary reflects a resounding consent to a "Yes" to life in every stage of her earthly development. In the beginning, Mary's "Yes" to the angel's Annunciation is her desire for a new humanity, and her desire

---

21. Moore, *Contagion of Jesus*, 178.
22. Moore, *Contagion of Jesus*, 81.

could only have been possible unless she was unencumbered by the negative weight of original sin. Moore asserts that her invitation by God through the angel and her subsequent mission from Pentecost onward clearly marks the need for believers to bring Mary into full and conscious participation in the operations of her Son.[23]

Mary's perspective makes her the model for the whole church in its identity and mission. Far from the pure and sentimental image of Mary formed in the minds and hearts of monastic communities over centuries, including an over-emphasis on her virginity, Mary is a far richer model for the disciples of Jesus. As a mature Christian believer, Moore despises images of Mary, whose function is to make the virtue of chastity central to the monastic community.[24] Moreover, the latter image of Mary is out of step with the community, where women are discounted and abused through an entrenched system of patriarchy.[25] Moore asserts the "Madonna" image of Mary in the church suffers from a distorted projection. The projection views Mary as innocent and unthreatening. It downplays her subversive voice and strong-mindedness as displayed in the Magnificat. The consequence of the projective idealization of a passive Mary has been a Church that had talked up her receptive, listening, and obedient soul before God and downplayed her prophetic witness.[26] This one-sided emphasis has an unhelpful consequence. On the one hand, Church officials have encouraged a positive subjectivity for women, even to the point of promoting their voices, and yet, on the other hand, practically, the Church authorities have tried to keep women conforming and obedient to male power.

Further, Church officials often couch issues to do with faith and moral life in the language of clear, rational thought but without reference to feelings and the heart.[27] Referring to Lonergan's reflection that our lack of attention and devotion to Mary has a lot to say about a negation of the feelings within ourselves, Moore concludes: "Rome's appalling insensitivity to feeling [as such] which creates an unhealthy gap between rationality and sentimentality [has often been] noted as the two salient features of official Roman Catholicism."[28] In the subjectivity of Mary, we

23. Moore, *Contagion of Jesus*, 86.
24. Moore, *Contagion of Jesus*, 74.
25. Moore, *Contagion of Jesus*, 86.
26. Moore, *Contagion of Jesus*, 56.
27. Moore, *Contagion of Jesus*, 87.
28. Moore, *Contagion of Jesus*, 88.

find someone who is not ignorant, passive, and unknowing. Mary is an active and knowing person. All disciples need a similar psychological formation and spiritual transformation. Her transformation made it possible for her to say "Yes" to the messenger of God.[29] It reveals Mary as possessing self-awareness. For Mary, her subjectivity and complete self-awareness are centered in the phrase "being in Christ" and freedom from the "wobble" of original sin, thus giving a clue to what we ought to be cultivating when we form people within the church.

Mary becomes, for us, a Trojan horse figure overturning a distorted culture. The neglected role of women in a culture of distorted patriarchy needs addressing. Mary's consent to God and her contemplative stillness makes her a worthy model belonging to God. As our mother and first among her Son's disciples, we can appreciate Mary as someone sent to heal the phallocentric distorted culture of the church. Therefore, Mary's motherhood to Jesus and the Church is her advocacy for all women. For women, advocacy means a rediscovery of female subjectivity, a call for men to accept and integrate the feminine within their own psychic lives, and for men and women to appropriate the freedom that Paul speaks about when he proclaims that for those in Christ, there is neither male nor female. The renewed culture will not be one where the oppressed become the oppressors, according to a Hegelian twist, but where women and men are united in an equal partnership.

Reflecting on his own experience of devotion to Mary, Moore adds a biographical note. He states that as he centers his prayer and meditation on Mary, he discovers her more intensely, especially when he pays attention to his embodiment through focusing.[30] Concerning his relationship with women, he states: "What I have been given most deeply to understand about myself is a meeting place between a man and a woman within . . . I can now look back on my life as one of conflict between them and I am only seeing this now because they are coming to peace. I celebrate this peace in the Song of Songs that I read daily and always freshly."[31] Further, in the later part of his life, through his blog, Moore writes about Mary on the feast of the Assumption.[32] Moore's context for writing is to unpack again the significance of the pain-body in our lives and its complete opposite, the Body of Christ. Elsewhere, Moore calls the pain-body "feeling bad

---

29. Moore, *Contagion of Jesus*, 89.
30. Moore, *Contagion of Jesus*, 94.
31. Moore, *Contagion of Jesus*, 97–98.
32. Moore, "2012–2014 Blog," Aug 15, 2012.

about feeling good" and is closely related to original sin, and the proneness to self-punishing attitudes. The "feeling bad about feeling good" is the very voice of original sin. Somewhere in childhood, people pick up the idea that our desire is bad, and adults communicate the message to the child that we are born with bad desires. We grow with an addiction to unhappiness.[33] Moore concludes that Mary is the body shown free of all these distortions. She is the image of the body of Christ.

THE BODY OF CHRIST

For Moore, the most enduring image for the church is the image of the body of Christ. At the Second Vatican Council, several images of the church, due to a renewal in biblical studies, became prominent: the church as the pilgrim people of God (Heb 11:13–16); the church as unleavened bread (1 Cor 5:7); the church as a gathering of hosts and guests (Luke 22:30); the church as a letter from Christ (2 Cor 3:2–3); the church as the house of David, the remnant of the elect (Luke 2:4, 10–11); the church as the flock of the Shepherd (Luke 12:32); the church as locus of the Holy Spirit (Eph 2:22); the image of the church as the New Jerusalem, the cornerstone (Eph 2:19–22), the temple, the Holy City and Mount Zion (Rev 21:21–22); the church as a bride (Eph 5:25): the church as a fellowship of saints (Phil 4:21–23); the church as the place where God is creating a new humanity (Eph 4:24).

Throughout his writings, Moore does not directly address his image of preference. However, there are indications that the image of the body of Christ (1 Cor 12; Rom 12:4–5) was most important to him. First, I note that Moore used the term *body* in five different yet linked contexts. I spoke to Moore's insights into human embodiment in chapter 1. He uses "body" to talk about pain-body and body shift. These are Tolle-inspired terms, and focusing is a technique to aid our recognition of body-pain. We are our bodies or embodied people, and the positive and negative feelings of the psyche make themselves felt through the body. Therefore, an attunement to our body is vital if we want to name what is hurting us and seek to be healed.

The second use of the term *body* is about Christ: his broken body on the cross and his transformed body in the resurrection.[34] I explored the

---

33. Moore, "2012–2014 Blog," Jun 11, 2012.
34. Moore, *Body of Christ*, 37–57, 69–87.

meaning of Christ's crucified body and resurrected body in chapters 7 and 8. Moore affirms that the church cannot separate the Jesus of liturgy and dogma from the Jesus of dangerous memory, who freely chose the cross. If we cannot know Jesus in the church in all our nakedness, as he was naked, then we will not be committing to the real Jesus.[35] Again, Moore links the mystical (our dissolution) and the social (the body of the church and her mission to the suffering). Further, the resurrection encounter is synonymous with the call by Jesus to be a community of disciples. He states that Jesus socialized their awakening (and transformation) to the ultimate mystery in the communion of the church, an awakening typically experienced in a person's solitude. He made being together the place of communion with ultimate mystery.[36] The "being together" of ecclesia is the place where we meet the mystery. For Moore, the church born of the resurrection "socializes for the disciples the mystical touch of God."[37]

The third use of the term *body* is about the Eucharist. I will speak to this in the latter part of the chapter. The fourth use of *body* concerns membership in the body of Christ, the church, through baptism. In several places, Moore makes positive reference to the Protestant scholar Bishop John A. T. Robinson and his scholarship around Paul's understanding of the body.[38] Robinson's book *The Body: A Study in Pauline Theology* appeared in 1953 with the acclaim of several Catholic scholars, including F. Prat and Fr. P. Benoit.

Moore suggests that being in the body of Christ causes us to increase to others a range of tenderness and rethink Paul's insight that "when one member suffers, the others suffer with it. In this way, no reasoning has to take place between the report of a friend's loss and pain and my prayer for him. In the body as I now learn to inhabit it, I can feel his loss and some of his pain. I am 'in the body' as I am 'in touch,' 'in one system of communication.'"[39] He is saying that if we genuinely feel ourselves to be members of the body of Christ, then we will be suffering along with others because of a current of communication and connection between those in the same body.

---

35. Moore, "Night Thoughts," 240.
36. Moore, "Night Thoughts," 238–39.
37. Moore, "Night Thoughts," 239.
38. Moore, *Body of Christ*, 15.
39. Moore, *Body of Christ*, 15.

According to Robinson, salvation is historically conditioned by two factors: first, the soul of salvation, who is Christ and who remains eternally the same; and second, the church, the body of Christ which changes concretely throughout human history. Robinson's insight corresponds very closely with Moore's bipolar church. On the one hand, there is the church as a sign of salvation, and at the heart of the church is the risen Lord; on the other hand, there is the church as a human community ever in need of refinement and restructuring to meet the needs of the time. Religious conversion must be both a personal and a community affair. As a personal affair, conversion means surrendering our lives to Christ. As a community affair, conversion means that each person in the church has his center in other people. The church is not an aggregation of individuals but rather a reality of interdependence.

According to Robinson, Paul's theology of the body is threefold: the body of the flesh, the body of the cross, and the body of the resurrection.[40] There are two keywords in Paul's writings concerning the body of the flesh: *soma* and *sarx*. *Soma* or "body" refers not only to something that each person has but something that each person is. *Soma* stands for humanity in solidarity with the rest of creation and created to be with God. By contrast, *sarx* or "flesh" suggests that humanity exists in a state of weakness and mortality in his worldliness and solidarity with earthly existence. *Sarx* can be either a neutral or a sinful connotation. As neutral, it refers to people living *for* the world, allowing their being in the world to govern their whole life and conduct. As sinful, *sarx* is an attitude that denies creaturehood over against God. Both *soma* and *sarx* designate different aspects of our human relationship with God.[41] *Soma* stands for man in solidarity with creation but made for God. *Sarx* stands for man in solidarity with creation but distanced from God.

Concerning the body of the cross, the starting point to understanding the meaning of the body is the Incarnation, where God sent his Son into a human situation of death, sin, and subjugation to the law. Christ identified with the body of the flesh and mankind's fallen state but without sin. He defeated sin, enslavement, and the curse of the cross. The death of Christ is the defeat of evil because his death consists of the liberation from the flesh. The redemptive work of Christ is reproduced in the life of the Christian through baptism. It is through baptism that the

---

40. McBrien, *Church in the Thought*, 29.
41. McBrien, *Church in the Thought*, 30–31.

Christian enters the one body, and it is through the body of Christ that a man can be saved through the body of the cross.[42]

Concerning the body of the resurrection, Paul brings together the eucharistic body of Christ, the body of Christ, which is the church, and the Christian hope of the resurrection and renewal in their own body. Paul's use of the term *body* to speak about the church is not so much a designation of a collectivity or corporate entity. It is instead to be compared with a human corporeal body. Robinson asserts:

> Paul uses the analogy of the human body to elucidate his teaching that Christians form Christ's body. But the analogy holds because they are in literal fact the risen organism of Christ's person in all its concrete reality. What is arresting is his identification of this personality with the church. But to say that the church is the body of Christ is no more of a metaphor than to say that the flesh of the encounter Jesus or the bread of the Eucharist is the body of Christ. None of them is "like" His body (Paul never says this): each of them *is* the body of Christ in that each is the physical complement of the one and same Person and Life. They are all expressions of a single Christology. It is almost impossible to exaggerate the materialism and crudity of Paul's doctrine of the church as literally now the Resurrection body of Christ.... The body that he has in mind is as concrete and as singular as the body of the Incarnation. His underlying conception is not of a supra-personal collective, but of a specific personal organism. He is not saying anything so weak as that the church is a society with a common life and governor, but that its unity is that of a single physical entity: disunion is dismemberment. For it is in fact no other than the glorified body of the risen and ascended Christ.[43]

EUCHARIST, MASS, AND SACRIFICE

In the previous section, I noted that Moore linked four contexts for using the term *body*. The fourth context I wish to explore is the eucharistic body of Christ. Moore grounds his understanding of the Eucharist in Aquinas's phrase *O Sacrum Convivium*, the Sacred Love Feast. The expression "the Sacred Celebration" captures several elements that Moore

---

42. McBrien, *Church in the Thought*, 31–32.
43. Robinson, *Body*, 51.

understands to be part of any eucharistic theology; demonstrates how we have distorted the meaning of "sacrifice"[44]; emphasizes the context of the Last Supper as a shared ritual meal and Jesus' body and blood as the love feast. In chapter 8, I spoke about the two understandings of sacrifice: first, the dark side of sacrifice as destroying victims on the altars of our disesteem felt self-rejection, apathy, and malice; second, for humankind, sacrifice had become a means of appeasement by blood, a form of hating ourselves, and a way of violently shaping the world.[45] In the light of the resurrection, the sacrifice of Jesus "dissipates the shadow of ancient sacrifice, and facing us with the painful, beautiful truth that in all our sacrificing it is ourselves and not God that we have been trying to appease."[46] Jesus' death is a sacrifice only as an act of thanksgiving and love. His death on the cross is a sacrifice only on his terms, as "a feast of love."[47] Jesus makes the ancient form of sacrifice obsolete and offers the only sacrificial rite that his people are to know, the "love feast on the forgiving eternally alive victim."[48]

In trying to understand the meaning of the Eucharist, the Catholic Church has always tied what Jesus did at the Last Supper to what happened on Calvary, and the confluence of these two key insights brought about a third expression, the sacrifice of the Mass. In the Reformation controversies, the Protestants emphasized the "once for all" nature of Christ's sacrifice against Catholics, who, for Protestant reformers, seemed to be saying that the Mass was a reenactment of Calvary, emphasizing that the sacrifice of the Mass was the sacrifice of Calvary repeated. Both sides were expressing a needed insight. For the reformers, the death of Jesus is "once and for all." Jesus does not have to die again on the cross. For Catholics, there is an intimate link between the ritual and sacred action of the Mass and what Jesus did on Calvary.

Similarly, the sacrifice of the Mass is the sacrifice of Calvary since the Mass is "the drama of God's love swallowing up our ritualized violence in a rite that is only banquet, is there, celebrated regularly throughout the world, to cure us of the sacrifices on which our civilization is built."[49] The Mass is the only kind of sacrifice that Catholics are meant

---

44. Moore, "New Convivium," 40.
45. Moore, "New Convivium," 42.
46. Moore, "New Convivium," 41.
47. Moore, "New Convivium," 41.
48. Moore, "New Convivium," 42.
49. Moore, "New Convivium," 43.

to know. Therefore, when Catholics think of sacrifice, Moore insists that both the idea of taking a life, in this case, the innocent victim in Jesus, and the laying down of one's life freely must always be kept in tension.[50] The needed tension takes away the distorted and primordial association in the human heart that links self-transcendence with self-rejection.[51] We think that to please God, something must be destroyed in us. Instead, the disciples come to understand that Jesus, the Victim, rises with forgiveness to inaugurate "the New Covenant and the new convivium."[52] God changes our action, which seeks only to destroy another out of self-rejection into sorrow, the offer of forgiveness, and a love feast. Moore states: "Out of this absolution, wherever it is experienced, comes the love for our enemies, the new and eternal life, the Resurrection of the dead. Its sacrament is the Eucharist, in which his flesh given for us is bread given for us, his blood wine. This healing murder is proclaimed among us only by a shared meal."[53]

EUCHARIST: THE SACRIFICE OF CALVARY

While writing *The Body of Christ*, Moore is weighing into a debate in the wider church over whether the Eucharist, theologically speaking, is best understood as a sacred meal or a sacrifice. Moore is typically suspicious of the word *sacrifice*. The word *sacrifice* immediately brings to mind the suffering inflicted on some hapless victim. The sacrifice of Jesus can only be understood as a free act by Jesus, with the result that Jesus took to himself our sins, so that by turning evil into good, we might benefit from the birth of new meaning in his actions. Yet conversely, the crucifixion is also an act by victimizers seeking to overcome good with evil. Moore states again: "The crucifixion was a human sacrifice offered by the powers of this world religious and secular, whose rule has death as its instrument—its baton as one Jewish writer calls it—under the aegis of Caiaphas the High Priest. This sacrifice of our humanity to the powers that be is by its victim, stood on its head, in such wise that the victim, in

---

50. Moore, "New Convivium," 46.
51. Moore, "New Convivium," 48.
52. Moore, "New Convivium," 48.
53. Moore, "New Convivium," 51.

defiance of the prime requirement for [the] sacrifice of non-personhood, the thingness of the victim, is protagonist and priest."[54]

For many in the church and present at the eucharistic celebration, the divinity of the victim confers sacrificial status on Calvary. For Moore, the action of Jesus on Calvary denotes an act of self-sacrificing love designed to dissolve the legitimacy of our sacrifice of others, undertaken by us on the altar of our disesteem, by which we create victims, out of our feelings of threat and fear. On the cross, Jesus "dissolves" this idea of sacrificial status.[55] Any sacrificial status is dissolved since Jesus lays down his life of his own accord, only to take it up again.[56] Moore insists that even when the Eucharist is called a sacred meal or "the bread of life,"[57] the self-sacrificing action of Jesus is giving birth to new meaning despite the suffering he would endure. The Eucharist is linked both to the Last Supper as a meal and to Calvary.

EUCHARIST AND THE TRUE SELF

Moore also ponders on what newness comes about in us through the Eucharist. Moore states that the action of Jesus

> nourishes something new in us, the true self evoked by the vindicated non-vindictive, and forgiving victim pressing on the soul of the disciple the risen condition of having died into the life beyond life. Jesus feeds the soul not metaphorically but by bestowing the food that "the eternal in man"—to quote Scheler—needs. This rooting of the eucharistic meal in the emancipation from sacrificial religion is conveyed by the liturgy properly performed and understood, [which] shows its nourishing character from the very start of the ritual.[58]

Just as the action of Jesus stands our sacrificing of others on its head and transforms it into revelatory new humanity, our "participation [in the Eucharist] stands the action of food and drink on its head so that this

---

54. Moore, *Body of Christ*, 12.
55. Moore, *Body of Christ*, 7.
56. Moore, *Body of Christ*, 13.
57. Moore, *Body of Christ*, 12.
58. Moore, *Body of Christ*, 7.

food transforms us into itself."[59] The "something new" being nourished within us is our being taken into the "love-revolution of Jesus."[60]

What does it mean to be drawn into his love revolution? Moore shares his feelings about celebrating the Eucharist: "I am letting myself be dragged kicking and screaming into an act of love that terrifies me."[61] Jesus invites us to take and eat the bread, which is his body for us and to drink the wine, which is his blood for us. Moore paraphrases the action of Jesus in these words: "'I love you as God loves you, to bloodshed. I break myself as bread for you to share and become bread that is broken for each other.'"[62] The words "my body for you" resonate deeply within our being, and we begin to appreciate our most fundamental desire: to be myself for another.[63] It is the desire we are made for, and it is why we remain frustrated until Jesus releases the desire within us.

EUCHARIST AS SACRED MEAL

At the Last Supper, bread is broken and shared, and wine is blessed and shared, and the ritual sharing is a meal. Moore affirms: "Just think again of Jesus at supper for seeing his death as releasing him into his fullness, this fact immediately spontaneously taking the form, to the shock of the fearful disciples, of 'my body for you—eat it! and 'my blood for you, drink it! . . . Jesus passionately ritualizing his own death into Resurrection."[64] Again, Moore states: "People who taught me theology in Rome were so centered on the death in the meal that they forgot it *was* a meal, and thought it was a 're-enactment,' re-presentation and a string of such words of the death. What they missed was that for centuries, Christians referred to the Eucharist as the sacrifice of Christ, not the event of Calvary."[65]

The shift in focus from understanding the Last Supper as a ritual meal to understanding it as a sacrifice or prayer of thanksgiving legitimately emphasizes what is special and unique in the meal. Still, the shift is not meant to create two mutually exclusive meanings in one action.

---

59. Moore, *Body of Christ*, 13.
60. Moore, *Contagion of Jesus*, 53.
61. Moore, *Contagion of Jesus*, 53.
62. Moore, *Contagion of Jesus*, 53.
63. Moore, *Contagion of Jesus*, 54.
64. Moore, "2012–2014 Blog," Nov 8, 2012.
65. Moore, "2012–2014 Blog," May 7, 2012.

A New Awareness

However, as soon as the celebration of the Eucharist is understood along the same lines as the Old Testament symbolism of the priest entering the Holy of Holies, with the people outside as spectators, then the meaning of the Eucharist can become misunderstood. Moore quotes Eamon Duffy:

> [It seems, therefore, that] the Eucharist's basic structure was unequivocally that of a meal, and this was the position adopted by Guardini and most other theorists of liturgical reform from the 1930s onwards. Immediately, however, the dogmatic theologians detected a problem. Was not this precisely the position Luther had adopted in renaming the Mass, the Lord's Supper, and hence was not this the view condemned at Trent? Did not an account of the Mass as, in essence, a meal, reduce or obliterate its sacrificial character?[66]

According to Moore, Cardinal Ratzinger argues that the meaning of the Mass is reduced by calling it a meal. In Ratzinger's mind, the consequence of calling it a meal is a downgrading of its sacrificial character. Moore argues that the ritual meal aspect and the sacrificial nature need not be mutually exclusive: "That which identifies the bread and wine with Jesus's body and blood . . . is the prayer that is celebrating the victory over death, a paean of life beyond life as we know it."[67] For Moore, the way to get from the bread and wine, by way of feeling, to Calvary's extraordinary character and reality, made luminous by Easter, is a source of constant reflection. The thanksgiving prayer of the Mass articulates well what Ratzinger calls the transformation of existence, even of death, into thanksgiving. To bring about transformation, Jesus takes the only universal symbol, the shared meal, to expose that "most human thing to our banality."[68] Our banality occurs when we mistake respectable citizenship with discipleship, assume positions of competence and power in the church rather than becoming Easter people, or discourage people from receiving Holy Communion.

EUCHARIST: THE WAY OF RITUAL MEAL

Moore often mentions and praises the eucharistic theology of P. F. Fitzpatrick, published in his book *In Breaking of Bread*. For this reason, I will

---

66. Duffy, "Benedict XVI," 202.
67. Moore, *Body of Christ*, 8.
68. Moore, *Body of Christ*, 8.

briefly highlight Fitzpatrick's insights on the Eucharist and the way of ritual. Fitzpatrick offers several insights into the Eucharist and what he calls the way of ritual. He states: "[At the Last Supper] the ritual Christ now bequeathed to his disciples he is about to leave, comes from himself in the setting of a ritual familiar to them already—the Passover meal— a commemoration of the ancient preservation and liberation of God's people. It is in this ritual complexity, inherited from a distant past, developed by Christ, and enjoined upon those who follow him, that I see the best way towards an understanding of his Eucharistic presence."[69]

Fitzpatrick turns to Aquinas for insight. For Aquinas, the Eucharist represents and commemorates Christ's saving work. The eucharistic celebration is not another sacrifice; instead, we can call the Eucharist a sacrifice (immolation) because it represents Christ's passion, which was a sacrifice. We can call the Eucharist a sacrifice since we share in the fruits of the Lord's passion through it. The life of the Spirit leads to spiritual nourishment.[70] Fitzpatrick states: "Eucharist represents the saving work of Christ, as a sign of our union with him, as a means of our sharing in what he has done for us, a means that is analogous to bodily nourishment."[71]

Fitzpatrick notes that, for Aquinas, the emphasis of the Eucharist is on spiritual eating. Spiritual eating begins with having faith and love. Having faith is more fundamental than the Eucharist as sacramental eating, which signifies it. Therefore, Aquinas postulates that while the patriarchs did not eat Christ sacramentally, they ate Christ spiritually through faith and love. The primary focus is spiritual eating, spiritual since the Eucharist enables us to share in the saving work of Christ, and eating since the Eucharist involves the transformation of ourselves who are the eaters. Transformation has as its object the release of bondage and eternal life, which will consummate the deliverance that Christ came to bring. The consummation is no less than God, who will be "all in all" as we wait in joyful hope for his coming. Spiritual eating intends and represents its perfection. At present, we have it imperfectly, as signified in the Eucharist. Spiritual eating is the way "in approaching the Eucharistic presence by way of ritual—the spiritual eating which [brings about our union] with Christ by faith and love that is indispensable for salvation,

---

69. Fitzpatrick, *In the Breaking*, 196.
70. Fitzpatrick, *In the Breaking*, 197.
71. Fitzpatrick, *In the Breaking*, 197.

union that has the Eucharist for its sacramental sign in this present life and the life everlasting for its consummation."[72]

Fitzpatrick also indicates that since the sacramental sign and that which it signifies exceeds the range of what can be adequately understood, we can only find the truth of what is celebrated within the ritual through our participation.[73] Simply "looking" at the ritual is not where we will find the truth. Therefore, we would not arrive at its inner meaning by looking at the meal and noting a similarity with the everyday human activity of eating. We find the truth through joining the ritual and our complete and conscious participation. In that ritual, we discover our desire for God, a quest for what is not touched by the destructive forces of time and change. We seek God, and God reveals himself as seeking our friendship, as open and almost vulnerable to our love. Therefore, the difficulty with apprehending the truth of the ritual meal simply by looking is grounded in two aspects. First, it is due to our darkness and negation that hides deep in the human condition and that causes us to turn away from the truth. Second, it pertains to being confronted with an excess of light so that we are embarrassed by the dimension of love and its calling.[74]

We understand the ritual meal under two dynamics: eating food and enacting a sacred ritual. First, the food consumption of this sacred meal displays the incomplete nature of our lives, which always needs regular replenishment. It shows our dependence on the earth, and upon what the earth provides while at the same time bearing witness to the skills and force which we bring to bear upon the earth, what it supports, and the effort we consume to prepare the food. The obtaining and preparation of food calls for assigning roles in the community so that we might eat the food. The meal is "a communal acknowledgment of our needs, our abilities, our dependency upon each other, our mutual trust."[75] Given all these factors, it is only fitting that Jesus should have linked the ritual meal to our quest for God and our awareness of God. We share something pleasant during the meal, expressing our needs and achievements. The meal becomes an occasion where our sharing meets our need for nourishment, surpassing the reach of our skills alone, and opens us to discovering friendship. The meal becomes an occasion where those who

72. Fitzpatrick, *In the Breaking*, 198–99.
73. Fitzpatrick, *In the Breaking*, 199.
74. Fitzpatrick, *In the Breaking*, 200.
75. Fitzpatrick, *In the Breaking*, 201.

eat are united to something greater than any life they can attain on their own.

Second, as a sacred ritual, Christ takes the rite he and his friends inherited and goes beyond it in a way that only Christ can. The old Passover, a meal and ritual by which people remember, share, and embody the liberating power of God, is now transformed in the Last Supper since "the new age of the deeper rescue is inaugurated by sharing in something greater."[76] Jesus and his disciples now come to Last Supper meal after their many meals together throughout his public ministry. Fitzpatrick states: "Just as the Passover ritual both embodies and transcends their ordinary meals so did this last Passover . . . [the ritual] they shared with Christ both embodied and transcended the Passover meals which they like their ancestors has shared over the years."[77] The symbolic elements of the lamb, the unleavened bread, the cups of wine, and the blood put on the door posts or sprinkled over the people in the Sinai covenant are all used or surpassed in what Jesus institutes at the Last Supper. Taken up by Christ, the ritual language of the Passover already transcends the day-to-day meaning of a meal. Christ proclaims his death for our salvation. He gives the Passover bread to his disciples and asks them to eat it and tells them that he is himself, in the bread, the Lamb of the new Passover given up for them. He gives the cup to them as the Passover ritual prescribed. They are to share it, for it is his blood shed for them, sealing the new covenant, more significant than the covenant of Sinai.

Only by participating in the way of ritual might we be led towards what lies beyond this ritual. The ritual uses and respects the place of ritual in human life. It does not commit the fallacy of replacement nor deny the fundamental nature of ritual by talking in terms of appearances or denying the meaning of the words used. The way of ritual does not eliminate the mystery; on the contrary, it acknowledges the mystery by its very inadequacy.[78] Therefore, the Eucharist cannot be reduced to some technique by which substances and accidents are manipulated. The way of ritual neither reduces the Eucharist to human terms nor makes it into a divinely induced rearranging of human distinctions that have become distractions. The way of ritual allows us to take on board our primary concern, the saving work of Christ and how his presence exceeds anything explicable in terms of memory, fellowship, or devotion.

76. Fitzpatrick, *In the Breaking*, 202.
77. Fitzpatrick, *In the Breaking*, 203.
78. Fitzpatrick, *In the Breaking*, 204.

What words we use will have resonances that go beyond our powers of verbal expression, but we must not deny their minimal meaning. The eucharistic presence must be dealt with in terms of signs that the way of ritual allows for.[79]

Thus, Christ's presence in the Eucharist is "a ritually [achieved] sign of his presence among those with whom he already shares his risen life in the hope of joy."[80] As we enter into the way of ritual, we find it invites us to embark on a journey toward the rite instituted by Christ. A journey of that sort cannot consist in denying the meaning of the words describing its course, any more than a poem can exercise force by refusing the words that comprise it. We must let each stage of the ritual keep its significance and take seriously the complex associations of the eucharistic rite. We must accept it as a rite of eating and drinking. This is a rite made by Christ into an eating and drinking of his body and blood. Thus, ritual gives us a way into "[Christ's] saving presence in us a sign where he acts in and through us . . . . In the ritual meal . . . built upon inherited rites, he unites himself to us in a way that cannot be reduced to friendship to memory or to any activity or convention of ours."[81]

The way of ritual stands in contrast to a disguised approach. It reveals the mystery of God's love in Christ. It is a progressive revelation of Christ and not a disguise. It obligates us to take ritual on its terms, that is, a sacred way distinct from ordinary time and yet not divorced from those activities. It invites us to accept that ritual is first touched by what we make of the world, then second, goes beyond the world through what Christ does, and third, touches the way the world is to be dealt with by us. The way of ritual tries to exhibit the Eucharist as a sign of God's love for us in our great need and darkness.[82]

THE WORDS OF JESUS AND TRANSUBSTANTIATION

Moore contrasts two perspectives that might inhabit our horizon of understanding the Eucharist that bring us to two different goals. Moore's concern is in communicating a sense of the Eucharist that helps us appreciate what Jesus is doing for us. Broadly, Moore's two approaches are:

79. Fitzpatrick, *In the Breaking*, 204.
80. Fitzpatrick, *In the Breaking*, 205.
81. Fitzpatrick, *In the Breaking*, 206.
82. Fitzpatrick, *In the Breaking*, 207.

Jesus becomes bread and bread becomes Jesus. When we approach the Eucharist via "Jesus becomes bread," then, according to Joachim Jeremias, Jesus is saying: "This piece of bread, is what I, crucified, am, for you to share."[83] Moore endorses Jeremias' interpretation. However, we have misunderstood the words of Jesus, especially when priests began to emphasize the word "is" over the four words "This is my body." The emphasis is the aftermath of religious controversies with other Christian churches and their understanding of the Eucharist. The emphasis changes the ritual role of the words. If we can recapture the complete sense of the words of Jesus, "This is my body," we will be better able to appreciate the self-identification of Jesus with bread and wine and the sacred ritual meal aspect of the Eucharist.

Conversely, the other direction is to say that "bread becomes Jesus." For Moore, transubstantiation is the answer to the question, How is it possible that bread becomes Jesus? Transubstantiation is the teaching of the church that the substance of bread and wine offered at the Eucharist is changed into the body and blood of Jesus Christ. The efficacy of the words of Christ and the action of the Holy Spirit brings about change. However, the "eucharistic species" remain unaltered (CCC 283). The term itself was first used in the thirteenth century at Lateran IV (1215). Under the influence of Aristotelian thought, theologians distinguished between the Eucharist's substance (the body and blood of Christ) and the accidents of bread and wine (accidents such as weight, color, texture, etc.). As the theory goes, accidents remain, even as the bread and wine are changed into the body and blood of Christ. The doctrine was reaffirmed at the Council of Trent (1551), but the term was never intended to explain how the change takes place, but rather, to provide a term that describes what takes place.

The Second Vatican Council linked the Eucharist to the church's teaching on the Real Presence of Christ within the church. As Christ is present in the church in many and various ways, the Eucharist surpasses all others. Pope Paul VI, in *Mysterium Fidei*, affirms that Christ's presence in the Eucharist is substantial and, through the Eucharist, Christ becomes present whole and entire, God and man (n. 39). The Real Presence of Christ in the Eucharist flows from his total self-gift on the cross and his will to make the gift effective for all people throughout history.

---

83. Moore, *Contagion of Jesus*, 52.

Moore has no problem with the term *transubstantiation*. He is doubtful as to its power to illuminate and draw us into the mystery. The word itself comes from an age when a metaphysical framing of doctrines was taken for granted. Moreover, this framing does not speak to our contemporary culture, and if theology mediates between a cultural matrix and the meaning and significance of religion within that context, then we must search for a framework that speaks to the people of contemporary culture. Otherwise, staying with the word *transubstantiation* will not do justice to the Eucharist as an event that takes place within the world of meaning that we inhabit.

EUCHARIST AND SEX

The Eucharist also speaks to our sexuality. The words of Jesus, "This is my body for you," reflect an understanding of sexual love that stands in opposition to "This is your body for me."[84] For there to be good sex, our physical body and the sexual love that comes from it needs to move towards an intentionality of "love, of sacrifice, of self-gift."[85] Love is at the heart of sex and the words of Jesus describe the true intentionality of the body. Lastly, the words of Jesus indicate our being drawn into his way of desire and the bliss of the Father.[86] Jesus' desire for the Father compels him to celebrate with friends his coming release from death. Eucharist is "the full explication of the desire whereby we are constituted as human. It creates the meal out of its exuberance in Jesus."[87] We are invited to be caught up in his desire for the universe.

MOORE, LITURGICAL REFORM, AND EUCHARIST

For many centuries in the life of the church, people refrained from receiving the Eucharist, and so, while the transformation occurred according to the words of Jesus, the "take and eat" did not occur. It was Pius X who had to recall the church faithful to more frequent Holy Communion. Moore reminds us of Aquinas's words that the sacrament is meant to be taken and eaten. Since the Second Vatican Council, the church has

---

84. Moore, *Contagion of Jesus*, 54; "My Body for You," 211.
85. Moore, *Contagion of Jesus*, 54.
86. Moore, "2012–2014 Blog," Dec 21, 2012.
87. Moore, "2012–2014 Blog," Jan 21, 2013.

initiated a massive reform of the eucharistic celebration. The Eucharist is both the transformation of bread and wine at the Last Supper into the body and blood of Jesus as well as being linked to the victim slain for sinners and on account of sin. Moore states:

> So liturgical reform if it is deemed necessary, is not done by choosing a "good" period in the past and taking this as a model. Nor, however, can it be done without a model, a basic idea of how Jesus' action at the Last Supper is to be done today.... Liturgical reform has to be based on a model that is none other than the ritual meal and acted and spoken by Jesus, and past forms of the Mass used as models insofar as they are faithful to his ritual as a meal whose content is his crucified body and his blood shared.[88]

For this reason, the Tridentine Mass does not make clear the essential and ritual meal character of the Last Supper, but obscures it and so must be deemed deficient. The only real model is the model of Jesus' special ritual meal.

Inasmuch as humanity breaks Jesus on the cross, by means of humanity's instrument of world order, Jesus expresses his love by breaking bread at a love feast with friends.[89] Therefore, Moore's approach is to speak of the Eucharist as Jesus' "self-identification" with bread and wine. In other words, for Moore, Jesus becomes bread through self-identification. It is also a form of identification that sides with the victims of history, and thus, demonstrates a new and frightening kind of love. Jesus' love is frightening to us because of our desire to cling to life, and, in our effort to live, we wed ourselves to systems that preserve life by violence and thus have victims.[90] When we eat the bread and drink the cup, we are joined to a love that tries to undermine the system we live by, and our eating and drinking empowers us to be open to a completely new way of living. It is an act of love that is "unique, revelatory, and world-changing."[91] Jesus undermines by love any system that we, knowingly or unknowingly, are a part of that creates victims. It is the same system that sacrifices people to appease, supposedly, an angry God.

In the next chapter, I will explore Moore's understanding of the doctrine of the Trinity.

---

88. Moore, *Contagion of Jesus*, 56.
89. Moore, *Contagion of Jesus*, 51.
90. Moore, *Contagion of Jesus*, 50.
91. Moore, *Contagion of Jesus*, 50.

11

Moore and the Trinity

INTRODUCTION

In his writings, Moore gave a great deal of time for theological reflection on a key doctrine of the Christian faith: the doctrine of the Blessed Trinity. In this chapter, I aim to compare the theological reflections made by Moore about the Trinity with a traditional theology of the Trinity. In chapter 8, I said that it would be difficult to assess Moore's redemption theology without first giving a brief account of Lonergan's theology of redemption. Moore's contribution to redemption theology was never meant to be comprehensive. I feel the same way when speaking to Moore's theological contribution to an understanding of the Trinity. To better understand Moore's insights concerning the Trinity, what is first required is a brief but important overview of a traditional theology of the Trinity. I will present a traditional theology of Trinity through the insights of Anthony Kelly and Neil Ormerod, since both have written extensively and comprehensively on the Trinity.

TRINITY AND ART

The mystery of the Trinity has been an object of intense speculation and doctrinal definition over many centuries. However, it must be said that clergy preaching at Sunday Mass, especially on Trinity Sunday, rarely are able to penetrate the mental block caused by the term *Trinity*. For many people, the problem is connecting the theology of the Trinity to their everyday lives and concerns of faith. It is also the problem of wanting to imagine a reality of faith that cannot be imagined but only understood.

Notwithstanding such an exigency, a good place to start is with art, which relies on imagination and the immediate emotional impact of the image on the observer. The artist Rublev produced a now famous icon, *Philoxenia*. *Philoxenia* is an icon depicting the three angels who visit Abraham and Sarah as recorded in the book of Genesis. Abraham offers them hospitality. Abraham and Sarah have long given up the hope of having children and grow anxious as to how God's promise of making their descendants as many as the stars of heaven will come about. Anthony Kelly states that the icon suggests that "the divine communion is an open circle enfolding the believer and creation into itself; it invites the beholder to come from the outside and into the realm of ultimate love."[1] Michael Paul Gallagher suggests that the God atheists reject is the one named by Moore as a Christian Zeus. It is not the God who is three persons relating to each other in love. In the icon, the three angelic figures are sitting around a table, pointing towards a chalice, symbolizing the Trinitarian life connected to the cross of Christ. Gallagher suggests they are "inviting us to join them and enjoy their communal life of creating and healing."[2]

IMMANENT AND ECONOMIC LIFE OF THE TRINITY

Theological discourse about the Trinity implies two trajectories: the intra-Trinitarian life (ad intra or immanent Trinity or the Trinity in itself) and the extra-Trinitarian life (ad extra or economic Trinity or the Trinity for us and our salvation). In the former, we are seeking to talk about God in Godself. In the latter, we are seeking to understand the missions of the Father through our appreciation for the Word and the Spirit in the world and creation. Whichever is our focus the aim of a theology of the Trinity is that, through faith, we may participate in the life of God, whose love is sustaining and transforming the world. Therefore, it must be clearly stated that faith does not have as its aim a problem to be solved, in the case of the doctrine of the Trinity, the problem of the three in one. The starting point is an act of awe and wonder before the greatness of God and the presence of the Spirit-filled risen Lord, who "animates, unsettles,

---

1. Kelly, *Trinity of Love*, 2.
2. Gallagher, "Reflection," 1.

heals and expands everything we routinely call 'real-life'" so that we may be accepted into communion with God.³

TRINITY AND THE CHURCH

All Christian theology begins with the community of the church. The church is not simply a social institution. It is a community initiated by the call of the Father. Its meaning derives from the Christ crucified and risen. The Holy Spirit animates its structures. The Trinity as a communal life of self-giving love is the energy, form, and motive of the life of the church; the energy is that which empowers the church to move outward and forward; the form is the Incarnate and crucified Christ; the motive is the goal of final communion of the Church when God will be everything to everyone (1 Cor 15:58).⁴ Through inhaling the Spirit or "Holy Breath," the church is drawn to the mysterious origin from which the Spirit comes so we may be centered in Christ, in whom all things hold together (1 Cor 1:17).⁵ Yet, inasmuch as the Trinity exercises a centripetal force on the believer, it also exercises a centrifugal force, sending both the Word and the Spirit in mission so that believers may bring the compassion and communion of the Father, Son, and Holy Spirit to all history and culture, and thus address the problem of evil in the world.

TRINITY AND CRITICAL CATEGORIES

Theology must be ever aware of an uncritical acceptance of extra-theological conceptions for speaking about God lest distortions occur to our understanding of the faith. To simply accept prevailing cultural notions, and assume a position of being "not critically aware of the pre-theological preconceptions in the culture in which it works," we may, at best, become mistaken about the truths of the faith, or at worst, legitimate the reigning ideology of our time.⁶ For example, when the modern notion of "person" is applied to the Trinity, Kelly cautions that "the divine mystery can appear as a committee of consent rather than the one God in three

---

3. Kelly, *Trinity of Love*, 2.
4. Kelly, *Trinity of Love*, 4.
5. Kelly, *Trinity of Love*, 4.
6. Kelly, *Trinity of Love*, 15.

persons."[7] Likewise, when the intra-Trinitarian life as relational becomes the template for social relations in the world, we may end up turning something we need to speak sparingly of into a social Trinitarianism that does not respect the otherness of God and the limits to understanding the inner life of God. In our desire to present a theology of the Trinity, it must be kept in mind that we are not beginning with some abstract idea of God. We are beginning with our experience of Christ risen and the Spirit, God's divine self-communication in human history for our healing and the promotion of our self-transcendence through the gifts of faith, hope, and love. Our intelligence must be critically attuned so that confusion about what we believe does not reign.

TRINITY AND THE FUNCTIONS OF MEANING

Following on from Lonergan, Kelly affirms that our theological meaning-making around the doctrine of the Trinity fulfills four functions: cognitive, constitutive, communicative, and effective.[8] These functions were outlined in chapter 1. Cognitive meaning places the focus on an accurate conception and away from a false and inadequate conception of the Trinity. Constitutive meaning emphasizes how the Trinity changes our identity through our adherence to the faith. Communicative meaning focuses on the kind of community of mission we become through our appreciation for the Trinity. Effective meaning focuses on the ways we set about to change the world through our faith in the Trinity.

TRINITY, ANALOGY, AND METAPHOR

Theology aims to deliberate truth from its most inspiring vision and energize our commitments to love and justice for people and the world. Whenever we do theology, we must be attentive to the fact that we are seeking to speak about infinite realities with a finite mind. Therefore, inasmuch as we can theologize, our employment of an analogical imagination is essential. However, analogy must also combine with a desire to interrelate all the mysteries of our faith with each other by establishing an interconnection into "one Mystery of love."[9] Analogy and the intercon-

---

7. Kelly, *Trinity of Love*, 15.
8. Kelly, *Trinity of Love*, 19.
9. Kelly, *Trinity of Love*, 20–21.

nections of the mysteries of faith serve the task of healing, liberating, and transforming the world. These analogies become the basis for a praxis congruent with analogical thinking. Analogy seeks to render a clear, more speculative and precise understanding of our faith. However, it must also be stated that people are inspired more by metaphor and symbol than by the precision of analogy. Metaphor opens the imagination, and since it is the case that in religious matters, love precedes knowledge, metaphors have a vital role to play for the preacher.

TRINITY AND BIBLICAL CATEGORIES

When speaking about the Trinity, Christian theology must begin with the biblical account. However, beginning with the New Testament, we notice that the Scriptures present both an "iconic" and "schematic" approach, in contrast to what much later became a systematic approach in the doctrines of the faith. Iconic rhetoric focuses on an image of the Divine and its relationship to our salvation as something that can inspire and move us to love. A schematic approach to rhetoric takes a more systematic way without being fully aware of the problematic nature of what is being presented.[10] For example, when it comes to speaking about the Trinity, the Johannine account of Jesus' Last Supper discourse is more schematic than Paul's Trinitarian greeting at the beginning or end of some of his letters. In John 17 and following, the Trinity is presented as a unity of Father, Son, and Spirit in a communion of life through interrelated divine "personalities."[11]

Further to this, Moore, as I indicated in chapter 7, gives a Trinitarian experience of the disciples whose desire is awakened, made desolate, and then transformed through their encounter with the earthly, crucified, and risen Lord. What becomes clear from our reading of the New Testament is that the texts serve a kerygmatic and doxological purpose.[12] The language of the New Testament also reflects an apologetic period in the life of the church who are trying to understand in faith something completely new to them and impart that understanding to the society around them. The biblical writers exercise a great deal of creative effort to word their

---

10. Kelly, *Trinity of Love*, 37.
11. Kelly, *Trinity of Love*, 39.
12. Kelly, *Trinity of Love*, 59.

experience of Christ since they are engaged with articulating a new revelation about someone they believed in and in whose being they existed.

Behind both the rhetoric of the iconic and the schematic stands another rhetoric altogether, namely, God's story unfolding in human history. In terms of the Trinity, it is the story of the Father, Son, and Spirit as three dramatic personae taking to themselves, by a divine initiative, the people of God in a story that includes faithfulness, failure, and redemption. For John, God's story starts with the Father, who reveals himself in the divine Word through the power of the Spirit and who brings about a union of Jesus risen with the disciples.[13] There is tremendous joy experienced through participating in Jesus' story, and it is the joy "of being included in the original story of the oneness existing between the Father and the Son. It results from the praxis of koinonia as it narrates the meaning of the divine communion in a way that includes all who will come to believe throughout the whole of human history."[14] In the New Testament, the iconic and schematic use of symbols is designed to evoke a passionate response to a distinctive God.

TRINITY AND DOCTRINAL PRECISION

In the period beyond the New Testament, a new mode of rhetoric that is less symbolic becomes important. It is the doctrinal mode of rhetoric. The doctrinal mode is grounded in a more theoretical differentiation of meaning, with more abstraction, so as to attain a clearer and more critical appreciation of the biblical symbols. The doctrinal mode requires a more disciplined intellectual stance so as to overcome confusion within the community about what the church believes. It undertakes this stance by exercising a greater precision of words and a philosophical control of meaning. In chapter 1, I spoke about the theoretic realm of meaning whose aim is a greater control of the meaning of terms and their relation to each other. Immediately, we see a breakaway from an evocative symbolic world with its kerygmatic and doxological emphases. In the doctrinal mode, the mantra is almost "do it with precision or let confusion grow."[15]

Not surprisingly, there are different emphases even as a more doctrinal mode takes hold. Saint Irenaeus decides to focus his attention on the

---

13. Kelly, *Trinity of Love*, 40–41.
14. Kelly, *Trinity of Love*, 44.
15. Kelly, *Trinity of Love*, 69.

revelation of the Trinity in the world for us and our salvation, and not on the intra-Trinitarian life. He argues that "only God could reveal the manner in which the Word Son originated within the Divine Mystery. It was not given to the human mind to have such knowledge."[16] Working within an understanding of the "Monarchia" of the one God, the question arises: Were the "three" simply all modes of successive manifestations of the one?[17] An appeal to the Scriptures did not help since texts could be cited to justify conflicting positions. Variously, Tertullian, Origen, and Arius gave diverse answers to questions asked about the relationship between the three in the Trinity and their relationship to their one Divine nature.

TRINITY AND THE EARLY COUNCILS

It was the bishop of Constantinople, Athanasius, holding up against the Arian suggestion that, since the Father generates the Son, then the Son could not be God as the Father is and, therefore, must be less than God the Father, that brought an even greater precision to the doctrine of the Trinity. Eventually, in the Councils of Nicaea (325), Constantinople (381), and Chalcedon (451), answers were given, but not in the sophisticated concepts of philosophical systems. The affirmations of the council fathers were a judgment on the divine reality as the Christian faith had come to know it. Judgments are affirmations of truth to toward which greater philosophical precision might apply.

Kelly cites John Courtney Murray, who states that what motivated the fathers was

> this conviction of the realism of the Word of God—that it is a real word with the real meaning . . . [and realism] sustained Athanasius in working out the celebrated formula which explained the sense inherent in the dogma stated by the Council of Nicaea. His study of the Scripture disclosed to him, as to Basil later, a general proposition. All the affirmations made by the scriptures about . . . [God the] Father are also made about the Son, with one exception, the Son is not the Father. In particular, the scriptures affirm about the Son what they affirm about the Father that he has as his own, the two powers that are uniquely divine and proper only to God, the power to give life and the power to judge the heart of man. If, then, everything that is true

---

16. Kelly, *Trinity of Love*, 68.
17. Kelly, *Trinity of Love*, 69.

about the Father is likewise true about the Son, except that the Son is not the Father, it follows that the Son *is* all that the Father *is* except for the name of the Father.[18]

TRINITY AND THE NICENE CREED

I now come to the proclamation of the Nicene Creed. These are the affirmations defined at the Council of Nicaea concerning the Father, Son, and Holy Spirit that grounded the formulation and subsequent developments of belief. The unity of the Godhead is implicit. Symbols and metaphors such as "begetting" and "light from light" are still employed. But a greater doctrinal precision is reached. It begins with God the Father and not the one Divine being. God the Son is not created but begotten. The generation of the Son by the Father is not some contingent act of the will. The Son is "God from God" and "true God from true God." There are a number of technical words also used, including the word *homoousios*, meaning "consubstantial," "of one substance," or "of one being," so that God the Son is consubstantial with God the Father.

The Father begets God the Son eternally, and so, the Son is not made or created by the Father. The term *begotten* comes from John 1:14 and so is faithful to the biblical account. Ormerod states that the term expresses a relationship, one with its origin in the Father and its endpoint in the Son, but the Father is not the Creator of the Son. It is akin to a father-to-son relationship but also very unlike a son-to-father relationship since it is "eternal."[19] The ancient world is working with a mistaken biology that understood the Father as the sole source of any new child.

Further, the Creed speaks about God from God and Light from Light. Later, theology would use the word "procession."[20] The Son proceeds from God the Father, and the Son is "one being with the Father," that is, *homoousios* or consubstantial or "of one substance." The phrase "of one substance" has nothing to do with material connotations of substances. According to Ormerod, it denotes more the sense used in a court of law when a lawyer states: "The substance of the matter at hand is this."[21] Understanding the meaning of substance in this way, the lawyer is

---

18. Kelly, *Trinity of Love*, 78.
19. Ormerod, *Trinitarian Primer*, 41.
20. Ormerod, *Trinitarian Primer*, 42.
21. Ormerod, *Trinitarian Primer*, 42–43.

pointing to the intrinsic intelligence and reasonableness in his argument. The Nicene Creed does not mention the words *person* or *hypostasis* and *prosopa*. When, at a later stage, the word *person* is adopted, it designates more of a distinction but without definition. "Person" applied to the Trinity is not equivalent to our modern-day meaning of personhood.[22] It should be noted that while the Creed starts with the pre-existent Christ and moves to Christ coming into the world for our salvation, our experience is the other way around.

Later, God the Holy Spirit is affirmed. It was the Cappadocian fathers who helped secure the status of God the Holy Spirit, and the Spirit's mode of origin within the Divine Mystery. The Holy Spirit is called "the Lord and giver of life, who proceeds from the Father and the Son equally with the Father and the Son he is adored and glorified." Again, the divinity of the Holy Spirit is affirmed. The Spirit proceeds from the Father and the Son and is of one substance with them both.

Ormerod states that the trouble with all these distinctions is that we do not have a clear image of the Trinity to hang onto when, often, as humans, we rely on images to understand.[23] He states: "The only guidance we have is to hang on to what is true, not what we may imagine. In that sense, the teaching of Nicaea requires us to ask about what our criteria for reality are. Do we find it in suitable images or in correct understanding?"[24]

TRINITY: PROCESSIONS AND RELATIONS

We end up with an understanding of the Trinity, which serves to differentiate the three Divine Persons who are all equally sharing in one divine nature. There is a real distinction between Father, Son, and Holy Spirit yet they all equally share the one divine nature. To formulate this unity-in-distinction, we can say: What is said of one person is said of the other persons except that the Father is the Father and not the Son or the Spirit, the Son is the Son and not the Father or the Spirit, and the Spirit is the Spirit and not the Father or the Son. They are not in different places since God is not contained by location. They are not located at different times because God is eternal. Different quantities do not characterize

---

22. Ormerod, *Trinitarian Primer*, 44.
23. Ormerod, *Trinitarian Primer*, 50.
24. Ormerod, *Trinitarian Primer*, 51.

them since they are equally divine. Equally, they share power, greatness, wisdom, eternity, and divinity.

The two processions are the Father begetting the Son and the Spirit proceeding from the Father and the Son. The Father and the Son breathe forth the Spirit. Their personal identity is their mutual relationship. Further, while the Father is the Father of the Son and the Son is the Son of the Father, the Spirit is not the Spirit of the Father in the same way as the Father generates the Son. The Father does not beget the Spirit.

The two processions give rise to four relations. The Father generates the Son, and the Son proceeds from the Father. There is a relation of paternity from Father to Son. But the Son is the Son of the Father, so there is a relation of filiation from the Son to the Father. Thus, so far, we have two relations. Then, there is a third relation. The Father and the Son as one co-principle spirate the Holy Spirit, and the Holy Spirit receives (active) spiration from the Father and the Son. Then, there is a fourth relation. There is a relation of passive spiration from the Holy Spirit to the Father and the Son. These relations are logically related. There is no filiation without paternity and no paternity without filiation; there is no active spiration without the reception of spiration, and there is no passive spiration without an active spiration.

The final formulation includes two processions, three persons, four relations (Father to Son, Son to Father, Father and Son to Spirit, and Spirit to Father and Son), two missions (the mission of the Son and the Spirit), and one God, with one divine nature. In terms of the first procession, there is a difference between the relationship of the Father to the Son and the Father to the Spirit. Ormerod asserts that the relationship between the Father and the Son is mutually defining of their identity.[25] What can be said of the Father can also be said of the Son, and what can be said of the Son can also be said of the Father, except the Father is not the Son, and the Son is not the Father. If the Father's person is defined in relationship to the Son, it cannot be defined in its relation to the Spirit. According to Ormerod, Augustine did not want the identity of the Spirit to collapse into the identity of the Son. So, Augustine proposed that the Holy Spirit proceeds from the Father and the Son.[26]

---

25. Ormerod, *Trinitarian Primer*, 55.
26. Ormerod, *Trinitarian Primer*, 54.

A New Awareness

TRINITY, TWO MISSIONS, AND CREATED PARTICIPATIONS

Through an account of the relations between the persons, we can now provide an understanding of how God relates to his creation. We start with the two missions. The missions are God's interaction with the created world. The Son is the one who the Father sends into the world. To be the Spirit is to be the one whom the Father and the Son send into the world. In the divine missions of Jesus and the Holy Spirit, God is revealed in the world. The Father sends the Son to reveal the Father, and the Father and Son send the Spirit to help us to live out our participation in the divine life.

The missions are the processions within the Trinity but with a created term. What makes a procession mission-oriented is the addition of a created term in the world. I can't venture into a full treatment of the missions as created participation of the two processions and the four relations (paternity, filiation, active spiration, and passive spiration). But briefly, the working hypothesis for the four created terms is the Incarnation, sanctifying grace, the habit of charity, and the light of glory.[27] While the tradition from Aquinas affirms the created terms of Incarnation and sanctifying grace, Bernard Lonergan, in his Trinitarian theology, adds the created terms of the habit of charity and the light of glory.[28]

The created terms are both contingent and created. For example, the Incarnation of the Son is the procession of the Son from the Father in the relation of paternity with the created term of the Incarnation. The Father did not have to send the Son to assume human nature. The Father creates the contingent conditions necessary for the truth to be present in the world and in the Incarnation, and the contingent condition is a human nature for the Son to assume. The indwelling of the Holy Spirit in the hearts of the believer is the procession of the Holy Spirit from the Father and the Son by active spiration with the created term of sanctifying grace through which the believer is made pleasing to God. The habit of charity is the reception of the Father and the Son by the Spirit by passive spiration with the created term of acts of love in the believer and a habitual change to the believer's being. The light of glory is the filiation from the Son to the Father with the created term of the light of glory by which the Son sees the Father in the beatific vision. Ormerod states that all these

---

27. Blackwood, "Lonergan's Trinitarian Theology," 11–15.
28. Ormerod, "(Non-Communio) Trinitarian," 460.

created terms are present in the human being Jesus of Nazareth.[29] Blackwood asserts: "If the secondary act of the Incarnation, sanctifying grace, the habit of charity and the light of glory make it true to say that there are relations between us and the Trinitarian persons . . . then, those four created supernatural realities make it true to say that our interpersonal relations include the Trinitarian persons."[30]

TRINITY AND THE PSYCHOLOGICAL ANALOGY

To better appreciate the insights being proposed by Moore toward formulating a theology of the Trinity, I must mention one final aspect. The two great figures of Augustine and Aquinas spoke eloquently about the Trinity. As mentioned earlier, theology uses analogies. It is our faith trying to respond to the demands of understanding. Analogy helps us to formulate a theological hypothesis or theory. It does not aim to provide us with greater certainty but with a greater understanding of our faith.[31]

One of the earliest uses of analogy for understanding the Trinity is what has come to be known as the "psychological analogy," first formulated by Augustine, occurring in his major work *On the Trinity*.[32] Augustine begins with the faith affirmation that humankind is made in the image and likeness of God. He proposes that we can turn to the spiritual dimension of being human to find a better analogy of the Trinity. Aquinas would refine this analogy centuries later. To appreciate the analogy, we must first know a little about the process of knowing and we must understand our understanding.[33] In chapter 1 on Moore and Lonergan, I indicated that understanding the process of knowing does not easily come to people. Ormerod states that it is not easy to grasp how we understand, deliberate and take action over some matter or, as Ormerod puts it, "coming to give a definition of something; coming to express approval or disapproval or what we call forming a judgment of value coming to a decision for either sending or doing good."[34] We talk about a new concept arising within consciousness through an insight gained for the first time.

29. Ormerod, "'For in Him,'" 813.
30. Blackwood, "Lonergan's Trinitarian Theology," 17.
31. Ormerod, *Trinitarian Primer*, 62.
32. Ormerod, *Trinitarian Primer*, 69.
33. Ormerod, *Trinitarian Primer*, 70.
34. Ormerod, *Trinitarian Primer*, 70.

A New Awareness

Augustine calls this an "inner word," that is, not the word finally spoken in language but the endpoint of a process from data to questions to understanding to formulating a concept.

Augustine also talks about "knowledge with love." Prior to making a judgment of truth and value, we set about to weigh the evidence against our insight to affirm what is the case and explore what is worthwhile so as to take a course of action.[35] After much deliberation, there comes a moment when all our efforts require a judgment of value, call it "a point of finality, of closure and [this process] moves to an inner judgment."[36] There is a "yes." Augustine uses this as an analogy for understanding the generation or procession of the Son from the Father as knowledge with love. God's inner "yes" is Jesus, who is "the judgment of value which affirms the divine goodness and everything that divine goodness does."[37]

Now, when we come to an inner judgment of value and are ready to say yes to something that we have judged to be good, it releases a proper love for that object which we have judged to be good. The first moment of the process is our judgment of its goodness. The second moment is a sigh of inner contentment or "yes" that it is good. This moment in the human mind is Augustine's analogy for the procession of the Spirit. Thus, the procession of the Spirit is not so much like speaking outwardly the spoken Word, but expressing outwardly "the inner sigh of divine contentment that is released by the Word as a judgment of value."[38]

Augustine is well aware of the axiom: nothing is loved unless it is first known. In the axiom, Augustine is expressing the mutual involvement of the mind and the will in our actions. He is not saying that often, we love without first knowing the object we are loving and, therefore, we should stop until we do know the object well enough. Rather, he is saying that "nothing is responsibly loved unless it is first known." Responsible love commits to someone because he or she knows that person and so knows the needed depth of their commitment so as to love them well.[39] The procession of the Spirit is, by analogy, a responsible, mature, well-grounded love and a love grounded in the truth. The Spirit is not

---

35. Ormerod, *Trinitarian Primer*, 71.
36. Ormerod, *Trinitarian Primer*, 71–72.
37. Ormerod, *Trinitarian Primer*, 72–73.
38. Ormerod, *Trinitarian Primer*, 73.
39. Ormerod, *Trinitarian Primer*, 78.

only God's love given to us but also the inner responsible and divine love released by the "inner word" of judgment spoken by the Father.[40]

In the final analysis, we must never forget that we are dealing with an analogy. Our human knowing is limited. God's knowledge is perfect, and the expression of that knowledge in the divine Word is perfect, such that God's Word is no less than God.[41] There is no temporal sequence of God. Therefore, while our understanding, formulation of a concept or inner word, and our love in what we judge to be of value happens within time, for the Trinity, there is no time. We must always keep in mind that the processions of the Son and the Spirit are simultaneous. What analogy does is give a reasonable account of the understanding subject (the Father), the Word spoken by the subject (the Son), and the Spirit sighed through the Word by the same subject (procession from the Father and the Son). Ormerod concludes that divine love is rich in intelligence, and divine intelligence is full of love.[42]

MOORE AND THE TRINITY

By means of this brief introduction to the theology of the Trinity, I am better able to unpack the insights that Moore brings to the task of theologizing on the doctrine. Again, I admit that my contribution is very modest.

First, in a very early essay published in the 1947–48 edition of *The Downside Review*, Moore pleads for a return to a biblical theology of the Trinity, a priority for the "event-dialogue" of the biblical text over the theological hypothesis on the inner life of the Trinity.[43] The article uses the language of the "Holy Ghost" as well as the Spirit (*geist* is originally Germanic, meaning "Spirit") to symbolize the Third Person of the Trinity.[44] Moore appeals to scholars to move away from speaking about the intra-Trinitarian life through the use of such terms as person, processions, substance, and relations and urges them to move toward exploring the Scriptures themselves. He is not saying that the terms are mistaken. He has in mind the faithful and their appropriation of the Trinity for their

---

40. Ormerod, *Trinitarian Primer*, 74–74.
41. Ormerod, *Trinitarian Primer*, 75.
42. Ormerod, *Trinitarian Primer*, 80.
43. Moore, "Blessed Trinity," 21.
44. Moore, "Blessed Trinity," 17.

journey of faith. In his mind, if the doctrines of our faith and the manner they are communicated do not inspire us to greater sanctity, then we are neglecting an important dimension of their existence. We are neglecting the importance of communicative meaning. I would imagine that he is thinking about the ordinary believer in the pew or the monk newly arrived at the monastery, who, without theological sophistication, is trying to make sense of the Trinity practically for their lives and trying not to succumb to those blank looks spoken about earlier.

Moore suggests that the biblical texts could be fruitful for understanding "the distinctiveness of the Persons" from the perspective of the economic Trinity. He is echoing a precise and wise approach to the inner life of the Trinity, namely, that what we say about the intra-Trinitarian life must first find resonance within the Scripture. For Moore, the place to start our exploration is in the Gospel of John and especially the Last Supper discourse. It is Christ at the Last Supper who is offering us an invitation to conversion and an invitation into a participation with the Trinitarian life and, through participation, an "insider" understanding of the doctrine of the Trinity.[45] Moore suggests that we are to interpret "Christ's words introducing the Persons in the supper-room, as the spontaneous expression, we might almost say the overflow, of his own essential mystery."[46] The way, via the Scriptures, reveals Christ as the center of the cosmos, drawing all things to himself with the humility of Truth itself.[47] Thus, on the night before his passion, Christ reveals who the Father is in relation to Himself and the Holy Spirit. He reveals that the Father is to be found in the Son. He reveals what the intention of the Father is in sending the Son for our salvation and the sending of the Spirit for our sanctification. For Moore, "the mystery of Christ is . . . the mystery of the Persons."[48] The relationship between the Father and the Son, and the Mystery of the Spirit of the Father and the Son, spoken later in the early church by means of more technical words, is revealed by the words of Christ at the Last Supper. Contemplation on Christ leads to the Father and the mind is enabled to enter "spirit-wise into the mystery of Christ."[49]

Again, Moore prioritizes reflection on our own religious experience within the community of the church. The Mystery of Christ is not

---

45. Moore, "Blessed Trinity," 18.
46. Moore, "Blessed Trinity," 19.
47. Moore, "Blessed Trinity," 19.
48. Moore, "Blessed Trinity," 21–22.
49. Moore, "Blessed Trinity," 21.

only to be understood through theological reflection; it must also be embodied in the church (John 17:11) and can only be embodied in the church if Christ is at the heart of the church (John 14:15-19). Further, God declares himself as family, not through that symbol, but through the creative act of adoption by which we are given knowledge of the Trinity and love for the Trinity through becoming the sons and daughters of God. It is the very experience of adoption that is a primary source for our knowledge of the Holy Spirit as a distinct Person.[50]

For Moore, all other analogies of the Trinity, including those constructed by Augustine and Aquinas, are secondary. He concludes: "If, then, we are not thinking as members, drawing on the special knowledge which membership confers and is, we cannot attach a real meaning to the statement that God is three."[51] The knowledge we gain through lived membership does not come from doctrinal theology. Doctrinal theology aims to make the truths of the faith clearer and more reasonable. Knowledge comes from Christ inviting us into the depths of the Trinity. Such is Moore's mystical approach. At that depth, Christ invites us to share the communion of an extended family, over which he sends the Holy Spirit so that his joy may be in us. There is, therefore, a profound link between the economy of salvation, lived in the church and the Trinity *ad intra*.[52]

Second, Moore includes a chapter titled "Beata Trinitas" in his book *The Inner Loneliness*. In this chapter, he accentuates the incomprehensibility of God, something that we should never forget when we are seeking to understand God. As Moore says, "God is God," and we must be ever vigilant of "the inveterate temptation to make God comprehensible."[53] He then turns to the psychological analogy put forward by Augustine and refined by Aquinas. He begins with Augustine's "understanding of conscious being . . . [as] knowing and loving." Since God is beyond knowing and loving, it would be best for us to understand God as behind our knowing and loving, not our knowledge about God as a result of our knowing and loving. Here, he is taking an approach to God which is echoed by the mystics as distinct from systematic theologians. Moore is affirming the mystics' experience of God, as well as what traditional natural theology acknowledges as God being the primary cause of all

---

50. Moore, "Blessed Trinity," 23.
51. Moore, "Blessed Trinity," 24.
52. Moore, "Blessed Trinity," 24.
53. Moore, *Inner Loneliness*, 110.

reality. Without God providently sustaining us every moment of our day, we would not know, love, or even exist.

For Moore, "God *is* knowledge and loving." God originates knowing and loving. Knowledge and love happen simultaneously in God, with no time or distance or pause between questions, understanding, concepts, judgments of fact, judgments of value, and acts of love. For us, we might take a great deal of time, with many iterations, before we appreciate the truth. Moore states that God is "complete, total, infinite in scope and in this infinity of joy one Word is spoken."[54] While in humans, responsible loving proceeds knowing, in God, infinite joy is already present, together with infinite love and infinite knowledge simultaneously. "God is a total binge of joy, love, wisdom, [and] intelligence."[55]

This statement should make us question whether we really know what knowing and loving is. When we do ask this question, we conclude that all knowledge and love spring from God's mysterious reality.[56] So, while we go about having interests, taking lovers, indulging our curiosities, until we enjoy somewhat the perspective of the mystic, "We don't know *why* this happens at all."[57] The *why* is to be found in our experience of the Mystery of God. Here, Moore is emphasizing that God's very being is incomprehensible. God's divine nature is beyond our every experience, and the prioritizing of God's knowing and loving before our knowing or loving is glimpsed in mystical experience.

Moore directly addresses the writings of the mystics on the Trinity. Our understanding of the processions within the Trinity is not a derived reality by analogy to knowing and loving in humans, but rather, our knowing and loving derives its understanding from who God is and knowing God through contemplation. For Moore, the mystic's religious experience seems to suggest that the psychological analogy needs to be stood on its head. Apropos of this, unless we are in tune with the Trinity as sitting behind all our knowing and loving and as the cause of it, we cannot appreciate the clue of the Holy Spirit. Therefore, the Spirit will come across as a "shadowy resultant on the first procession." The Spirit becomes a problem and a source of curiosity for us, rather than a mystery and source of wonder, making possible all our knowledge and love. Moore understands the teachings of the mystic, especially Meister

---

54. Moore, *Inner Loneliness*, 113.
55. Moore, *Inner Loneliness*, 113.
56. Moore, *Inner Loneliness*, 110.
57. Moore, *Inner Loneliness*, 111.

Eckhart, when the latter interprets the Trinity flowing out of the Godhead, signaling that our knowing and loving flow out of God. If we are to be right in our knowing and loving, we must try first to appreciate the knowing and loving of God.

Moore turns to Augustine's "inner word." As already mentioned, the "inner word" of the human mind is when a new concept is formed before spoken and when we make a judgment of value before acting on a chosen course of action. Moore suggests that the inner word is similar to when we "speak" to ourselves, inwardly, before sharing our thoughts with others. What is most important is that the inner word needs to be spoken. God the Father generates the Word without a hint of hesitation or delay. On our part as creatures, we can deny, suppress, avoid, or repress an inner word. Moore is making the point that the analogy keeps before our minds a different dynamism in God.

With reference to Augustine's "Nothing is loved unless it is first known," Moore invites us to turn our gaze toward "the mysterious intentionality of the person, a hunger for a meaningful life, an eros that obscurely dictates the explicating of the rich reality *so that* it may fully deploy itself in love."[58] He is unpacking the intentionality of human consciousness drawn forward by the unrestricted desire to know and value. Knowledge leads to deliberation of values, values lead to an affirmation of what is worthwhile, and an affirmation of what is worthwhile tells us what we love and how what we love can be put into action responsibly. Augustine's phrase "love and do what you will" is not saying that as long as we love, anything can be done in the name of love and without sufficient knowledge. "Love and do what you will" becomes actualized when love is responsibly done, and responsible love comes from a sincere seeking of knowledge and truth. Before we commit to love, we must first understand the reality we seek to love correctly and thoroughly. The importance of understanding everything we seek to love applies to our friendships, our children, and our partners in marriage. Simply taking a blind leap is not good enough and might create more harm than good. It is within this understanding of human intentionality that we can better appreciate the psychological analogy of the Trinity.

Third, in the article "Are We Getting the Trinity Right?" we find Moore experimenting with a new analogy for the inner life of the Trinity. He begins with the psychological analogy and raises the question as to

---

58. Moore, *Inner Loneliness*, 113.

the relationship between the Trinity and the social implications for the church and society. I note that Moore proposes these thoughts in terms of a question "are we getting it right." For Moore, we need an understanding of the three persons sharing the one divine nature that emphasizes their communion. But the difficulty in appropriating an understanding of the Trinity as a communion comes from another error. Our culture of individualism accentuates the individual over and above the collective as an either/or, and our relationships with one another in the world become suffused with rivalry and envy. Envy is the keyword for fallen relationships. For Moore: "Envy is what desire, our life force, exposes itself to as it comes to life at the sight of itself in another."[59] Moore is drawing from the insights of Girard concerning desire and its propensity toward rivalry.

Is Moore proposing that all desire is mimetic and ultimately leads to envy? I do not think that Moore is claiming that all desire leads to calamity or discord. I have touched on the broader question as to whether desire is always mimetic in chapter 6. He also states that desire is a source for our bonding, and I assume that by the word *bonding* he means a rich and flourishing intersubjective reality. He speaks about authentic humanness as a reality that is both personal and without rivalry or envy.

The question becomes: How do we attain authentic personhood? Moore proposes that our understanding of the intra-Trinitarian life is the key to our attaining authentic humanity. Conceiving God as without envy, we are helped to appreciate "a beyond-community creative of community in those it touches."[60] In God, we are saved from envy and all forms of radical unloving. The Father, Son, and Holy Spirit are saying to us, "We are not envious." A proper Trinitarian theology will be therapeutic for original sin and all its outworking. A Trinitarian, non-envious understanding of God is the source for the healing of discord and reveals God as "transerotic."[61] In God, there is an identity between each Divine Person and the relational person. In God's inner life, we find the basis for understanding the church as a communion.

Girard and Jean-Michel Oughourlian have worked on an anthropology to help articulate the individual/collective dialectic in humanity. They call it "interdividual" humanity. In his humanity, Jesus knew he shared the divine life of the Godhead through knowing that he was deeply loved by the Father, a profound experience of interdividual

---

59. Moore, "Are We Getting," 60.
60. Moore, "Are We Getting," 60.
61. Moore, "Are We Getting," 61.

existence. Jesus' intimacy with the heavenly Father nourished his self-love, which generated self-gift.[62] For Moore, a lack of self-love leads to envy in society. Self-love intends to send us towards others without fear and enter into relationships with security. When self-love is repressed and unacknowledged, it generates insecurity and a compulsive need to dominate others, where envy and rivalry reign. Self-love also is meant to send us in the direction of transcendent companionship. The cross is the site where both the darkness of envy and rivalry looms large and, by Jesus, where self-love leads to the full flowering of self-gift. As a self-gift, it is also the site where the bankruptcy of scapegoating due to envy is exposed for what it truly is.

The cross tells us a lot about the inner life of the Trinity. Moore proposes that desire as love flows through all the Divine Persons as a "divine-personal-in-each-otherness" or a "beyond-intraindividual" where desire as love is a total mutual gift between the persons of the Trinity. In God, there is no rivalry, and for God, desire is love. God is a pure gift. Pure gift is the opposite of envy. While our mimetic relationships descend into rivalry over the object, in God, the object is their mutual love. The endless and loving mimetic influencing in God produces a dance, a circular motion that completely witnesses the Three in One. The dance is the only "resolution" to our mimetic relationships becoming envious in our lives.[63] The "place" on earth for the Trinity's self-disclosure is a new humanity where transformation from envy to love has happened.

Fourth, in another article, "And There Is Only the Dance," Moore returns to his efforts to reframe a better understanding of the Trinity, this time citing the Trinitarian writings of Thomas Weinandy. Weinandy's understanding is not dissimilar to that of James Alison. Moore begins his analysis with the consciousness of God. God is infinite consciousness, that is, infinitely wise, happy, generous, knowing, loving, and all these properties or qualities occur simultaneously.[64] Again, from the perspective of the mystic, to understand human nature, we must first appreciate God's spiritual nature. It is not that God is like us but that we are like God. Scripture says: we are made in the image and likeness of God. If we are to come to knowledge, there must be a correspondence between the knower and the known through language. For humans, the process of correspondence may take a long time before it is resolved. For

62. Moore, "Are We Getting," 62.
63. Moore, "Are We Getting," 67.
64. Moore, "And There Is Only," 269.

God, the knower and the known happen instantaneously. God the Father generates God the Son instantaneously. As in the preamble, Moore, in an abbreviated way, links the relationship between knowledge and love to an analogous understanding of what we mean by saying the Father generates the Son and the Spirit proceeds from the Father and Son. For us, knowing is not the endpoint within human consciousness, and all knowledge moves to love, and love is ecstatic.[65] By analogy to human consciousness, the Spirit is the ecstatic love of the Father and the Son.

Ever seeking to be original, Moore presents another analogy for the intra-Trinitarian life. His analogy is based on the technique of focusing, which I spoke about in chapter 1. Usually, when focusing is employed, the person has come to some emotional blockage within themselves which they cannot identify easily, either to its origin or cause or to its resolution, but which they feel in their body or embodiment as pain. The person knows that the emotional blockage is contained in the body and it gives rise to further disesteem and felt self-rejection. It could be the case that a person may not even be conscious of there being a blockage, and the blockage remains "unconscious." The blockage may reveal itself by the person being stuck in some kind of general malaise or by the person doubling their efforts to find some pleasurable release from pain without knowing why. What is needed is a "body shift" from a troubled mind to a greater and clearer view of what one's inner pain is all about. The "body shift" happens when the embodied person sits and reflectively allows insight to emerge. When insight emerges into the emotional block, the cause of the pain and its possible elimination, together with the desire to change, can occur in a "body shift" and the person experiences a sense of well-being.

For Moore, the whole process becomes a new way of understanding the relationship between the Father, the Son, and the Holy Spirit. The Father is likened to the subject who is seeking release and healing through attunement to the body and waiting for insight. The Son is likened to the experience of attaining that knowledge for liberation. When release and healing occur, there is the sheer delight of liberation at getting it right. The Spirit is likened to the sheer delight of attaining knowledge, which brings a body shift or liberation and release. The Spirit is also the motive force of delight by which liberation is achieved through knowledge. The Father cannot come to knowledge and sheer

---

65. Moore, "And There Is Only," 271.

liberation without the Spirit. Moore is obviously trying to give greater prominence to the role of the Spirit.

Moore parallels the knowledge that the focusing process produces with the Father generating the Son through the Holy Spirit. The Spirit is the motive force for healing and the sheer delight in getting it right or getting knowledge right so as to be released from pain. In the traditional understanding of the second procession, the Holy Spirit proceeds from the Father and the Son. Moore proposes that if we were to adhere to an understanding of the Spirit as the delight of the Father, then the Father generates the Son with the Spirit and ends in a sheer delight in getting it right. He postulates this understanding as an alternative way of understanding the intra-Trinitarian life with the Holy Spirit at the beginning and end. Thus, the Father begets the Son through the Spirit. The Spirit proceeds from the Father and the Son as sheer delight through knowledge. The delight of the Holy Spirit points to the priority of love in God. In God, loving and knowing are simultaneous. In God, there is no "yes, but" as there is in human life. There is only a divine "yes" of love. By use of the analogy of focusing, Moore signals his preference for the understanding proposed by Weinandy and Alison, namely, the Son proceeds from the Father through the Spirit and the Spirit proceeds from the Father and the Son. Again, Moore's alternative understanding moves beyond the traditional understanding of the intra-Trinitarian life while still maintaining two processions and scope for the two missions.

Fifth, I turn finally to Moore's insights on the Trinity in his book *The Contagion of Jesus*. Moore highlights some of the key theological insights that have remained with him throughout his life. One key insight is that the disciples came to affirm the divinity of Jesus through first experiencing a transformation of desire, as discussed in chapter 8. The original Mystery of God revealed in Jesus now is known to them as a loving and life-giving force that raised Jesus, "as the Father revealed in the Son as the God who, by extending what he is into Jesus, now enters human consciousness as the love that keeps on being love, despite, and against all human limitations. Thus, the crucified and risen One begins to appear in the light of this, God."[66] Finally, the disciples realize that their new consciousness comes about from an experience of mysterious vitality, which grows into the disciple's awareness of the Holy Spirit, "uniting

---

66. Kelly, *Trinity of Love*, 53.

Father, Son, and themselves."⁶⁷ Moore's constructed and imaginative story of what went on within the disciples seems to be well attuned to biblical data from the perspective of interiority.⁶⁸ Moore concludes that the disciples are "thinking-about-God-differently because [they] are being changed into God, that is, the Holy Spirit."⁶⁹ It follows that unless the resurrection experience is changing each of us, then Jesus makes no sense, and we cannot really understand the Mystery of the Trinity. Similarly, the Son's equality to the Father within the Trinitarian life only makes sense when we become part of it through the Holy Spirit.⁷⁰ We come closer to the Spirit when we sense in ourselves our inner transformation. Likewise, when we get away from the perspective of inner transformation, multiple complexities concerning God begin to appear.⁷¹

Moore goes on to explore the importance of the Holy Spirit. He begins by reiterating a conviction in Girard's understanding of desire. It is the triangulation of desire that makes us inescapably involved in each other. Moore states elsewhere that "it is my seeing myself, my own desire, in you that is its awakening in me. It is your likeness to me that stimulates me to emulate you."⁷² Further, it is seeing our desire in another that prompts our desire to fashion another like ourselves.⁷³ Desire is a force working in us and between us, putting in our way models in which we can recognize the process of desire either as descending into violence or becoming an encouragement to our full humanity. Inasmuch as desire devolves into rivalry, we cannot attain our true humanity. Inasmuch as we surrender ourselves to the movement of the Holy Spirit, desire becomes a source of love and encouragement for each other.

Moore couches the problem of understanding the inner life of the Trinity in terms of the dichotomy between the notion of "person" and the notion of energy. To speak of the notion of God in terms of "person" means that we start with the Father-Son relationship. If God is symbolized through the image of fatherhood (usually the image of patriarchal religiousness) and thus the father-son relationship, the problem of envy arises. Envy arises, since, from the dawn of time, fathers and sons have

67. Kelly, *Trinity of Love*, 53.
68. Kelly, *Trinity of Love*, 54.
69. Moore, *Contagion of Jesus*, 15.
70. Moore, *Contagion of Jesus*, 18.
71. Moore, *Contagion of Jesus*, 19.
72. Moore, "Where the Spirit," 174.
73. Moore, "Where the Spirit," 175.

been rivals towards each other. Humankind has variously projected onto God the image of the authoritarian Father over the envious Son. If God is symbolized as energy (usually the image of liberalized religion), then there is a lack of person within God. We might even think of this energy as something we can tap.[74]

For Moore, there does not need to be a dichotomous either/or between paternity and filiation. There is room for both, and so the term *person*, on the one side, and energy, on the other side, can sit well with each other. The solution comes from a careful reading of the Gospel of John particularly in the Last Supper discourse. At the Last Supper, Jesus spells out his total openness to God in terms of a son-to-father relationship. The symbol of a son-to-father relationship also evokes the scapegoating of him by those who would put him to death on the cross. The son-father symbol held by those under the shadow of death is founded on a misunderstanding suffused with envy and rivalry. We cannot know the liberated desire of Jesus and the revelation of the true God as love from a position of envy, until we have felt the power of his resurrection. On the cross, Jesus stands on its head, both the scapegoating and the envious portrayal of God by humankind, evoked in the father-son symbol.

The Spirit is the follow-through to the self-gift of Jesus through the death he undergoes by reason of the world's violence.[75] Moore states that in the Gospel of John, "the Spirit is the convincing vitality or energy with which a person enjoys God as intimate Father with the certainty of the coequal Son."[76] The exaltation of the victim of the cross unties the invisible thrall and dread of death in us by the action of the Spirit. The disciples experience the release of the Spirit as their self becomes fully active. It is the Spirit who reveals to us the face of the Father through the humanity, brotherliness, and style of the Son. It is the Spirit who reveals the filiation of Jesus toward the Father. The Spirit reveals how Jesus lives filiation and lets himself be crucified by the powerful who oppose mutual openness.[77]

Likewise, the Spirit is "the infinite life that comes of the open relationship of the eternal Father and the coequal Son."[78] Only through the resurrection can the relationship between Father and Son be known by us, and only in the resurrection can knowledge and the spiritual

74. Moore, "Where the Spirit," 188.
75. Moore, "Where the Spirit," 192.
76. Moore, "Where the Spirit," 188.
77. Moore, "Where the Spirit," 177.
78. Moore, "Where the Spirit," 178.

awareness of the Spirit come to us.⁷⁹ Only by Jesus going to the Father can the Father and Son send the Spirit. As the Son is exulted at the right hand of the Father, so the Spirit leaps from them into our hearts. Even though there is sadness felt by the disciples on hearing that Jesus must go to the Father, there is an even greater joy to be revealed through the sending of the Spirit. The Spirit comes from the Father in the Son, and we are assimilated to Christ; that is, we are made part of his body. In the Spirit, the disciples will do even greater things than they see Jesus doing. The body of Christ becomes the new site for the revealing of the Father and the Son, but not without its suffering. This new revelation point is the Spirit of adoption in which "after the ageless mistrust and envious idolatry of man, we are able to cry our 'Abba, Father!'"⁸⁰ In the Spirit, the Adamic envy of God and our living in the shadow of death is dissolved. In the Spirit, creation obscured by Adamic envy comes into its own.⁸¹

Again, Moore is influenced by the work of James Alison, who starts with the father-son analogy. He prefers the father-son analogy to the mind-word analogy that comes to us through Augustine and Aquinas, although he is still content to hang onto the mind-word analogy. Why the preference for the father-son analogy? In the father-son analogy, we find ourselves using a human analogy for the resulting of the Spirit, "namely a father-son relationship *so open* that in its aura or resultant climate, people become themselves and grow. . . . As this open relationship of the human father and son becomes ever more open, it crosses the gulf between the created and the uncreated and becomes the sublime reality Jesus foresees in the discourse, the resultant *climate* or *energy* is a resultant *person*."⁸²

MOORE AND THE TRINITY: A CRITIQUE

Given all that is stated in my preamble on the theology of the Trinity, we can observe possible points of agreement and disagreement between Moore and more traditional approaches to the Trinity.

First, Moore presents significant insights into our approach to the doctrine of the Trinity. He appeals for a return to the symbols of Scripture so that our faith may be inspired and grow. In a situation of preaching,

---

79. Moore, "Where the Spirit," 178.
80. Moore, "Where the Spirit," 180.
81. Moore, "Where the Spirit," 184.
82. Moore, "Where the Spirit," 184.

where the preacher aims to fan into a flame the gift of faith, a preacher who pulls out the treatises of Augustine and Aquinas and reads from them as part of the content of his sermon would surely be missing the mark. Moore is echoing the insight by Kelly, that a theology of the Trinity has as its prime focus a contemplative listening to the invitation by God to participate in the communion of love. A contemplative reading of the scriptural texts can lead us to the point of surrender to the Mystery of God, who is three Persons in a communion of love.

Unfortunately, however, the biblical evidence alone does not answer other questions that brought about the Christological controversies and the reasons for the subsequent response of the church in a more technically precise language, which Kelly characterizes as "do it with precision or let confusion grow." So, in terms of faith-seeking understanding, Moore's approach, while aiding in our path of surrender to God, may not satisfy the mind's desire to understand.

Second, while appreciating Moore's concern to appropriate the insights of the mystics, I am not sure how these voices advance the task of faith seeking understanding of the Trinity in a way that addresses the early controversies that arose in relation to Christ. Moore is correct in that the mystic's encounter with God is usually expressed as an encounter with the incomprehensible. Their expression about God is usually in terms of what God is not (apophatic) rather in terms of what is (cataphatic). Further, the temptation of the mystic is to think about creation as some kind of emanation of God and become forgetful of the distinction between creature and Creator and seemingly postulate ourselves as part of the evolving consciousness of God. These mystical experiences create other difficulties in understanding faith, including pantheism and emanationism. However, another possible avenue of connection with the mystic may exist. If our sanctification is a created participation in the divine life of God, then perhaps the experience of the mystic could be expressed in terms of the four created participations spoken of earlier.[83]

Third, in more traditional approaches "person" as applied to God the Father, Son, and Spirit is more a distinction without definition. The way Moore uses "Person" in the Godhead, especially when echoing the mimetic theory of Girard as non-envious, seems to assume a contemporary understanding of personhood, which may be a problem. The shift

83. Ormerod, "Metaphysics of Holiness," 74–79.

from speaking about a person in the human context and "person" in the divine context could be easily confused.

Fourth, Moore puts a great deal of emphasis on mimetic desire, which, in his mind, inevitably leads to envy and rivalry. He uses the analogy of mimetic desire to speak about desire within God. Moore states that mimetic desire is triangular comprising model, respondent and object of desire, only in the Trinity, the object for the Divine Persons is mutual love. The model is the Father, the Son is the respondent, and the Holy Spirit is their mutual love. The difficulty is that Moore's imaginative theory verges toward a tritheism, and the way in which it is framed seems to suggest that the Holy Spirit is not a person but more of a property.

The question of what kind of contribution mimetic theory can make to intra-Trinitarian theology is complex and vexing. Admittedly, mimetic or elicited desire accentuates desire as emerging from an intersubjective space and is a neutral reality until it becomes mutually loving or greedy, leading to violence. The presumption by Girard is that such mimesis leads to violence and does not remain neutral. However, it could be argued that since it does also allow for the possibility of mutual imitation in love, mimetic theory would seem to provide a proper analogy for the intersubjective space of the Trinity.

Ormerod weighs into the question of applying the mechanism of mimetic desire to the intra-Trinitarian life. He begins his analysis by exploring Girard's use of internal and external mediation. The amount of distance between the model and the respondent distinguishes internal mediation and external mediation.[84] Ormerod calls these accounts descriptive and not explanatory and then seeks to give an explanatory account of them. He proposes the distinction between "conscious but not objectified" and "conscious and objectified." Within a Lonerganian view of consciousness, "conscious but not objectified" is identified in chapter 1 and chapter 5 in terms of psychology's "unconscious" mind. Again, from the perspective of consciousness, "conscious and objectified" is identified with reflective consciousness, or what Moore calls reflective self-awareness. Ormerod contends that most of what is identified by Girard in terms of envy and scapegoating occurs because of the unobjectified nature of the conscious state.[85] Alternatively, salvation requires

---

84. Ormerod, "Doran's *Trinity in History*," 56.
85. Ormerod, "Doran's *Trinity in History*," 56.

an objectification of these states made possible by Jesus' life, death, and resurrection, which exposes the scapegoat mechanism.

At this point, Ormerod distinguishes intersubjective spontaneity, on the one hand, and interpersonal relationships, on the other. Intersubjective spontaneity should not be confused with the intelligent, reasonable, responsible, and loving formation of interpersonal relationships, even if it may be an initial spark to interpersonal relations. Intersubjective spontaneity is a primordial basis for human interactions. Interpersonal relationship is a more considered and evaluated basis for human interactions.[86] When intersubjective spontaneity goes wrong, it goes wrong on the basis of not being attuned to attentiveness, intelligence, reasonableness, and responsibility. The problem with the mechanism of mimesis is not whether it is internal or external or double or whether there is distance or no distance. The problem is whether the person is conforming to the imperatives of consciousness. The desire to know, to value, and to love is not imitative; rather, "it is a natural participation in the divine nature as the source of all truth and goodness."[87] It is a participation in the divine nature because grace completes and perfects nature, dismantling the distorted condition of envy and rivalry and elevating nature to a horizon where the love of God has changed all our values.[88] The grace of religious conversion enables moral conversion, by which we choose values over satisfactions, and intellectual conversion, by which we seek the truth, including attunement with the operations of human consciousness.

Positively, mimetic theory signals that we ought to acknowledge the formative intersubjective context of desires and move away from any sense that we are autonomous, independent, and desirous human beings. It also alerts us to the truth that the passive imitation of the desires of others means that we are in danger of taking to ourselves disordered desires. What helps us to prevent breakdown by disordered desire is to subject them to intelligent thinking and responsible loving. Since our whole lives are ever a movement from inauthenticity to authenticity, irresponsibility to responsible loving and unintelligent thinking to intelligent thinking, then the task of becoming authentic will require an acceptance of God's grace in conversion. The created participation in the divine relations that ground a supernatural imitation of the Divine is not mimetic, but a gift

86. Ormerod, "Doran's *Trinity in History*," 57.
87. Ormerod, "Doran's *Trinity in History*," 58.
88. Ormerod, "Doran's *Trinity in History*," 58.

of God poured into our hearts by the Holy Spirit. I am not certain that Moore's analogy of the intra-Trinitarian life along the lines of mimesis helps once these distinctions are recognized.

Moore is very firm about one thing. What really needs to happen is that we stop imitating each other and begin to imitate Christ. Perhaps an answer to Moore might be couched in these terms. This imitation of Christ becomes possible through our participation in the Trinitarian relations, and that occurs when we imitate Christ, accept sanctifying grace, practice the habit of charity, and dwell in the hope of seeing God face to face. Blackwood asserts: "The healing that is achieved in sanctifying grace that is enacted in the habit of charity that has its historical origin in the Incarnation, and that finds its final manifestation in the light of glory is in its affective dimensions, a shift from the deadly scapegoating imitation of one another toward the holy imitation of the truly innocent victim, Jesus Christ."[89]

Fifth, Moore's adoption of an intra-Trinitarian understanding, as proposed by James Alison and Thomas Weinandy, even with the traditional terms of procession and mission, does not square up with the doctrinal gains in the tradition. On one hand, these proposals seem to give more prominence to the Holy Spirit in the Trinitarian life. One the other hand, they seem to work against the gains of the tradition. For example, Moore proposes to speak of the Father generating the Son through the Holy Spirit. The difficulty with this proposal is that we do not speak of this anywhere in the tradition. Ormerod sates: "We can say that the Father is the Father of the Son and the Son is the Son of the Father; but while we say that the Spirit is the Spirit of the Father, we never say that the Father is the Father of the Spirit."[90] Alternatively, while we say that the Spirit is the Spirit of the Son, we do not say that the Son is the Son of the Spirit. This insight alone renders this new understanding problematic.

However, I do appreciate Moore's desire for an understanding that makes the Holy Spirit more fully present in the generation of the Son, as if we were to complete the "dance" of God. If the created participations follow from the intra-Trinitarian processions, then this understanding may better ground Moore's desire to get the Holy Spirit working more fruitfully in our lives. Moore is obviously working from a desire to give greater prominence to the Holy Spirit, who has been conspicuously

---

89. Blackwood, "Lonergan's Trinitarian Theology," 16.
90. Ormerod, *Trinitarian Primer*, 54.

missing from the church's prayer and devotional life. However, a renewed appreciation for the place of the Holy Spirit does not need a rethink of traditional intra-Trinitarian theology. Our appreciation needs us to be more sensitive to the economy of salvation through meditating on the Scriptures, in which the full import of the missions of the Son and the Holy Spirit sent by the Father is revealed. In terms of intra-Trinitarian theology, it needs to revisit the connection between the created participations and the believer's life of holiness, especially in the created terms of the Incarnation of the Son and our imitation of him, the gift of sanctifying grace, and the habit of charity.

Sixth, regarding the word *interdividual* and the designation of the Trinity as a "beyond-intraindividual" life, I note that the word, penned by Girardian scholars, introduces a new term for an understanding of the Trinity. The meaning of the term may already be captured by the word *procession*, which is another way of speaking about the relationality of the Trinity. Since we are talking about God, every word that seeks to understand the Trinity in terms of relationality will necessarily be perfect in God. This new way of speaking about the inner life of the Trinity emphasizes communion in the love of God. Many of Moore's concerns indirectly come back to this "communion" metaphor for God. It is also a metaphor that has gained supremacy for speaking about the life of the church. Ormerod presents a fruitful set of insights for an alternative metaphor which may help our understanding as well as the kind of concerns raised by Moore in his writings.

Ormerod starts with the affirmation that the church is often depicted as the "icon" of the inner life of the Trinity.[91] Just as the inner life of the Trinity is a communion in love, so the church is called to be a communion in love. Communion ecclesiology flows out of communion in the Trinity. This understanding of the church is found throughout the New Testament. Ormerod has another suggestion, namely, to change the focus from the intra-Trinitarian communion of the persons to the created participations of the Trinity. The created participations are grounded in the intra-Trinitarian processions but flow outward into the created order.[92]

In terms of the church and the Trinitarian processions, it could be stated quite accurately that the church participates in the mission of the Son and the Spirit in the world, extending the Incarnation of the Son,

---

91. Ormerod, "(Non-Communio) Trinitarian," 448.
92. Ormerod, "(Non-Communio) Trinitarian," 449.

the sanctifying grace and the habit of charity of the Spirit into human history. The Son is sent by the Father to inaugurate the kingdom, and the Spirit is sent at Pentecost to continue to sanctify the church so that others may come to the Father and the Son. Here, we are already beginning to emphasize an understanding of the church that does not get much purchase: The church as missionary linked to the mission of Jesus and the advancement of the kingdom through self-sacrificing love and its motive force for mission, the Holy Spirit.[93] The mission of the church is located then as an extension of the missions of the Son and the Spirit concretely expression through the virtues of faith, hope, and love. This approach to understanding the church is very different from the usual emphasis on the "dance" of perichoresis or even the non-envious mimesis of the persons within the Trinity.

Ormerod argues that the two processions within the Trinity are linked to the two missions of the Son and the Spirit, but "procession and mission are rarely mentioned in *communio* ecclesiologies."[94] He states that "the processions are often viewed as a threat to the equality of the three Persons, implying some type of hierarchical ordering among them. Without the processions, however, the mission bears no intrinsic relationship to God's trinitarian life. To fail to attend to the processions severs a genuine trinitarian connection between the mission of the church and the processions/missions of the Son and the Spirit."[95] Also, *communio* ecclesiologies tend to both neglect consideration of the church's mission and prescind from historical details of the life of the church. We end up with an idealized form of the church in *communion* and the mistaken idea that because we say these words about the church, we are already there.[96]

Here is where Ormerod takes a brilliant turn. The traditional Trinitarian theology and its use of two processions, four relations, three persons, and one nature are designed to answer the questions of whether and how individual Persons of the Trinity relate to the created order.[97] Drawing from the work of Robert Doran and Bernard Lonergan, Ormerod locates "the theological realities of sanctifying grace and the virtues of faith, hope and charity as created participations in the trinitarian

93. Ormerod, "(Non-Communio) Trinitarian," 451–52.
94. Ormerod, "(Non-Communio) Trinitarian," 455.
95. Ormerod, "(Non-Communio) Trinitarian," 455.
96. Ormerod, "(Non-Communio) Trinitarian," 457.
97. Ormerod, "(Non-Communio) Trinitarian," 460.

relations. The relations between these realities of the Christian life reflect the relations between the trinitarian relations linking grace with charity and faith with hope. Inasmuch as a Christian is grounded in sanctifying grace and lives a life of faith, hope and charity, she is imitating the divine trinitarian relations and is truly, then, an icon of the Trinity."[98]

This connection between the Trinitarian relations and sanctifying grace enables us to connect to what Lonergan calls the "divinely originated solution to the problem of evil." I spoke to this term in chapter 8 in the context of a theological understanding of redemption. Ormerod asserts: "Viewed in this context, our sharing in the trinitarian life through created participations in the divine life, leading to a life grounded in grace and informed by the theological virtues, becomes a constitutive of element of the divinely originated solution to the problem of evil. The Trinity shares the divine life with us so that evil may be overcome in the world."[99] Further, the problem of evil is not simply a concern of the individual, for it permeates human history, culture, and society. The life of the theological virtues grounded in sanctifying grace "goes beyond our personal conversion away from evil to call us to engage in world transformation, to move toward the manifestation of God's kingdom on earth."[100]

This divine solution by God creates a community with multiple tasks or callings: the task to mediate God's love (prayer, sacraments, liturgy); the task to promote a life of generous and sacrificial love as a means to overcome evil by contemplating the life of the saints; the task to model a living hope that the adversities of the present struggle against evil are not the final word but reach into a greater life grounded in God's love; and the task to open our minds through faith to our communally held beliefs that go against the distorting ideologies within human existence, "by affirming our transcendent origin and end, our vocation to union with God and the means God has established toward reaching that union."[101]

In conclusion, Ormerod sums up the mission of the church:

> The work of the church as a whole is to promote lives grounded in grace and lived out in faith, hope, and charity. Inasmuch as the church undertakes this work, the church as a whole is an icon of the Trinity. The church as a whole, then, participates in created participations of the divine nature that are imitative of

---

98. Ormerod, "(Non-Communio) Trinitarian," 461.
99. Ormerod, "(Non-Communio) Trinitarian," 461.
100. Ormerod, "(Non-Communio) Trinitarian," 462.
101. Ormerod, "(Non-Communio) Trinitarian," 463.

the four trinitarian relations.... This theology provides an alternative to the claims of *communio* ecclesiology for presenting the life of the church as iconic of the life of the Trinity. The focus on grace and the three theological virtues, as genuinely trinitarian, provides a more robust and substantial account of the life of the church's mission to the world than a *communio* approach can sustain without losing any trinitarian depth.[102]

This theology of the Trinity grounds a Trinitarian spirituality in terms of the theological virtues of love, faith, and hope. The starting point is God's grace.[103] Grace is the gift of God, unearned and undeserved and which cannot be manipulated but in and by which we know ourselves as deeply loved. Grace is the gift of the Holy Spirit and relates to the divine procession of the Spirit, which proceeds from the Father and the Son. If the Spirit dwells in our hearts, so do the Father and the Son come to make their home in the believing heart (John 14:26). Ormerod states:

> This liberation of our desire through grace opens our hearts to love as God loves. Through the Father and Son dwelling in us, we become sources of the divine Spirit for the world. Without this grounding in grace, our actions become activism, and we burn ourselves out. On the other hand, without our engagement for others in charity, the gift of grace turns inward and festers in *self*-fulfilment. Grace and charity are linked as the Holy Spirit is linked to the Father and the Son.[104]

Apart from the procession of the Spirit and the gift of grace, the Son proceeds from the Father. Ormerod asserts: "The Word is God's 'Yes' to all that God is and does. We see this as the faithful obedience of Jesus who never stops saying 'yes' to God because he is the Incarnation of God is only 'Yes' to us."[105] This means that when "we say 'yes' to the gift of God's love poured into our hearts, Christ lives in us and we manifest a divine faith.... This is the nature of faith saying 'yes' to God in trust and obedience within the concrete circumstances of our lives. Through living a life of faith, we can truly say that God's Word, the eternal Yes, lives in our hearts, just as the Holy Spirit dwells in us as divine love."[106]

---

102. Ormerod, "(Non-Communio) Trinitarian," 463.
103. Ormerod, "Healthcare and the Response," 24.
104. Ormerod, "Healthcare and the Response," 26.
105. Ormerod, "Healthcare and the Response," 28.
106. Ormerod, "Healthcare and the Response," 28.

Finally, Ormerod speaks to the theological virtue of hope. Jesus shared a special intimacy with the Father. He never lost sight of the ultimate goal of his mission. Through our adoption as sons and daughters of the Father, we long for the day when we shall see God face-to-face. This is our hope. In the New Testament, hope is often associated with suffering and endurance and "when our common human optimism about the future hits a brick wall, we need a more powerful source of hope, one that transcends the limits of our present existence."[107] Without hope, our faith may falter in times of great suffering. Without faith, our hope has no clear grasp of our ultimate goal. Just as grace and charity are linked through the relationship of the Spirit to the Father and the Son, so faith and hope are linked through the relationship of the Son to the Father.[108]

Overall, I would say traditional Trinitarian theology answers the concerns presented by Moore. First, it gives greater prominence to the Holy Spirit by linking the procession of the Holy Spirit in the intra-Trinitarian life with the created participation of sanctifying grace. The prominence of the Holy Spirit is central to Moore's theology of the Trinity. Second, it addresses Moore's concern that we overcome the tendency towards envy and rivalry, which are manifestations of the problem of evil in the world. This approach addresses the problem of evil through our participation in the gifts of faith, hope, and love as an extension of the processions within the Trinity into their created participations.

Third, it presents an understanding of the church as grounded in the Trinitarian life and a model of the church that is not only called to be a communion of love grounded in the Divine Persons but a missionary church grounded in the two processions and the two missions of Son and the Holy Spirit and thus by God's grace, united to God through the created participations of the Trinity in the created order. This fits with Moore's concern for the church to be missionary, healing the wounds brought about by the problem of evil. Fourth, it emphasizes that the purpose of the church is to transform the current situation in the world into a new situation that comes closer to the kingdom of God on earth through self-sacrificing love, overcoming the evils of the present through redemptive suffering. In chapter 7, I noted Moore's understanding of Jesus as grounded in the inauguration of the kingdom of God. In chapter 8, I noted the connection between redemptive suffering in the church

---

107. Ormerod, "Healthcare and the Response," 30.
108. Ormerod, "Healthcare and the Response," 30.

and the cross, a link made by Moore throughout his writings and given particular emphasis in Lonergan's Mysterious Law of the Cross.

Finally, it links the gifts of faith, hope, and love to the processions and the two missions of the Son and the Spirit. The Spirit is given greater prominence as the love proceeding from the Father and the Son and the Trinity's created participation in the world through sanctifying grace. The Son is the "Yes" of faith proceeding from the Father through the created participation of the Incarnation. In as much as we say "yes" to God, we are continuing the Incarnation. By extension, the church is the continuing work of the Incarnation. The gift of hope correlates with the response of filiation from the Son to the Father in the beatific vision and our desire in hope to persevere through our suffering by focusing on our ultimate goal.

DOES GOD SUFFER?

I have chosen to put this question of whether there is suffering in God in the context of the Trinity. For Moore, the question arises in the context of those seeking to understand what they call "the consciousness of Christ." Coming at it from the perspective of the self-knowledge of Christ, the question as to whether God suffers could have been dealt with in chapters 7 or 8. I have chosen to deal with it here since the created participation of the Incarnation is involved, and since what happens to Christ also happens to the Father, only that it is Christ in his humanity who suffers rejection and death and not the Father or the Spirit.

The first thing that Moore seeks to clarify is the difference between consciousness, self-awareness, and reflective self-awareness or self-knowledge.[109] In chapter 1, I unpacked the meaning of these terms from Moore's perspective influenced by Lonergan. Then, Moore directly addresses the question as to whether God suffers in Christ. The traditional answer to the question of suffering in the Godhead has been a definite "no." Suffering is linked to change, finiteness, and contingency. God does not experience change, nor is God finite or contingent. What about Christ?

Moore starts his analysis with the question of suffering, noting that suffering has been falsely understood by believers as only of value if endured as a means to union with God. It has been thought of as something

---

109. Moore, "God Suffered," 122–37.

we must undergo out of a desire to imitate the sufferings of Christ.[110] Not only ought the Christian want to suffer, but he ought to want to suffer with God. Moore judges all positions grounded in this premise to be inadequate. These attitudes are grounded in the mistaken attitude that God has put a divine seal on suffering. For Moore,

> [The] Passion is the finger of this God laid on the depths of the soul and expanding it to infinite truth. The truth that God has suffered touches the Spirit that is made of truth by truth, for truth. A man suffering his loss of his life in this world is the most intimate thing of him and to say that it is given a new meaning by the Cross is true but quite inadequate. It is not merely transvaluated by God, but made God's own so that for man to be lost in this world is to be lost in God. . . . The Cross is God in this world of pain, but then it is this world of pain in God, into whom the soul of the sufferer is snatched and learns an incomprehensible grammar of sorrow and forgiveness. The Mystery that is the delight and strength of the soul is suffering not made new, but made God's. The suffering that is God's is not merely a new suffering, but a new thing, the one thing, to be called fire or light or the bread of life.[111]

Moore is affirming that not all suffering stirs up within us the despair of meaninglessness. There is a form of suffering that creates new meaning, and in the case of the cross, the new meaning is the startling revelation of God, who responds to evil with good, even to the point that the Father does not prevent Jesus' suffering and death on the cross. The suffering of Jesus is a unique form of suffering for humanity since the Sinless One endures suffering on account of sins and on account of sinners. In this respect, it is a suffering in which God suffers.

In the next chapter, I will explore Moore's approach to Christian sexuality.

---

110. Moore, "God Suffered," 138.
111. Moore, "God Suffered," 139.

12

Moore and Sexuality

INTRODUCTION

It would be safe to assume that from Moore's first days as a novice in the Order of Saint Benedict till his days in the parish of St. Mary's Liverpool, Benedictine community members did not engage in formal conversation on sex and sexuality. If there were any theological reflections on sexuality, they would have been in the context of canon law or moral theology classes. The class lecturers may have even conducted the lectures in Latin and would have approached the topic from the perspective of broad principles grounded in a natural law approach. Postulants and novices would have been warned about the sinfulness of masturbation, the importance of chastity, discouraged from particular friendships, and taught a theology of marriage that placed the birth and raising of children as the primary end of a marriage.

MOORE AND INTERVIEWS

I want to begin an exposition of Moore's theological understanding of sexuality with two interviews, one conducted on radio in 2011 and the other face to face, some months before he died in 2014. On Sunday, the thirteenth of February 2011, Moore was visiting Sydney, Australia, and consented to give a radio interview for a religious program on ABC Radio National to the interviewer, Noel Debien. Moore was ninety-four years old. Debien asked him a range of questions:

Debien: [How] has that monastic life and that deliberate decision to be single, to put aside one part of your life, which is particularly sex and desire . . . helped you overcome your own mental noise?

Moore: For me, the pressure of sex is very solitary. To be quite honest I fell in love with [The record of interview omits names and other associations at this point] . . . I'm gay, of course. [At this point, Moore pauses]. But gosh, you couldn't say that 50/60 years ago. That's the other thing, the enormous change that is happening there. But as I say, solitary sex and masturbation and stuff like that very simple stuff, nothing like a real decision of preference to marriage. I didn't have that. I snuck into the thing and everything I know I discovered it all in the other way around. I got in, the inwards [life] was developed with God, and now I want to get out, I wanted to get out. That's the nearest I can get to it.

Debien: How have you seen attitudes to spirituality, and sexuality that you just mentioned change over that time?

Moore: Real change doesn't happen in the head. It doesn't happen in ideas. It certainly doesn't happen with a new papal encyclical or anything like that, it just happens. Just the other day, Archbishop Vincent Nichols, the leading Catholic of England was interviewed and he was asked: "Will the church ever accept a gay union?" And he said, "I don't know, we don't see down the road." It's unbelievable. The head Catholic said that, how could he say that. Well, it isn't him. It's in the air. It's moving. . . .

Debien: I would like to ask you a very direct question. You're contemplated human sexuality very deeply. How right has the church got it in its current understanding of human sexuality and teaching.

Moore: There's a whole hilarious book which is the bedside reading of at least three women friends of mine called *Eunuchs for the Kingdom of Heaven.* . . . [When the author became a Catholic], she thought, I'm going to research what the church has been saying about sex down the ages, so she produced this book, simply church pronouncement moments at various levels of high authority, about sex. To sum it up, it is the monitoring of sexual experience in those who have it by those who aren't supposed to. That is what's going on. A major problem for these walleys was orgasm. If orgasm comes on too soon, at supper or something, what should you do? Orgasm was a real problem because orgasm suspends the reason, and that's terrible to suspend the reason, all hell breaks loose. All down the ages, we've got two sexual churches: the sexual church of those who are living in ordinary human relations, and then the sexual church of those funny celibate experts. . . .

Debien: How does sexuality fit into the life of a monk, given that there is, in part, a negation going on?

Moore: There is a very good answer, of course, it is Aelred of Rievaulx—it is a wonderful book, *Christian Friendship*. You see, the Catholic Church is being so stupid here. They don't realize that he came out with some definite statement of acceptance of homosexuality as an orientation. It already has traditionally— an old tradition—very cultivated, sophisticated, deep-rooted tradition of same-sex relationships. Not sexually active, but I'm sure they had problems with that and when they did, they had to deal with it. It was seen. But the point is, we've already got an enormous wisdom of bonding with the Catholic tradition throughout Christendom. There was a very regular practice of same-sex friendships, blessed in church, same-sex commitment that sort of thing supposedly. I was supposed to be chaste, but that wasn't the point. Emotionally—this emotional reality has long been well-known in the Catholic tradition at its best— that's the point. And now when at last the taboos lifted, it should be the church, above all, that has alternatives to promiscuity. It would be an absolute revelation.[1]

Moore gave the second interview to Vincent Manning as part of a doctoral thesis that Manning was writing on the impact of HIV/AIDS on the life of the church. He handed the thesis to St. Mary's University, Twickenham London, in October 2019, titled "Encountering Christ through the Passion of HIV: An Inquiry into the Theological Meaning of HIV in the Church."[2] He begins the interview by raising the overarching theme of attitudes to the body. Moore states: "Disgust with my body a tendency or impatience with my body, that sort of thing I would see that is very much aggravated by HIV." Moore tells his interviewer that he had struggled most of his life with self-acceptance and acceptability, where acceptability meant feeling loved just as he was before God. The traditional Catholic approach to sexuality in which he was formed as a young monk and priest, was profoundly flawed and pastorally unhelpful. Sexuality was viewed as a heresy of individualism. He remembers hearing the confessions of young couples preparing for marriage and asking them how far they went as if he were interviewing seminarians. He states: "If I

---

1. ABC Radio National, "Moore," 1–4.
2. Manning, "Encountering Christ," 131–35.

take the last 30 years. It is only fairly recently . . . that I have completely accepted myself as gay. If I go back before that, it was a sort of muddled Catholic consciousness, well I knew I like boys and men, the chemical fact was there, but my attitude to it [was more confusing]."

The interviewer asked Moore about the link between sex and sin. Moore responds by quoting Timothy Radcliffe, who, quoting from Charles Taylor, argued that our attitudes to sex are a relatively recent habit picked up from the Enlightenment thinkers and reinforced in the secular age "because of the Enlightenment concern with control and sex being the symbol of the individual loss of control." Moore also admits to his internalized homophobia, which is his misinformed reaction to the outbreak of AIDS while lecturing in the States. He talks to Manning about the insights gained from Tolle, especially his insight into what he calls the pain-body. The voice of anti-bliss insists that pain is appropriate, and many made it into a habit because they were not supposed to be happy. He also mentions the work of Alice Miller and her insights into childhood trauma at the root of personal and societal problems. Further, Moore speaks about the doctrine of original sin as a massively misinterpreted doctrine since the older traditional interpretation framed the human condition as a deserved punishment and viewed creation as inevitably fallen and dangerous, standing in opposition to the promise of Christ, who comes to bring life to all. It shapes an attitude beyond just the loathing or suspicion of one's body and causes people to resist all that life brings.

MOORE, INNER LONELINESS, AND SEX

Moore's central question is: What has God got to do with sex? He begins by linking two aspects: an affirmation of our specialness and sex. What drives people toward others in relationships is a sense of their specialness. Yet, Moore states that while specialness, on the one hand, urges us to form relationships with people, on the other hand, there exists a truth about the human condition few acknowledge, namely, "no one can know me as I know myself, no one can be present to me as I am thus present to myself. There is a loneliness in each of us that no other person can relieve."[3] Moore is working from the much-stated quote from Augustine's *Confessions*. Augustine states: "You stir man to take pleasure in praising you, because you have made us for yourself, and our heart is restless until

3. Moore, *Inner Loneliness*, 1.

it rests in you."[4] This religious insight points to the affirmation that all our longing, feeling, imagining, and desiring to know, value, and do what is good reach up to and find fulfillment in God. For this reason, to get in touch with our true inner self is to get in touch with a restlessness or inner loneliness that will only find rest in God. We feel lonely since we are situated as humans between the finite and the infinite.

According to Moore, there are three ways to notice this inner loneliness or restlessness.[5] The first way postulates an indirect attentiveness to inner loneliness. The person notices it as simply a lingering discontentment but, sadly, interprets it as something that acts to take away their sense of specialness and nothing more. The cry goes up: life is ultimately dissatisfying, and we have to live with this realization by asserting our specialness, thus snatching what comfort we can along the way through whatever can give us pleasure and meaning. We have to be meaning-makers through self-assertion. Becker's immortality projects said as much. Alternatively, this indirect sense of inner loneliness can bring people to the point of desperation where they seek relief from suffering through a self-medicating approach in the form of alcohol or non-prescribed medications.

The second way postulates another kind of awakening to this inner loneliness. It seeks a remedy for it in another person, say a spouse or close friend, a treatment that will never be fully satisfied since no person or persons can sustain us ultimately. Nietzsche also captures the possible reactions to the first and second ways when speaking about the madman who runs through his town, shouting out the devastating consequences of what our self-assertion brings upon us.[6] Yet another consequence of our self-assertion is that it brings with it the denial of death.

The third way awakens in us the realization that this deep and inescapable feeling of restlessness points toward a religious truth and is not without reason. However, through trust and patient attention, our presence and our vulnerability lead us to search for God, the mysteriously desiring and desired One who is the source and terminus of our inner loneliness. Then, God leads us to love our neighbor as ourselves. Here, we affirm the connection between self-love and self-gift. Our search to assuage our inner loneliness leads us to God, and God leads us back to our neighbor. Thus, God is central to a good sex life.

4. Augustine, *Confessions*, I.i.1:3.
5. Moore, *Inner Loneliness*, 14–15.
6. Moore, *Inner Loneliness*, 16.

For Moore, God is the only companion who can fully dispel this inner loneliness. God is "the One who is." Each of us is an idea in the mind of God, and God causes the idea of us to be. Denis Edwards states: "This description of God as the cause of all that exists is brought into dialogue with the inner loneliness. Then God is seen as the one who by nature is concerned with my existence. The lonely human person desires that there be one who by nature is person and friend in an unlimited way. My lonely self-awareness is grounded in one who is the idea of me, and of all reality, existing."[7] I discussed this extensively in chapter 3.

Further, when we meet God and God's desire to "be-for" we will experience more intensely our relationship to others, for "experiencing myself as 'special' absolutely and 'for God,' for the ultimate mystery, I have a much fuller conviction of my specialness as a gift to others. . . . It follows that until a person has that fullness of self-love, which is only found in being for God, he or she is correspondingly restricted in the power to love the neighbor."[8] If Moore's axiom "to be myself for another" is his way of defining a human being, then here is Moore's way of "defining" God, namely, "God is the other within that ends an otherwise ineluctable inner loneliness."[9] Moore knows very well that we cannot strictly define God, but he wants to affirm that this "infinitely mysterious reality partners our inner loneliness and that nothing else can."[10] Knowing this Partner from within, we know our worth not only from ourselves but from the ground of all that is, deepening our conviction about our value and the value of others.

This Partner is a Being who is involved with us and for us. God's being Godself and being for us are identical. However, once we are caught in the gaze of this God, we find that God has interests everywhere and for everything, even for our sex life. We do not have to embark on a path of autonomous self-assertion against others to maintain our worth. Instead, deepening our sense of the value of others fills us with trust and moves us away from mistrust. Our strangeness to each other does not have to be a threatening experience. Intimacy with others starts with intimacy with God, and this beginning makes intimacy with others much freer, even with others with whom one is not particularly close (universal love).[11]

7. Edwards, *What Are They Saying?*, 57.
8. Moore, *Inner Loneliness*, 13.
9. Moore, *Inner Loneliness*, 18.
10. Moore, *Inner Loneliness*, 18.
11. Moore, *Inner Loneliness*, 19.

A New Awareness

SEX, SELF-LOVE, AND SELF-GIFT

Moore affirms that sex, self-love, and self-gift are intrinsically linked. This union is not of our making. God creates this dynamic polarity in us, but they go out of alignment. Self-love unshared generates further insecurity and unease, such that we want everything our way. The desire to dominate comes from a repressed psyche wherein we banish proper self-love.[12] This distorted self-love brings about self-hatred. The problem, then, becomes a deep distrust of happiness, a blindness to free unconditional joy in the human mind, and, ultimately, a refusal to accept the connection between self-love and self-gift. We do not want to admit that something in our life is not our own making. We prefer to make life difficult rather than being grateful for it, for not being grateful is the surest sign that it is about our making. The lack of connection puts us at odds with our sexuality and our fear of losing control and being out of control. Freud recognizes this tension in sexuality, the fear of losing control, the desire to keep it in our control against the desire for union.[13]

For Moore, we can move forward on a fully human path in relation to sexuality and sexual activity when we accept the union between self-love and self-gift. This connection causes us to realize that we participate in a reality (God) for whom "'to be' *is* 'to love' (and) for whom 'to be' is 'to be for.'"[14] The distinction between flourishing and making others thrive does not exist in God. God does not have happiness; God is happiness. God's happiness is the happiness of all things. God's self-enjoyment is "outgoingness."[15] God's compassion is the compassion of desiring happiness in all things. If we participate in this mystery, then for us also, "to be" is also "to be for." Our mistrust of happiness is the biggest obstacle to believing in this kind of God. We do not believe in our spontaneous goodness. We do not think our deepest desire is to make another person happy. We may even seek to justify our disbelief by saying that happiness and the desire for boundless bliss is a selfish attitude. It is simply too good to be true. But were we to accept that our spontaneous goodness is natural and our desire for happiness is good, we would take a completely different approach to our lives and the world in which we live. Then, it

---

12. Moore, *Inner Loneliness*, 47.
13. Moore, *Inner Loneliness*, 67.
14. Moore, *Inner Loneliness*, 25.
15. Moore, *Inner Loneliness*, 36.

follows that "being well" and "being for" are one, and their unity derives from an identity of "being at all" with "being for all."

Moore concludes that the "human being, as spontaneous lover, is the image of the one who *is* love and I do have an inkling of what it would be to be the love of someone for whom I love. I sense with an altogether new intensity, that I *am*. To love is to feel in oneself the current that flows out of the heart of all existence."[16] The desire to be wholly understood and accepted, which arises from our inner loneliness, leads to an infinite love requirement that challenges and demands us to extend ourselves to others.[17] Thus, Moore understands compassion in this way: "Compassion is an infinite happiness trying to realize itself in a tortured world." If God's "to be" is to make us happy, then, participating in God, our "to be" is to make others happy. What is in God by nature is in us by our participation in the One who *is* it by nature.[18] This is the real world, the being of God, who is also the "why" of it all. Reality is not our desire for personal significance that becomes a motive for self-assertion and self-making through denying creatureliness and death. This is Becker's thoughtful insight and is the basis of our wrongful making of the world and human relationships. Our assertions of autonomy are not reality but an unintelligent anxiety-provoked reaction to the primary need for significance. Nor are we thrown into the world without guidance or a lifeline and made to look after ourselves only. Our need for meaning is a fundamental insecurity that brings us to the One whose "own being" is a "being for me" or a being with lovingness, in which the lovingness is the person's very being.[19]

MOORE, SEX, AND THE INCEST TABOO

Moore accounts for the split within self-love and the separation between desire as unlimited and desire to be controlled to the historical development of the incest taboo. First, in his account of early tribal life, when sexual awareness first emerged, the natural inclination was to seek sexual union with members of the same family. Sexual union within one's own family was grounded in security and safety. In the family, the sexual

---

16. Moore, *Inner Loneliness*, 30.
17. Moore, *Inner Loneliness*, 33.
18. Moore, *Inner Loneliness*, 34.
19. Moore, *Inner Loneliness*, 41.

explorer found a family-friendly mirror to validate the feelings that they were having at the birth of self-awareness. With the introduction of the incest taboo, young men were required to venture into a more threatening situation with the twin poles of passion and friendship.

In tribal societies, the incest taboo was a helpful mechanism of repression at a time of low self-awareness and high societal compliance, enshrined in ritual and tribal practices to encourage venturing into a broader social setting aided by tribal elders. Over many centuries, these beginnings of emerging sexuality and the growth of self-awareness have become a powerful private feeling that the maturing young person must integrate. The feelings left their original context within the community of the tribe. In the nuclear family of modern societies, the young man and woman "stumble on their sexuality as a purely private event and a new and powerful force erupting within and having no connection apparently with the already familiar world of brothers and sisters and parents."[20]

The mature, self-aware person knows that nature cannot tell us who we are and what we are to feel. What was once taboo guided by tribal elders now becomes repression. Moore concludes that sexual feeling "deprived of its friendly familiar mirror to validate itself in, is repressed, forced underground whence it exerts that compulsive tyrannical power which we have seen characterizes *all* repressed desire."[21] It is our sexual desire in its privatized and repressed form that feels similar to an unknown powerful force, and therefore threatening, that generates the fear of losing control and leads to the split between desire and control within self-love. Moore adds that this unease within us due to the powerful force of sexual desire is "symptomatic of the most fundamental unease of all, our unease with the huge, mysterious personal force in which 'we live and move and have our very being.'"[22] If we were less fearful of God, we would be more open to sex and sexuality. If we were more aware that God created us desiring and desirable creatures, we would be more at home with our sexuality. Thus, we need to find God for sex to be more fulfilling.

---

20. Moore, *Inner Loneliness*, 52.
21. Moore, *Inner Loneliness*, 52.
22. Moore, *Inner Loneliness*, 53.

SEXUALITY, SEXUAL IDENTITY, AND GOD

Moore links sexual identity with the profound experience of loneliness and our relationship with God. He views the Oedipus story as a myth describing how men and women developed from a tribal-based set of norms and practices around sexual identity to sexual identity as emerging from an inner experience and growth in self-awareness. During this shift in our psychic history, self-awareness is strong enough to pull away from the "psychic womb" of the tribe and to rely on one's own emotional experience as a measure of fulfillment.[23] Thus, we discover our sexual identity only through a relationship with God since only God can address our loneliness. While man and woman are to find meaning in each other, they will do so only by seeing their significance in God.[24]

Moore has always believed there must be a connection between sexuality and God. He provides a rudimentary map of sexual development in the early years of life, starting from zero to one year old when the child enjoys an oceanic consciousness with the mother. Moore calls this the "will" phase. From two to four, the separation phase begins, noted by Margaret Mahler. From four to five comes an identification with gender and the establishing of sexual identity. This is Freud's Oedipal phase. The male child suppresses the sexual opposite, their anima, thus repressing their female aspect, which is part and parcel of their psychic makeup. Here is where the incest taboo emerges since one's family members are too easily identified with their repressed anima.[25] Yet, even as we develop our sexual identity, an encasement of identity at the age of five, with no room to grow, equates to a fixation by the ego and the arresting of our proper sexual development.

Moore is convinced about the vital importance of sexual identity. We are woven into the "whole continuum of nature" through the three points of dependence on sustenance, sexuality, and mortality, three aspects of our embodied humanity.[26] They are the three great reminders of our creaturehood. Sexuality stands out among the three since it makes "a deeper road into personhood" and brings persons together.[27] Moore assesses that these three aspects of humanity not only remind us of our

23. Moore, *Inner Loneliness*, 57.
24. Moore, *Inner Loneliness*, 61.
25. Moore, *Inner Loneliness*, 72.
26. Moore, "Sex, God," 153.
27. Moore, *Inner Loneliness*, 73.

creaturehood, but they also accentuate "cosmic loneliness."[28] Again, nature can tell us what we are, but nature remains silent to the question of our identity: who we are. Our self-awareness drivers us to know why and to whom we belong. Nature is silent to these questions.[29] This silence creates the conditions for inner loneliness. One takes on the mantle of a "cosmic orphan." When people are caught up in the problem of loneliness and meaning, the answer can only come from God and each other through ownership of and negotiation with our contrasexuality. Society may assign men and women specific roles according to their gender as a way of making sense of our sexual identity. But we must look to one another and within to understand our sexual identity. The problem becomes: How does one align sex with passion and friendship, with sexuality as a powerful attraction to another, with sexuality as identity, and with sexual identity as the final addition of personhood?[30]

Since our sexuality accentuates our inner loneliness and makes us turn to one another, there remains the problem of how to do this well. In the myth of the garden, the biblical writer proposes that the immediate effect of losing touch with God and our creatureliness is a felt awkwardness between the sexes due to a linking of their loneliness with the loss of God.[31] This awkwardness is the root cause of all our sexual disorders. Being out of touch with God leads to being out of friendship with our body and all our desires. Shame generates lust. The problem is not so much a lack of self-control in sexual matters. The problem is being out of touch and therefore, "*out of friendship* with my body and its desires."[32]

MEN, WOMEN, AND DOMINATION

A very brief overview of Western society would have to conclude that for the last two thousand years, our culture has been preoccupied with male sexual identity. Men have couched female sexual identity in terms of metaphors like seductress, temptress, witch, and siren who lure men off course and onto the rocks.[33] Women's nonalignment to men in patriarchal

---

28. Moore, *Inner Loneliness*, 73.
29. Moore, "Sex, God," 153.
30. Moore, *Inner Loneliness*, 73–74.
31. Moore, *Inner Loneliness*, 74.
32. Moore, "Sex, God," 155.
33. Moore, *Inner Loneliness*, 74.

societies are hardly felt because they do not have a voice. The consequence of all these factors leads to men alienating themselves from women and seeing their own sexual identity, contrary to women, dominantly emphasized. Domination results in control as "the name of the game."[34] Consequent to these factors, men displace their felt alienation or inner loneliness through the domination of women rather than understanding their inner loneliness as pointing them toward God. Therefore, the story of the fall signals that a felt awkwardness between the sexes, arising from a refusal of creaturehood, also gives rise to the desire in men to control women. The Catholic Church today finds itself amid a shift in consciousness towards interiority and conversion. A distorted spirituality emphasizing self-control above all else, and control of women will fail to touch people. The only way to enjoy our sexuality and discover anew its positive spirit is by opening ourselves to the real God stripped of male projections.

Our sexual identity and our quest to understand it has moved from a tribal situation where leaders gave sexual identity to boys and girls to a modern society where people are self-aware, and identity is privatized. When culture relegates sexual identity to the private sphere of our lives, cosmic loneliness endures. But the only one who can answer our gnawing sense of cosmic loneliness is God. Because of this, sex and God are intimately connected.[35]

MOORE, THE FALL, AND SEXUALITY

Moore offers several insights concerning the reasons for our unease with our sexuality by examining the myth of the garden in the book of Genesis. A psychological and interiorly oriented interpretation of the Genesis story has been central to his understanding of original sin. Christians generally are familiar with the elements of the biblical story: the garden; Adam in an undifferentiated existence; the creation of Eve; the tree of the knowledge of good and evil; the command by God not to eat the fruit; the eating of the fruit, after which Adam and Eve feel shame at their nakedness; and finally, God's question to them, Who told you that you were naked? Moore interprets the anxiety felt by Adam and Eve to cover their nakedness as displaying an uneasiness with their sexuality.

---

34. Moore, "Sex, God," 156.
35. Moore, *Inner Loneliness*, 76–77.

They feel shame at being naked.[36] What was once a friend has now become a threat. He concludes that their loss of intimacy with God equates to a loss of friendship with their sexual desires. It will only be through overcoming a sense of inner loneliness, which no other human being can overcome and that only God can overcome, that they will rediscover sexual desire without shame or anxiety.

Again, Moore demonstrates that one's dislike for sex and sexuality results from not knowing God, where "like" means "being friendly with." This alienation from the true God causes humans to construct a patriarchal culture where men have found their sexual identity in God but where men project maleness onto God to dominate women.[37] In a distorted culture, men view sexual passion as something to be mastered rather than shared, celebrated, and enjoyed. Moore affirms:

> My sexual being is the first big revelation to me of my *natural* being, of my being a product of nature: and this provokes in me the realization that that which tells me *what* I am cannot tell me *who* I am. And this condition, of seeking from my environment to know who I am and hearing only silence is the most radical description of *loneliness* that there can be. Thus, sexual identity does not find its meaning through the opposite sex, because it is a loneliness that questions the stars. That is why men have put their domestic life at risk by hitching their wagons to stars, and why women now are at last beginning to do the same. What we have before us is a massive negotiation of a deep and ill-understood loneliness, a cosmic loneliness, a loneliness out of which we cannot lift each other. And we have met it before. It is the ineluctable loneliness that only an intimate experience of the Creator can end for us.[38]

Through this intimate experience with our Creator, the person is not split in their self-love. There is no fear of desire, especially the strong desires of our sexuality, namely, the desires the Creator has planted deep within us. We can venture toward one another with passion and friendship. We can appropriate a sexual identity that is more whole.

---

36. Moore, *Inner Loneliness*, 68.
37. Moore, *Inner Loneliness*, 58.
38. Moore, *Inner Loneliness*, 77.

SEXUAL IDENTITY, ORIGINAL SIN, AND MALENESS

For Moore, there is a relationship between original sin and sexual identity. Drawing from the Jungian authors Eugene Monick and James Wyly, Moore proposes that sexual identity is not adequately integrated into the psychosexual development of men at the early phases of human development.[39] This maldevelopment is linked to original sin. In this case, original sin establishes a wobble in the development of our sexual identity and into a stuckness and shutupness in an early stage of consciousness. Confining ourselves to this early stage of growth results in several biases within us that seek to get the better of others. The situation gives rise to male domination that comes in many forms, including the compulsivity to political power and the spread of pornography. One of vices of these biases is lust. The shutupness can give rise to a compulsivity prompting Saint Paul to speak about such sin as highly entrenched. The law of Moses will not be able to help since it compels us not to be compulsive out of fear of punishment. For Paul, only the Spirit of the risen Lord can free us. What we once saw as a problem with desire itself, we now see as a problem with the confinement and control of desire. The confinement of desire causes difficulty and an inability to never successfully or wholly affirm "the goodness of sexual pleasure."[40]

Moore states:

> There is a stage in the development of the male psyche when the man has discovered his sexual potency but is still, emotionally, subject to the mother. He may be sexually active, but within her parameters. . . . And the main thesis of my authors is that the male psyche in our Western culture has not developed beyond a relationship to woman that is shaped by the relationship of the young man to the mother. Obviously individual men outgrow this filial stance. But we are talking about a maturing process that needs to happen on a universal scale, where inertia is the rule. There is, after all, a dramatic disparity between the way a man relates to his spouse and the way, among men, he talks about women. . . . So long as the latter way of thinking remains immature, any advances made in the former are fragile, certainly are not strong enough to set the pace. The culture, its assumptions, society's law, the whole vast web of interconnected understandings that make a society, still represent, as women

39. Moore, "Bedded Axle-Tree," 212.
40. Moore, *Let This Mind*, 105.

know very well, an idea of the status of women, that is not that of equal partner with man. What I am suggesting is that this by now established subjugation of woman can be, and has to be, seen as the fixation of man in a state previous to equality with woman, the state, that is, of son subject to the mother, which assuredly is the opposite of the superior state but which, precisely through being in the inferior position, feels compelled to capture the superior position. The point is that equality is an emotional achievement.[41]

The pattern is "mother domination, split off of the phallos involving male inflation, and an anarchic phallos instilling a sense of limitless grandiosity, the crucial fact that phallos thus exiled can only disturb and destroy, cannot heal; the necessity for humiliation under the control of 'other gods'-as we should say, 'a higher power'; and the final reintegration of phallos, now the origin not of domination but of union."[42] A more authentic understanding of the male phallus must occur in our Western culture.

First, men need to acknowledge the problem. Currently, in the male culture, the phallos means male sexual energy prevented from growth by an emotional fixation on the mother, and so, exiled from the male psyche, the person finds expression in "symbols of domination, grandiosity, spires, obelisks, and the rest, to say nothing of nuclear missiles."[43] Moore proposes that until we unburden ourselves to one another as men and admit to each other the awe we hold in the male phallos, our male sexuality will never be fully integrated. The never-admitted male cult of the phallos has displaced itself into all the assumptions of a male-controlled world. It gives rise to the inflated lust for power in straight men and the more overt phallic quest in gay men.

Second, men need to resort to a higher power that is not equivalent to some humiliation of men. Men must accept that transformation happens because of a gift or grace.[44] Moore offers Mary, Mother of the Church, as an example of a mother who had no dominating relationship over her Son, even as she endured the consequences of her consent. She is the second Eve subject only to God, and her life pattern is God-dependent and spousal. Moore asserts: "We have lost touch with the woman

41. Moore, "Bedded Axle-Tree," 212–13.
42. Moore, "Bedded Axle-Tree," 214.
43. Moore, "Bedded Axle-Tree," 214.
44. Moore, "Bedded Axle-Tree," 223.

who inwardly makes a surrender to God terrifying in its totality, and outwardly is exposed to the gossip of neighbors."[45] In her stead, we have portrayed Mary's response to the Annunciation as one of a dignified lady holding a ladylike conversation with a visiting angel and collapsing her consent into something that disguises the terror toward what lay ahead. Restoring the mystery, the starkness and terror of Mary's consent, and the spousal dimension of her consent and taking away the image of the virginity linked to motherhood would go a long way to relating to Mary more deeply if a spiritual renewal is to happen.[46]

Third, there is a renewal that comes from surrendering to the risen Christ. Moore states:

> The center is where I come to know, in every fiber of my being, that I am gift. If I am a gift, there is a giver. And if I *am* the gift, there is no me to whom the gift is made. The giver then gives not "to me" but "to be," gives to be to that which is not, and thus is being itself in respect of which I am not.... Toward their supreme truth of myself as gifted, I am drawn as to a magnetic center. But the center has a power to draw that far exceeds all philosophical understanding, and that overcomes the huge resistance and systemic bias that we call sin. Here the sense of being nothing but gift, of not being anything for the giver to give to, of not having this solid substantive self that resists description as givenness-to-nothing, here at the center is the mystery that is Jesus, God's gift not to God, but to us.... (Jesus) empties himself because he is radically empty of self. This perfection of death is love and of love as death is the vibrant heart of all existence.... Jesus became the center for desire, became all of himself, once he had died: for then he could make himself known fully to his own.... It is of the first importance, for the whole work of transformation to which we are called in our time, to hold firmly in focus the presence of the risen Jesus, for it is in this presence that we come to know ourselves as gift, and it is only in so knowing ourselves that we can have that fullness of self-love that liberates phallos from the *libido dominandi*.[47]

---

45. Moore, "Bedded Axle-Tree," 221.
46. Moore, "Bedded Axle-Tree," 222–23.
47. Moore, "Bedded Axle-Tree," 223–24.

A New Awareness

SELF-AWARENESS, SEX, AND AROUSAL

Moore takes a further tilt toward understanding sexuality and arousal, again informed by a Jungian perspective. With our consciousness explosion into greater self-awareness, the newly emerging self identifies with its biological gender to secure its sexual identity. The self is fused to gender. Boys will identify with their penis and girls with their vaginas. When a man and a woman are attracted to each other, something more arises through sexual arousal: the desire for attention, stimulation, and physical pleasure. This same self has both male and female dimensions.

In chapter 5, I described Jung's understanding of the journey of individuation, a process whereby we discover that we are more than our personae and our masks or roles in life. Women who have invested so much in their children may need to come back to themselves and find their strengths and personal interests again. Men who have done so much in the career space, especially competitive environments, may need to discover their empathy again. Within each of us, we have our contrasexual opposite or ideal of women (anima) by which men are drawn to women and that men project onto women and the ideal of men (animus) by which women are drawn to men and that women project onto men. These situations of attraction and projection need intelligent and responsible negotiation by both men and women. Such negotiation happens by means of a larger self.

In sexual attraction, a man is in love with his maleness and the fact that he can sustain an erection. The female dimension of the man is the other aspect (anima). Moore calls the female aspect "*both* myself *and* another," and he acknowledges the female dimension as his "inner partner."[48] The "inner partner" of the man and his maleness come into an interplay between the man and the woman through sexual attraction. The "inner partner" is present so that men can experience the woman's desire for him and enlarge his feelings for her. It functions to bring the two persons into a relationship. It fuels the desire to live for each other. However, knowledge of the "inner partner" will not sustain a relationship in the long term. The woman who is physically standing before the man cannot be his inner partner. The inner partner is an archetype of the feminine for the man, just as her inner partner is an archetype of the masculine within the woman. The "inner partner" is an ideal. With the explosion of self-awareness into consciousness, the "inner partner" must

48. Moore, "Original Sin, Sex," 90.

take a back seat and a negotiation with the historical person in front of them must take place.

At this point, Moore brings the garden story into a Jungian perspective. The story of Adam and Eve depicts the woman Eve brought to Adam as if drawn from his inner partner (anima). Adam recognizes her as "bone of my bone flesh of my flesh." There is no distinction within consciousness between dreaming and waking at this point of the story.[49] Adam feels the woman to be part of himself. If the creation of Eve is akin to being in a dream, the fall is akin to waking from a dream and a differentiation between waking and dreaming within consciousness. Moore surmises that for this reason, the garden story is incestuous since the feeling is one of being mated with one's inner partner. However, at the narrative's end, the flaming sword preventing the couple from returning to the garden is meant to explain the restriction of the incest taboo.[50]

From a mysterious oneness in the garden, they now move beyond the garden into an awareness of being two separate people, only this time, there is a craving that the man feels. It is the craving for sameness between the woman Eve before him, now a distinct identity, and his "inner partner." In the "fallen" condition, the woman Eve has a strangeness about her through Adam's eyes and the man Adam has a strangeness about him for the woman. She is not the same as the man's "inner partner" or his "bone of my bone." Suppose one was completely in touch with the woman before him historically as well as his inner partner; the woman before him would not seem so strange. But he is not. And this all occurs because of the birth of self-awareness, highlighting growth in consciousness, while at the same time lowlighting the "inner partner."[51] Beyond the garden and through our birth in self-awareness, we cannot feel each other's desire as our own. The advent of self-awareness demotes the "inner partner" and demotes God. It accentuates our separateness. If the man is to find bliss, regain oneness, and overcome estrangement "with his or her own life in the other," he cannot return to the garden. Self-awareness is here to stay. He can only move forward. To move forward is to negotiate the woman before him with his archetypal inner partner. To go back to the garden is to lose self-awareness.

It is only in the experience of death that union and moving beyond estrangement is possible. In this case, the death experience is not "on

49. Moore, "Original Sin, Sex," 93.
50. Moore, "Original Sin, Sex," 91.
51. Moore, "Original Sin, Sex," 92.

the other side" or in a world after death.[52] It is not death as a physical cessation of life. The experience of death that brings about the union between man and woman is dying to one's ego consciousness many times throughout one's life, thus transforming. To believe in God is to believe in life changed through Jesus. For us, living after the fall, the situation is "Paradise lost to the dream" or equating dream with waking as well as "Paradise thrust into waking by the Son."[53] In Jesus risen, we receive a foretaste of an age to come, awakened to limitless dimensions.[54] In the words of Paul: "There is no more male or female, slave or free, Greek or Jew, but only, and in all, Christ" (Gal 3:28). We move from death to life and into a non-estrangement between men and women.

SEXUAL DESIRE AND THE THEOLOGY OF THE BODY

Moore turns his attention to *The Theology of the Body* by John Paul II. The book is a profound philosophical work and worthy of reading. However, Moore sums up the document's overall direction in these words: the principle of "a lifelong commitment of man and woman to each other with a procreative outcome."[55] In his estimation, John Paul II keeps the whole approach to human sexuality "closed to the Garden of Love." For the pope, any sex at full blast is equivalent to lust. The pope's language did not speak to people about their own experience. If good sexual desire is taking a risk and making a fool of oneself, exposing oneself, and entering a "game," which is a prelude to entering the mystery of love, wrong sexual desire is not seeking pleasure but a desire for rivalry. Rivalistic desire occurs when one fails to recognize that "this submerged likeness to you surfaces and comes together with your likeness to me."[56] In other words, sex is "a drama of confluence in which people's desire for each other is fired by the desire they are awakening in each other."[57] So, if sexual desire is triangulated, according to mimetic theory, then "John" and "Mary" are models and respondents, and the object is their mutual attraction.

---

52. Moore, "Original Sin, Sex," 92.
53. Moore, "Original Sin, Sex," 97.
54. Moore, "Original Sin, Sex," 97.
55. Moore, "Word for Sexual Desire," 207.
56. Moore, "Word for Sexual Desire," 209.
57. Moore, "Word for Sexual Desire," 209.

If sex is the halfway house between desire and union, Moore states, "desire is love trying to happen."[58] He affirms that "sexual desire is the hint of the ultimate mystery of us that is love. And this quality of mystery shows itself in sexual desires, feeling different from just ordinary wanting things."[59] Unfortunately, the official Church often goes from sex to having a baby, avoiding the whole subject of sexual desire. If desire is love trying to happen, then it is as if each person is consenting to their desire to reach a higher activity. Such higher activity is none other than a different level of being.[60] Moore also proposes that the intent of "desire is love trying to happen" is part of the nature of contemplative prayer. As I noted in chapter 3, Abbot Chapman calls contemplative prayer an "idiotic state," that is, "the state of desire on the way to being love."[61]

In light of John Paul II's theology of the body, we have a substantial theology giving us insight into the meaning and value of the body, human sexuality, and married life.[62] John Paul II speaks about Adam possessing a deep existential solitude. God, understanding Adams's aloneness, brings forth Eve, the woman, from "bone of my bone." In the garden, their sexual expression also expresses their intimacy with God. The pope describes how, after the fall, Adam and Eve lost intimacy with God through disobedience. Humankind's being out of touch with God means also being out of touch within themselves so that they can no longer order their lower-level nature to their higher-level nature. They can no longer have the higher order of their being (committed love) befriending the lower order (sexual pleasure). The result is a failure of the lower order to obey the requirements of the higher order (sexual pleasure within the sexual act but open to the gift of children). The lower order deteriorates into a lust-filled rebellion against the higher demand.[63] The pope, then, postulates that Adam and Eve become embarrassed at their animality (sexual genitals) and, feeling the shame of being naked, cover themselves. Thus, in the pope's mind, disobedience (eating the fruit when told not to) and shame (feeling naked) are linked to lust. With the breaking of the lower level to its proper ordering by the higher level, lust is born. The drama for the pope begins in disobedience proceeds to lust,

58. Moore, "Word for Sexual Desire," 212.
59. Moore, "Word for Sexual Desire," 205.
60. Moore, "Word for Sexual Desire" 222.
61. Moore, "Word for Sexual Desire," 222.
62. Moore, "Crisis of an Ethic," 169.
63. Moore, "Crisis of an Ethic," 162.

and lust gives rise to shame. Sex and sexual activity become shameful because of a breakdown due to disobedience and lust.[64]

Moore presents an alternative interpretation of the myth of the garden using the terms of *shame* and *lust*. He assesses the understanding by John Paul II as downgrading the value of sex in itself. He agrees with the pope that Adam and Eve suffer a clouding of their minds and hearts due to the rejection of their creaturely status. Their denial of creatureliness follows the serpent's affirmation that should they eat the fruit, they will be like gods. Their denial of creaturehood has them shamefully judging their sexual organs after eating the fruit. Their sexual organs are a sign to remind them of their animality, something they cannot abide by once the fruit has been eaten. From shame at their sexual organs, lust follows.

For Moore, the progression is first, the denial of creaturehood; second, shame at the sexual organs that embarrass them with their animality far below a godlike status; and finally, lust. He postulates that the approach taken by John Paul II has the effect of communicating that sexual desire should be something curbed through control. This curbing puts a negative tone on sex. Moore, meanwhile, affirms that married couples find overindulging in sexual activity the least of their worries. It is more the case that couples are challenged to fan into a flame their sexual activity, which is a critical element in their intimacy.[65] In his words, we all desire to be desired by the one we desire. The fulfillment of genuine desire requires a continual dying of the ego. Dying to the ego means decentering the ego and making God the center of our lives. Lust is not the sexual passion that claims autonomy over the control of the will. Lust is the sexual passion that derives from falsely claiming to be God or assuming godlike status.

Moore considers Augustine to have gotten sex wrong through his interpretation of the myth of the garden. Augustine misses the insight that Adam and Eve end up in lust because they are caught in a denial of their creaturehood. In Moore's eyes, Augustine forgot that God created sex for men and women to enjoy and to turn into a life commitment. Sex is the halfway house between desire and love. The commitment of love underpins the relational nature of desire, the importance of mutual desirability, and the intention of desire.[66] The task of men and women is to restore genuine desire and accomplish its intentionality toward love.

64. Moore, "Crisis of an Ethic," 163.
65. Moore, "Crisis of an Ethic," 166.
66. Moore, "Crisis of an Ethic," 167.

The task is not, as the pope implies, to bring sexual passion under the control of the will. For Moore, sexual disrespect is akin to "cheating," that is, where one is "not making a fool of myself, not exposing myself, not taking a risk not entering the game, which is the prelude to the mystery. I don't capture another person for myself sexually, the way I do this in the market. I do it in a way offensive to life's mystery embodied in me."[67] In other words, "wrong sex" is a state where sex falls short of being a mutual attraction reaching up to the mystery of love.

MOORE, SEX, AND SEXUAL DESIRE

Moore turns his attention toward sexual desire itself. The standard view of classical antiquity is that a human is a rational animal. We are distinguished from the animal world by our reason. The body and the pleasures of the body are viewed as a threat to rationality. Moore earlier diagnoses our felt danger as actually the fear of being out of control in the face of powerful psychic sexual forces. The fear results in a split in our self-love between desire and control. The Roman Catholic Church, through its teaching Magisterium, recognizes the intense form of pleasure known as male orgasm as fitting within the marital act and directed toward procreation. The conclusion is that oral sex, anal sex, and mutual masturbation, which also are forms of sexual pleasure that contribute to sexual intimacy, are considered to be not open to life and so morally prohibited. Enjoyment and pleasure facilitate the relational dimension of marriage but may have little to do with procreation. However, Moore affirms that a more holistic approach would take great care to accentuate that pleasure from sexual activity is part of a multidimensional approach to sexual intimacy, even though it sometimes has no regard for procreation.

Within such a context, Moore seeks to readdress an unbalanced approach to sexual intimacy. He views the problem in these words: "that the Church when it talks of sex is talking a language that does not touch their [the faithful's] experience of it."[68] This lack of communication betrays a mind behind the teaching that does not honor sexual desire for what it is, namely, how people awaken sexually to each other.[69] He wants to explore sexual desire as a vital force channeled into mutual attraction. He asks:

---

67. Moore, "Word for Sexual Desire," 208.
68. Moore, "Word for Sexual Desire," 203.
69. Moore, "Word for Sexual Desire," 203–4.

"Why should I thank God for an erection, or for the more diffused bodily pleasure of a woman?" Moore turns to Girard and the mimetic nature of desire. Desire without rivalry involves the couple in an intense mutual attraction whose "intentionality is love."[70] Moore states: "Sex is the way it is because it is the halfway house between desire in the raw . . . and love."[71] We can express desire in this manner since the wanting of sexual desire is like no other wanting. Each of us wants to let the other know that we feel excited. Eros (passion, desire, and attractive arousal) moves toward or "gets a whiff of agape." However, sexual desire is also a hint of the ultimate Mystery of God, which is love. It leads us out of the shallow and into "deeper waters."[72]

SEX, FLESH, AND SPIRIT

Christian Scriptures have been used over the centuries to speak to sexual passion through Saint Paul's reference to "the flesh." Equating sexual passion with flesh has been a source of great confusion leading to various understandings of the nature of sex. In Gal 5:16 and following, Paul contrasts the opposites of flesh and spirit. A commonsense interpretation of the text by homilists often presents a dichotomy between flesh and spirit: "There is a spiritual part of me that inclines to unselfish behavior and worship and delights in spiritual things, and there is another part of me that is centered on physical gratification in all its forms; and these two are opposed engaging in the long tug-of-war for my consent. The purpose of prayer and spiritual discipline is to ensure the victory of the first, higher part of me, over the second, lower part of me."[73] Moore assesses the difficulty with this interpretation. The interpretation suggests that physical gratification or fleshly pleasure is sinful. Thus, the interpretation moves away from an understanding which affirms that sexual pleasure is a gift of God.

Moore's reading of Paul's "flesh" is quite different from the reading made by homilists who bear down on the sins of the flesh and, in so doing, often downgrade sexual pleasure. For Moore, God has given us our embodiment as a gift. The flesh is not the whole of human nature. The flesh is a situation in which we understand what we are and who we are through

---

70. Moore, "Word for Sexual Desire," 205.
71. Moore, "Word for Sexual Desire," 205.
72. Moore, "Word for Sexual Desire," 206.
73. Moore, *Let This Mind*, 97.

a partial view of human nature. The sin of the flesh comes from a partial view of human nature raised to be the full view of human nature. What is a vital dimension of human nature can quickly and mistakenly come to mean the whole of human nature. The partial view raised to the position of the full view is the flaw Paul is seeking to redress. When the flesh is the whole view of human nature, a more extensive statement affirming the spirit's importance is neglected. In this case, flesh as a dimension of human nature is elevated by homilists to mean the whole of human nature. Unfortunately, the flesh is not only equated with the whole of nature but, for many, the flesh is equivalent to sex and sexual pleasure. This false interpretation of the flesh further posits a view that understands the satisfaction of the flesh as something to be denied.[74] Such a position does not answer the question, What has sexual pleasure got to do with our lives even when it is subsumed into a more extensive view?

Moore places his understanding of the flesh into a broader context. He affirms that just as a distortion can happen in our understanding of the proper purposes of money and power when placed into a narrow context, so too distortion can happen in our understanding of sex when put into a limited context. The limited context is the other side of the boundary set by the momentous crisis of Oedipal development. The boundary stands between moving forward to other developments, on the one hand, and thinking of the Oedipal crisis as the final crisis. The Oedipal crisis is not the final development point in a person's life. The person who views the Oedipal crisis as the final growth is consenting to a refusal "to grow, to take new shapes," which Moore understands as sin.[75] Since the Oedipal crisis requires self-negation, repression, sexual estrangement, and obedience to cultural-social-familial biases, the tendency of sin is equating such psychic mechanisms with our final growth. Here, the accusing voice of original sin claims dominion in our lives with the accusation, "So, what else is there."[76] In the Pauline understanding, living according to the flesh results from adhering to a distorted voice that consequently shuts the door to a fuller view of sex and sexuality.

Moore reframes sin: all wickedness is spiritual and not, as many homilists assert, "of the flesh." All sin is centrally self-closure rather than spiritual openness. It is a set of spiritual attitudes that confine us in a pattern where we refuse to grow. Conversely, life in the spirit inspires

74. Moore, *Let This Mind*, 98.
75. Moore, *Let This Mind*, 99.
76. Moore, *Let This Mind*, 99.

attitudes away from the mistaken conviction that we are "unchanging parameters of those passions."[77] Thus, there is no tug-of-war between the flesh and the spirit, the lower and higher levels. There is a dialectical tension between "real desire and an inertial tendency to stay where we are." God's Spirit puts pressure on our radical desire to grow, and this affirmation completely stands in contrast to what Paul calls "the way of the flesh," that is, our inertial tendency to stay where we are. So, living by the flesh is equivalent to living by our appetites, which are God-given and good, but then also remaining in a pattern that is meant to be only the beginning of a long-life growth process. Moore's psychological perspective for this scriptural point is that living according to the spirit is "the Oedipally initiated but not final shaping of our attitudes to ourselves, to each other, and to life."[78]

CELIBATE PRIESTHOOD AND SEXUALITY

There are three other issues concerning sex and sexuality, which become a significant focus in Moore's writings. These are the celibate priesthood, homosexuality in the Church, and, to a lesser extent, *Humanae Vitae*, and the question of contraception. I will deal with the first two issues. The issue of *Humanae Vitae* and the Church's teaching on contraception occupied Moore's writings in the Catholic periodical *The Tablet* in the 1960s. For most Catholics today, the issue is not a high priority.

First, in chapter 9, I presented the insights of Marie Keenan and A. W. Richard Sipe regarding the dark and harmful nature of sexual abuse by clergy within the Catholic Church. Moore speaks highly about their insights. Here, I want to offer Moore's insights into celibacy as a way of living sexuality. As mentioned in chapter 9, over many years and in various periods of his life, the question of mandated celibacy for male clergy remained a concern for Moore. Moore was conscious of the inadequacy of the formation program for clergy and religious before the 1960s. The training emphasized one's obligations to observe and exercise the Benedictine vows, especially the vow of chastity. The emphasis by formators at that time was on obedience to God, to one's superiors, and to one's vows, and little to no focus on self-knowledge of our sexual nature and the

---

77. Moore, *Let This Mind*, 99.
78. Moore, *Let This Mind*, 100.

deep roots that sexuality makes into our identity.[79] The insight that one could be a priest but also Christian and sexual had not yet fully emerged. Moore's insights around sexuality and clergy were articulated in the context of an unhelpful clerical club mentality, and subsequently, where priests leaving the priesthood often abandoned their religious faith and practice. In the 1960s, when the Catholic Church was experiencing an exodus of clergy and religious from its ranks, reaching its apex in the 1970s, Moore was a priest in a parish. He was determined to speak about sex and sexuality in an exploratory manner and undo the culture of repression that characterized the past.

Moore called for a considered spirituality to address the "erosion."[80] The metaphor of "erosion" described the state of the church in which men and women no longer could abide by mandatory celibacy and no longer felt they had the tools to live the vow. A spirituality addressing erosion would explore the relationship between the rational and non-rational, the conscious and the unconscious, and an integration of feeling, thinking, and evaluating. Any spirituality would have to speak about the institutional and the personal dimensions of accepting celibacy.

Moore examines the institutional perspective from the insights of Sipe.[81] Celibacy is the state of non-marriage and abstinence from sexual activity. The voluntary sacrifice of all sexual pleasure is an extreme form of religious asceticism when undertaken over a whole lifetime. It is one mode of coming to terms with one's sexuality. In the Catholic Church, a man ordained to the priesthood must follow the discipline of celibacy and the church's expectation of them is to live celibate lives "for the sake of the Kingdom." The exemplar for celibate living was the humanity of Jesus. He was comfortable with his humanity and capable of relating to people at a deep level. He allowed intimate contact between himself and others. The men and women of his life were able to be vulnerable with him and felt that his chaste manner could be trusted. His encounter with women especially was sensual but never unchaste and this manner revealed him to be in tune with his embodiment.

Sipe asserts that there are several essential criteria for recognizing whether a person is ready for a celibate life. First, obtaining a narrative history of the candidate's developmental patterns is critical, and exploring

---

79. Moore, "Sex, God," 154.
80. Moore and Maguire, *Dreamer*, 68.
81. Moore, "2012–2014 Blog," Sep 12, 2012.

this history should precede any celibate intention, with the understanding that early experiences vitally influence a person's eventual sexual celibate adjustment pattern. Sipe states: "Family background, education, ethnic and cultural fixes, character traits, sexual preferences, unique talents, loves and hates all come into play. In addition, self-knowledge is fundamental to any successful celibate pursuit."[82] A well-balanced formation program would be attentive to each person's history and assess the student's fitness for priesthood partially based on its findings.

Second, there is a recognition that celibacy is dynamic and, therefore, requires on the part of the celibate, continuing personal assessment. It is a process of internalizing and actualizing the celibate ideal from intention to achievement. The person seeking to be celibate begins with an image of celibacy personified in a person believed to be practicing abstinence. The process toward embracing celibacy involves the attainment of a degree of self-knowledge. It measures one's capacity to live with the sexual discipline and deprivation necessary to be celibate. Self-awareness readies a person to proceed further in seeking knowledge about the process of celibacy and what it involves realistically.[83]

Third, sexual achievement is accountable and measurable. Sipe asserts: "Out of all its manifest variations permutations individualization, frustrations, failures, or perversions, certain qualities measure its authenticity: service complete, self-honesty, awareness of the oneness of the human condition and the capacity to love."[84] A well-adjusted formation program attuned to the celibate lifestyle before and after a vow will attend to these factors to guide an ongoing self-evaluation. Suppose there is no such program or the program lacks these criteria. In that case, no one is helping the candidate to make an informed decision before he takes the vow, nor is anyone allowing them to continue to live a celibate lifestyle after the vows.

More generally, there are a host of concerns regarding the practice of mandatory celibacy and how it may not be lived out as best as it could be. Within the crisis of celibacy, Moore identifies historical and theological factors that have contributed to the poor state of lived celibacy. First, the failure of the official Church to communicate a more positive understanding of sex and sexuality was partly due to the historical development of celibacy by the great reformer, Pope Gregory VII, who imposed

---

82. Sipe, "Celibacy," 1.
83. Sipe, "Celibacy," 1–2.
84. Sipe, "Celibacy," 2.

monasticity on all the clergy, making them celibate secular monks with breviaries.[85] While those laws were promulgated to put a stop to simony and clerical marriage, thus protecting the property of the church, they also contributed to unintended negative consequence for generations of clergy who were insufficiently helped to live the vow and in many cases failed in their celibate commitment.

Second, these monks, in their turn, preached a monastic spirituality to the married. Generally, the history of the Church has been one where the voice of the laity has not been listened to effectively by the official Church. In our modern times, sex, from the laity's perspective, connotes pleasure, relationships, babies, and marriage. For the official Church, marriage for the sake of family receives the highest consideration.[86] Part of the mentality behind the official position is a formation by clergy in stoic thinking, namely, "sexual enjoyment is only permissible if involved in procreation."[87] In Moore's experience, the laity has a higher estimation of sexual pleasure as an important means to sustain their married relationship. For the official Church, "the best becomes the only permissible when the babies are prepared for."[88]

Third, there has been a failure on the part of clergy to communicate a positive attitude toward sexuality coming out of a misinterpretation of the terms *flesh* and *spirit* in the writings of Paul. The contrast between the flesh and the spirit, the illegitimate pull of the flesh contrasted to the legitimate awakening of the body, and its relationship to a sexual embodiment are poorly understood. Moore affirms that an awakening of the body means that we come to appreciate the body's beauty, strength, accuracy in tenderness for one another, and its power to initiate and sustain loving relationships.[89] He assesses that denying male sexuality would be akin to allowing the church to "unman" its clergy simply by being against the body.

Fourth, the decision to be celibate must be underpinned by a proper formation program, before any decision is made by the candidate. Formation requires an open and honest education on sex and sexuality. The losses of sexual intimacy and family life must be explored. Men want to become priests because they desire to serve God through being ardent

85. Moore, *Contagion of Jesus*, 144.
86. Moore, *Contagion of Jesus*, 145.
87. Moore, *Contagion of Jesus*, 145.
88. Moore, *Contagion of Jesus*, 146.
89. Moore and Maguire, *Dreamer*, 71.

yet gentle gospel servants. Their felt sexuality will find its fulfillment in the service of love. However, Moore worries that mandatory celibacy without honest conversation leaves the possibility that, since the urge for sexual love will not be fulfilled, celibacy will be "maintained only by an act of the will."[90]

The personal perspective is equally as important. What is needed is a cultural shift within the Catholic Church in sexual matters that comes only with the birth of new awareness. According to an older priestly spirituality, priests were required to embrace celibacy and taught that by prayer and renunciation, the grace of ordination, fraternal support among celibate friends, and obedience to their religious leaders, their vocation would hold them firmly to the reality of God. Moore concludes that these links no long work. A new awareness of sexuality must begin by knowing the body and appreciating our embodiment. He admits: "I do not know my body, the body in which others know me, and some love me, and in which I, bewildered, love."[91] The combination of being alienated from one's body and trapped in a pattern that no longer connects one to the reality of God weighs heavily on Moore's mind and heart. It is only in the body that a person is loved and lovable. We can only find a way to move forward through a new self-awareness and self-appropriation of our conscious and unconscious dynamics. From a Freudian and Jungian perspective, Moore asserts that the unconscious dynamic is vitally important since the body is the place of the unconscious.[92]

In tune with Moore, Au states:

> Honest awareness and discipline at these moments can help us to do what is appropriate for ourselves as well as for others. If we pay attention to our emotional and physiological reactions to sexual stimuli, we will know when we are getting aroused and when we need to retard our actions for the sake of reflection. Reflection allows us the chance to decide what we want to do about our growing sexual arousal and of responsible ways of responding, if we are to love chastely. We need to know how our sexual arousal is influenced by such factors as our moods and fantasies, or alcohol or other drugs.[93]

---

90. Moore, *Body of Christ*, 54.
91. Moore and Maguire, *Dreamer*, 90.
92. Moore and Maguire, *Dreamer*, 91.
93. Au, *By Way*, 153.

For Moore, part of the process of re-education into sexuality is the freeing of sexual feelings.[94] By freeing, he is referring to an honest appreciation for our sexual feelings. He does not mean an attitude of "letting it rip"; rather, it is about

> a very positive effort to let myself feel good about the sexual feeling that I now am asking my body about.... Just as tension in the body—stiff neck or tightness in the belly—is my body trying to get my attention, so sexual arousal is my body seeking attention. We laugh such an idea out of court saying that the body here is being only too successful in getting attention. And thus predictably, we miss the point, that with sexual arousal the body seeks my attention to its and my primary need, which is to connect with someone else, to pass from death to life in loving. But just as with pain, it only succeeds in getting my attention by upsetting me.[95]

Moore's approach, therefore, is to

> befriend the way I feel just as this moment, however, messed up and allow my feeling to speak and surprise me so that I breathe a sigh of relief. It is only then that I begin to know what it is that we are referring to when we speak of acting "from within." And when we catch on to this, freedom becomes a quality, and experience of self, a state of mind, like joy and peace; and this is the freedom that controls.... It has nothing to do with what we call free will, unless we mean that these free people are the only ones who exercise free will. With the truly free person or connotation of dominance, of breaking-in, has vanished and self-control, self and not another in control, takes its place among the fruits of the Spirit.[96]

To befriend our sexual feelings is to take ownership of our erotic nature. Moore's orientation complements the insights of Au on the importance of a proper eroticism in our lives. Au proposes that our lives can be imagined as living between two gardens.[97] The first garden affirms the radical goodness of human embodiment and its erotic associations. The radical goodness of the first garden maintains that eros fuels our need for an intimate connection with others. Sexuality is a relational power

---

94. Moore, "My Body for You," 205.
95. Moore, "My Body for You," 206.
96. Moore, "My Body for You," 208.
97. Au, *By Way*, 141–43.

that bonds us to others with affection and care. The virtue of chastity at the center of celibacy affirms the radical goodness of sexuality so that we may come close to each other. Chastity seeks to mold people into lives marked by love. In celibacy, clergy abstain from the physical expression of sexuality; however, their sexuality is put in the service of love and personal relationships.

Again, Moore affirms the insights of the Christian feminism biblical scholar Phyllis Trible.[98] For Trible, the book of the Song of Songs, the context of the first garden, "speaks from lovers to lovers with whispers of intimacy, shouts of ecstasy, and silences of communication" and we are invited to enter this garden of delight.[99] The Song of Songs redeems a story about human sexuality that had gone awry. In its poetry, Trible states: "The visual must be heard; the auditory seen. Love itself blends sight, sound, sense, and non-sense. In these ways, the voices of the Song of Songs extoll and enhance the creation of sexuality in Genesis 2."[100] Furthermore, women are the principal creators of the poetry of eroticism.

The second garden is where Adam and Eve find themselves after the fall. The second garden is marked by shame at their nakedness and sexual alienation, the drudgery of hard work, the imbalance of power between men and women, stemming from their disconnection from God. In the words of Trible the narrative subject of Gen 2:7—3:24 is a story of the struggle between life and death. Life means

> unity, fulfillment, harmony, and delight. It is not, however, a paradise of perfection or purity untouched by loneliness, responsibility or finitude. To the contrary it is fulfillment within limits, a fulfillment that includes imperfections, makes distinctions, sets up (boundaries) hierarchies, and tempers joy with frailty. Death (Thanatos) is the loss of life. It means discord, strife, hostility, and danger. As a result, imperfections become problems, distinctions become opposites, hierarchies become oppressions, and joy dissipates into unrelieved tragedy.[101]

If we are to reclaim the first garden, we must not deny the erotic. To deny the erotic within us, including the erotic in clerical celibacy, will lead to problems. Only by encountering the erotic can clergy overcome sexual disesteem, fear, and anxiety. An awareness of the erotic means an

---

98. Moore, *Contagion of Jesus*, 97.
99. Trible, *God and the Rhetoric*, 144.
100. Trible, *God and the Rhetoric*, 145.
101. Trible, *God and the Rhetoric*, 74.

awareness of the body and a sensitivity to what Moore calls the pain-body. Through an acceptance of embodiment, clergy are better able to understand the unconscious and appreciate that listening to the body leads to greater self-knowledge. Just as importantly, eroticism separated from interpersonal intimacy and reduced to selfish pleasure can only do harm. Therefore, clergy should be aware of any eroticism that is self-enclosing or generated from fear. Clergy should be careful to avoid prostitution and pornography. Moore often depicts the hope of the disciples of Jesus, in terms of the gift of the Spirit, following upon their dissolution and emptying. Chaste love is born of resurrection hope.

When celibacy is concerned only with abstaining from intercourse through using willpower, it is time for a new setting. Suppression, denial, and repression are powerful psychic mechanisms for avoiding difficult questions. Suppression may help us distance ourselves from improper sexual fantasies and control our sexual desires for the sake of clearly chosen authentic values. However, suppression is never helpful as a means to avoid important questions. Denial can lead to fixation and sexual obsession blinding people from the broad building of wholesome relationships. Fixation leads to the impersonal use of others for one's own sexual gratification. Repressing the erotic runs the risk of becoming "rigid, listless, or angry people, whose frustrated sexual drive leads more often to neurotic symptoms than to loving behaviors."[102] If we find ourselves celibate clergy struggling with our vows and the only response from within is the voice that says, "Well, what did you expect!" then life will remain unfulfilled. Priests can then assume that the voice of the pain-body will become the dominant voice within. For Moore, the voice of the pain-body is the voice making itself heard wherever celibacy is experienced as commanded, but not loved.[103]

Moore asserts that the only way that one can be healed is through the conviction that we are loved exactly as we are and that being loved unconditionally is the only thing that matters. He adds, "I cannot be convinced that I am loved exactly as I am unless I can feel myself exactly as I am, and by accepting myself as I feel myself. And the only way I do feel myself exactly as I am is to give my body space to speak or come up with the blessed exact image of what I am doing to it that it doesn't like, that prevents it from being my joy, my freedom, my connection with the

---

102. Au, *By Way*, 145.
103. Moore, *Body of Christ*, 54.

body of us all that faith knows as the body of Christ crucified and risen in us."[104] Moore is convinced that a relationship exists between sex and love. He states:

> We can say that sex is really about love. We can say that where love is lacking sex becomes the exercise of power over others. We can name centuries of priestly training based on the fear of sex that denies it the possibility of becoming love, so that it readily declines into wanting power over others, and what better subjects than children, the powerless? I ask now why does all this line of explanation have about it that awful combination of truth with hopelessness so that the best thing we can muster in place of being judgmental is a state of professed moral impotence, its characteristic word 'sad,' which is becoming the preferred word for ecclesiastical authority required to make a statement about clerical misdemeanors . . . . But when we get out of the head into the body, the notion of energy presents itself *as* what has been allowed to stagnate, and as what could start to move again to our healing.[105]

For Moore, the realities of love, sex, and the body interplay. He links the word *body* to its eucharistic context, the Church as the body of Christ, and the words of affirmation from one human to another. The spirituality of a mature approach to sexuality must be grounded in an appreciation for the eucharistic words of Christ, "This is my Body for you," as the dialectical opposite of "This is your body for me."[106] In the former, we are expressing a conviction in tune with Jesus: "This, bread and wine, is what I, crucified, am for you, with a love that makes obsolete a million years of bloody sacrifice placating a God of threat and revealing a loving Father."[107] When the eucharistic meaning of the body is grasped, the lover "I most deeply want to be, given an enabling energy shift, comes into the sacrificial movement of Jesus."[108]

Celibacy requires an ongoing process of growth and cannot be assumed to be something conferred simply by the grace of ordination. Any growth process requires knowing the map or territory ahead, familiarizing oneself with the signposts that give direction, and recognizing the dead

---

104. Moore, "My Body for You," 209.
105. Moore, "My Body for You," 209–10.
106. Moore, "My Body for You," 211.
107. Moore, "My Body for You," 211.
108. Moore, "My Body for You," 212.

ends. A vital key to fully human formation is the release of all disesteem and self-punishment and the balancing of self-love and self-gift. Moore states priests "who mature beyond [disesteem and self-punishment] are the salt of the earth, humorous, compassionate and life-enhancing."[109]

MOORE AND HOMOSEXUALITY

A final issue regarding sex and sexuality that concerns Moore personally and profoundly is sexual orientation, especially for homosexual persons and their standing within the Catholic Church. To put the question in context, I want to turn to the work of Salzman and Lawler. They begin by affirming that there are five foci by which theologians draw moral knowledge: Scripture, tradition and Tradition, reason, and experience. Both traditionalist and revisionist moral theologians have recourse to these sources. Traditionalists place a weighty priority on the hierarchical teaching of the Church to interpret the tradition. Thus, Scripture, reason, and experience become subject to the Magisterium's interpretation. While accepting the latter, Revisionists take a dialectical approach to these sources. However, there is a presumption of truth in favor of what the Magisterium teaches. All teaching must be critically reflected on and appropriated in the light of sound scriptural exegesis, the reasonable insights of the physical, social, and human sciences and the cultural/social and relational experiences of the faithful.[110]

Magisterial teaching on homosexuality is found in the *Catechism of the Catholic Church* (1993); and three documents of the CDF: the *Vatican Declaration on Certain Questions of Sexual Ethics* (Latin title: *Persona Humana*) (1975); the letter on *The Pastoral Care of the Homosexual Person* (1986); and *Considerations Regarding Proposals to Give Legal Recognition to Unions between Homosexual Persons* (2003). Based on these sources, the Catholic Church condemns homosexual acts as "intrinsically disordered" (CCC 2357). The teaching Church highlights that the constant witness of Scripture has condemned homosexual acts as seriously flawed. Further, the magisterial teaching on homosexual acts and relationships is grounded in three arguments: natural law, procreation, and complementarity. The natural law argument asserts that there is an essential order in nature grounded in a heterosexual interpretation of

---

109. Moore, *Body of Christ*, 54.
110. Salzman and Lawler, *Sexual Person*, 214–15.

male and female sexuality.¹¹¹ The procreation argument is grounded in an understanding that every sexual act must be open to life and love. It interprets openness to life in purely a biological sense and, therefore, immediately linked to the transmission of life as a hoped-for consequence of intercourse.¹¹² The complementarity argument is grounded in the determination that homosexual acts violate men's and women's heterogenital and reproductive complementarity. In other words, the biological structure of men and women is such that a heterosexual relationship complements the reproductive desire of people.¹¹³

In contemporary discussion, there has arisen in theological circles a distinction between a homosexual orientation and homosexual behavior. The former is a psychosexual condition produced by genetics, psychological factors, and social-cultural influences. Homosexual orientation is generally understood to be an emotional and psychosexual propensity towards others of the same sex.¹¹⁴ It is considered more a way of being in the body than a way of behavior. According to Salzman and Lawler, the biblical passages most often cited condemning homosexuality as a behavior assume that heterosexuality is the natural condition of every person. However, in a modern understanding of homosexuality, there is an opposing viewpoint. Homosexuality is not a perversion but an inversion of the heterosexual. Homosexual people, by no choice of their own, do not naturally share a heterosexual orientation and, therefore, cannot be held morally accountable.

These preliminary insights serve as a context for Moore's understanding of homosexuality. Moore's most prodigious first writings on homosexuality come in an article given at a Lonergan Workshop titled "A Word for Sexual Desire: Order Is in Things Not over Things." Moore grounds his insights on the work of Girard and his earlier axiom: desire is love trying to happen. Sex is the midpoint between raw desire and love.¹¹⁵ Starting with John Paul II and his theological reflections on the body, Moore concludes that for all its profound insights on sexuality and human embodiment, it lacks any content about sexual desire itself. He assesses it as a "disembodied" theology of the body.¹¹⁶ Not only does John

111. Salzman and Lawler, *Sexual Person*, 226–27.
112. Salzman and Lawler, *Sexual Person*, 227–28.
113. Salzman and Lawler, *Sexual Person*, 228–30.
114. Salzman and Lawler, *Sexual Person*, 216.
115. Moore, "Word for Sexual Desire," 205.
116. Moore, "Word for Sexual Desire," 207.

Paul II not deal with the "fuel" of sexuality, but he does not mention the millions of people worldwide whose sexual desire is oriented to people of the same sex. The consequence is that homosexuals show up on the pope's map as "non-persons."[117]

Moore suggests that homosexual behavior deemed wrong suffers primarily from presenting homosexual acts as a form of "cheating." By cheating, the pope is putting into the month of the person who is homosexual the statement, "I do it [sex] in a way offensive to life's mystery embodied in us."[118] By contrast, Moore suggests that wrong sex is disordered sexual desire. But if sexual desire is a halfway house between raw desire and love, then sexual desire and sex can best be understood as "people's desire for each other . . . fired by the desire that they are awakening in each other."[119] Sex, at its best, internalizes the desired one. There is no more wonderful event than to be desired by the one desired.

From the Girardian perspective of mimesis, the object of desire is the other person or, as Moore states, "it's Peter for John and John for Peter." The object internalized is the other or what we would call "mutual admiration." Moore states that the couple are "imitating each other's imitation of each other."[120] In the Girardian sense, the imitation by the respondent can be either envy or rivalry, on the one hand, or wanting to be like the loving model, on the other hand. In the latter, affection and imitation can grow into love. Sexual love can grow into a larger-than-life experience that we call God's love or devolve into envy, brutality, and violence. If sexual love is central to loving, then an "implicit definition of sex as relationship, of sex as attraction between people, will have to be affirmed."[121] In Moore's assessment, the mind of the Church does not seem to affirm a relationship-centered definition.

If sexual desire is the halfway house between raw sex and love, "homosexuality may look more like a sexual excess than a sexual deviance [since] . . . gay men do seem to suffer from too much mutual admiration which characterizes sexual desire."[122] This new focus on the joy of sex with its inner intentionality toward loving commitment causes Moore to conclude that the official church and the laity are not speaking the same

117. Moore, "Word for Sexual Desire," 208.
118. Moore, "Word for Sexual Desire," 208.
119. Moore, "Word for Sexual Desire," 209.
120. Moore, "Word for Sexual Desire," 210.
121. Moore, *Contagion of Jesus*, 144.
122. Moore, "Word for Sexual Desire," 211.

language. Whereas the emphasis of the official Church has been that sexual desire is a "baby trying to happen," it now seems that "it is the homosexual fact that forces the Church to take sexual desire seriously as thresholding love."[123] The Church's emphasis on sexual desire linked mainly to procreation contributes to the position that homosexual love is "intrinsically disordered." Moore's Girardian perspective judges the Catholic position as wrong and offensive. For him, homosexual love "is the working of God in them bringing them into his love, which of course is the only climate babies can grow into becoming real men and women."[124]

Moore also turns his attention to some consequences that follow from the Church's stance on homosexuality, but this time to do with the distorting effect of the Church's teaching on the social institution of the Church. These distorting effects were subsequently documented in a book by Frederic Martel, *In the Closet of the Vatican: Power, Homosexuality, Hypocrisy*, published in 2019, five years after Moore's death. The social dysfunction named is the creation of a clerical gay subculture within the Church, even in the heart of the Vatican, that makes straight clergy members feel unwelcome. This distorted role reversal is getting a reaction from Church authorities who are calling for a screening out of all gay candidates from priestly candidacy and formation. In earlier years, well before the publication of Martel's book, Moore took the time to ask his friend James Alison, a noted theologian with a ministry to gay and lesbian people, whether such rumors were true. At the time of asking the question, Alison, familiar with the workings of the Vatican, admits to no knowledge of such matters. However, Martel's book, several years after Moore's question, exposes the double lives of priests and the intended and unintended consequences of extreme homophobia. Martel concludes that the resulting schizophrenic attitude to homosexuality in the Church is hard to fathom. His study affirms that the more a prelate is homophobic, the more likely he is gay.

Overall, Moore assesses the negative approach to homosexuality within the Church as a form of taboo. With any taboo, the issue is a threat to that society. The mechanism of taboo works in a manner that as people talk about it more and more, against the intention of the taboo, the more acceptance grows. Until then, the subject must be left in the dark. Moore also postulates that the homosexual taboo arises out of

---

123. Moore, "Word for Sexual Desire," 213.
124. Moore, "Word for Sexual Desire," 214.

a misinterpretation of the human body within the biblical worldview. In biblical times, people viewed the male as carrying the "seed" of life, and the woman was only the ground where the seed germinated. To spill the "seed" on the ground or into another male body was considered an abomination akin to murder. If the taboo today is understood in this light, and Scripture is used as a justification against homosexuality, then these texts need sincere reinterpretation. But most importantly for Moore, today's taboo creates victims. It discriminates against a whole class of persons whom some within the Church find threatening. While the official Church turns to natural law to justify its key positions, for Moore, natural law is grounded in a flourishing life or "the demands of an unselfish life."[125] He argues that if natural law is grounded in an unselfish life, there exists a body of evidence to demonstrate that homosexuality and homosexual relationships can engage in a committed and covenanted life.

---

125. Moore, *Contagion of Jesus*, 161.

Bibliography

ABC Radio National. "Dom Sebastian Moore." Feb 12, 2011. https://www.abc.net.au/radio/programs/sundaynights/dom_sebastian-moore/7741902.

Alison, James. *The Joy of Being Wrong: Original Sin through the Eyes of Easter.* New York: Crossroad, 1998.

Arcamone, Dominic. *Conversion as Transformation: Lonergan, Mentors, and Cinema.* Eugene, OR: Pickwick, 2020.

———. *Religion and Violence: A Dialectical Engagement through the Insights of Bernard Lonergan.* Eugene, OR: Pickwick, 2015.

Augustine. *Confessions.* Translated by Henry Chadwick. New York: Oxford University Press, 1991.

Au, Wilkie. *By Way of the Heart: Towards a Holistic Christian Spirituality.* New York: Paulist, 1989.

———. *Urgings of the Heart: A Spirituality of Integration.* New York: Paulist, 1995.

Bakewell, Sarah. *At the Existentialist Café: Freedom, Being, and Apricot Cocktails.* New York: Other Press, 2016.

Becker, Ernest. *The Denial of Death.* New York: Simon and Schuster, 1973.

Blackwood, Jeremy. "Lonergan's Trinitarian Theology with Prologue." https://www.academia.edu/19608017/Lonergans_Trinitarian_Theology_with_Prologue.

Burrell, David B. "Torment as Method." In *Jesus Crucified and Risen: Essays in Spirituality and Theology in Honour of Dom Sebastian Moore,* edited by William P. Loewe and Vernon J. Gregson, 13–17. Collegeville, MN: Liturgical, 1998.

Carpenter, Dan. "Recovering Dom Sebastian." *Dan Carpenter Literarium,* Dec 20, 2019. https://dancarpenterpoet.wordpress.com/2019/12/20/discovering-dom-sebastian.

Cavadini, John C. "Neoplatonism." In *Encyclopedia of Catholicism,* edited by Richard P. O'Brien, 910–11. New York: HarperCollins, 1989.

Chapman, John. *Spiritual Letters.* Introduction by Sebastian Moore. New York: Burns and Oates, 2004.

Chenu, P. M. D. "Ratio Superior et Inferior: A Note on the Interaction of Theology and Philosophy." *The Downside Review* (1942) 260–65.

Conn, Walter E. *The Desiring Self: Rooting Pastoral Counseling and Spiritual Direction in Self-Transcendence.* New York: Paulist, 1998.

———. "Understanding the Self in Self-Transcendence." *Pastoral Psychology* 46 (1997) 3–17.

BIBLIOGRAPHY

Doran, Robert M. *Intentionality and Psyche*. Vol. 1 of Theological Foundations. Milwaukee, MN: Marquette University Press, 1995.
———. "Jungian Psychology and Christian Spirituality I: Christian Spiritual Transformation: Self-Transcendence and Self-Appropriation." In *Intentionality and Psyche*, vol. 1 of Theological Foundations, 391–412. Milwaukee, MN: Marquette University Press, 1995.
———. "Jungian Psychology and Christian Spirituality II: The Jungian Psychology of Individuation." In *Intentionality and Psyche*, vol. 1 of Theological Foundations, 413–29. Milwaukee, MN: Marquette University Press, 1995.
———. "Jungian Psychology and Christian Spirituality III: Psychology and Grace." In *Intentionality and Psyche*, vol. 1 of Theological Foundations, 431–46. Milwaukee, MN: Marquette University Press, 1995.
———. "Mimesis." http://www.robertmdoran.com/The%20Trinity%20in%20History%204%20Mimesis.pdf.
———. "Psychic Conversion." In *Intentionality and Psyche*, vol. 1 of Theological Foundations, 25-70. Milwaukee, MN: Marquette University Press, 1995.
———. *Theology and Culture*. Vol. 2 of Theological Foundations. Milwaukee, MN: Marquette University Press, 1995.
Duffy, Eamon. "Benedict XVI and the Eucharist." *New Blackfriars* 88 (2007) 195–212.
Dunne. Tad. "Desire." 2008. http://taddunne-writings.weebly.com/uploads/1/8/6/3/18634728/desire.pdf.
———. "Rights." 2022. http://taddunne-writings.weebly.com/uploads/1/8/6/3/18634728/rights.pdf.
———. *We Love you Matty: Meeting Death with Faith*. Amityville, NY: Baywood, 2000.
Edwards, Denis. *What Are They Saying about Salvation?* New York: Paulist, 1986.
Fellows of the Woodstock Theological Center. "The Realm of Desire: An Introduction to the Thought of Bernard Lonergan." Washington, DC: Woodstock Theological Center, 2011. https://lonerganresource.com/media/pdf/books/4/The%20Realms%20of%20Desire%20-%20An%20Introduction%20to%20the%20Thought%20of%20Bernard%20Lonergan.pdf.
Fitzpatrick, P. J. *In the Breaking of Bread: The Eucharist and Ritual*. Cambridge: Cambridge University Press, 1993.
Fox, Matthew. *The Pope's War: Why Ratzinger's Secret Crusade Has Imperilled the Church and How It Can Be Saved*. New York: Sterling Ethos, 2012.
Gallagher, Michael Paul. "Contexts and Horizons of Desire: Sebastian Moore's Contribution to Fundamental Theology." *Lonergan Workshop* 14 (1998) 59–72.
———. *Free to Believe: Ten Steps to Faith*. London: DLT, 1989.
———. "A Reflection on Rublev's Icon of the Trinity." *Liturgy*, 2011. https://liturgy.co.nz/virtualchurch/rublevstrinity1.html.
———. *Struggles of Faith*. Dublin: Columba, 1990.
Girard, René. *Deceit, Desire and the Novel*. Baltimore: Johns Hopkins University Press, 1966.
———. *The Girard Reader*. Edited by James G. Williams. New York: Crossroad, 1996.
———. "The Girard-Schwager Correspondence, 1974–1991." In *René Girard and Raymund Schwager: Correspondence 1974–1991*, edited by Scott Cowdell et al., 78–99. Translated by Chris Fleming and Sheelah Trefle Hidden. London: Bloomsbury, 2018.

BIBLIOGRAPHY

———. *I See Satan Fall like Lightning*. Translated by James G. Williams. Maryknoll, NY: Orbis, 2004.

———. *Violence and the Sacred*. Baltimore: Johns Hopkins University Press, 1977.

Girard, René, et al. *Things Hidden since the Foundation of the World*. London: Continuum, 2003.

Gray, Susan. "A New Theology of Women? Lonergan's Approach to Human Authenticity and Catholic Teaching on Womanhood." *The Longergan Review* 7.1 (2016). https://www.academia.edu/35612020/A_New_Theology_of_Women_Lonergans_Approach_to_Human_Authenticity_and_Catholic_Teaching_on_Womanhood.

Hammarskjöld, Dag. *Markings*. Translated by W. H. Auden and Leif Sjoberg. London: Faber and Faber, 1965.

Heaney, Maeve Louise. *Suspended God: Music and the Theology of Doubt*. New York: T. & T. Clark, 2022.

Hughes, Glenn. "The Denial of Death and the Practice of Dying." Ernest Becker Foundation, Oct 1, 2014. https://ernestbecker.org/becker-in-the-press-test-2/.

A More Beautiful Question: The Spiritual in Poetry and Art. Columbia: University of Missouri Press, 2011.

———. "On Desire." *VoegelinView*, Sep 24, 2021. https://voegelinview.com/on-desire/

———. *Transcendence and History: The Search for Ultimacy from Ancient Societies to Postmodernity*. Columbia: University of Missouri Press, 2003.

Hughes, Glenn, and Sebastian Moore. "The Affirmation of Order: Therapy for Modernity in Bernard Lonergan's Analysis of Judgment." *Lonergan Workshop* 8 (1990) 109–33.

———. "Hamlet and the Affective Roots of Decision." *Lonergan Workshop* 7 (1990) 179–202.

Hunt, Anne. *Trinity: Nexus of the Mysteries of Christian Faith*. Maryknoll, NY: Orbis, 2005.

Ignatius of Loyola. "Prayer of Surrender." *My Catholic Life!* blog. https://mycatholic.life/catholic-prayers/prayer-of-surrender/.

Keenan, Marie. "Evidence to the Australian Royal Commission into Institutional Responses to Child Sexual Abuse." https://www.childabuseroyalcommission.gov.au/sites/default/files/IND.0675.001.0001.pdf.

———. "Sexual Abuse and the Catholic Church." Nov 2014. https://www.academia.edu/86333415/Sexual_abuse_and_the_Catholic_Church.

Kelly, Anthony P. *An Expanding Theology: Faith in a World of Connections*. Sydney, NSW: E. J. Dwyer, 1993.

———. *Touching on the Infinite: Explorations in Christian Hope*. Blackburn, VIC: Collins Dove, 1991.

———. *The Trinity of Love: A Theology of the Christian God*. Wilmington, DE: Michael Glazier, 1989.

Kierkegaard, Søren. *The Sickness unto Death*. London: Penguin, 1989.

Kirwan, Michael. *Discovering Girard*. London: Darton, Longman and Todd, 2004.

———. "Eucharist and Sacrifice." *New Blackfriars* 88 (2007) 213–27.

———. *Girard and Theology*. London: T. & T. Clark, 2009.

Lawrence, Fred. "Dedication to Sebastian Moore, osb." *Lonergan Workshop* 14 (1998) viii–ix.

Loewe, William P. "Encountering the Crucified God: The Soteriology of Sebastian Moore." *Horizons* 9 (1982) 216–36.

———. *Introduction to Christology*. Collegeville, MN: Liturgical, 1996.
Lombardo, Lucien. "Some Observations of Alice Miller's 'The Body Never Lies.'" The Natural Child Project. https://www.naturalchild.org/articles/alice_miller/bnl_review_3.html.
Lonergan, Bernard. "Cognitional Structure." In *The Lonergan Reader*, edited by Mark Morelli and Elizabeth A. Morelli, 38–386. Toronto: University of Toronto Press, 1997.
———. *Insight: A Study in Human Understanding*. Edited by Fredrick E. Crowe and Robert M. Doran. Vol. 3 of *Collected Works of Bernard Lonergan*. Toronto: Toronto University Press, 1997.
———. *The Lonergan Reader*. Edited by Mark Morelli and Elizabeth A. Morelli. Toronto: University of Toronto Press, 1997.
———. *Method in Theology*. Toronto: University of Toronto Press, 1996.
———. *A Second Collection*. Edited by William F. J. Ryan and Bernard J. Tyrrell. London: DLT, 1974.
———. "Self-Appropriation." In *The Lonergan Reader*, edited by Mark Morelli and Elizabeth A. Morelli, 340–62. Toronto: University of Toronto Press, 1997.
———. *Understanding and Being*. Edited by Frederick E. Crowe and Robert M. Doran. Vol. 5 of *Collected Works of Bernard Lonergan*. Toronto: Lonergan Research Institute, 1990.
Longenecker, Dwight. "Picking a Bone with René Girard." The Imaginative Conservative, Jun 5, 2021. https://theimaginativeconservative.org/2021/06/picking-bone-with-rene-girard-dwight-longenecker.html.
Manning, Vincent. "Encountering Christ through the Passion of HIV: An Inquiry into the Theological Meaning of HIV." PhD diss., 2019. https://academia.edu/44257440/Encountering_Christ_through_the_Passion_of_HIV.
McBrien, R. P. *The Church in the Thought of Bishop John Robinson*. London: SCM, 1966.
Meissner, W. W. *Freud and Psychoanalysis*. Notre Dame: Notre Dame University Press, 2000.
Melling, Joseph. "Sebastian Moore: A Life in Movements." *The Downside Review* (Oct 2018) 1–4.
Merton, Thomas. *Conjectures of a Guilty Bystander*. New York: Doubleday, 1989.
Miller, Alice. "The Feeling Child." Interview by Dianne Connors, OMNI Publications International, March 1987.
Miller, Jerome. A. *The Way of Suffering: A Geography of Crisis*. Washington, DC: Georgetown University Press, 1988.
Miller, Mark. "Why the Passion? Bernard Lonergan on the Cross as Communication." Diss., 2008. https://www.semanticscholar.org/paper/Why-the-passion%3A-Bernard-Lonergan-on-the-cross-as-Miller/aa5a33d4588aac6d9b0c9560ce3392b1ad3ee543.
Mitchell, Stephen A., and Margaret J. Black. *Freud and Beyond: A History of Modern Psychoanalytic Thought*. New York: Perseus, 1995.
Moore, Sebastian. "2008 Sebastian Moore Blog." Oct 12, 2008. https://www.scribd.com/document/233134725/Sebastian-Moore-Blog.
———. "2012–2014 Blog." https://dom-sebastian-moore.tumblr.com.
———. "Analogy and the Free Mind." *The Downside Review* 76 (1958) 1–28.
———. "And There Is Only the Dance: Reflections on the Trinity." *The Downside Review* (Oct 2001) 269–96.
———. "Are We Getting the Trinity Right?" *The Downside Review* (Jan 1999) 59–72.

———. "The Bedded Axle-Tree." In *Jesus Crucified and Risen: Essays in Spirituality and Theology in Honour of Dom Sebastian Moore*, edited by William P. Loewe and Vernon J. Gregson, 211–25. Collegeville, MN: Liturgical, 1998.
———. "Bishop's Dilemma: The Cruel Irony of Deterrence." *Commonweal* (1982) 484–85.
———. "The Blessed Trinity: A Plea for Biblical Theology." *The Downside Review* (Winter 1947/1948) 17–25.
———. *The Body of Christ: The Shudder of Blissful Truth*. London: Darton, Longman and Todd, 2011.
———. "The Body Speaks in God Is a New Language." *Lonergan Workshop* 16 (2000) 153–71.
———. "A Catholic Neurosis?" *The Clergy Review* 56 (1961) 641–47.
———. "Christian Self-Discovery." *Lonergan Workshop* 13 (1978) 187–213.
———. "Christ Today." *Catholic World* 206 (1967) 109–10.
———. "The Communication of a Dangerous Memory." *Lonergan Workshop* 6 (1987) 55–61.
———. *The Contagion of Jesus*. Edited by Stephen McCarthy. London: Darton, Longman and Todd, 2007.
———. "Contemplation in a World of Violence II." *The Merton Journal* 8 (2001) 24–29.
———. "The Crisis of an Ethic without Desire." In *Theology and Sexuality: Classic and Contemporary Readings*, edited by Eugene F. Rogers Jr. 162–63. London: Blackwell, 2002.
———. "Critical and Symbolic Realism: Lonergan and Coleridge." *Lonergan Workshop* 12 (1996) 147–78.
———. *The Crucified Is No Stranger*. London: Darton, Longman and Todd, 1977.
———. "Crucifixion: Accident or Design?" *Contagion: Journal of Violence, Mimesis and Culture*. 5 (1998) 155–63.
———. "Death as the Delimiting of Desire: A Key Concept for Soteriology." In *The Challenge of Psychology to Faith*, edited by Steven Kepnes and David Tracy, 51–56. New York: Seabury, 1982.
———. "The Discovery of Metaphysics—One Man's War." In *Spirit as Inquiry: Lonergan Festschrift*, edited by Frederick E. Crowe, 120–24. Chicago: Saint Xavier College, 1964.
———. "The Doxology of Joy." *Lonergan Workshop* 13 (1997) 141–59.
———. "The Easter Egg." *New Blackfriars* (1967) 517–20.
———. "The Empty Tomb Revisited." *The Downside Review* 99 (1981) 239–47.
———. "Experiencing the Resurrection." *Commonweal* 109 (Jan 29, 1982) 47–49.
———. *The Fire and the Rose Are One*. New York: Seabury, 1980.
———. "For a Soteriology of the Existential Subject." In *Creativity and Method: Essays in Honour of Bernard Lonergan*, edited by Matthew L. Lamb, 229–47. Milwaukee, MN: Marquette University Press, 1981.
———. "For Bernard Lonergan." *Compass: A Jesuit Journal*. Spiring (1985) 9.
———. "The Forming and Transforming of Ego: An Explanatory Psychology of Soteriology." *Lonergan Workshop* 8 (1980) 165–189.
———. "Four Steps Towards Making Sense of Theology." *The Downside Review*. April (1993) 79–100.
———. "F. R. Leavis: A Memoir." *Method: Journal of Lonergan Studies* 1.2 (1983) 214–22.
———. "Gerard Manley Hopkins." *The Downside Review* (Oct 1944) 184–95.

———. *God Is a New Language*. Westminster, MD: Newman, 1967.
———. "God Suffered." *The Downside Review* 77 (1958–59) 122–40.
———. "Haughton, Sartre and Holbrook." *New Blackfriars* (1967) 157–58.
———. "The 'infallible' temptation." *Commonweal* (Oct 1986) 525–27.
———. *The Inner Loneliness*. New York: Crossroad, 1982.
———. "In Water and in Blood." *Lonergan Workshop* 11 (1995) 91–103.
———. "Jesus and the Buddha." *The Merton Journal* 8 (2001) 24–29.
———. *Jesus the Liberator of Desire*. New York: Crossroad, 1989.
———. "Jesus, the Liberator of Desire: Reclaiming Ancient Images." *The Downside Review* (1990) 1–19.
———. "The Language of Love." *Lonergan Workshop* 3 (1982) 83–105.
———. *Let This Mind Be in You: The Quest for Identity through Oedipus to Christ*. New York: Harper and Row, 1985.
———. "Life, Death and Resurrection Notes towards a Theology of the Redemption." *The Clergy Review* 58 (1963) 203–16.
———. "My Body for You." *The Furrow* 51.4 (2000) 203–13.
———. "The New Convivium." *The Downside Review* (Jan 1996) 40–55.
———. "The New Life." *Lonergan Workshop* 5 (1985) 145–62.
———. "Night Thoughts of a Christian." *The Downside Review* (1994) 235–42.
———. *No Exit*. Glen Rock, NJ: Newman, 1968.
———. "Notes and Comments: The Historical Jesus and the 'Sensus Plenior.'" *Heythrop* 2 (1972) 173–77.
———. "Original Sin, Sex, Resurrection and Trinity." *Lonergan Workshop* 4 (1983–84) 85–98.
———. "Our Love Is Crucified." *The Downside Review* (Jan 1998) 27–43.
———. "Out of This World." *The Clergy Review* 50 (1965) 579–89.
———. "Person and Metaphysics." *New Blackfriars* 49 (1968) 233–36.
———. "The Poetry of the Word." Unpublished essay.
———. "Psychoanalysis and Religious Experience: Four Perspectives." *Horizons* 13 (1986) 400–405.
———. "Realism or Empiricism?" *The Clergy Review* 46 (1961) 98–103.
———. "Reflections on the Thought of Sartre." *The Downside Review* (1953–54) 146–52.
———. "Reflexions on Death I." *The Downside Review* (1951–52) 184–95.
———. "Reflexions on Death II." *The Downside Review* 71 (1952–53) 14–24.
———. *Remembered Bliss: A Book of Spiritual Sonnets*. Belfast: Lapwing, 2014.
———. "The Resurrection: A Confusing Paradigms-Shift." *The Downside Review* 98 (1980) 257–66.
———. "Rhythm and Psalmody." *The Clergy Review* (Fall 1945) 72–77.
———. "The Search for the Beginning." In *Christ, Faith and History: Cambridge Studies in Christology*, edited by S. W. Sykes and J. P. Clayton, 79–94. Cambridge: Cambridge University Press, 1972.
———. "The Secular Implications of Liturgy." In *The Christian Priesthood*, edited by Nicholas Lash and Joseph Rhymer, 215–29. London: Darton, Longman and Todd, 1970.
———. "Self-Love: The Challenge to Theology." *Compass: A Jesuit Journal* 8 (1990) 32–35.
———. "Sex, God, and the Church." In *Celibate Loving: Encounters in Three Dimensions*, edited by Mary Anne Huddlestone, 152–57. New York: Paulist, 1984.

———. "Some Principles for an Adequate Theism." *The Downside Review* 95 (1977) 201–13.

———. "Spirituality and the Primacy of the Dramatic Pattern of Living." *Lonergan Workshop* 8 (1990) 279–96.

———. "Thoughts in Defence of the Mystical." *The Merton Journal* 19 (2012) 15–23.

———. "Towards a Eucharistic Definition of Sacrifice." *The Downside Review* (1950–51) 428–39.

———. "What God Has Joined and Man Has Put Asunder." *Lonergan Workshop* 17 (2002) 163–73.

———. "Where the Spirit of the Lord Is, There Is Freedom." *Lonergan Workshop* 14 (1998) 173–95.

———. "Why Did God Kill Jesus?" *The Downside Review* (Jan 1994) 15–25.

———. "A Word for Sexual Desire: Order Is in Things Not over Them." *Lonergan Workshop* 18 (2005) 203–24.

———. "The Word of God: Kerygma and Theorem, a Note." *Heythrop* (1964) 268–75.

Moore, Sebastian, and Anselm Hurt. *Before the Deluge*. Glen Rock, NJ: Newman, 1968.

Moore, Sebastian, and Kevin Maguire. *The Dreamer Not the Dream*. Paramus, NJ: Newman, 1970.

———. *The Experience of Prayer*. London: Darton, Longman and Todd, 1969.

Morelli, Elizabeth. "Reflections on the Appropriation of Moral Consciousness." *Lonergan Workshop* 13 (1997) 161–89.

Morelli, Mark. *Self-Possession: Being at Home in Conscious Performance*. Chestnut Hill, MA: Lonergan Institute, 2015.

O'Connor, Peter. *Understanding Jung: Understanding Yourself*. North Ryde, NSW: Methuen, 1985.

O'Malley, John W. "Vatican II: Did Anything Happen?" In *Vatican II: Did Anything Happen?*, edited by David G. Schultenover, 52–91. New York: Continuum, 2007.

Ormerod, Neil. "Desire and the Origins of Culture: Lonergan and Girard in Conversation." *Heythrop* 54 (2011) 784–95.

———. "Doran's *The Trinity in History*: The Girardian Connection." *Method: Journal of Lonergan Studies* 4 (2013) 47–59.

———. "The Eucharist as Sacrifice." In *The Eucharist: Faith and Worship*, edited by Margaret Press, 42–55. Strathfield, NSW: St. Paul's, 2001.

———. "For in Him the Whole Fullness of Deity Dwells Bodily: The Trinitarian Depths of the Incarnation. *Theological Studies* 77 (2016) 803–22.

———. *Grace and Disgrace: A Theology of Self-Esteem, Society and History*. Sydney: E. J. Dwyer, 1994.

———. "Healthcare and the Response of the Triune God." In *Incarnate Grace: Perspectives on the Ministry of Catholic Health Care*, 22–35. St. Louis: Catholic Health Association, 2017.

———. *Introducing Contemporary Theologies: The What and the Who of Theology Today*. Sydney: E. J. Dwyer, 1997.

———. Is All Desire Mimetic/Lonergan and Girard on the Nature of Desire and Authenticity." In *Violence, Desire and the Sacred*, edited by Scott Cowdell et al., 251–62. New York: Continuum, 2012.

———. "The Metaphysics of Holiness: Created Participation in the Divine Nature." *Irish Theological Quarterly* 79 (2014) 68–82.

———. "A (Non-Communio) Trinitarian Ecclesiology: Grounded in Grace, Lived in Faith, Hope, and Charity." *Theological Studies* 76 (2015) 448–67.

———. *A Public God: Natural Theology Reconsidered*. Minneapolis, MN: Fortress, 2015.

———. "René Girard, Unlikely Apologist: Ormerod Commentary on Kaplan." https://syndicate.network/symposia/theology/rene-girard-unlikely-apologist/.

———. *A Trinitarian Primer*. Strathfield, NSW: St. Paul's, 2011.

———. "Vatican II—Continuity or Discontinuity? Toward an Ontology of Meaning." *Theological Studies* 71 (2010) 609–36.

Pagola, Jose Antonio. *Jesus: An Historical Approximation*. Translated by Margaret Wilde. Miami: Convivium, 2012.

Prodigal Kiwi(s) Blog. "Dom Sebastian Moore OSB Interviewed." Mar 8, 2011. https://prodigal.typepad.com/prodigal_kiwi/2011/03/dom-sebastian-moore-osb-interviewed.html.

Quang, Tuan Lee. "The Encounter with Jesus Crucified and Risen in the Soteriology of Sebastian Moore." Unpublished diss., Catholic University of America, Washington, DC, 2011.

Raub, John Jacob. *Who Told You That You Were Naked?* New York: Crossroad, 1995.

Rees, Daniel. "The Monastic Mission in the Twentieth Century." In *Monks of England: The Benedictines in England from Augustine to the Present Day*, edited by Daniel Rees, 235–50. London: SPCK, 1997.

Robinson, John A. T. *The Body: A Study in Pauline Theology*. Philadelphia: Westminster, 1952.

Roy, Louis. *Embracing Desire*. Eugene, OR: Wipf & Stock, 2019.

———. *Engaging the Thought of Bernard Lonergan*. London: McGill-Queens University Press, 2016.

———. "Three Faith Dynamisms." *New Blackfriars* 81 (2000) 541–48.

Salzman, Todd A., and Michael G. Lawler. *The Sexual Person: Toward a Renewed Catholic Anthropology*. Washington, DC: Georgetown University Press, 2008.

Sheldrake, Philip. "Desire." In *The New SCM Dictionary of Christian Spirituality*, edited by Philip Sheldrake, 231–32. London: SCM, 2005.

Sipe, A. W. Richard. "Celibacy Today: Practice and Pretense, Mystery, Myth, Miasma." Mar 11, 2008. http://www.awrsipe.com/click_and_learn/2008-03-11-celibacy-today.html.

Sipe, A. W. Richard, et al. "Clerical Spirituality and the Culture of Narcissism." Aug 30, 2013. http://www.awrsipe.com/reports/2013/Spirituality-and-the-Culture-of-Narcissism.pdf.

Sotejeff-Wilson, Kate. "Dr Kate Sotejeff Remembers the Theologian and Poet." Mar 25, 2014. https://www.dartonlongmantodd.co.uk/magazine/2011-domo-sebastian-moore-obituary.

Stewart, Gordon. "God as Policeman or Lover." *Views from the Edge* (blog), Dec 27, 2014. https://gordoncstewart.com/2014/12/27/god-as-policeman-or-lover/.

Tolle, Eckhart. *The Power of Now: A Guide to Spiritual Enlightenment*. Novato, CA: New World Library, 1989.

Trethowan, Illtyd. "A Contemporary Personalist." In *Jesus Crucified and Risen: Essays in Spirituality and Theology in Honour of Dom Sebastian Moore*, edited by William P. Loewe and Vernon J. Gregson, 19–30. Collegeville, MN: Liturgical, 1998.

Trible, Phyllis. *God and the Rhetoric of Sexuality*. Philadelphia: Fortress, 1988.

Webb, Eugene. *The Self Between: From Freud to the New Social Psychology of France.* Seattle: University of Washington Press, 1993.

———. *Worldviews and Mind: Religious Thought and Psychological Development.* Columbia: University of Missouri Press, 2009.

Wolff-Salin, Mary. *Journey into Depth: The Experience of Initiation in Monastic and Jungian Training.* Introduction by Sebastian Moore. Collegeville, MN: Liturgical, 2005.

Index

Aelred of Rievaulx, 298
Alison, James, 13, 343, 345, 348, 352, 396
Arcamone, Dominic, 23 fn 16, 34 fn 57, 35 fn 60, 55 fn 35
Au, Wilkie, 110, 388
Augustine, St., 16, 59
Alberigo, Giuseppe, 292

Beattie, Tina, 288–89
Becker, Ernest
    fear of death and, 102
    denial of death and, 103, 105–6
    heroic self-image and, 107
    Kierkegaard and, 106
    immortality systems and, 104
    self-absorption and, 103
    vital lie and, 104–5
Beckett, Samuel, 42–43
Benedict XVI (pope), 269, 286, 291, 293, 295, 296
Blondeau, Alexander T., 1
Burrell, David
    on Moore's Method, 66–67

Casaldaglia, Pedro, 297
Carpenter, Dan
    Moore and 18–19
    on writing style, 18–19
Chapman, John, 88–90, 94, 379
church
    as body of the Cross, 310–311
    as body of the flesh, 310
    as body of the Resurrection, 311
    as bully, 302
    as community of friends, 302–3
    as disciples of Jesus, 304–5
    as dream, 300–301
    as lovers, 30
    Bipolar, 299–300
    continuity and discontinuity debate and, 292–93
    fear and, 296–98
    friendship and discipleship, 305–5
    Matthew Fox and, 296
    Mary and, 305–8
    monolithic consciousness and, 276
    patriarchy and, 285–90
    personal renewal and, 269–72
    Robinson, A.T. John and, 309
    sacraments and, 274–76
    self-sacrificing love and, 255
    siege mentality and, 265
    symbolic life and, 274–77
    wider society and, 290–291
    Vatican II and, 291
Conn, Walter, 32–33, 130, 152, 145–47
Consciousness
    as oceanic, 135
    definition of, 22
    empirical, 26
    imperatives of, 110
    intellectual, 26
    levels of, 26

INDEX

Consciousness (continued)
  moral, 27
  polymorphism of, 27–28
  presence to self and, 46
  rational, 27
  stages of 37
contemplation
  prayer and, 55, 77, 84, 161–62, 177, 216
  as idiotic state, 379
  as nothing in particular, 93–94
  as silence, 94
conversion
  affective, 34
  as traumatic, 80
  definition of, 34
  ego and, 149–50
  intellectual, 35
  moral, 34
  neurosis and, 80
  psychic, 35
  psychological, 35, 81
  rebirth and, 82
  religious, 34–35
  self-transcendence and, 80
Cozzens, Donald, 298
critical realism
  idealism and, 38
  naive realism and, 38
  reality and, 38
culture
  classicist notion of, 294
  denial of death and, 117
  empirical notion of, 294
  general notion of, 63
  historical consciousness and, 294
  of consumerism, 94
  of modernity, 43

dark night, 89, 225
death
  anxiety and, 103
  as dissolution, 202
  as our mystery, 122
  as punishment, 122
  as threat, 112
  dependency and, 112
  denial of, 121
  distorted heroism and, 107
  distorted notions of, 123–25
  fear and, 102–3, 202, 214
  hero systems and, 103
  humility and, 105
  images of God and, 125–27
  immortality systems and, 104
  of current ego, 155, 156, 159
  on the death of meaning, 102
  physical extinction and, 103
  sin and, 227
  the cross and, 218–19
  trust in God and, 105
Debien, Noel, 17
desire
  bias and, 192
  CDF and, 15
  death and, 256–57
  desirability and, 91
  direct awakening and, 91
  Dunne and, 167–69
  Girard and, 180–86
  God and, 175, 177
  Hughes and, 169
  innate, 191
  love and, 176
  power and, 174
  Roy and, 178–80
  Self-love and, 177
  Sheldrake and, 169–70
dialectic
  contradictories and, 64
  contraries and, 64–65
  notion of, 33
  of self-love and self-gift, 110
  role of religion and, 65
disciples
  as emptied, 303
  awakening of desire and, 224, 256, 259
  desolation of desire and, 69, 125, 224, 257–58
  psychic transformation and, 150, 159
  transformation of desire and, 69, 259, 345
Doran, Robert, x, 144–45, 354
Dunne, Tad

INDEX

on death, 123–27

Edwards, Denis, 1, 365
ego
    Alice Miller and, 137
    ego states and, 158–60
    consciousness and, 145–47
    conversion and, 149–50
    as conscious, 154
    as unconscious, 154
    dying of, 149–50
    Freud and, 131–32
    German idealism and, 129–30
    Jung and, 138
    Margaret Mahler and, 135–36
    psychology and, 130–31
Eliot, T. S., 8, 18, 71, 164, 189, 266
eucharist
    as body, 309
    liturgical reform and, 322–23
    poetry and, 76
    ritual meal and, 316–20
    sacred meal and, 315–16
    sacrifice and, 311–13
    sacrifice of Calvary and, 313–14
    sex and, 322
    transubstantiation and, 320–322
    true self and, 314–15

flesh, 226, 278
    as soma, 310
    as sarx, 310
    Paul's understanding of, 382–84
Fingarette, Herbert
    on anxiety, 134–35
    on ego, 135
Fitzpatrick, P. F., 316–20
focusing
    attention to body and, 154, 173, 303
    body shift and, 39
    definition of, 39
    feelings and, 38–41
    healing and, 344
    pain-body and, 100
    reconciliation and, 303
    trinity and, 345
Frankl, Victor, 4
Freud, Sigmund
    pleasure principle and, 161
    structure of the personality and, 131–32
    Oedipus Complex and, 133–34
    reality principle and, 161

Gallagher, Michael Paul, 12, 52, 167
garden
    myth of the, 370, 371, 377–78, 380
    of the Fall, 390
    of human embodiment, 389–90
Girard, Rene
    metaphysical desire and, 183
    mimetic desire and, 181
    on desire and God, 184
    rivalry and, 181–82
    scapegoating and, 184
    triangulation of desire and, 181
    on desire and God, 184–86
God
    direct awakening to, 90–92
    indirect awakening to, 90, 177
Goldsmith, Charlie, 13
Gratry, Pere A., 16
Gray, Susan
    on women in the church, 285–87
Gregson, Vernon, 1–2, 13
Guzie, Tad, 13

Hammarskjold, Dag, 59
Harvey, Peter, 11
Haughton, Rosemary, 15
Heaney, Louise, 2–3
Hegel, Fredrich, 115
Hopkins, Gerard Manley, 15
horizon
    notion of, 33
    care and, 33
    conversion and, 34–35
    radical change and, 80, 100
Hughes, Glenn, 41–44, 72, 107, 108, 119, 169
Hulbert, James, 1
Hunt, Anne
    on the Trinity, 1
    on Moore's Method, 67–68
Hunt, Anselm, 11

INDEX

Jesus
  ecstasy of, 83
  as confrontational, 205–6
  as form of God, 231–32
  as model of desire, 188
  as sinless, 225–28
  as the True Self, 66, 94, 101, 154, 159, 211, 216, 219, 223, 225, 230
  as victim, 186, 189, 219
  death of, 218–19
  empty tomb and, 264–67
  forgiveness and, 84, 220–221
  freedom and, 83, 230
  hidden ground of, 93
  incompleteness and, 223
  inverted soteriology and, 209–12
  liberation of desire and, 224–25
  New Quest and, 204
  obedience and love in, 236, 238, 240
  Old Quest and, 204
  scapegoating and, 249–50
  self-sacrificing love, 314
  personal significance and, 217
  poetry and, 75–76
  self-identification of, 63, 213, 226, 321, 323
  self-love, self-gift and, 228–29
  sorrow and, 219–20
  suffering and, 222
  symbol of True Self and, 154
  the cross and, 206–8
  the kingdom and, 206
  the resurrection and, 208–9
  true self and, 61, 66, 152, 216–17, 314
  ultimate significance and, 218
John Paul II (pope), 378–80, 394
Jung, Carl
  on archetypes, 144
  on contrasexuality, 142–44
  on ego and individuation, 139
  on ego-personae, 139–40
  on ego and self, 138
  on shadow and ego, 140–42
  on symbols, 163

Keenan, Marie, 280–282
Kierkegaard, Soren, 43, 106
Komonchak, Joseph, 292
Krombach, Benedict, 73–74

Lawrence, Frederick, 13
Leavis, F. R, 20, 71
Le Quang, Tuan, 1
Loewe, William, 1
Lonergan, Bernard
  acts of meaning and, 28
  basic sin and, 239
  carriers of meaning and, 29
  common sense and, 30
  concrete performance and, 23
  consciousness and, 22
  conversion and, 21, 75, 79–80
  empirical consciousness and, 26
  functions of meaning and, 28
  ideal of knowledge and, 23
  insight and, 26
  intellectual consciousness and, 26
  intellectual pattern and, 47
  interiority and, 31
  liturgy and, 75
  meaning of meaning and, 28
  moral consciousness and, 26
  mysticism and, 21
  patterns of experience and, 44–45
  rational consciousness and, 26
  realms of meaning and, 30–32
  redemption and, 233–34
  self-appropriation and, 22
  self-presence and, 22
  self-transcendence and, 25, 110
  subject as object and, 23
  subject as subject and, 23
  theological method and, 48
  theory and, 30–31
  transcendence and, 31–32
  turn to the subject and, 21–22
Longenecker, Dwight, 19
love
  as boundless, 95
  as responsible, 341
  as self-donation, 190
  breaking bread and, 323
  dependency and, 113

INDEX

directionality of desire and, 176
eros-love and, 170
feast of, 311–12
love *of* self vs love *for* self, 151
mysticism and, 96
priesthood and, 278
self-sacrificing, 255, 314
self-transcendence and, 80

Maguire, Kevin, 11–12
Mahler, Margaret
    mother separation and, 135–36, 198
    mother trust and, 162
    natural narcissism and, 111
    neurosis and, 135
Marchetto, Archbishop Agostino, 292–93
McCarthy, David, 19
Melling, Joseph, 8
Merton, Thomas, 93
Miller, Alice, 157–58
Miller, A. Jerome
    on crisis, 97, 101
    on ethic of control, 98, 100
    on the Sacred, 97–98
Morelli, Mark
    on dramatic patterns, 45
    on life as drama, 61–62
    on mystical patterns, 46, 95
Moore, Sebastian
    adult guilt and, 116
    Alice Miller and, 153–54
    being a bully and, 14
    being in love and, 82
    classicist notion and, 64
    contemplative prayer and, 83–84, 90, 93–94
    consciousness and, 37
    contrasexuality and, 163–64
    conversion and, 21, 81–82
    cosmic consciousness and, 46
    creaturehood and, 117–22
    critical realism and, 37–38
    feelings and, 172–74
    death and, 41
    desire and, 170–71, 186, 187, 189
    desire for God and, 90
    drama of salvation and, 63
    dramatic pattern and, 45–46, 61–62
    Eckhart Tolle and, 75, 96–101
    empirical notion and, 64
    Ernest Becker and, 108–10
    existential subject and, 35
    Freud and, 161–62
    Girard and, 186–90
    God desiring us and, 92
    homosexuality and, 17
    "I am" and, 46
    individuation and, 166
    infantile guilt and, 116
    inner loneliness and
    intellectual pattern and, 47
    intentionality and, 163
    interdependence and
    interiority and, 68–69
    inverted soteriology and, 209–12
    Jung and, 153, 162–66
    law of the cross and, 247
    love and, 96, 176–77
    Mahler and, 154–57
    Mary, 15, 77, 306, 307, 308
    mystical pattern and, 46
    Noel Debien interview and, 17, 360–363
    on academic life, 12–13
    on being a mistake, 40
    on CDF and fear, 16–17
    on conscious and unconscious, 52–53, 68–69
    on desire, 170–17, 172, 173, 174
    on disesteem, 40, 100, 195
    on disordered narcissism, 173
    on ego and consciousness, 145–47
    on first knowing, 37
    on focusing, 38–40
    on genuine religion, 100
    on his mother, 10, 17–18
    on homosexual feelings, 10, 17
    on Jesus of history, 204
    on Lonergan, 20–21
    on monastic life, 10, 13
    on myth of dominance, 292
    on new awareness, 4
    on Neoplatonism, 96
    on oneness and separateness, 136–37, 155–56

INDEX

Moore, Sebastian (continued)
   on original sin, 117–18
   on parish life, 11–12
   on patriarchy, 287–88
   on personal significance, 60
   on power, 115–16
   on psychic self-discovery, 165
   on reflective self-awareness, 37, 148–49
   on second knowing, 37
   on self-absorption and God, 112–14
   on self-awareness, 36, 52, 54, 148
   on self-worth, 81
   on the act of judgment, 42
   on the cross and resurrection, 206–9
   on the message of Jesus, 205–6
   on the shadow, 164–65
   on the true self, 98–99
   on the turn to the body, 41
   on ultimate significance, 60
   on his wobble, 14
   on women, 14–15
   original sin and, 194
   panic and, 40
   personal experience and, 51
   personal significance and, 108
      Mary, 15, 77109
   poetic themes and, 74–78
   poetry and, 69–74
   power and, 174–75
   pre-religious awareness and, 57–60
   punishment and, 246–47
   psyche and, 163
   redemption and, 243–44
   sacrifice and, 189–90
   satisfaction and, 244–45
   self-gift and, 109
   self-love and, 177
   religious conversion and, 81
   the fall and, 164
   social politics and, 115–16
   spiritual pain and, 40
   theological method and, 56
   Timothy Radcliffe and, 263
   trinitarian suffering and, 358–59
   trinity and, 337–58
   true self and, 151–52, 154
   turn to the subject and, 21

   Vincent Manning interview and, 262–63
mystical religiousness, 92
myth, 35, 53, 185, 196, 197, 275, 276, 277, 292, 301, 369

narcissism
   as distorted, 151
   cosmic specialness and, 104
   culture and, 111
   Margaret Mahler and, 111
   natural, 103, 111
   self-absorption and, 103, 104, 111–12
neoplatonism, 96
Nietzsche, Frederich, 43

O'Malley, John, 293
Ormerod, Neil
   on church as communio, 353–54
   on church as mission, 353–54
   on continuity and discontinuity debate, 295–96
   on innate desire, 193
   on mimetic desire, 193
   on sacrifice, 252–253
original sin
   as death wish, 195, 215
   creaturehood and, 117
   development and, 198, 373
   feeling bad and, 77, 94, 308, 383
   interiority and, 371
   John Jacob Raub and, 200–202
   Mary and, 305
   myth of Adam and, 199–202
   myth of the Garden and, 196–97
   self-awareness and, 22, 52, 195–96
   separation crisis and, 198
   sexual identity and, 198

poetry
   elemental meaning and, 53
   conversion and, 75
   courage and, 73
   culture of disbelief and, 73
   disesteem and, 77
   Jesus and, 75–76
   liturgy and, 75

INDEX

mystery of God and, 72
sexuality and, 78
symbols and, 69, 71
Tolle and, 75
truth and, 74–75
prayer
    chanting psalms and, 85
    contemplation and, 83
    direct awakening to God and, 91
    dwelling of God and, 93
    Freud and, 161–62
    John Chapman and, 88–90
    Lectio Divina and, 84
    life and, 85–86
    love and, 87–88
    luminous identity and, 91–92
    monastic life and, 84–85
    nothing in particular and, 91
    unknown God and, 86–87
priesthood
    catholic dream and, 278
    celibacy and, 278
    contemplation and, 278
    psychic life and, 278
    sexual abuse and, 279–85

Ratzinger, Joseph (Cardinal), 16, 49, 296, 297, 316
redemption
    as law of the cross, 242–43
    as liberation, 235
    as meritorious obedience, 236
    as mystery, 234
    as necessity, 234
    as sacrificial, 236
    as satisfaction, 232–40
    as substitutionary, 238
    as transaction, 235
    as vicarious satisfaction, 240–242
    cross and, 259–62
    desire and, 256–58
    divinity and Jesus and, 258–59
    resurrection and, 236–37
    self as gift and, 254
    unified field theology and, 235
Riuni, Camillo, 293
Robinson, Geoffrey, 298
romantic religiousness, 92

Roy, Louis
    on desire, 178–79
    on consciousness-in, 37
    on consciousness-of, 37
    on happiness, 179–80
    on mystical consciousness, 37
    on religious faith, 57–58

Salzman and Lawler, 393–94
self
    as intending, 146
    as object of inquiry, 146
    "me" and, 147
    "I" and, 146–47, 148
    self-against and, 31, 188
    self-as-gift and, 34, 62, 110, 114, 150, 174, 188, 228, 229, 322, 343, 347, 364, 366, 393
    self-for, 31, 34, 118, 231
    true self and, 151–55
self-appropriation
    critique of culture and, 24
    identification of, 25
    learning and, 25
    orientation and, 25
self-love, 81, 149, 158, 177, 179, 187, 188, 190, 229, 343, 365, 366, 367
self-sacrificing love
    kingdom and, 354, 357
self-transcendence
    consciousness and, 25, 32–33
    desire and, 170
    Jesus and, 83
    imperatives of consciousness and, 110
    self-discovery and, 80
sexuality
    arousal and, 176
    befriending the erotic and, 389
    domination and, 370–371, 374
    flesh and, 382–83
    God and, 363–67, 370
    grace and, 374
    homosexuality and, 393–97
    incest taboo and, 164, 198, 367–69, 377
    inner loneliness and, 363, 366
    inner partner and, 377–78

INDEX

sexuality (continued)
    Jesus and 375
    John Paul II and, 378–81
    love and, 392
    lust and, 379–80
    Mary as model and, 375
    original sin and, 373–76
    phallos and, 374
    pleasure and, 164, 373, 379, 381, 382, 383, 385, 387
    priesthood and, 384, 393
    self-gift and, 366–67
    sexual awareness and, 376–78
    sexual desire and, 381–82
    sexual identity and, 369–70
    shame and, 379–80
    spirit and, 384
    Song of Songs and, 390
    the Fall and, 371–73
    the flesh and, 382–84
Sipe, A. W. Richard, 282–85, 384–86
sin
    disengagement from God and, 117
    disengagement from others and, 118
    ego consciousness and, 223–24
    fear of change and, 226
    fear of intimacy and, 226
    freedom and, 226
    resistance and, 226
    self-rejection and, 226
    suffering and, 222
    will to non-being, 159, 224, 225, 228
Swiatecka, M. Jadwiga, 72
symbol
    cross and 211, 212, 325
    body and, 271
    death of Jesus and, 219
    Jesus and, 216, 217, 218, 289, 316, 319
    trinity and, 331, 337, 339, 347

theology
    affectivity and, 58
    analogy and, 50
    as autobiography, 60–61
    anxiety and, 66–67
    church and, 54–55
    culture and, 54, 63
    definition of, 63
    disciples of Jesus and, 62
    doctrines and, 58
    dogmatic, 49
    evolutionary worldview and, 54
    general categories and, 65–66
    God as real and, 51
    history and, 48–49
    images of God and, 52, 53
    interiority and, 67–68
    metaphysics and 48
    method and, 48–49
    myth and, 53
    personal experience and, 51
    philosophy and, 50
    poetic consciousness and, 69–70
    prayer and, 55, 56, 57
    religious experience and, 55
    scholastic method and, 48, 50
    special categories and, 65
    surrender to God and, 58
    theopoetics and, 70
    the unconscious and, 53
Trible, Phyllis, 288, 390
trinity
    analogy, metaphor and, 327–28
    art and, 324–25
    as interdividual, 353
    biblical categories and, 49, 328–29
    church and, 326
    created participations and, 334–35
    critical categories, 326–27
    divine solution to evil and, 355–56
    doctrinal precision and, 329
    early councils and, 330–331
    functions of meaning and, 327
    Nicene creed and, 331–32
    Ormerod and, 353–57
    processions, relations and, 332–33
    psychological analogy and, 335–37
    theological virtues and, 356, 357, 358
Tolle, Eckhart, 34, 46, 75, 96–100, 151, 308

Voegelin, Eric, 166

Webb, Eugene
    on Ernest Becker, 107–8
Weinandy, Thomas, 352